ECONOMIC ISSUES, PROBLEMS AND PERSPECTIVES

TOWARDS A SOCIETY WITH A MORE FAIR ECONOMY OR AN ECONOMY WITH A MORE SOCIAL FACE

THE CONTRIBUTION OF SCIENTIFIC SOCIAL KNOWLEDGE TO THE ALTERNATIVE MODELS OF SOCIOECONOMIC DEVELOPMENT

ECONOMIC ISSUES, PROBLEMS AND PERSPECTIVES

Additional books in this series can be found on Nova's website under the Series tab.

Additional e-books in this series can be found on Nova's website under the e-book tab.

Economic Issues, Problems and Perspectives

Towards a Society with a More Fair Economy or an Economy with a More Social Face

The Contribution of Scientific Social Knowledge to the Alternative Models of Socioeconomic Development

José António Filipe
Nikos Nagopoulos
Kostas Rontos
and
Ioannis Vavouras
Editors

nova publishers
New York

Library of Congress Cataloging-in-Publication Data

Towards a society with a more fair economy or an economy with a more social face : the contribution of scientific social knowledge to the alternative models of socioeconomic development / editors, Josi Antsnio Filipe, Nikos Nagopoulos, Kostas Rontos, and Ioannis Vavouras.

pages cm. -- (Economic issues, problems and perspectives)

Includes index.

ISBN 978-1-63482-900-7 (hardcover)

1. Economic development--Social aspects. 2. Equality. 3. Economics--Sociological aspects. I. Filipe, Josi Antsnio.

HD75.T694 2015

338.9--dc23 2015016920

Published by Nova Science Publishers, Inc. † New York

CONTENTS

Preface **vii**

Chapter 1 Governance Quality: Theory, Determinants and Policy Issues **1**
Kostas Rontos, Maria-Eleni Syrmali, Flora Tsapala and Ioannis Vavouras

Chapter 2 Socioeconomic and Political Aspects of Overall Development Worldwide: Measurement and Interconnections **39**
Kostas Rontos, Flora Tsapala and Ioannis Vavouras

Chapter 3 Endogenous Growth, Social Economy and Social Enterprises as a Means of Reversing the Traditional Model of Regional Development **57**
Nikos Nagopoulos and Kostas Rontos

Chapter 4 Corporate Social Responsibility: A Theoretical and Legal Background **69**
Nikolaos Bloskas

Chapter 5 The Emergence of CSR in Greece at Local Level: Synergies between SMEs and Local Authorities **81**
Miltiadis Stampoulis and Vassiliki Dimitriou

Chapter 6 Environmental Education, Environmental Policy and Socioeconomic - Sustainable Development **103**
Niki Psoma

Chapter 7 Commons, Anti-Commons, Cooperation and Fair Economy: A Reflection **117**
José António Filipe

Chapter 8 Mediterranean, Region, Development: Three Key Words and a Brief Commentary **133**
Luca Salvati

Chapter 9 A Queue Model for Idle Motorcars Management Considering an Energy Sources' New Scenario **143**
Manuel Alberto M. Ferreira, José António Filipe and Manuel Coelho

Chapter 10 Exploring Environmental Convergence in Complex Socio-Ecological Systems: A Brief Commentary **153**
Luca Salvati

Case Studies Worldwide **165**

Chapter 11 Case Study: Social Economy and Entrepreneurship: The Case of Greece (or Evidences from Greece) **165**
Kostas Rontos and Nikos Nagopoulos

Chapter 12 Case Study: An International Study on CSR in Five Countries (Portugal, Bulgaria, Brazil, India and Greece): Effects on Economic Development, Environmental Sustainability and Social Welfare **175**
Nikos Nagopoulos, Kostas Rontos, Desislava I. Yordanova, Manuel Coelho, José António Filipe, Manuel Alberto M. Ferreira, Selvarasu A. Mutharasu and Ivo C. Figueredo

Chapter 13 Case Study: Environmental Education Centers in Greece **215**
Niki Psoma

About the Contributors **229**

Index **237**

PREFACE

It is beyond any doubt that we live in economies characterized by extreme differences not only in the distribution of economic capacities such as income and wealth but also in the distribution of skills and knowledge and in many cases even in the extent of political power and rights. The everyday life proves it. Some accept that this outcome of the operation of market forces either competitive or non-competitive is a fair outcome. However, the prevailing thesis is that capitalism is by its nature an unfair socioeconomic system and that the economy should have a more social face or that societies should live in more fair economies. The issue is how we could achieve this objective. We argue that the most powerful means is scientific social knowledge. Scientific social knowledge is the core factor of socioeconomic development, the basic prerequisite to create more fair economies.

It has to be realized that a balanced and sustainable overall development of nations is the only way to overcome the various problems that humanity faces today. In this respect it has been established long ago that unrestricted economic growth is not a sufficient condition for the overall advancement of nations. It is required to switch our priorities to development. Development is a much wider concept than growth that incorporates as well the social and the political transformation and advancement of countries. The identification and more importantly the analysis of these sociopolitical transformations is associated with major difficulties. It must be realized, however, that this problem should not be the reason for policymakers and academic researchers to reduce their concern for the social and political dimensions of overall development.

Actually, in modern societies there exist additional needs for an effective reduction of income and wealth inequalities and for a more fair distribution of the economic result of human activities, for an effective reduction of state corruption, for a better social security system and what is called "social state", for health and education systems of high quality, for increased government effectiveness and for high standards of political rights and democracy in order the state to satisfy social needs more efficiently. The effective satisfaction of these needs is required, so that citizens are enabled to enjoy high standards of living and to live in more fair economies. Only when we take into serious consideration these issues we could argue convincingly that development is sustainable in the long-run.

The aim of the present volume is to provide some contribution to this objective, knowing the shortcomings of the task highlighted above.

In: Towards a Society with a More Fair Economy
Editors: J. A. Filipe, N. Nagopoulos, K. Rontos et al.
ISBN: 978-1-63482-900-7

Chapter 1

GOVERNANCE QUALITY: THEORY, DETERMINANTS AND POLICY ISSUES

***Kostas Rontos*[1,*], *Maria-Eleni Syrmali*[2], *Flora Tsapala*[1] *and Ioannis Vavouras*[2,3]**

[1]University of Aegean, Mytilene, Greece
[2]Panteion University of Social and Political Sciences, Athens, Greece
[3]Hellenic Open University (DEO 34), Patras, Greece

ABSTRACT

The objective of this paper is to provide guidance concerning the underlying determinants of cross-country variation in institutional quality and the accompanying performance of governance institutions. Based on theoretical perspectives from the prevailing good governance and institutions literature, this study adopts a solid conceptual approach and examines the disparate theoretical views under a unified framework. The analysis suggests that the quality of governance varies across countries mainly due to differences in countries' levels of economic development, political freedoms and levels of social development. As expected, these factors do not have a symmetric impact on governance structure but vary depending on the specific dimension of governance under consideration. The impact of economic development is stronger for the control of corruption, the rule of law and regulatory quality as far as the examined governance dimensions are concerned. Political development is strongly related to political stability and absence of violence as well as voice and accountability. A very interesting finding is the high correlation of social development as depicted by the relevant human development index with the level of government effectiveness. Therefore, attaining and sustaining good governance is not a one dimensional process whereas an integrated and coherent policy framework should be universally adopted due to the complex nature of the concept. Accordingly, good governance is a challenging task as it is associated not only with economic development but also with a wide variety of noneconomic factors of social and political nature. Strengthening and maintaining governance is achieved only through the adoption and effective implementation of the appropriate long-run policies. In a similar vein, concrete policy guidelines lie at the core

[*] Corresponding author: Email: K.Rontos@soc.aegean.gr.

of the good governance agenda. As a result, policy prescriptions should target a broad list of comprehensive governance reform efforts. More specifically, these are economic development, improved social standards and political development in order to achieve government effectiveness, anti-corruption safeguards, high standards of legitimacy and accountability, among other attributes of governance systems.

Keywords: Governance, Economic Development, Political Freedom, Social Development, Governance Indicators, Institutions

1.1. Introduction - Theoretical Background

1.1.1. Introducing Governance

The issue of governance has become a major concern for scientific research among international organizations, aid agencies and academic institutions. More specifically it has been mainstreamed on the development agenda by the World Bank[1] in the 1990s and in the decades that followed it has become a major concern for theoretical and empirical research. After the end of the Cold War, global and regional emphasis on democratization and the advancement of human rights have created demands for more accountable and transparent political institutions and a reformed judiciary (World Bank 1998, pp. 25-26). In the policy world, it has emerged out of the disappointments of a long stream of reforms applied to borrowing countries that failed mainly because they did not consider the importance of institutions and governance issues[2]. More specifically, Africa's development problems and the inefficiency of international aid were attributed to a governance crisis, whereas governance refers to the exercise of political power to manage a nation's affairs[3] (World Bank 1989, p. 60). In the same study it is supported that improved governance standards require political renewal whereas emphasis is given to fighting corruption by strengthening accountability, capacity building, sound policy fundamentals and institutional frameworks in order to improve structural weaknesses. This deep insight prevalent in the literature on growth and institutions intensified pressures upon a new development agenda targeting a lengthy list of governance objectives. Therefore, concrete policy recommendations lie at the core of the good governance agenda. These policy guidelines include economic development, improved social capabilities and political development in order to achieve high standards of legitimacy and accountability, tackle corruption and improve the performance of public institutions.

---

[1] The good governance agenda has been given a prominent role in the World Bank strategy. The World Development Report 1997 lays out a policy agenda to enhance the performance of governments by designing effective rules and restraints, checking arbitrary state actions and combating entrenched corruption (World Bank 1997, p. 3). It is also supported that neither good policies nor good investments are likely to emerge and be sustainable in an environment with dysfunctional institutions and poor governance (World Bank 2000, p. vii).

[2] See also Woods (2000).

[3] The African Development Bank (AfDB 1999, p. 2) extends the World Bank definition in order to adjust it to the new global environment. It defines governance as the manner in which power is exercised to manage a nation's affairs in relation to other nations whereas good governance cannot be considered a closed system due to the prevalence of globalization.

The scientific awareness over the role of governance and institutions can also be broadly viewed as an integral part of the ongoing research for the "deeper" determinants[4] of economic growth and development. Acemoglu (2005, pp. 397) discriminates between the proximate explanations of comparative growth and the fundamental or deeper causes. The first are supported by standard economic models of factor accumulation and innovation, whereas the second emphasize the importance of factors like economic institutions, geography and culture. Even if capital accumulation or technological innovation account for significant differences in long-run levels of per capita output across countries, they do not answer truly causal questions concerning the success or failure of certain societies to take the actions necessary to accomplish such accumulation or innovation (ADB 2010, p. 3). Similarly, North and Thomas (1973, p. 2) argue that factors liked innovation, economies of scale, education and capital accumulation are not causes of growth, they are growth instead. To further explore these issues, the emerging field of the economics literature concerning the deep determinants of growth described above, is called the new institutional economics. Beginning with the work of Douglass North as point of reference, the new institutional economics attempts to build on and extend neoclassical economics by integrating institutional analysis, in order to explain the role of institutions in long-term economic performance (North, 1990).

1.1.2. Defining Governance

While the notion of governance[5] has gained prominence in the literature and is extensively discussed among scholars and policymakers, there is little agreement on the essence of the concept. Governance is a multidisciplinary phenomenon[6] associated with a variety of economic, social and political factors, such as high per capita income, high human development standards and democratic institutions. Due to its elusive nature there is not a clear consensus on the concept. As such, there is no universally agreed definition of governance (Anne Mette Kjaer 2004, Ch. 1), neither a generally shared understanding of the concept[7]. On the contrary, international agencies and researchers follow their own definitions depending on the conceptual spectrum under which they analyze the phenomenon. Consistent with the multidimensional and multifaceted nature of the theme, governance can be conceptualized in various ways emphasizing different perspectives and with varying hypotheses about the links between governance and general development, which also escapes an internationally accepted definition (OECD 2009, p.11). Based on this premise, the sociopolitical context of good governance has not been generally approved and is contentiously debated.

---

[4] Rodrik (2004, p. 133).

[5] The term governance has its roots in the greek infinitive κυβερνάν (kubernân) (meaning to pilot or to steer) which was used in a metaphorical way by Plato to indicate the process of steering the citizens. This is where the latin term gubernare stems from, which also constitutes the origin of the word governance in different languages (European Commission, Étymologie du terme "gouvernance"), http://ec.europa.eu/ governance/docs/ doc5_fr.pdf.

[6] Governance is at the intersection of many fields in social sciences including development studies, economics, international relations, law, political science, public administration and sociology (Bevir 2011, p. 1; Dixit 2009, p. 6).

[7] For a concise overview of the relevant literature definitions, see United Nations (2007), Dethier (1999).

Although it is difficult to agree on a precise definition, the most common of them prevailing in the relevant literature are presented in the following paragraphs. Governance is defined by the World Bank as the manner in which power is exercised in the management of a country's economic and social resources for development (World Bank 1991, p. 1). In more concrete terms, the World Bank's involvement in governance has primarily focused on sound development management emphasizing public sector reform, public expenditure control and privatization[8]. Therefore, good governance infrastructure is fundamental in creating, operationalizing and maintaining an environment of strong and equitable development whereas it is a central supplement to sound economic policies. However, this definition is characterized as somewhat narrow as it does not take into account the political system and civil liberties as well as the role of civil society (Johnston 1998, p. 87). It is also considered as limited focused on the ability of governments in being responsive to citizens and providing them with core services. According to Kaufmann, Kraay and Mastruzzi (2010, p. 3) this definition is limited centered on public sector management issues. On the contrary, as discussed by Keefer more emphasis should be given to causal or more fundamental concepts which enclose the incentive structure that guides the actions of political actors (Keefer 2004, p. 3). The World Bank identifies three distinct aspects of governance: (i) the form of political regime, (ii) the process by which authority is exercised in the management of a country's economic and social resources for development, and (iii) the capacity of governments to design, formulate, and implement policies and discharge functions (World Bank 1994, p. xiv).

One of the most widely used definitions of governance in the literature is provided by the World Bank. Governance is defined as the traditions and institutions by which authority in a country is exercised. This broad definition includes: (a) the process by which governments are selected, monitored and replaced, (b) the capacity of the government to effectively formulate and implement sound policies, and (c) the respect of citizens and the state for the institutions that govern economic and social interactions among them[9] (Kaufmann, Kraay and Lobatón 1999, p. 1). The governance indicators that have been developed in this context capture six key dimensions of institutional quality or governance, and measure[10], through two indicators each, the political, economic and institutional dimensions of governance (Kaufmann 2005, p. 82). Overall, six dimensions of governance emerge which are the following[11]:

1. **Voice and Accountability** expresses perceptions of the extent to which citizens of a country are able to participate in selecting their government, as well as freedom of expression, freedom of association and a free media.

[8] Quibria (2006, p. 102).

[9] According to Baland, Moene and Robinson (2009, p. 4602) this definition of governance is very broad and gives emphasis not only on state capacity and the ability of the government to implement autonomous decisions often associated with governance, but also on the form of political institutions which determine who governs and what choices they make.

[10] Measuring governance performance could assist with setting standards for improvement and achievement as well as indicating where funds could have been better used and where policy might prove most effective (Besançon 2003, p. 2).

[11] The Worldwide Governance Indicators introduce sustainability metrics as they incorporate social, economic and political concerns related to sustainability. The elements captured by the index, such as accountability, political voice and political stability among other attributes of governing systems, are important over both the shorter as well as the longer term and therefore are of crucial importance from a sustainability perspective (World Economic Forum 2011, pp. 52-53).

2. **Political Stability and Absence of Violence/Terrorism** expresses perceptions of the likelihood that the government will be destabilized or overthrown by unconstitutional or violent means, including politically-motivated violence and terrorism.
3. **Government Effectiveness** expresses perceptions of the quality of public services, the quality of the civil service and the degree of its independence from political pressures, the quality of policy formulation and implementation, and the credibility of the government's commitment to such policies.
4. **Regulatory Quality** expresses perceptions of the ability of the government to formulate and implement sound policies and regulations that permit and promote private sector development.
5. **Rule of Law** expresses perceptions of the extent to which agents have confidence in and abide by the rules of society, and in particular the quality of contract enforcement, property rights, the police, and the courts, as well as the likelihood of crime and violence.
6. **Control of Corruption** expresses perceptions of the extent to which public power is exercised for private gain, including both petty and grand forms of corruption, as well as capture of the state by elites and private interests.

The OECD definition of governance is in accordance with the World Bank definition to denote the use of political power and exercise of control in a society in relation to the administration of its resources for economic and social development (OECD 1995, p. 14). This broad definition encompasses the role of public authorities in establishing the framework in which economic agents operate and in determining the allocation of benefits and the nature of the relationship between the ruler and the ruled[12]. According to the OECD good governance refers to the rule of law, efficient public sector management and corruption control.

According to the European Commission governance refers to the state's ability to serve the citizens. It concerns the rules, processes, and behavior by which interests are shaped, resources are administered, and power is exercised in society. The way public functions are accomplished, public resources are managed and public regulatory affairs are conducted is the major issue to be addressed in that framework. Despite its open and wide character, governance has a practical value related to the core aspects of the functioning of any society and political and social system and in this respect it can be characterized as a basic measure of stability and performance of a society as well as of quality and performance of any political and administrative system[13] (Commission of the European Communities 2003, pp. 3-4). Thus, institutional sustainability and capacity building are the primary elements of the good governance agenda[14].

According to the United Nations Development Programme (UNDP 2007, p. 1) governance is the system of values, policies and institutions by which a society administers its economic, political and social matters through synergies within and among the state, civil

[12] The OECD highlights three aspects of governance, which are identical to those of the World Bank's (1994) report presented above (OECD 1995, p. 14).

[13] In the same vein, the Commission's governance policy advice includes five principles for establishing more democratic governance. These are openness, participation, accountability, effectiveness and coherence (Commission of the European Communities 2001, p. 10).

[14] Commission of the European Communities (2003, p. 17).

society and private sector. It describes the rules, institutions and practices that set limits and provide incentives for individuals, organizations and firms. Despite the profusion of definitions of governance in the literature, it is possible to distinguish three fundamental types of governance. First, the political or public governance, the authority of which is the state, the government or the public sector and concerns the process by which the society manages its affairs. Second, the economic governance, whose authority is the private sector, and relates to the policies, the processes or organizational structures that are necessary to produce and distribute services and goods. Third, the social governance, whose authority is the civil society including citizens and non-for-profit organizations, and is connected to a system of values and beliefs that are indispensable for social behaviors to be materialized and for public decisions to be made (United Nations 2007, p. 2).

1.1.3. Governance's Aspects

Governance is supported by its economic, political and administrative aspects. Economic governance refers to the decision-making processes that affect a country's economic activities and its affairs with other countries. Political governance is the procedure of decision-making in order to formulate policy. Administrative governance is the system of policy implementation. Incorporating all three dimensions, good governance refers to the processes and structures that guide political and socio-economic relationships (UNDP 1997, p. 4). As can be derived from this definition, governance permeates all areas of economic and sociopolitical life and considers governance, policy formulation and implementation tightly intertwined.

The IMF's concentration on governance issues refers to their contribution to macroeconomic stability and sustainable growth in member countries (IMF 1997, p. 1). A more comprehensive insight of governance issues in the IMF's primary activities and policy perspectives suggests that governance generally encompasses all aspects of the way a country is governed, including its economic policies and regulatory capacities, as well as adherence to the rule of law[15]. In terms of economic growth and development, governance refers to the constituent elements of the notion of institutions. Important parts of governance, defined as such, incorporate the political institutions of a society which refer to the process of collective decision-making and to the checks on politicians and on politically and economically powerful interest groups. Moreover, state capacity is included, which is the capability of the state to provide public goods in diverse parts of the country. The regulation of economic institutions is also examined, which refers to the way the state intervenes in encouraging or discouraging economic activity by various different economic players (Acemoglu 2008, p. 1).

Governance expresses the level of institutional quality in a country. From a development perspective, governance issues are inseparable from ways and means to promote institutional reforms and induce a profound institutional change (Bonaglia, Braga de Macedo and Bussolo 2001, p. 6). Therefore, the literature examining the implicit factors of institutional quality is used as a frame of reference for the determinants of governance infrastructure as well[16]. From

[15] Corruption, defined as the abuse of public authority or trust for private benefit, is closely examined[15] (IMF 2013, p. 1).

[16] Baland, Moene and Robinson (2009, p. 4600).

an empirical perspective, the relationship between governance and its determinants has been left rather imprecise, with a notable absence of a concrete theoretical framework to guide empirical work[17]. Impediments to empirical research concerning governance and institutional quality can be attributed to conceptual and measurement problems whereas the way these themes are defined determines what gets modeled and measured[18]. As already denoted, there is not such a compact measure of institutional quality and government performance. As a consequence, in the relevant theoretical and empirical literature a specific dimension of governance is usually examined as for example corruption, which is a crucial aspect of governance, the rule of law, the level of political stability, regulatory efficiency and bureaucratic delays[19]. The results of this chapter are in line with the findings of Al-Marhubi (2004) who investigates the determinants of governance taking into consideration economic factors as well as exogenous and historically predetermined variables. In the present chapter emphasis is given to analyzing the factors contributing to each specific dimension of governance taking into account not only the level of economic growth but structural characteristics as well which are expressed by the choice of the relevant sociopolitical variables. Therefore, in order to improve governance systems the resultant policy means are not only of economic nature. Structural adjustments are moreover needed depending on the particular dimension of governance examined.

1.1.4. Establishing the Targets of the Study

Nevertheless, the recent empirical literature provides guidance concerning the underlying factors explaining the cross-country variations in institutional quality and the accompanying emergence of governance institutions. This chapter follows the prevailing literature by adopting a solid conceptual base and examining the disparate theoretical perspectives under a unified framework. More specifically, this chapter builds on the economic, political and cultural theories of institutions and government quality developed by La Porta et al. (1999) in order to explain their disparities across countries[20]. Economic theories hold that institutions are created on the basis of efficiency[21], that is, when the social returns of creating institutions exceed the transaction costs of doing so[22] (La Porta et al. 1999, p. 223). A direct testable hypothesis of these theories is that as the scale of economic activity expands, rising levels of economic growth bring about better institutions and government performance improves[23]. Political theories focus on redistribution rather than efficiency and hold that policies and

[17] Al Marhubi (2004, p. 394).

[18] A similar view has been expressed about corruption, which constitutes a fundamental pillar of governance (Jain 2001, p. 73).

[19] The contributions by Mauro (1995), Knack and Keefer (1995), Barro (1996), Treisman (2000), Acemoglu, Johnson and Robinson (2001), Rivera-Batiz (2002), Gradstein (2004), among others, are used as a reference point in the literature.

[20] The notion of good governance and the quality of government are closely interlinked (Rothstein and Teorell, p. 166).

[21] Despite the fact that this theory is an important part of reality it is at best incomplete as many extractive and inefficient governments exist around the world (La Porta et al. 1999, p. 227).

[22] For example, a government protects private property when the returns to this protection exceed the cost of police (La Porta et al. 1999, p. 227).

[23] However, in the literature the opposite relationship is also examined, that is the causal relationship from better governance to improved development outcomes (Hall and Jones (1999), *Chong and Calderón (2000)*).

institutions are designed by those in power to retain it and to transfer resources to themselves. According to political theories, those in power devise institutions and government policies in their own interests to create and extract rents and redistribute power. In a sense, the political system or the political macrostructure is responsible for determining the political motivation of all players in a state system and it is the very reaction of these factors that determines the behavior of state bureaucracy (Lederman, Loayza and Soares 2005, p. 10). Cultural theories state that societies hold beliefs that shape collective actions and government (La Porta et al. 1999, p.223). Social beliefs are a salient feature in the case of cultural theories as far as the formation of institutions is concerned[24]. Therefore, it is important to investigate the particular social structure where beliefs and ideas are articulated and contribute to the development of government capabilities. To put it differently, the essence of governance is the way in which state-society relations are structured and managed and the way citizens perceive the rules that guide their interaction with public officials as regards the achievement of their welfare, which is also the basic question guiding the assessment of governance in the government sphere[25] (Hyden, Court and Mease 2004, p. 99).

To give operational precision governance is examined in a certain economic, political, social and institutional context that influences its quality and evolution. The scope of the paper is to investigate the determinants of governance for all countries of the world for which the required data are available, that is 173 countries, building on three strands of the governance literature, whereas data seem to validate the theoretical predictions. The first strand focuses on the level of economic development as measured by the gross national income per capita in purchasing power parities or current international dollars. The second strand refers to the political determinants of governance approached by the range of political rights and the extent of civil liberties. The third strand analyzes the social aspects of governance proxied by the non-income human development index, which combines measures of life expectancy and educational attainment. The analysis suggests that all the above factors are of primary importance in determining the level of governance worldwide and should not be examined in isolation from each other. Policy implications that have emerged out of the empirical analysis reveal that different combinations of economic, social and political factors contribute to governance performance not uniformly but depending on the specific governance dimension under consideration. Generally, maintaining good governance is achieved only through the adoption and the effective implementation of the appropriate long-run policies of economic, social and political nature.

1.2. Data and Methodology

1.2.1. Methods of Statistical Analysis

To explore the factors that determine each dimension of governance in the global context, regression modeling was used with the six dimensions of governance taken as the dependent

[24] More specifically, cultural theories argue that some societies form beliefs and ideas that are conducive to good government, whereas others do not (La Porta et al. 1999, p. 229).

[25] In particular, according to this line of thought this question refers to whether the regime is so structured that citizens see that government cares about their welfare and security, either individually or collectively (Hyden, Court and Mease 2004, p. 99).

variables. Actually, six linear regressions of this kind were constructed each of them having as dependent variable one of the six dimensions of governance presented above. Concerning the regression approach, the multiple linear regression model of the following general specification was used:

$$Y = bo + b1.X1 + b2.X2 + \ldots + bn.Xn + e$$

Gross National Income per capita in purchasing power parities or current international dollars (GNI.pc.ppp), the political rights index (PR), the civil liberties index (CL) and the human development index (HDI) were used as independent variables, the same in every formula to express economic, political and social aspects of influence on each single dimension of governance. All variables used are discussed below in detail.

We must point out that social and political factors although considered by theory as crucial towards the advancement of the overall development of countries are mostly underestimated in empirical work. One of the most important reasons for this is that the social and political dimensions of development cannot be easily defined and measured in contrast to its economic dimension. The economic dimension is examined from a growth standpoint and is expressed in quantitative terms with widely accepted indexes, such as real income per capita, which are produced by international agencies and national statistical authorities for the vast majority of countries worldwide. In contrast to the economic aspect, there is no wide agreement on the measurement of the social and political dimensions of development, which can only be quantified with the use of proxy variables in the relevant empirical literature (Rontos and Vavouras 2013a, p. 51). Despite the existing severe measurement difficulties, sociopolitical variables are of primary significance, since the concept of governance is complex and associated with a variety of factors of social and political nature.

1.2.2. The Data Used

Next to these points, details for the data, on which the aforementioned variables are based, and their sources are given below.

Dependent and independent variables which are employed for the analysis have been derived for 173 countries. It is the total number of countries for which data for all these variables existed in the year 2012. It could therefore be considered as a worldwide analysis of the determinants of governance quality. The variables have been extracted from official statistics and other well-known international data sources as it is explained below.

To express governance[26], the relevant Worldwide Governance Indicators (WGI) dataset is used compiled by the World Bank. It should be acknowledged that it is the most extensively used dataset and has emerged as a standard point of reference in the relevant empirical literature. It covers a broad spectrum of the six governance dimensions given above which neatly capture the good governance agenda framework as delineated by the World Bank. These aggregate indicators combine the views of a large number of enterprise, citizen

[26] For a comprehensive overview of the most popular indicators employed in empirical research as well as some of the estimation problems that can arise when using these governance measures, see Williams and Siddique (2008).

and expert survey respondents in high income and developing countries. They are based on a variety of data obtained from 31 individual data sources produced by a variety of survey institutes, think tanks, non-governmental organizations, international organizations and private sector firms. The dataset covers governance indicators for 215 economies over the period 1996–2012[27] produced by Kaufmann, Kraay and Lobatón (1999). The values of the indicators lie between -2.5 and 2.5, where higher values correspond to better governance. Actually, the variable has been transformed to a standard normal one (with mean 0 and standard deviation 1), so that cross-country and over time differences in the measurement scale are avoided[28]. Despite the fact that this indicator measures subjective perceptions regarding the quality of governance and it is not the outcome of a quantitative objective measurement[29], it is of great importance since it reveals how governance is being perceived.

Gross National Income per capita in purchasing power parities or current international dollars (GNI.pc.ppp) is used to approximate the level of economic development in each country. GNI.pc.ppp is gross national income (GNI) converted to international dollars using purchasing power parity rates. An international dollar has the same purchasing power over GNI as a U.S. dollar has in the United States. GNI.pc.ppp is very useful in economic analysis when the objective is to compare broad differences between countries in living standards since purchasing power parities take into account the relative cost of living in various countries, while nominal GNI (or GDP) does not integrate any such considerations. GNI.pc.ppp is an indicator widely used in international comparisons of economic development. The data used refer to the year 2012 and are provided by the World Bank[30] and for that year cover 214 economies.

To approximate the quality of democracy in each country the political rights index (PR) is used estimated by the Freedom House organization. Political rights enable people to participate freely in the political process, including the right to vote freely for distinct alternatives in legitimate elections, compete for public office, join political parties and organizations and elect representatives who have a decisive impact on public policies and are accountable to the electorate. The scale of the PR index ranges between 1 and 7. Countries and territories with a rating of 1 enjoy a wide range of political rights, including free and fair elections whereas countries and territories with a rating of 7 have few or no political rights because of severe government oppression, sometimes in combination with civil war[31]. The

[27] The Worldwide Governance Indicators dataset is provided by the World Bank every two years from 1996 up until 2002 and on an annual basis since then. See, http://info.worldbank.org/ governance/wgi/ index.aspx#home.

[28] More specifically, the data sources are rescaled and combined to create the six aggregate indicators using the unobserved components model statistical tool. A key feature of the methodology is that it generates margins of error for each governance estimate. For a more comprehensive description of the methodology and related analytical issues, see Kaufmann, Kraay and Mastruzzi (2010).

[29] Despite their wide use, WGI have some limitations. Major reasons for concern include the likelihood of correlation of errors among sources, lack of comparability over time, data subjectivity and as a result sample bias and insufficient transparency (Arndt and Oman 2006, pp. 65-72). Langbein and Knack (2010) claim that worldwide governance indicators instead of measuring six distinct concepts of governance they appear to be measuring the same broad concept. Thomas (2010, p. 46-47) raises concerns on construct validity, that is whether the indicators are valid measurements of what they purport to measure. Kurtz and Schrank (2007, pp. 544-545) suggest that the dominant worldwide governance indicators are problematic, suffering from perceptual biases, adverse selection in sampling and conceptual conflation with indicators of policy choice resulting from survey design and aggregation problems (pp. 544-545).

[30] See, http://data.worldbank.org/indicator/NY.GNP.PCAP.PP.CD.

[31] For more details see Methodological Summary (Freedom House, 2012).

data used for the PR index refer to the year 2012 and for that year cover 195 countries and 14 territories.

To approximate the extent of civil liberties in each country the civil liberties index (CL) is used estimated by the Freedom House organization. Civil liberties allow for the freedoms of expression and belief, associational and organizational rights, rule of law and personal autonomy without interference from the state. The scale of the PR index ranges between 1 and 7. Countries and territories with a rating of 1 enjoy a wide range of civil liberties, including freedom of expression, assembly, association, education, and religion. Countries and territories with a rating of 7 have few or no civil liberties[18]. The data used for the CL index refer to the year 2012 and for that year cover 195 countries and 14 territories.

It must be stressed that the average of the PR and CL ratings is known as the "freedom rating" index (FR) and determines the overall status of a country as a free, partly free and not free. Countries are characterized as free countries (F) if they score 1.0-2.5 in the 1-7 scale, partly free countries (PF) if they score 3.0-5.0 in the 1-7 scale and not free countries (NF) if they score 5.5-7.0 in the 1-7 scale. However, since the two indexes focus on different aspects of democracy and freedom and since there are some deviations between the PR and CL ratings for several countries, the two separate ratings were used instead of the average FR index.

The human development index (HDI) is used as a summary measure of the level of human development. It is estimated by the United Nations Development Programme (UNDP) and it measures the average achievements in a given country in three relevant dimensions of human development: a long and healthy life, access to knowledge and a decent standard of living. It is a composite index with life expectancy in birth, mean years of schooling, expected years of schooling and gross national income (GNI) per capita as its main components[32]. Despite its inherent limitations the index is a useful comparative measure of the level of human development. According to this index countries are classified in four categories: very high human development, if the value of the index is higher than 0.900, high human development if the value of the index lies between 0.800 and 0.899, medium human development, if the value of the index is between 0.500 and 0.799 and low human development, if the value of the index is lower than 0.500. The data used for the HDI index refer to the year 2012 and are provided by the UNDP and for that year cover 187 countries. Since the HDI includes as one of its main components GNI per capita that has already been used as the basic variable of economic development, the variable HDI based on non-income measures is employed, that is the HDI excluding its income dimension or component.

All dependent and explanatory variables of the regression models are quantitative, measured in the scales suggested by the organizations that produce them. The normality of the dependent variable was tested, while linearity, multicollinearity, heteroscedasticity and autocorrelation checks were also carried out. The explanatory power of the model was expressed by the adjusted coefficient of determination (R^2). The stepwise procedure used by the SPSS package was employed for building the models, with a probability of F equal to 0.05 as a criterion to enter a variable and equal to 0.10 as a criterion to remove a variable. The economic significance (the direction of the effect) of a variable was also a criterion for its approval.

[32] http://hdr.undp.org/en/data.

1.3. RESULTS OF EMPIRICAL ANALYSIS

The results of our empirical analysis are provided separately for each dependent variable expressing the six dimensions of governance.

1.3.1. Dependent Variable: Political Stability and Absence of Violence/Terrorism (PSAVT)

By using GNI.pc.ppp (000), CL, PR and HDI as predictors, we obtained the following regression results (model 3 of table 1):

$$\text{PSAVT} = 0.554 - 0.465\ \text{CL} + 0.021\ \text{GNI.pc.ppp (000)} + 0.167\ \text{PR} \qquad (1)$$
$$R_{Adj}^2 = 0.579$$

Stepwise procedure did not include HDI into the model as it does not add to the explanatory power of the model in a statistically significant level.

According to their b coefficients (– 0.465, 0.021) CL and GNI.pc.ppp are in the expected direction, indicating that in a certain country of the studied group, the higher the income per capita is, the higher the political stability and absence of violence/ terrorism is and the higher the civil liberties are, the higher the political stability and absence of violence/terrorism is and vice versa.

However, PR's coefficient is not in the expected direction (0.167) and that is the reason to remove the certain variable from the model. Actually, we keep model 2 of Table 1:

$$\text{PSAVT} = 0.508 - 0.283\ \text{CL} + 0.022\ \text{GNI.pc.ppp (000)} \qquad (1a)$$
$$R_{Adj}^2 = 0.566$$

The b's coefficients of CL and GNI.pc.ppp are statistically significant ($t_{CL} = -9.634$, $p = 0.000 < 0.001$ and $t_{GNI.pc.ppp} = 6.343$, $p = 0.000 < 0.001$). Additionally, the constant coefficient is statistically significant as well ($t = 3.736$, $p = 0.000 < 0.001$).

According to their b coefficients (– 0.283 and 0.022) CL and GNI.pc.ppp in model 2 are in the expected direction, indicating that in a certain country of the studied group, the higher the income per capita is the higher the political stability and absence of violence/terrorism is. The higher the civil liberties are, the higher the political stability and absence of violence/terrorism is and vice versa. Stepwise procedure did not include HDI into the model as it does not add to the explanatory power of the model in a statistically significant level.

The model has an acceptable total explanatory performance, as the coefficient of determination $R^2_{CL,\ GNI} = 56.6\%$. CL is the first explanatory variable which entered the model, explaining most of the dependent's variation ($R^2_{CL} = 46.7\%$). GNI.pc.ppp adds a 9.9% in the equation's goodness of fit.

Tolerance statistics are high and VIF are low (VIF < 10) for all independent variables, indicating no serious multicollinearity problems (table 1).

Conditional index for the last dimension is low (5.590 < 15) and Eigenvalue is near 0 but not equal to it, both indicating not serious multicollinearity. The CL variable is the only one associated with high variance proportions in the last dimension.

Table 1. Basic results of the model

Coefficients[a]								
Model		Unstandardized Coefficients		Standardized Coefficients	t	Sig.	Collinearity Statistics	
		B	Std. Error	Beta			Tolerance	VIF
1	(Constant)	1.092	.111		9.812	.000		
	CL.2012	-.363	.029	-.685	-12.305	.000	1.000	1.000
2	(Constant)	.508	.136		3.736	.000		
	CL.2012	-.283	.029	-.535	-9.634	.000	.818	1.223
	GNI.PC.PPP.2012_1000	.022	.003	.352	6.343	.000	.818	1.223
3	(Constant)	.554	.135		4.091	.000		
	CL.2012	-.465	.079	-.879	-5.870	.000	.109	9.155
	GNI.PC.PPP.2012_1000	.021	.003	.343	6.262	.000	.814	1.228
	PR.2012	.167	.068	.362	2.468	.015	.114	8.764

[a] Dependent Variable: Political Stability and Absence of Violence/Terrorism.

Table 2. Collinearity diagnostics of the final stepwise model

Collinearity Diagnostics[a]						
Model	Dimension	Eigenvalue	Condition Index	Variance Proportions		
				(Constant)	CL.2012	GNI.PC.PPP.1000
2	1	2.356	1.000	.02	.03	.05
	2	.568	2.036	.00	.11	.50
	3	.075	5.590	.97	.86	.45

[a] Dependent Variable: Political Stability and Absence of Violence/Terrorism.

Taking into consideration the above criteria, we could conclude that there are not serious multicollinearity problems in the model. Durbin-Watson test did not indicate autocorrelation as $d = 2.005 > d_U = 1.72$ and $4\text{-}d = 1.995 > d_U = 1.72$ with explanatory variables $K = 2$, $a = 0.05$ and $n = 173$.

Additionally, studentized deleted residuals seem to follow the normal distribution according to all statistics and tests (skewness statistic = -0.117, std. error = 0.185, kurtosis statistic = 0.105, std. error = 0.367) and Kolmogorov-Smirnov statistic = 0.046, df = 173, p = 0.20). The distribution of studentized deleted residuals is shown in Figure 1.

Finally homoscedasticity assumptions seem, more or less, to be followed according to the scatter-plot in Figure 2.

The aforementioned results suggest that the model 1a has a good explanatory performance, the coefficients appear to have statistical and economic significance and the assumptions for the model approval are followed. Because of that we approve the model indicating the existence of linear dependence of political stability and absence of violence/terrorism on CL and GNI.pc.ppp (000).

1.3.2. Dependent Variable: Voice and Accountability (VA)

By using GNI.pc.ppp (000), CL, PR and HDI as predictors, we obtained the following regression results (model 3 of Table 3):

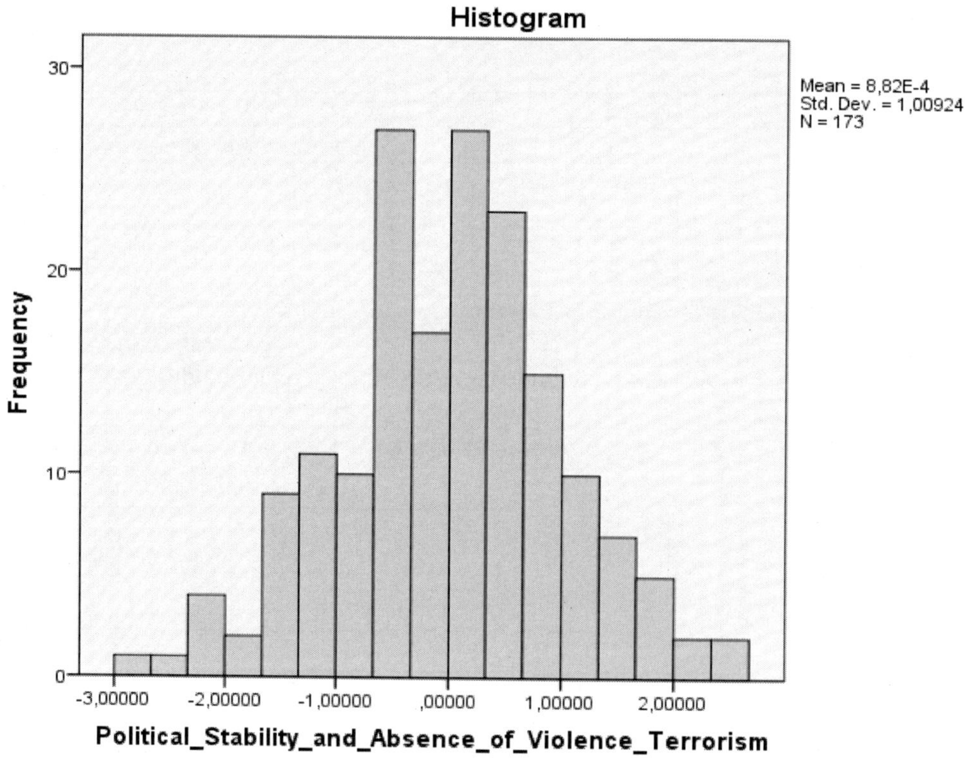

Figure 1.

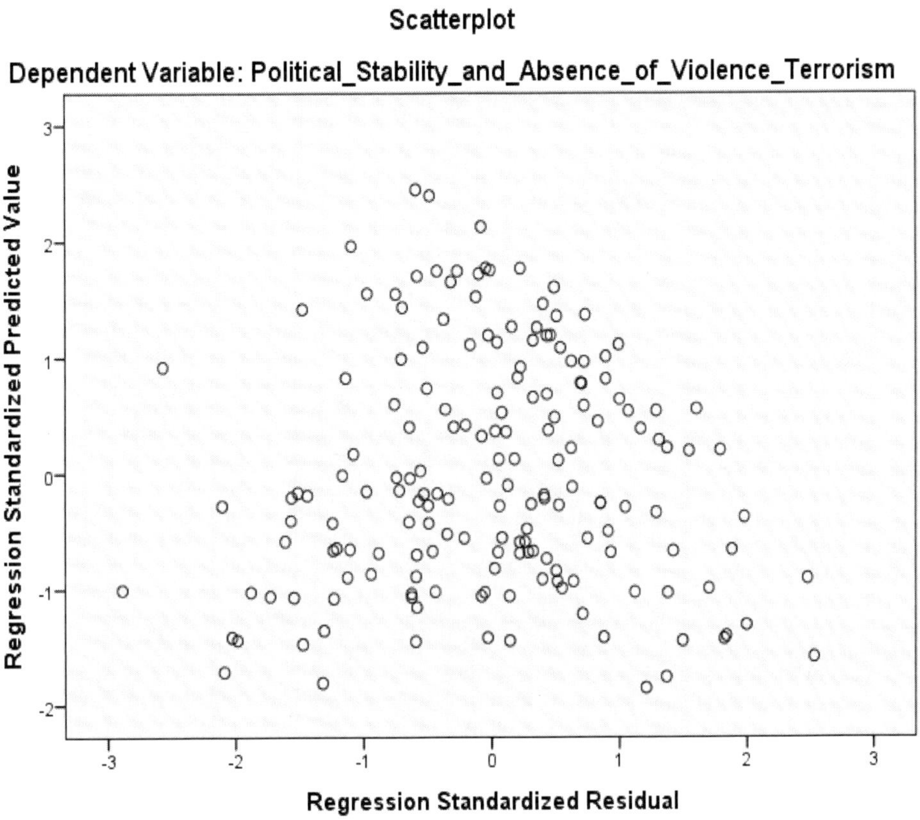

Figure 2.

$$VA = 1.296 - 0.345CL + 0.011GNI.pc.ppp\ (000) - 0.116PR \quad (2)$$
$$R_{Adj}^2 = 0.959$$

According to their b coefficients (- 0.345, 0.011, – 0.116) CL, GNI.pc.ppp and PR are in the expected direction, indicating that in a certain country of the group studied, the higher the political rights and civil liberties are, the higher the voice and accountability is and vice versa. Moreover, the higher the income per capita is the higher the voice and accountability is. Stepwise procedure did not include HDI into the model as it does not add to the explanatory power of the model in a statistically significant level. The b's coefficients of CL, GNI.pc.ppp and PR are statistically significant ($t_{CL} = -14.007$, $p = 0.000 < 0.001$, $t_{GNI.pc.ppp} = 10.554$, $p = 0.000 < 0.001$ and $t_{PR} = -5.514$, $p = 0.000 < 0.001$). Additionally, the constant coefficient is statistically significant as well ($t = 30.770$, $p = 0.000 < 0.001$).

The model has an excellent total explanatory performance, as the coefficient of determination $R^2_{CL, GNI, PR} = 95.9\%$. CL is the first explanatory variable which entered the model, explaining most of the dependent's variation ($R^2_{CL} = 92.8\%$). GNI.pc.ppp adds a 2.4% and PR adds a 0.7% in the equation's goodness of fit.

Table 3. Basic results of the model

Coefficients[a]								
Model		Unstandardized Coefficients		Standardized Coefficients	t	Sig.	Collinearity Statistics	
		B	Std. Error	Beta			Tolerance	VIF
1	(Constant)	1.615	.041		39.396	.000		
	CL.2012	-.511	.011	-.964	-47.066	.000	1.000	1.000
2	(Constant)	1.327	.045		29.372	.000		
	CL.2012	-.472	.010	-.889	-48.359	.000	.818	1.223
	GNI.PC.PPP.2012_1000	.011	.001	.174	9.433	.000	.818	1.223
3	(Constant)	1.296	.042		30.770	.000		
	CL.2012	-.345	.025	-.651	-14.007	.000	.109	9.155
	GNI.PC.PPP.2012_1000	.011	.001	.180	10.554	.000	.814	1.228
	PR.2012	-.116	.021	-.251	-5.514	.000	.114	8.764

[a] Dependent Variable: Voice and Accountability.

Tolerance statistics are high and VIF are low (VIF < 10) for all independent variables, indicating no serious multicollinearity problems (Table 3). Conditional index for the last dimension is low (14.882 < 15) and Eigenvalue is near 0 but not equal to it, both indicating not serious multicollinearity. Both CL and PR variable are associated with high variance proportions in the last dimension.

Table 4. Collinearity diagnostics of the final stepwise model

Collinearity Diagnostics[a]							
Model	Dimension	Eigenvalue	Condition Index	Variance Proportions			
				(Constant)	CL. 2012	GNI.PC.PPP. 2012_1000	PR. 2012
3	1	3.185	1.000	0.01	0.00	0.02	0.00
	2	0.701	2.131	0.00	0.00	0.45	0.01
	3	0.099	5.672	0.86	0.01	0.49	0.05
	4	0.014	14.882	0.12	0.98	0.03	0.94

[a] Dependent Variable: Voice and Accountability.

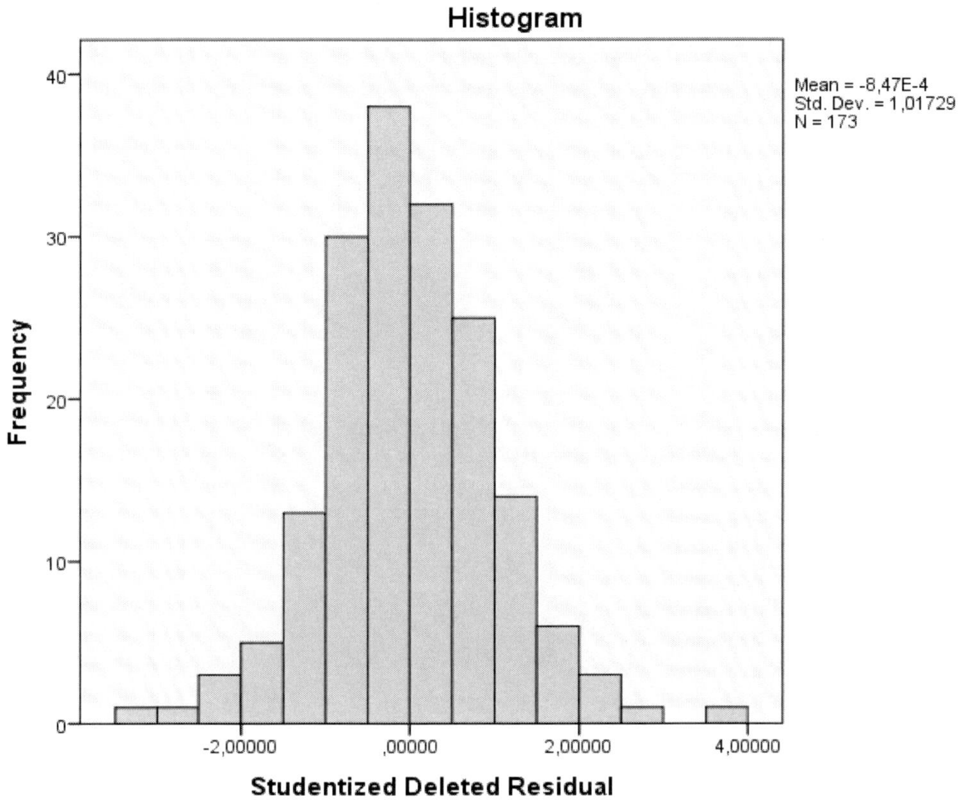

Figure 3.

Taking into consideration the above criteria, we could conclude that there are not serious multicollinearity problems in the model. Durbin-Watson test did not indicate autocorrelation as d = 1.822 > d_U = 1.74 and 4-d = 2.178 > d_U = 1.74 with explanatory variables K = 3, a = 0.05 and n = 173.

Additionally, studentized deleted residuals seem to follow the normal distribution according to all statistics and tests (skewness statistic = 0.091, std. error = 0.185, kurtosis statistic = 1.125, std. error = 0.367) and Kolmogorov-Smirnov statistic = 0.043, df = 173, p = 0.20). The distribution of studentized deleted residuals is shown in figure 3.

Finally homoscedasticity assumptions seem, more or less, to be followed according to the scatter-plot in figure 4.

The aforementioned results suggest that the model has a good explanatory performance, the coefficients appear to have statistical and economic significance and the assumptions for the model approval are followed. Because of that we approve the model indicating the existence of linear dependence of Voice and Accountability on CL, PR and GNI.pc.ppp (000).

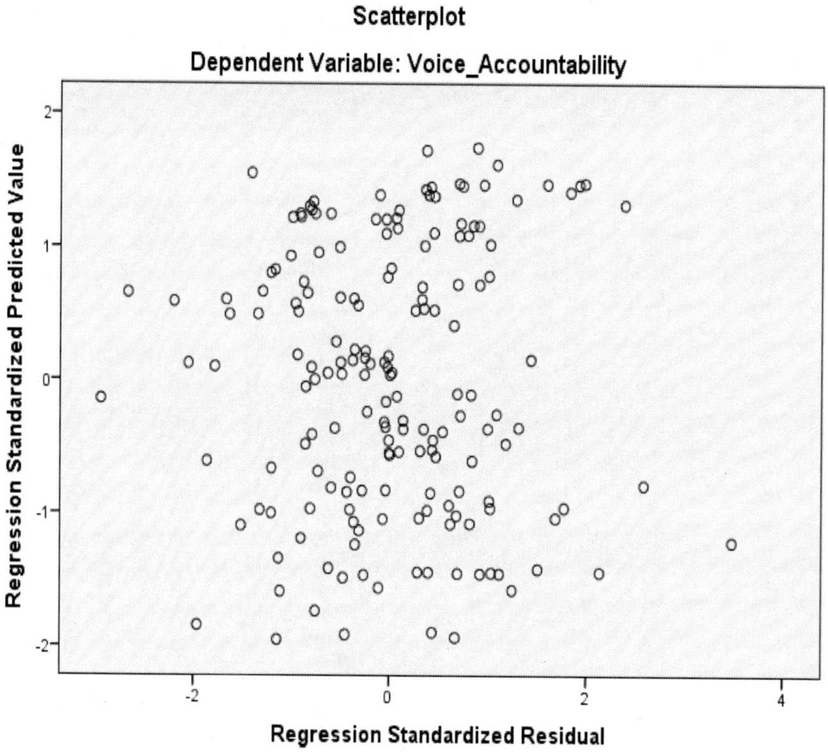

Figure 4.

1.3.3. Dependent Variable: Regulatory Quality (RQ)

By using GNI.pc.ppp (000), CL, PR and HDI as predictors, we obtained the following regression results (model 3 of table 5):

$$RQ = -0.224 + 0.028\ \text{GNI.pc.ppp (000)} - 0.217\ CL + 0.758\ HDI \qquad (3)$$
$$R_{Adj}^{2} = 0.753$$

According to their b coefficients (0.028, - 0.217, 0.758) GNI.pc.ppp, CL and HDI are in the expected direction, indicating that in a certain country of the studied group, the higher the income per capita or the human development is, the higher the regulatory quality is. Moreover, the higher the civil liberties are, the higher the regulatory quality is and vice versa. Stepwise procedure did not include PR into the model as it does not add to the explanatory power of the model in a statistically significant level. The b's coefficients of CL, GNI.pc.ppp and HDI are statistically significant ($t_{GNI.pc.ppp} = 7.797$, $p = 0.000 < 0.001$, $t_{CL} = -9.186$, $p = 0.000 < 0.001$, and $t_{HDI} = 2.101$, $p = 0.037 < 0.05$). Additionally, the constant coefficient is not statistically significant at conventional significance levels ($t = -0.870$, $p = 0.386 > 0.05$).

Table 5. Basic results of the model

Coefficients[a]								
Model		Unstandardized Coefficients		Standardized Coefficients	t	Sig.	Collinearity Statistics	
		B	Std. Error	Beta			Tolerance	VIF
1	(Constant)	-.686	.064		-10.724	.000		
	GNI.PC.PPP. 2012_1000	.045	.003	.758	15.176	.000	1.000	1.000
2	(Constant)	.276	.100		2.747	.007		
	GNI.PC.PPP. 2012_1000	.033	.003	.559	13.209	.000	.818	1.223
	CL.2012	-.238	.022	-.465	-10.993	.000	.818	1.223
3	(Constant)	-.224	.258		-.870	.386		
	GNI.PC.PPP. 2012_1000	.028	.004	.469	7.797	.000	.398	2.514
	CL.2012	-.217	.024	-.424	-9.186	.000	.673	1.486
	HDI.2012	.758	.361	.139	2.101	.037	.328	3.053

[a] Dependent Variable: Regulatory Quality.

The model has a very good total explanatory performance, as the coefficient of determination $R^2_{CL,\ GNI,\ HDI} = 75.3\%$. GNI.pc.ppp is the first explanatory variable which entered the model, explaining most of the dependent's variation ($R^2_{GNI.pc.ppp} = 57.1\%$). CL adds a 17.7% and HDI adds a 0.5% in the equation's goodness of fit.

Table 6. Collinearity diagnostics of the final stepwise model

Collinearity Diagnostics[a]							
				Variance Proportions			
Model	Dimension	Eigenvalue	Condition Index	(Constant)	GNI.PC.PPP. 2012_1000	CL. 2012	HDI. 2012
3	1	3.306	1.000	0.00	0.01	0.01	0.00
	2	0.575	2.397	0.00	0.21	0.10	0.00
	3	0.109	5.503	0.03	0.40	0.54	0.04
	4	0.010	18.484	0.97	0.38	0.35	0.96

[a] Dependent Variable: Regulatory Quality.

Tolerance statistics are high and VIF are low (VIF < 10) for all independent variables, indicating no serious multicollinearity problems (table 5). Conditional index for the last dimension is 18.484, slightly higher than 15, and Eigenvalue is close to 0, both indicating some but not serious multicollinearity. The HDI variable is the only one associated with high variance proportions in the last dimension.

Taking into consideration the above criteria, we could conclude that there are not serious multicollinearity problems in the model. Durbin-Watson test did not indicate autocorrelation as $d = 1.886 > d_U = 1.74$ and $4\text{-}d = 2.114 > d_U = 1.74$ with explanatory variables $K = 3$, $a = 0.05$ and $n = 173$.

Additionally, studentized deleted residuals variable seems to face some but not very serious kurtosis problems (skewness statistic = -0.733, std. error = 0.185, kurtosis statistic = 1.365, std. error = 0.367). Additionally, Kolmogorov-Smirnov test did not verify normality (K-S statistic = 0.071, df = 173, p = 0.035). The distribution of studentized deleted residuals is shown in figure 5.

Finally homoscedasticity assumption seems, to be followed according to the scatter-plot in figure 6.

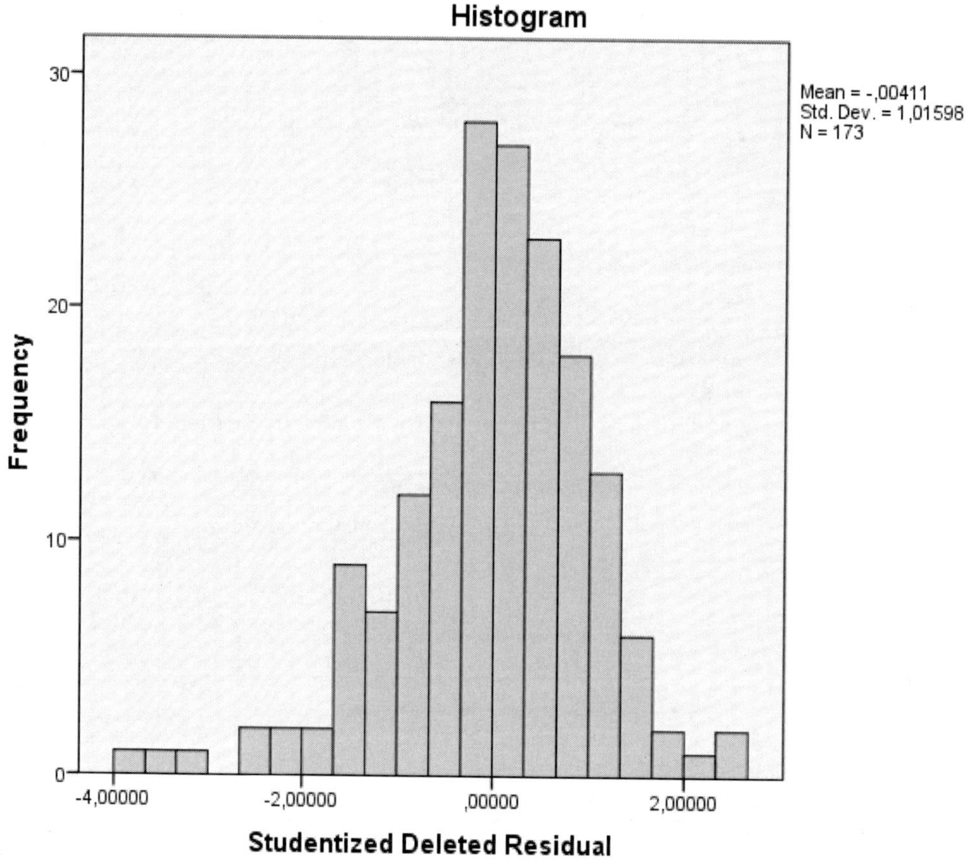

Figure 5.

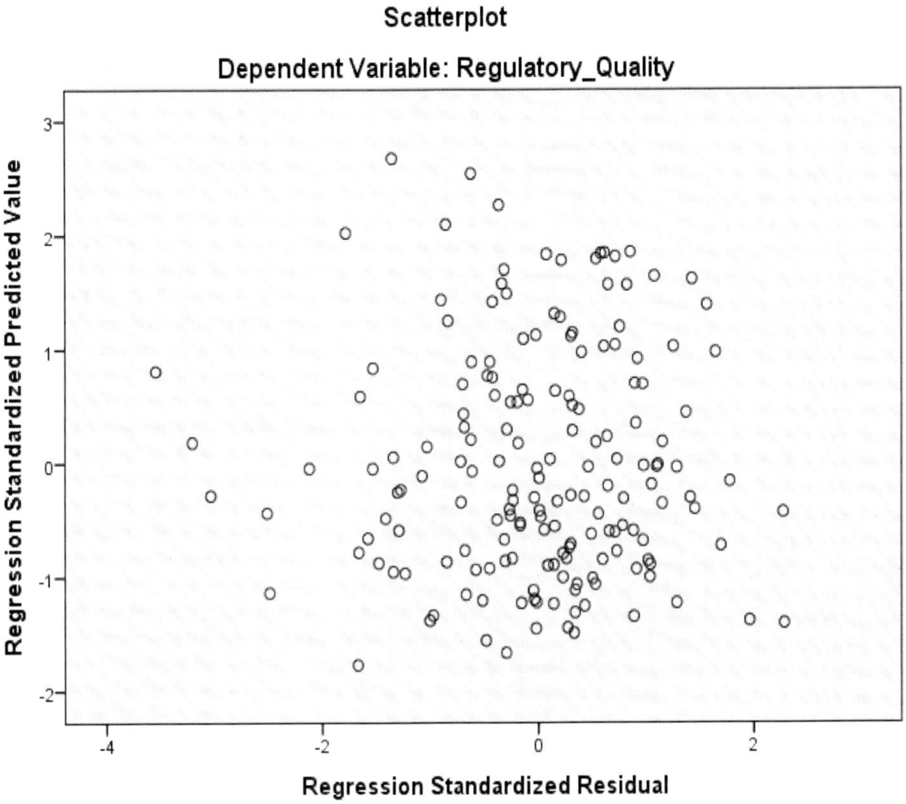

Figure 6.

The aforementioned results suggest that the model has a very good explanatory performance, the coefficients appear to have statistical and economic significance and the assumptions for the model approval are followed, with normality assumption and statistical significance of the constant coefficient as exceptions. Because of that we approve the model indicating the existence of linear dependence of Regulatory Quality on GNI.pc.ppp (000), CL and HDI, overcoming the aforementioned problems.

1.3.4. Dependent Variable: Rule of Law (RL)

By using GNI.pc.ppp (000), CL, PR and HDI as predictors, we obtained the following regression results (model 2 of table 7):

$$RL = 0.227 + 0.037\ \text{GNI.pc.ppp (000)} - 0.254\ \text{CL} \quad (4)$$
$$R_{Adj}^{2} = 0.822$$

According to their b coefficients (0.037, - 0.254) GNI.pc.ppp and CL are in the expected direction, indicating that in a certain country of the studied group, the higher the income per capita is and the higher civil liberties are the higher the rule of law is. Stepwise procedure did not include PR and HDI into the model as they do not add to the explanatory power of the model in a statistically significant level. The b's coefficients of GNI.pc.ppp and CL are statistically significant ($t_{GNI.pc.ppp}$ = 16.648, p = 0.000 < 0.001, t_{CL} = -13.458, p = 0.000 < 0.001). Additionally, the constant coefficient is statistically significant as well (t = 2.598, p = 0.010 < 0.05).

The model has a very good total explanatory performance, as the coefficient of determination $R^2_{GNI, CL}$ = 82.2%. GNI.pc.ppp is the first explanatory variable which entered the model, explaining most of the dependent's variation ($R^2_{GNI.pc.ppp}$ = 63.4%). CL adds a 18.8% in the equation's goodness of fit.

Tolerance statistics are high and VIF are low (VIF < 10) for all independent variables, indicating no serious multicollinearity problems (Table 7). Conditional index for the last dimension is low (5.590 < 15) and Eigenvalue is near 0 but not equal to it, both indicating not serious multicollinearity. The CL variable is the only one associated with high variance proportions in the last dimension.

Table 7. Basic results of the model

Coefficients[a]								
Model		Unstandardized Coefficients		Standardized Coefficients	t	Sig.	Collinearity Statistics	
		B	Std. Error	Beta			Tolerance	VIF
1	(Constant)	-.799	.061		-13.041	.000		
	GNI.PC.PPP.2012_1000	.049	.003	.797	17.277	.000	1.000	1.000
2	(Constant)	.227	.087		2.598	.010		
	GNI.PC.PPP.2012_1000	.037	.002	.593	16.648	.000	.818	1.223
	CL.2012	-.254	.019	-.479	-13.458	.000	.818	1.223

[a] Dependent Variable: Rule of Law.

Table 8. Collinearity diagnostics of the final stepwise model

Collinearity Diagnostics[a]						
Model	Dimension	Eigenvalue	Condition Index	Variance Proportions		
				(Constant)	GNI.PC.PPP.2012_1000	CL.2012
2	1	2.356	1.000	.02	.05	.03
	2	.568	2.036	.00	.50	.11
	3	.075	5.590	.97	.45	.86

[a] Dependent Variable: Rule of Law.

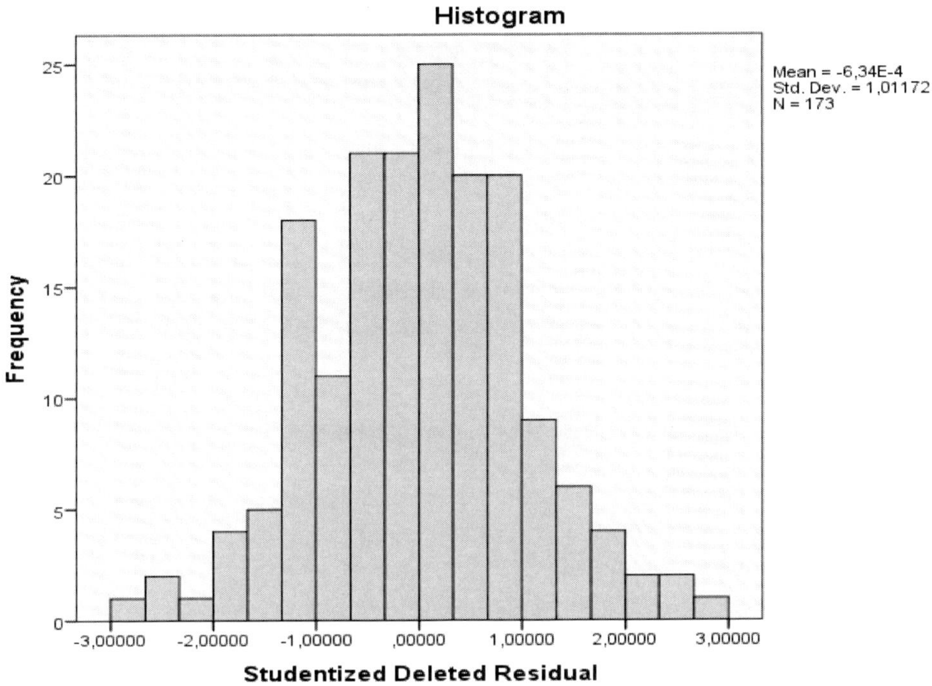

Figure 7.

Taking into consideration the above criteria, we could conclude that there are not serious multicollinearity problems in the model. Durbin-Watson test did not indicate autocorrelation as $d = 2.008 > d_U = 1.72$ and $4\text{-}d = 1.992 > d_U = 1.72$ with explanatory variables K = 2, a = 0.05 and n = 173.

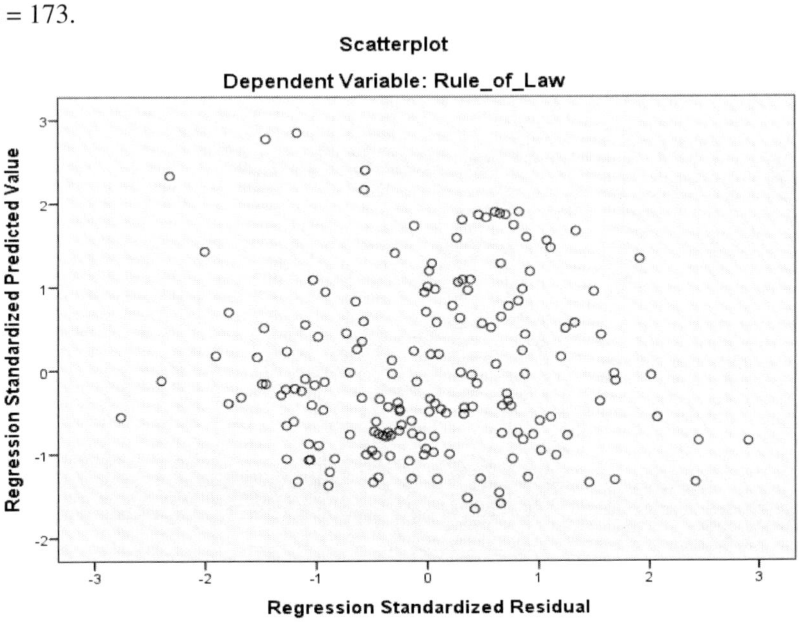

Figure 8.

Additionally, studentized deleted residuals seem to follow the normal distribution according to all statistics and tests (skewness statistic = 0.015, std. error = 0.185, kurtosis statistic = 1.90, std. error = 0.367) and Kolmogorov-Smirnov statistic = 0.035, df = 173, p = 0.20). The distribution of studentized deleted residuals is shown in Figure 7.

Finally homoscedasticity assumptions seems to be followed according to the scatter-plot in Figure 8.

The aforementioned results suggest that the model has a very good explanatory performance, the coefficients appear to have statistical and economic significance and the assumptions for the model approval are followed. Because of that we approve the model indicating the existence of linear dependence of Rule of Law on GNI.pc.ppp (000) and CL.

1.3.5. Dependent Variable: Control of Corruption (CC)

By using GNI.pc.ppp (000), CL, PR and HDI as predictors, we obtained the following regression results (model 2 of table 9):

$$CC = 0.164 + 0.038\ GNI.pc.ppp\ (000) - 0.236\ CL \qquad (3)$$
$$R_{Adj}^{2} = 0.751$$

According to their b coefficients (0.038, - 0.236) GNI.pc.ppp and CL are in the expected direction, indicating that in a certain country of the group studied, the higher the civil liberties are, the lower the level of corruption is and the higher the income per capita is, the lower the level of corruption is and vice versa. Stepwise procedure did not include PR and HDI into the model as they do not add to the explanatory power of the model in a statistically significant level. The b's coefficients of GNI.pc.ppp and CL are statistically significant ($t_{GNI.pc.ppp}$ = 14.069, p = 0.000 < 0.001, t_{CL} = -10.269, p = 0.000 < 0.001). Additionally, the constant coefficient is not statistically significant at conventional significance levels (t = 1.542, p = 0.125 > 0.05).

Table 9. Basic results of the model

Coefficients[a]								
Model		Unstandardized Coefficients		Standardized Coefficients	t	Sig.	Collinearity Statistics	
		B	Std. Error	Beta			Tolerance	VIF
1	(Constant)	-.789	.066		-11.944	.000		
	GNI.PC.PPP.2012_1000	.050	.003	.776	16.074	.000	1.000	1.000
2	(Constant)	.164	.106		1.542	.125		
	GNI.PC.PPP.2012_1000	.038	.003	.592	14.069	.000	.818	1.223
	CL.2012	-.236	.023	-.432	-10.269	.000	.818	1.223

[a] Dependent Variable: Control of Corruption.

Table 10. Collinearity diagnostics of the final stepwise model

Collinearity Diagnostics[a]						
				Variance Proportions		
Model	Dimension	Eigenvalue	Condition Index	(Constant)	GNI.PC.PPP.2012_1000	CL.2012
1	1	1.686	1.000	.16	.16	
	2	.314	2.317	.84	.84	
2	1	2.356	1.000	.02	.05	.03
	2	.568	2.036	.00	.50	.11
	3	.075	5.590	.97	.45	.86

[a] Dependent Variable: Control of Corruption.

The model has a very good total explanatory performance, as the coefficient of determination $R^2_{GNI,\ CL} = 75.1\%$. GNI.pc.ppp is the first explanatory variable which entered the model, explaining most of the dependent's variation ($R^2_{GNI.pc.ppp} = 59.9\%$). CL adds a 15.2% in the equation's goodness of fit.

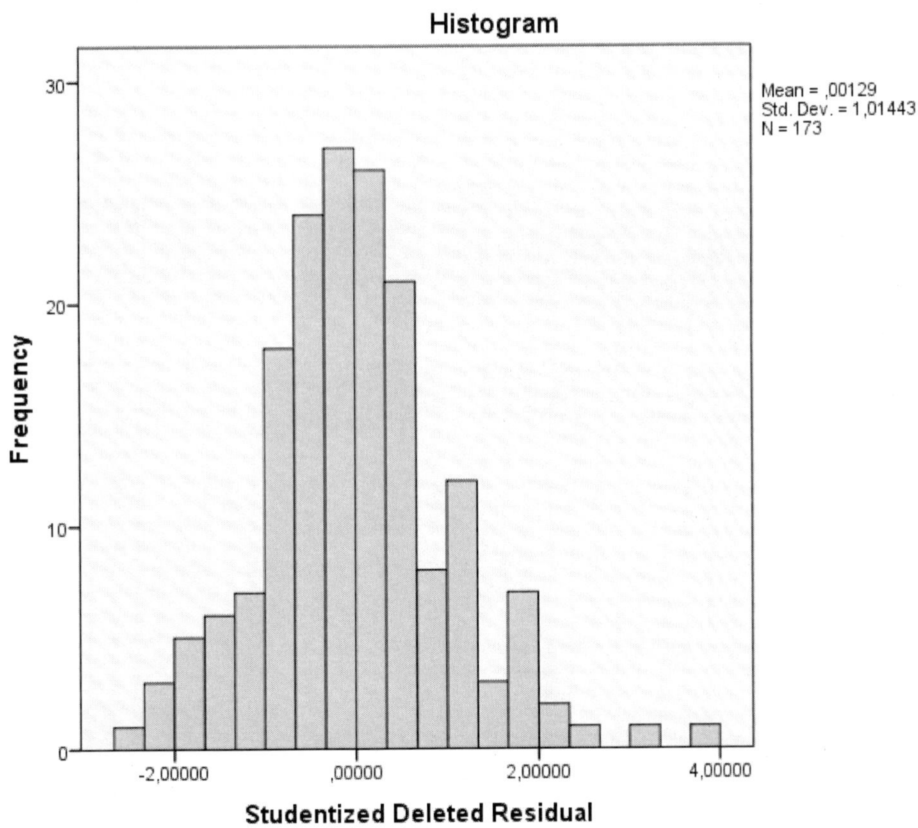

Figure 9.

Tolerance statistics are high and VIF are low (VIF < 10) for all independent variables, indicating no serious multicollinearity problems (Table 9). Conditional index for the last dimension is low (5.590 < 15) and Eigenvalue is near 0 but not equal to it, both indicating not serious multicollinearity. The CL variable is the only one associated with high variance proportions in the last dimension.

Taking into consideration the above criteria, we could conclude that there are not serious multicollinearity problems in the model. Durbin-Watson test did not indicate autocorrelation as $d = 2.005 > d_U = 1.72$ and $4\text{-}d = 1.995 > d_U = 1.72$ with explanatory variables K = 2, a = 0.05 and n = 173.

Additionally, studentized deleted residuals seem to follow the normal distribution according to all statistics and tests (skewness statistic = 0.520, std. error = 0.185, kurtosis statistic = 1.205, std. error = 0.367) and Kolmogorov-Smirnov statistic = 0.061, df = 173, p = 0.20). The distribution of studentized deleted residuals is shown in figure 9.

Finally homoscedasticity assumptions seem to be followed according to the scatter-plot in figure 10.

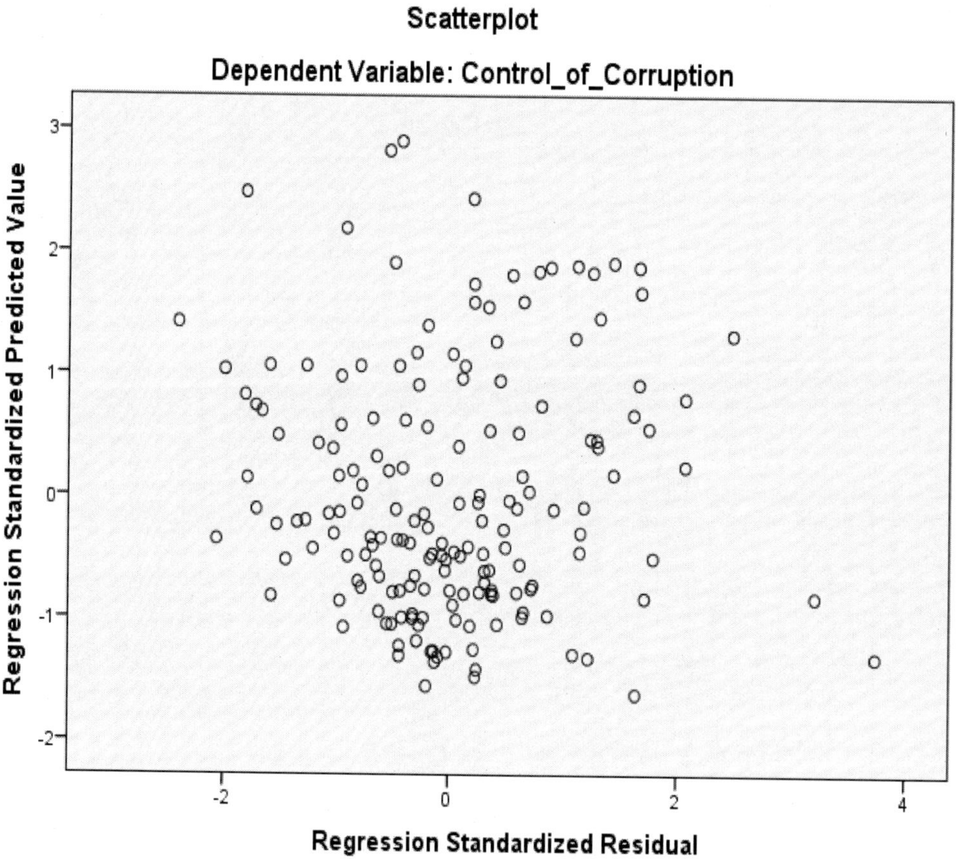

Figure 10.

The aforementioned results suggest that the model has a good explanatory performance, the coefficients appear to have statistical (with the constant coefficient as an exception) and economic significance and the assumptions for the model approval are followed. Because of that we approve the model indicating the existence of linear dependence of Control of Corruption on GNI.pc.ppp (000) and CL, overcoming the significance problem of the constant coefficient.

1.3.6. Dependent Variable: Government Effectiveness (GE)

By using GNI.pc.ppp (000), CL, PR and HDI as predictors, we obtained the following regression results (model 3 of Table 11):

$$GE = -0.752 + 1.411\ HDI - 0.192\ CL + 0.028\ GNI.pc.ppp\ (000) \quad (6)$$
$$R_{Adj}^{2} = 0.753$$

According to their b coefficients (1.411, - 0.192, 0.028) GNI.pc.ppp, CL and HDI are in the expected direction, indicating that in a certain country of the studied group, the higher the civil liberties, the higher the government effectiveness is and vice versa. Moreover, the higher the income per capita and HDI are, the higher the government effectiveness is. Stepwise procedure did not include PR into the model as it does not add to the explanatory power of the model in a statistically significant level. The b's coefficients of CL, GNI.pc.ppp and PR are statistically significant ($t_{HDI} = 4.372$, $p = 0.000 < 0.001$, $t_{CL} = -9.054$, $p = 0.000 < 0.001$ and $t_{GNI.pc.ppp} = 8.607$, $p = 0.000 < 0.001$). Additionally, the constant coefficient is also statistically significant ($t = -3.261$, $p = 0.001$).

Table 11. Basic results of the model

Coefficients[a]								
Model		Unstandardized Coefficients		Standardized Coefficients	t	Sig.	Collinearity Statistics	
		B	Std. Error	Beta			Tolerance	VIF
1	(Constant)	-3.080	.176		-17.536	.000		
	HDI.2012	4.530	.253	.808	17.926	.000	1.000	1.000
2	(Constant)	-1.705	.242		-7.047	.000		
	HDI.2012	3.401	.269	.607	12.642	.000	.674	1.484
	CL.2012	-.186	.025	-.352	-7.346	.000	.674	1.484
3	(Constant)	-.752	.231		-3.261	.001		
	HDI.2012	1.411	.323	.252	4.372	.000	.328	3.053
	CL.2012	-.192	.021	-.363	-9.054	.000	.673	1.486
	GNI.PC.PPP. 2012_1000	.028	.003	.449	8.607	.000	.398	2.514

[a] Dependent Variable: Government Effectiveness.

Table 12. Collinearity diagnostics of the final stepwise model

Collinearity Diagnostics[a]							
				Variance Proportions			
Model	Dimension	Eigenvalue	Condition Index	(Constant)	HDI. 2012	CL. 2012	GNI.PC.PPP. 2012_1000
1	1	1.969	1.000	.02	.02		
	2	.031	7.989	.98	.98		
2	1	2.753	1.000	.00	.00	.02	
	2	.232	3.441	.00	.06	.43	
	3	.015	13.587	.99	.94	.55	
3	1	3.306	1.000	.00	.00	.01	.01
	2	.575	2.397	.00	.00	.10	.21
	3	.109	5.503	.03	.04	.54	.40
	4	.010	18.484	.97	.96	.35	.38

[a] Dependent Variable: Government Effectiveness.

The model has a very good total explanatory performance, as the coefficient of determination $R^2_{CL,\, GNI,\, HDI} = 81.3\%$. HDI is the first explanatory variable which entered the model, explaining most of the dependent's variation ($R^2_{HDI} = 65.1\%$). CL adds a 8.2% and GNI.pc.ppp adds a 8.0% in the equation's goodness of fit.

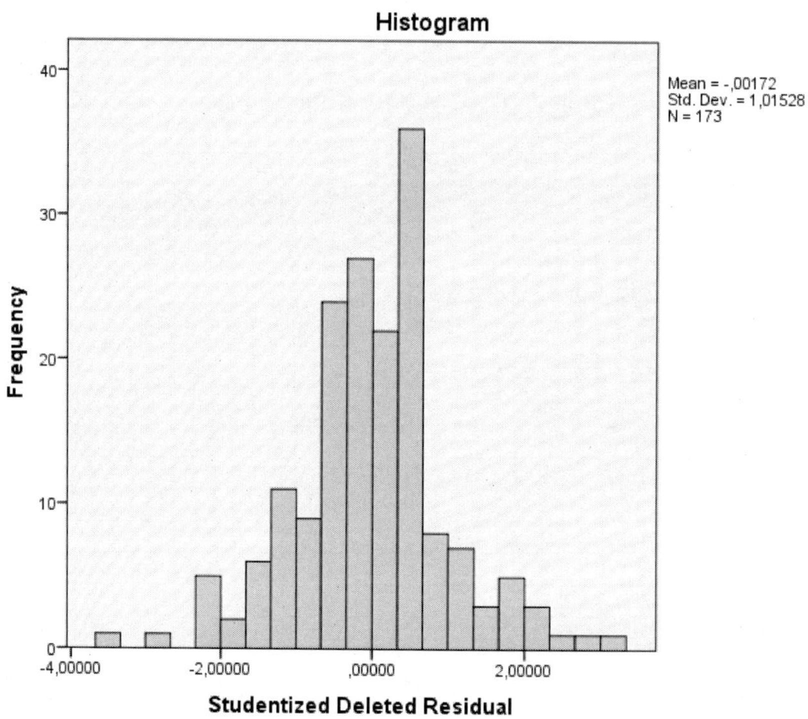

Figure 11.

Tolerance statistics are high and VIF are low (VIF < 10) for all independent variables, indicating no serious multicollinearity problems (Table 11). Conditional index for the last dimension is 18.484, slightly higher than 15, and Eigenvalue is near 0, both indicating some but not serious multicollinearity. The HDI variable is the only one associated with high variance proportions in the last dimension.

Taking into consideration the above criteria, we could conclude that there are some but not serious multicollinearity problems in the model. Durbin-Watson test did not indicate autocorrelation as $d = 2.059 > d_U = 1.74$ and $4\text{-}d = 1.941 > d_U = 1.74$ with explanatory variables $K = 3$, $a = 0.05$ and $n = 173$.

Additionally, studentized deleted residuals variable seems to face some but not very serious kurtosis problems (skewness statistic = -0.068, std. error = 0.185, kurtosis statistic = 1.152, std. error = 0.367). Additionally, Kolmogorov-Smirnov test did not not verify normality (K-S statistic = 0.089, df = 173, p = 0.002).

The distribution of studentized deleted residuals is shown in figure 11.

Finally homoscedasticity assumptions seem to be followed according to the scatter-plot in figure 12.

The aforementioned results suggest that the model has a good explanatory performance, the coefficients appear to have statistical and economic significance and the assumptions for the model approval are followed. Because of that we approve the model indicating the existence of linear dependence of GE on GNI.pc.ppp (000), CL and HDI.

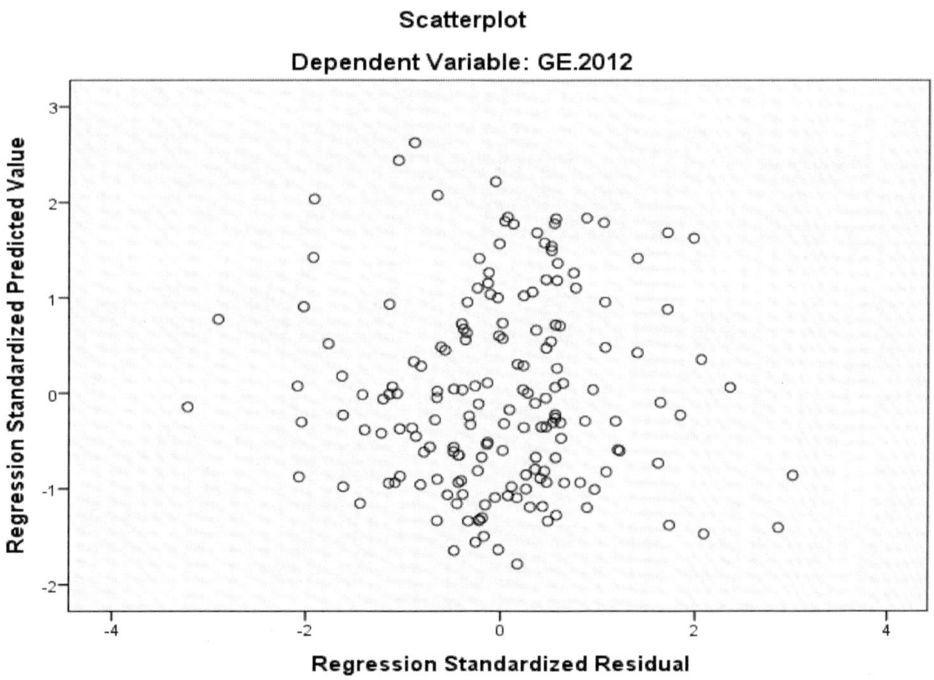

Figure 12.

Concluding the results, we should mention that more or less the six regression equations have a good performance, even if some multicollinearity or normality problems seem to appear for some of them. The importance of the models' explanatory power and the emergence of some theoretically very important variables (as HDI) as significant explanatory factors for the first time in our research are some very good reasons to overcome some (not very serious) technical problems.

CONCLUSION

This chapter explores the underlying determinants of governance outcomes worldwide based on approaches emerging from the prevailing theory of the good governance and institutions literature. The results suggest that the quality of governance varies across countries due to differences in countries' levels of economic development, extent of political rights and civil liberties as well as their respective levels of human development. The aforestated factors determine the overall level of institutional quality. Moreover, these inclusively examined factors do not have a symmetric impact on governance structure but vary depending on the specific dimension of governance under consideration. Poor governance is not exogenously assigned[33] whereas insufficient governance capacities and failures largely unveil the existence of economic and political weaknesses as well as institutional and social underdevelopment. An alternative policy interpretation is that government performance is in part determined by economic development[34] whereas it is also shaped by the systemic variation in the political and social conditions of individual countries, especially those related to the level of non income human development. In spite of the existence of context specific governance weaknesses prevalent in each country, there is scope for the emergence of overarching principles that embody principles of economic development, democracy, equitable and sustainable human development. Accordingly, concrete policy measures lie at the core of the good governance agenda targeting a lengthy list of governance objectives including improved social standards, increased economic and political development in order to achieve high levels of government effectiveness, anti-corruption safeguards, high standards of legitimacy and accountability among other attributes of effective governance systems.

Even though there seems to exist a high correlation between governance quality and income levels, not all countries facing the same economic conditions exhibit similar governance capacities. The following prominent country examples confirm the theoretical framework and the choice of the empirical model. Qatar and United Arab Emirates in spite of the prevailing high income levels perform poorly in all governance aspects according to the relevant indicators previously examined. It should be emphasized that the level of political freedom is low in these two countries and both are characterized as not free[35]. Consequently,

[33] Baland, Moene and Robinson (2009, p. 4601).

[34] As far as the worldwide governance indicators project is concerned it must be pointed out that good governance characteristics are not the privilege of rich countries only but of developing economies as well. For example, it is indicated that emerging economies like Botswana, Chile, and Estonia in specific governance dimensions, as it is the control of corruption, score better than countries such as Greece and Italy which are considered industrialized countries (IBRD 2006, p. 3). This argument supports the view that good governance is not only shaped by economic factors but of social and political nature as well.

[35] The taxonomy of countries as free, partly free and not free is based on the Freedom House (2012).

as it has been already pointed out, apart from the economic environment political aspects of development should also be seriously taken into account as far as the welfare of economies is concerned. Singapore even though considered partly free experiences one of the most low corruption levels in the world. Apart from being a high income country, this outcome could be also attributed to social factors and the achievement of very high human development standards as comprised by the relevant non income human development index[36], which are however beyond the scope of this chapter.

It is useful to unbundle the most basic relationships that emerge out of the empirical analysis between each of the six dimensions of governance and the employed economic, political and social predictor variables. As far as the economic factors are concerned, the results indicate that income per capita is positively associated with all the six dimensions of the predicted governance variable but it is most strongly correlated to the degree of corruption, the rule of law and the regulatory quality. As expected, the two variables, namely control of corruption (CC) and GNI.pc.ppp, are positively related: higher values of GNI.pc.ppp are associated with higher values of CC that is lower perceived levels of corruption. From a parallel point of view, the level of corruption is an extensive one in low income countries. This is not necessarily because their inhabitants present a natural proclivity towards this phenomenon, but because the conditions of life make them prone to it (Lalountas, Manolas and Vavouras 2011, p. 11). In other words, in low income economies, corruption is to some extent a survival strategy[37]. In these countries, increasing personal income is a strong motive and is becoming stronger due to conditions of utter deprivation most often combined with political instability and weak social structure. However, the effective control of corruption should not be misinterpreted and considered as a "quasi luxury good" the demand of which increases once the level of economic development rises to a certain level but it is achieved only through the adoption and effective implementation of the appropriate long-run policies (Rontos and Vavouras 2013b, p. 6). Moreover, as far the rule of law and regulatory quality are concerned it appears that their constituent elements and, more particularly, the protection of property rights and contract enforcement, the independent functioning of the justice, the respect of citizens for the accompanying governance institutions and the capacity of the state to formulate and enforce a coherent policy framework are more prevalent in high income societies.

The political system represented mainly by civil liberties, seems to be another critical factor that affects the level of governance globally. More specifically, the level of civil liberties seems to be negatively associated with all the six dimensions of governance, that is the higher protection of civil liberties the higher the quality of governance. However, it should be pointed out that the most strong negative correlation is present between civil liberties on the one hand and political stability and the level of voice and accountability on the other. The higher the civil liberties (that is the country is associated with reduced political freedoms) are, the higher are the risks for politically-motivated violence and political destabilization. As far as the political rights index is concerned it is also correlated to the political dimension of governance. Concerning voice and accountability the sign of the relationship is negative as predicted by theory since higher values of the political rights index

[36] According to data as far as the human development index is concerned for the year 2012 Singapore ranks thirtieth (30th) out of 187 countries, whereas it scores in the fourth (4th) place among all Asian economies examined, after Korea, Japan and Hong Kong.

[37] Rose-Ackerman (1999, p. 72).

correspond to lower political development. It could therefore be argued that achieving and maintaining high governance standards and political development is a process facilitated by the smooth functioning of democratic political institutions and civil liberties. Notions such as freedom of expression, associational rights, constitute but a few of the principal elements for the operation of a politically free state. The more open the democracy is, that is the more free the electoral process, the higher the political pluralism and participation and the higher the personal autonomy and individual rights, the more the phenomenon of weak governance is limited. The long-run health of the political system often requires internal checks and balances whereas openness and transparency are the best ways of ensuring that such structural mechanisms develop[38]. Along the same line, governments will become more effective in providing social and economic infrastructure when they can be held accountable to citizens who can freely express their opinions[39].

The strong correlation of the economic dimension of governance, namely government effectiveness and regulatory quality with the human development index should be highlighted. Government effectiveness is closely associated with the human development index whereas this finding indicates the role of social environment in the quality of policy formulation and enforcement. Social structures as captured by the human development index are related to the quality of public services provided and the credibility of government's commitment to such policies. Higher educational attainment levels are considered to promote governance, as a better educated population is more likely to participate in public decision making and to demand better governance (Busse and Gröning 2009, p. 77). Human development is also positively correlated to regulatory quality. Narrowing deficits in health, education and living standards are positively associated with the capacity of the government to implement sound policies. Human capital building, which is shaped by the accumulation of its basic ingredients, is therefore closely connected with increased governance capacities[40]. Investing in basic social infrastructure including education and health, emerge as drivers of navigating towards sustainable human development, which is critical for promoting an adaptive governance structure.

When patterns of poor governance systems prevail and become institutionalized their control is extremely difficult whereas the political difficulties of reform become even more challenging (*Bräutigam* and *Knack 2004, p. 256)*. Fighting endemic, deeply rooted structural weakness should involve profound economic and institutional reforms as well as structural adjustments as effective guides for remedying the root causes of the governance failure (Abed 1998, p. 1). In practical terms, the analysis implies that implementing universal policy recommendations to all countries indiscriminately regardless of their economic, social and political background proves to be ineffective and unresponsive. To put it differently, in case that governance flaws are deeply embedded in the political and social dynamics of a country there is unlikely to be a generic blueprint suitable for all reforms in all countries as it overlooks the possibility that the way institutions function may be subject to timing and domestic content (Grindle 2010, p. 11). Consequently, initiatives taken to promote good governance must be responsive to individual sociopolitical traits of countries whereas they

[38] Islam (2006).

[39] Dijkstra (2013, p. 9).

[40] Countries with high levels of the human development index are associated with low levels of corruption (Rose-Ackerman 2005, p. 210), which is a fundamental aspect of governance.

should be supported by a deliberate policy mix, targeted reforms and structural adjustments which must have internal driving forces and cannot be left on exogenous factors.

The above analysis has highlighted that achieving and mainly maintaining good governance is a challenging task as it is associated with a wide variety of economic as well as noneconomic factors of social and political nature. There is scope then for the emergence of national governance frameworks that embody principles of democracy, equitable human development and sustainability. These governance requirements are also a key element as far as development cooperation practice and aid conditionality is concerned[41]. From a sustainable perspective strengthening governance is achieved only through the adoption and effective implementation of the appropriate social and political reforms. The more unitary, concrete and stable the country is, the harder it becomes for phenomena that can paralyze state structures to prosper. On the contrary, countries characterized by economic instability and social inequalities and a fluid and changing environment in the allocation of political power, are those countries in which dysfunctional governance structures, such as corruption, find fertile ground to infiltrate and materialize. The governance challenges are even greater in developing countries as not only the most appropriate rules have to be identified but these policies have also to be supported by appropriate governance capabilities in order to enforce them, which in poor countries are correspondingly weak (Khan 2012, pp. 5). Good governance objectives should therefore target a broad list of comprehensive governance reforms, including reducing corruption, reinforcing the rule of law and increasing the accountability and effectiveness of public institutions. Likewise, concerns of political freedom should be fully incorporated into future policy purposes and strategies while policymakers should ensure that all citizens have secure access to the basic requirements of human development.

REFERENCES

Abed, G. (1998). Governance issues and transition economies. Prepared for the Conference on "Challenges to Economies in Transition: Stabilization, Growth and Governance", Bishkek, May 27-28, 1998.

Acemoglu, D. (2008). Interactions between governance and growth. In *Governance, growth, and development decision-making*, The World Bank.

Acemoglu, D., Johnson, S. & Robinson, J. (2001). The colonial origins of comparative development: An empirical investigation. *American Economic Review, 91*(5), 1369-1401.

Acemoglu, D., Johnson, S. & Robinson, J. (2005). Institutions as a fundamental cause of long-run growth. In P. Aghion & S. Durlauf (Eds.), *Handbook of Economic Growth*. Elsevier, North-Holland.

African Development Bank (1999). Bank Group Policy on Good Governance.

Al-Marhubi, F. (2004). The determinants of governance: A cross-country analysis. *Contemporary Economic Policy, 22*(3), 394-406.

[41] Democratic governance should be approached holistically due to its multidimensional nature, taking into account political, economic, social, cultural factors, which also must be reflected in development cooperation practice (Commission of the European Communities 2006, p. 6).

Arndt, C. & Oman, C. (2006). *Uses and abuses of governance indicators*. OECD Development Centre, Paris.

Asian Development Bank (1995). Governance: Sound development management. ADB.

Baland, J-M., Moene, K. O. & Robinson, J. A. (2009). Governance and development. In *Handbook of Development Economics*. *5*, 4597-4656, Elsevier, North-Holland.

Barro, R. (1996). Democracy and Growth. *Journal of Economic Growth*, *1*(1), 1–27.

Besançon, M. (2003). Good governance rankings: The art of measurement. Cambridge, Massachusetts: World Peace Foundation and WPF Program on Intrastate Conflict and Conflict Resolution. *WPF Reports*, No. *36*, Harvard University.

Bevir, M. (2011). *Governance as theory, practice, and dilemma. I*n *M. Bevir (*Ed), *The SAGE Handbook of Governance*. SAGE Publishing, London.

Bonaglia, F., Braga de Macedo, J. & Bussolo, M. (2001). How globalization improves governance. *OECD working paper*, No. *181*.

Bräutigam, D. A. & Knack, S. (2004). Foreign Aid, Institutions, and Governance in SubSaharan Africa. *Economic development and cultural change*, *52*(2), 255-285.

Busse, M. & Gröning, S. (2009). Does foreign aid improve governance? *Economics Letters*, *104*(2), *76-78*.

Chong, A. & *Calderón*, C. (2000). Causality and feedback between institutional measures and economic growth. *Economics and Politics*, *12*, 69–82.

Commission of the European Communities (2001). European governance - a white paper. *COM(2001)*, 428 final, Brussels.

Commission of the European Communities (2003). Communication from the Commission to the Council, the European Parliament and the European Economic and Social Committee. Governance and development. *COM*, 615 final, Brussels.

Commission of the European Communities (2006). Communication from the Commission to the Council, the European Parliament, the European Economic and Social Committee and the Committee of the Regions. Governance in the European consensus on development - Towards a harmonised approach within the European Union, *COM*, 421 final, Brussels.

Dethier J-J. (1999). Governance and economic performance: A survey. *ZEF Discussion Paper on Development Policy*, No.5, University of Bonn, Germany.

Dijkstra, G. (2013). Paradoxes around Good Governance. *Inaugural Lecuture* (March 2013).

Dixit, A. (2009). Governance institutions and economic activity. *American Economic Review*, 99(1), 5-24.

Freedom House (2012). *Freedom in the world 2012: The Arab uprisings and their global repercussions.*

Gradstein, M. (2004), Governance and growth. *Journal of Development Economics*. *73*, 505–518.

Grindle, M. (2010). Good governance: The inflation of an idea. *Faculty Research Working Paper Series*, RWP10-023, Harvard Kennedy School.

Hall, R. & Jones. C. (1999). Why do some countries produce so much more output per worker than others? *Quarterly Journal of Economics*, *114*, 83-116.

Hyden, G., Court. J. & Mease, K. (2004). *Making sense of governance: Empirical evidence from 16 developing countries*. Boulder, Co: Lynne Riener.

International Bank for Reconstruction and Development (IBRD)-The World Bank (2006). A decade of measuring the quality of governance. Washington, DC: The World Bank.

International Monetary Fund (1997). Good governance: The IMF's role. Washington, DC: IMF.

International Monetary Fund (2013). The IMF and good governance: A Factsheet. http://www.imf.org/external/np/exr/facts/gov.htm.

Islam, R. (2006). Does more transparency go along with better governance? *Economics and Politics*, *18*(2), 121-167.

Jain, A. (2001). Corruption: A review. *Journal of Economic Surveys*, *15*(1). 71–121.

Johnston, M. (1998). What can be done about entrenched corruption? In B. Pleskovic and J. Stiglitz (eds.), *Annual World Bank Conference on Development Economics*. Washington, DC: The World Bank.

Kaufmann, D. (2005). Myths and realities of governance and corruption. *Global Competitiveness Report 2005-2006*, 81-98, World Economic Forum.

Kaufmann, D., Kraay, A. & Lobatón, P. (1999). Governance matters. *Policy Research Working Paper Series 2196*, World Bank.

Kaufmann, D., Kraay, A. & Mastruzzi, M. (2010). The worldwide governance indicators: methodology and analytical issues. *Policy Research Working Paper No. 5430*, World Bank.

Keefer, P. (2004). A review of the political economy of governance: From property rights to voice. *World Bank Policy Research Working Paper No. 3315*, World Bank.

Khan, M. (2012). Governance and growth: History, ideology and methods of proof. In N. Akbar, K. Botchwey, S. Howard & J. Stiglitz (Eds.), *Good Growth and Governance in Africa: Rethinking Development Strategies*. Oxford: Oxford University Press.

Kjaer, A. M. (2004). *Governance*. Cambridge: Polity Press.

Knack, S. & Keefer, P. (1995). Institutions and Economic Performance: Cross-Country Tests Using Alternative Institutional Measures. *Economics & Politics*, *7*(3), 207-227.

Kurtz, M. & Schrank, A. (2007). Growth and Governance: Models, Measures, and Mechanisms. *The Journal of Politics*, *69*(2), 538-54.

La Porta, R., Lopez-de-Silanes, F., Shleifer, A. & Vishny, R. (1999). The Quality of Government. *Journal of Law, Economics & Organization*, *15*(1): 222-279.

Lalountas, D. A., Manolas, G. A. & Vavouras, I. S. (2011). Corruption, globalization and development: How are these three phenomena related? *Journal of Policy Modeling*, *33*, 636-648.

Langbein, L. & Knack, S. (2010). The worldwide governance indicators: Six, one, or none? *Journal of Development Studies*, *46*(2), 350-370.

Lederman, D., Loayza, N. V. & Soares, R. R. (2005). Accountability and corruption: Political institutions matter. *Economics & Politics*, *17*, 1-35.

Mauro, P. (1995). Corruption and Growth. *Quarterly Journal of Economics*, *110* (3), 681-712.

North, D. (1981). *Structure and change in economic history*. New York: W.W. Norton & Co.

North, D. (1990). *Institutions, institutional change and economic performance*. Cambridge: Cambridge University Press.

North, D. & Thomas, R. P. (1973). *The rise of the Western world: A new economic history*. Cambridge: Cambridge University Press.

Organisation for Economic Co-operation and Development (1995). Participatory development and good governance. *Development Co-operation Guidelines Series*, OECD, Paris.

Organisation for Economic Co-operation and Development (2009). Donor approaches to governance assessments: 2009 Sourcebook. OECD, Paris.

Quibria, M. G. (2006). Does governance matter? Yes, no or maybe: Some evidence from developing Asia. *Kyklos*, *59*(1), 99-114.

Rivera-Batiz, F. (2002). Democracy, governance and economic growth: Theory and evidence, *Review of Development Economics*, *6*(2), 225-247.

Rodrik, D., Subramanian, A. & Trebbi, F. (2004). Institutions rule: The primacy of institutions over geography and integration in economic development. *Journal of Economic Growth*, *9*(2), 131-165.

Rontos, K. & Vavouras, I. (2013a). Socioeconomic and political development: Their measurement and connections, *Global Journal of Human Science Political Science*, *13*(5).

Rontos, K. & Vavouras, I. (2013b). Corruption control as a quasi luxury good. *Discussion Papers DEO34*.

Rose-Ackerman, S. (1999). *Corruption and government: causes, consequences, and reform.* New York: Cambridge University Press.

Rose-Ackerman, S. (2005). The Challenge of Poor Governance and Corruption. *Revista Direitogv*, Special Issue 1, 207-266.

Rothstein, B. & Teorell, J. (2008). What is quality of government? A theory of impartial government institutions. *Governance: An International Journal of Policy, Administration and Institutions*, *21*(2), 165-190.

Thomas, M. (2010). What do the worldwide governance indicators measure? *European Journal of Development Research*, *22*, 31-54.

Treisman, D. (2000). The causes of corruption: A cross-national study. *Journal of Public Economics*, *76*, 399-457.

United Nations (2007). Public governance indicators: A literature review. Department of Economic and Social Affairs, United Nations, New York.

United Nations Development Programme (1997). Governance for sustainable human development - A UNDP policy document. .

United Nations Development Programme (2007). Governance indicators – A users' guide (Second edition).

Williams, A. & Siddique, A. (2008). The use (and abuse) of governance indicators in economics: A review. *Economics of Governance*, *9*(2), 131-175.

Woods, N. (2000). The challenge of good governance for the IMF and the World Bank themselves. *World Development*, *28*(5), 823-841.

World Bank (1989). *Sub-Saharan Africa: From crisis to sustainable growth*, Washington, DC: The World Bank.

World Bank (1991). Managing development: The governance dimension - A Discussion Paper, Washington, DC: The World Bank.

World Bank (1994). *Governance: the World Bank experience*, Washington, DC: The World Bank.

World Bank (1997). *World Development Report 1997: The state in a changing world.* Washington, DC: The World Bank

World Bank (1998), *Beyond the Washington consensus: Institutions matter, World Bank Latin American and Caribbean Studies*, Washington, DC: The World Bank.

World Bank (2000). *Reforming Public Institutions and Strengthening Governance: A World Bank Strategy*, The World Bank.

World Economic Forum (2011), *The Global Competitiveness Report 2011-2012.*

Zhuang, J., de Dios E. & Lagman-Martin, A. (2010). Governance and institutional quality and the links with economic growth and income inequality: With special reference to developing Asia. *ADB Economics Working Paper Series*, No. 193.

In: Towards a Society with a More Fair Economy
Editors: J. A. Filipe, N. Nagopoulos, K. Rontos et al.
ISBN: 978-1-63482-900-7

Chapter 2

SOCIOECONOMIC AND POLITICAL ASPECTS OF OVERALL DEVELOPMENT WORLDWIDE: MEASUREMENT AND INTERCONNECTIONS

Kostas Rontos[1,*], Flora Tsapala[1] and Ioannis Vavouras[2,3*]

[1]University of Aegean, Mytilene, Greece
[2]Panteion University of Social and Political Sciences, Greece
[3]Hellenic Open University (DEO 34), Patras, Greece

ABSTRACT

The objective of the paper is to detect and analyze the basic factors of overall development worldwide. We argue that overall development has three dimensions; that is economic, social and political. By following the method of factor analysis, six variables are considered of high importance for the overall development of nations. These variables are the level of income per capita, the degree of human development, the extent of government effectiveness, the level of perceived corruption, the range of political rights and the extent of civil liberties. The aforementioned variables are integrated into two basic factors or pillars of development, namely the socioeconomic and the political. The analysis unveils that both factors are of crucial importance for the overall development. Based on these two broad criteria of development, our empirical research in the form of cluster analysis distinguishes four groups of countries that are described and discussed. The basic conclusion emerging from cluster analysis is that although an effective strategy towards overall development demands integrated policies incorporating both the socioeconomic and the political dimensions of development, most countries have not achieved both of them. The major policy implication emerging from our analysis is that a balanced and sustainable overall development seems to require not only the promotion of economic development, as the traditional theory of growth implies, but the simultaneous advancement of social and political development of nations.

Keywords: Socioeconomic Development, Political Development, Corruption, Human Development, Government Effectiveness, Factor Analysis, Cluster Analysis

---

* Corresponding Author: Email: vavouras@panteion.gr.

2.1. Introduction

2.1.1. Overall Development and Its Dimensions

The traditional empirical analysis approaches, measures and evaluates development mainly from its economic point of view. Social and political factors, although widely considered as important for the advancement of the overall development of countries, are either underestimated or even totally ignored in relevant empirical work. Several reasons lead to this outcome. The most significant one is that contrary to the economic dimension of development that can be relatively easily defined and measured, the sociopolitical dimension can hardly be defined and measured. Economic development as a quantitative variable is widely identified with economic growth and is measured by international organizations and national statistical services for all countries of the world with relatively simple and generally acceptable indexes, such as real income per capita, while social and political aspects of human action can only be expressed by more complicated procedures on which there is no wider agreement.

However, it has been established long ago that economic growth, although considered a necessary, is not a sufficient condition for the overall development of nations. Development is generally recognized as a wider concept incorporating as well the social and the political transformation and advancement of countries. The identification and much more the analysis of these sociopolitical transformations is associated with major difficulties. This problem should not reduce the concern for the investigation of the social and political dimensions of overall development. Modern societies realize the existence of additional needs for the reduction of income and wealth inequalities and for the more fair distribution of the economic result of human activities, for the more effective reduction of the level of public sector corruption, for a better social security system and what is called "social state", for a higher quality of health and education systems, for a better governance and for high standards of political rights and civil liberties and democracy in general. The effective satisfaction of these needs enables citizens to enjoy high standards of living.

The recent worldwide economic crisis of 2007-2008 has emphatically unveiled that whenever and wherever an economic crisis is associated with a social and political crisis, even the economic crisis itself is deeper and more long lasting. In this way economic disturbances or shocks characterized as symmetric, that is disturbances of economic activity that have simultaneous impacts on all countries, might have country specific or asymmetric consequences. Economic shocks might turn to have differential effects on various countries by affecting some of them more deeply than others, and therefore they might require a different macroeconomic policy mix. Even though economic shocks might be symmetrical in their origins, they might have asymmetrical effects on various courtiers due to their differentiated sociopolitical environment. The countries more deeply affected by the 2007-2008 economic crisis and sovereign debt crisis that followed seem to be those where the levels of social and political development are not considered as very high.

2.1.2. Measuring Economic, Social and Political Development

It is important to note at this point that relatively recently international agencies and organizations have developed methodologies to measure variables that express social and political dimensions of development. It must be stressed that overall development is a multidimensional concept associated with a variety of social, economic and political factors or variables. In the following part of this section we discuss the variables that have been used in our factor analysis as the main characteristics or attributes of the level of overall development of nations.

The variable most widely used in empirical research as the best indicator of the level of economic development is real income per capita. Various international organizations[1] classify countries as developed or developing according to their prevailing or average real income per capita levels. Although real income per capita is criticized as an inadequate indicator of economic development, mainly because it is an inefficient measure of the average living standards and quality of life prevailing in a country, it is generally recognized as the best available measure of the average level of economic development associated with a given country. However, apart from economic development the notion of overall development in a specific country is also associated with the degree of human development. That is by the level of health, the degree of access to knowledge and the level of well-being prevailing in a given country, as a wider concept than economic development. Human development generally refers to the expansion of people's freedoms and capabilities to live their lives as they choose (UNDP, 2009).

The notion of overall development is also associated with the degree of government effectiveness since an effective public sector promotes all the three dimensions of development specified above. Kaufmann et al. define governance as "the traditions and institutions by which authority in a country is exercised. This includes the processes by which governments are selected, monitored and replaced; the capacity of the government to effectively formulate and implement sound policies; and the respect of citizens and the state for the institutions that govern economic and social interactions among them" (Kaufmann, Kraay and Mastruzzi, 2009).

Another variable that we consider to be associated with all the three dimensions of overall development is the level of perceived public sector corruption prevailing in a country. It is broadly defined as the abuse of public power for private benefit (Tanzi, 1998) or the abuse of public office for private gain (Martinez-Vazquez, Arze del Granado and Boex, 2007). The World Bank defines public sector corruption as the abuse of public authority for private interest (World Bank, 1997) while OECD defines it as the misuse of public office, roles or resources for private benefit, material or otherwise (OECD, 1996)[2]. The determining factors of corruption are numerous. The most important ones are the level of economic development, the type of political authority, the quality of governance, the quality of the institutional framework, the effectiveness of the justice system, the degree of globalization, the level of competition, the structure and the size of public sector, as well as the cultural qualities, the geographic location and history. Widespread corruption largely unveils the

[1] Such as the United Nations, the World Bank and the OECD.

[2] A definition provided by the nongovernmental organization Transparency International that covers corruption in both the public and the private sectors of the economy is the misuse of trusted power for own profit (Transparency International, 2011).

existence of institutional and political weaknesses as well as economic and social underdevelopment.

Corruption might be the single most significant barrier to both democratization and economic development of countries.The general attitude towards corruption is also determined by the level of individual morality that is by the system of individual behavioral and moral attributes (Rontos, Salvati and Vavouras, 2013a). Basically, corruption is detrimental to economic growth and development by adversely affecting investment. It must be stressed however that some early works on the subject argued that corruption improves economic efficiency and therefore promotes economic growth operating as the necessary "grease" to lubricate the wheels of state bureaucracy[3]. The extent of the consequences the phenomenon has on economic development is largely determined by the existing institutional framework (de Vaal and Ebben, 2011). On another account, corruption is a "disease" which is caused by poverty, that is controlled only when economies develop (Treisman, 2000; Paldam, 2002). However, we argue that corruption is extensive in low income countries, not because their inhabitants present a natural proclivity towards the said phenomenon, but because the conditions of life make them prone to that (Lalountas, Manolas and Vavouras, 2011).

It is also accepted that there exists a strong connection between the level of overall development and the quality of democracy or the quality of the political system. Underdevelopment is widely considered to be both a symptom and a cause for the malfunctioning of democratic institutions. Moreover, democracy and the consequent public accountability reduce the costs of development. In a sense, the political system or the "political macrostructure" determines the political motivations of all players in the state system and it is the very reaction of these factors that finally determines the behavior of state bureaucracy (Lederman, Loayza and Soares, 2005). As a result, a highly developed and well-functioning democracy serves as a tool for increasing the level of overall development (Zhang, Cao and Vaughn, 2009).

2.1.3. The Target of the Study

Our primary objective in this chapter is to examine all the above factors, that is income per capita, human development, government effectiveness, public sector corruption, and political freedom in the forms of political rights and civil liberties, as the main determinants of overall development and the specific ways that their combination in several levels classifies countries and determines the patterns of their development. Our analysis reveals that all the above factors are correlated and in general are of crucial importance in determining the extent of overall development worldwide[4]. As it will be shown, factor analysis reveals the existence of two distinct factors of overall development. The political development comprising political rights and civil liberties and the socioeconomic development comprising the remaining four variables.

[3] See for example Leff (1964) and Huntington (1968).

[4] This outcome is compatible with our argument on the importance of these variables as determinants of the overall level of development presented in a relevant work. See Rontos, Salvati and Vavouras (2013b).

2.2. CARRYING OUT THE EMPIRICAL WORK

2.2.1. Data and Variables Used

The empirical analysis is based on six variables that have been derived for 176 countries (see list of countries in Table 3)[5]. It is the total number of countries for which data for all these variables existed in the year 2010. As a result the analysis could be considered as a worldwide one. The variables have been derived from official statistics and other reliable and well-known international data sources as it is explained below in more detail.

1. To approximate the level of economic development in each country and to render international comparisons possible the variable gross national income per capita in purchasing power parities or current international dollars was used (GNI.PC.PPP). The data used refer to the year 2010 and are provided by the World Bank (2010a) and for that year cover 215 economies.
2. The human development index (HDI) has been used as a summary measure of the level of human development. It is estimated by the United Nations Development Programme (UNDP) and it measures the average achievements in a given country in three dimensions of human development: a long and healthy life, access to knowledge and a decent standard of living. The data used refer to the year 2010. They are provided by the UNDP (2010) and for that year cover 169 countries and 25 territories. Since the HDI includes as one of its main components GNI per capita that has already been used as the basic variable of economic development, we used the variable HDI.NONINCOME, that is the HDI excluding its income dimension or component.
3. To express the degree of government effectiveness in each country the relevant World Bank Government Effectiveness indicator (GE) has been used. GE is one of the six composite indicators of broad dimensions of governance, the so called “worldwide governance indicators” (WGI) covering over 200 countries since 1996 and produced by Kaufmann, Kraay and Mastruzzi (World Bank, 2010b).
4. To express the extent of corruption prevailing in each country the corruption perceptions index (CPI) has been used. CPI is the most extensively used index for relevant empirical studies. It is a composite indicator, based on a variety of data derived from 13 different surveys carried out by 10 independent and reputable organizations. The major strength of the CPI lies in this combination of multiple data sources in a single index, a fact that increases the reliability of each country’s score (Lambsdorff, 2006). The data used for the CPI refer to the year 2010 and as it has already been stated are provided by Transparency International (2010) and for that year cover 178 countries or territories.
5. To approximate the quality of democracy in each country the “political rights” index (PR) has been used. The index is based on the evaluation of three sub-indexes, namely electoral process, political pluralism and participation and functioning of government. The index is estimated by the Freedom House organization (2013). The data used for the PR index refer to the year 2010 and are provided by the

[5] The methodology of this paper was originally presented in Rontos and Vavouras (2013).

organization Freedom House (2010) and for that year cover 194 countries and 14 territories.

6. To approximate the extent of civil liberties in each country the "civil liberties" index (CL) has been used. The index is based on the evaluation of four sub-indexes, namely freedom of expression and belief, associational and organizational rights, rule of law, and personal autonomy and individual rights. The index is also estimated by the Freedom House organization (2013). The data used for the CL index refer to the year 2010 and are provided by the organization Freedom House (2010) and for that year cover 194 countries and 14 territories.

2.2.2. Methods of Statistical Analysis

The analytical steps include first a factor analysis and second a non-hierarchical cluster analysis. Factor analysis was used to detect the internal relations and structures among the above six variables by grouping and reducing their number. The statistical measure Kaiser-Mayer Olkin (K.M.O.) of sampling adequacy and Bartlett's Test of Sphericity were calculated. Principal components analysis was employed to extract the number of factors, with Eigenvalues>1 taken as a criterion, which was verified by Scree Plot. Conducting factors rotation the maximum likelihood method was used as extraction method and Varimax with Kaiser Normalization as rotation method.

Then, a non-hierarchical k-means cluster analysis (CA) was carried out with the aim at separating countries in a few groups exhibiting homogeneous socioeconomic and political patterns. The clustering criteria were the scores of the factors extracted from the above analysis calculated according to the Bartlett method. The optimal number of clusters was chosen according to the Cubic Clustering Criterion (CCC) and the Variance Ratio Criterion (VRC). Both criteria suggested the same number of clusters.

2.3. Empirical Results of the Study

2.3.1. Factor Analysis Results

Factor analysis, applied on 176 countries inserted in the model, suggests the existence of two factors according to the Eigenvalues criterion and verified by the Scree Plot (Figure 1). As a result, factor analysis confirms our hypothesis of the existence of two distinct factors of development, the socioeconomic and the political one. Note that initially 86.49 % of the variation is explained by the model.

The statistical measure Kaiser-Mayer Olkin (K.M.O.) indicates the data suitability, the existence of adequate endogenous correlations and the adequacy of the sample, ranging in 0.784. At the same time, Bartlett's Test Sphericity = 988, 15, df = 105, p = 0.00 verifying the possibility of variable correlation, by using factor analysis.

It is important to note, that the two factors retained, show that the total variance finally explained by the model is 80.5% and that we have only 19.5 % loss Factor 1 explains the 46.2 % of the total variance and factor 2 the rest 34.3.

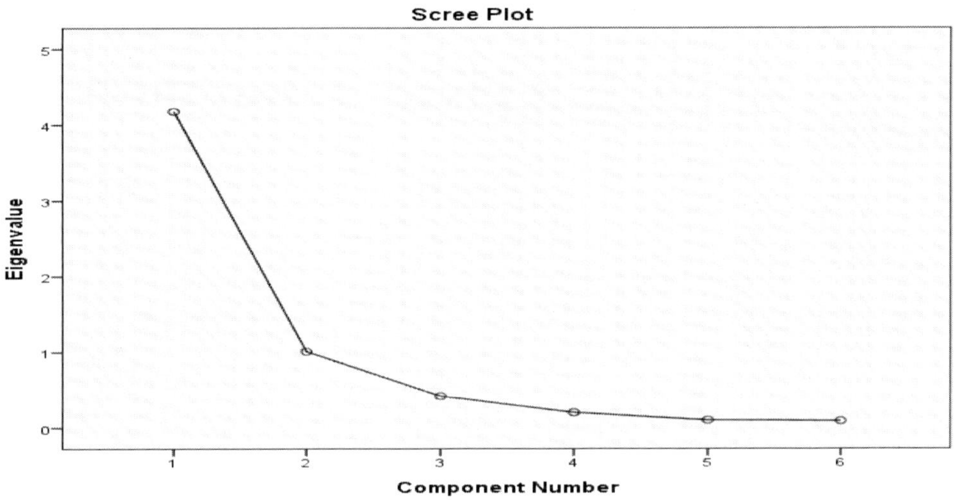

Figure 1.

Table 1. Rotated factor matrix

	Factor	
	1	2
GNI.PC.PPP.2010	.879	-.143
CPI.2010	.852	-.398
GE.2010	.805	-.438
HDI.NONINCOME.2010	.666	-.266
CL.2010	-.346	.922
PR2010	-.254	.873

The results from the use of the Varimax Rotation with Kaizer Normalization method are analyzed below. The resulted factors could be labeled as follows:

- **Factor 1: Socioeconomic aspects of development** Four variables are loaded on this factor: GNI.PC.PPP, CPI, GE, and HDI.NONINCOME, that represent actual socioeconomic aspects of development and count factor loadings which range from 0.879 to 0.666. All variables have very high loads, which fluctuate more than 0.6.The perceptual variables and their factor loadings are presented in the Table 1.
- **Factor 2: Political aspects of development**. Two variables are loaded on this factor: CL and PR, which represent actual political aspects of development and have very high loads (0.922 and 0.873 respectively- Table 1).

In Figure 2 it is shown how the six variables are located in a rotated factor space.

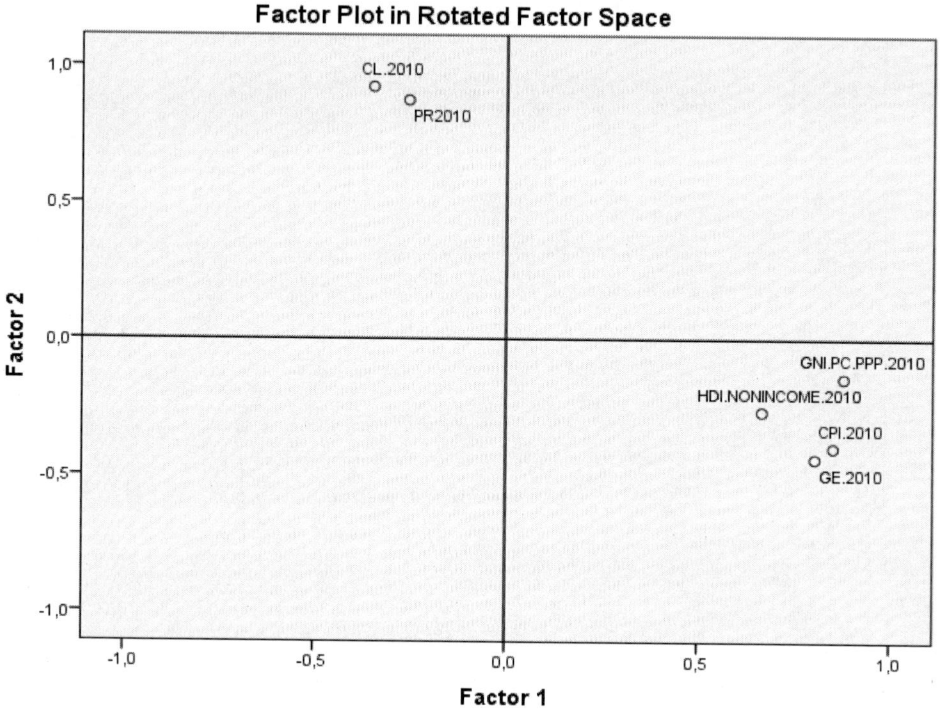

Figure 2.

2.3.2. Cluster Analysis Results

Cluster analysis identified four groups of homogeneous countries according to our socioeconomic and political criteria as they are determined by the scores of the two aforementioned factors (Table 2). As it has already been stated, the full list of countries according to the cluster membership is shown in Table 3.

Table 2. Results of cluster analysis: Average value by factors' score and cluster

Factors	Clusters			
	1	2	3	4
Factor 1: Socioeconomic development	-.30821	1.46801	2.18501	-.59533
Factor 2: Political development*	1.10621	-.78835	1.59198	-.62630
Number of countries (N = 176)	55	31	9	81

*According to the scale of PR and CL a positive average score means low political development and vice-versa.

Table 3. Cluster membership by country

Cluster 1	Cluster 2	Cluster 3	Cluster 4
Macau	Australia	Bahrain	**Countries with high GNI**
Timor – Leste	Austria	Brunei	**(Higher than the median**
Afghanistan	Barbados	Hong Kong	**GNI.PC.PPP = 4,625 $)**
Algeria	Belgium	Kuwait	
Angola	Canada	Oman	Albania
Armenia	Chile	Qatar	Argentina
Azerbaijan	Cyprus	Saudi Arabia	Bosnia and Herzegovina
Belarus	Denmark	Singapore	Botswana
Bhutan	Estonia	United Arab	Brazil
Burundi	Finland	Emirates	Bulgaria
Cambodia	France		Costa Rica
Cameroon	Germany		Croatia
Central African	Iceland		Czech Republic
Republic	Ireland		Dominica
Chad	Israel		Dominican Republic
China	Japan		Ecuador
Colombia	Korea (South)		El Salvador
Congo –	Luxembourg		FYR Macedonia
Brazzaville	Malta		Greece
Cote d'Ivoire	Netherlands		Guatemala
Cuba	New Zealand		Hungary
Democratic Rep, of	Norway		Italy
Congo	Portugal		Jamaica
Djibouti	Seychelles		Latvia
Egypt	Slovenia		Lebanon
Equatorial Guinea	Spain		Lithuania
Eritrea	Sweden		Maldives
Ethiopia	Switzerland		Mauritius
Gabon	United Kingdom		Mexico
Gambia	United States		Montenegro
Georgia	Uruguay		Namibia
Guinea			Panama
Haiti			Paraguay
Iran			Peru
Iraq			Poland
Jordan			Romania
Kazakhstan			Serbia
Kyrgyzstan			Slovakia
Laos			South Africa
Libya			Trinidad and Tobago
Malaysia			Turkey
Mauritania			Ukraine
Morocco			Venezuela
Myanmar			
Pakistan			
Russia			
Rwanda			
Somalia			

Table 3. (Continued)

Cluster 1	Cluster 2	Cluster 3	Cluster 4
Sri Lanka Sudan Swaziland Syria Tajikistan Thailand Tunisia Turkmenistan Uzbekistan Vietnam Yemen Zimbabwe			**Countries with low GNI (Lower than the median GNI.PC.PPP = 4,625 $)** Bangladesh Benin Bolivia Burkina Faso Cape Verde Comoros Ghana Guinea – Bissau Guyana Honduras India Indonesia Kenya Kiribati Lesotho Liberia Madagascar Malawi Mali Moldova Mongolia Mozambique Nepal Nicaragua Niger Nigeria Papua New Guinea Philippines Samoa Sao Tome and Principe Senegal Sierra Leone Solomon Islands Tanzania Togo Tonga Uganda Vanuatu Zambia

According to cluster analysis described above we can observe the following clusters:

Cluster 1 includes a considerable number of 55 countries characterised as mainly socially and economically disadvantaged and very politically disadvantaged in Africa, Asia and Latin America. Most of them are considered as third world countries. Afghanistan, Armenia,

Cameroon, Central African Republic, Colombia, Cuba, Egypt, Ethiopia, Georgia, Iran, Iraq, Vietnam are examples of them. However, two countries included in this group are not considered as third world countries, namely China and Russia.

Cluster 2 includes a total of 31 countries characterised as developed and consolidated democracies placed mainly in the European Union and in the Northern America with high economic and social development and considerable high political development (the lowest score of factor 2 on average among clusters). Examples of countries belonging to this cluster are Australia, Austria, Belgium, Canada, Denmark, Germany, Finland, France, Japan, Netherlands, Spain, Sweden, South Korea, United Kingdom and the United States.

Cluster 3 includes a limited number of 9 countries described as those showing a considerably higher socio-economic development (the highest score of Factor 1 on average among clusters) but already unstable political systems (the highest score of Factor 2 on average among clusters). To this cluster belong some very rich oil exporting countries of the Middle East (Bahrain, Qatar, Kuwait, Saudi Arabia and United Arab Emirates). However three non-oil exporting high income countries are also included in this cluster, namely Hong Kong, Singapore and Brunei.

Cluster 4 which is the most populated includes 81 countries associated with very low levels of socio-economic development (the lowest score of Factor 1 on average among clusters) but showing also fairly good levels of political development. However, this forth cluster presents an extended variation in strictly economic terms as they are represented by GNI.PC.PPP. Actually the range of GNI.PC.PPP among the 78 countries of the cluster (3 of the 81 with missing income were omitted) is 31,300 $, while the interquartile range is 10,970 $. With a median value of 4,625 $, countries as Slovakia, Czech Republic, Greece and Italy have extremely high GNI values (21,870-31,740 $), while some others as Mozambique, Malawi, Sierra Leone, Niger and Liberia have extremely low GNI values (900-440 $). The fact that the score of the socioeconomic factor, which was used for countries' clustering (together with political factor), came from the combination of GNI and three more variables (CPI, GE, HDI) may explain this variation of the strict economic variable (GNI) of the model. Due to this heterogeneity, we could classify the countries in cluster four in two sub-groups (Table 3), according to the median value of their respective GNI.PC.PPP.

The ANOVA analysis presented in Table 4 indicates, that overall, each of the factor's score used in the present clustering, i.e., the socioeconomic and political one differs significantly across the clusters (p-value = 0.00 for both factor scores). However, according to F values, the variable contributing slightly more to cluster's differentiation is the political development.

Table 4. ANOVA analysis

	Cluster		Error		F	Sig.
	Mean Square	df	Mean Square	df		
Factor 1: Socioeconomic development	47.903	3	.281	172	170.298	.000
Factor 2: Political development	47.050	3	.251	172	187.713	.000

2.3.3. Presentation and Analysis of Thematic Maps by Continent Clustering Countries

Maps 1-7 that follow represent the clustering of all countries of the world according to their socioeconomic and political development (Map 1), as well as the clustering of African countries (Map 2), Asian countries (Map 3), European countries (Map 4), North American countries (Map 5), Oceanian countries (Map 6) and South American countries (Map 7) according to these two factors. It can be observed that according to the methodology developed in the present paper North American Countries and countries of the Western Europe are included in cluster 2, countries of Southern America and Eastern Europe are included in cluster 4.1, while countries of Asia and Africa are mainly included in clusters 1 and 4.2. The most astonishing is Map 4 according to which Europe is not actually divided into center and periphery as the vast bulk of empirical research accepts, but into Eastern (cluster 4.1) and Western (cluster 2). This emerging "gap" between Eastern and Western Europe is going to inhibit all efforts to achieve real convergence in Europe. Some countries of the European periphery, namely Spain, Portugal, Iceland and Ireland characterised as developed and consolidated democracies seem to fulfil the conditions that guarantee their long-run overall development while some others such as Greece, Bulgaria, Romania and Poland are characterised by low levels of socioeconomic development that seems to inhibit their long-run overall development. This outcome presents the most serious problem that Europe is going to face. Real European convergence is emerging as a very difficult task.

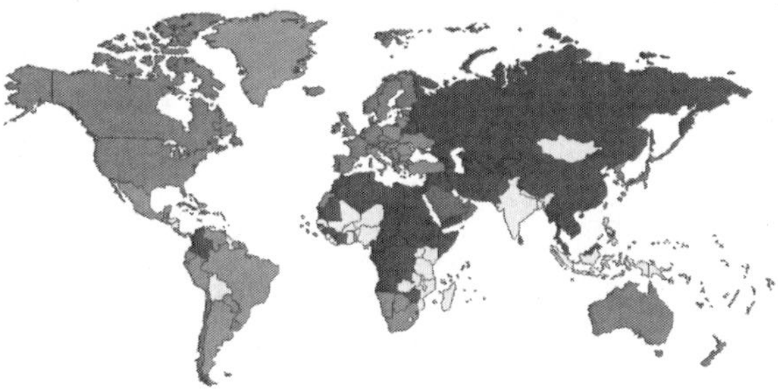

Map 1: Clustering countries at global level according to the socio-economic and political development

- Cluster1: Countries socially and economically disadvantaged
- Cluster2: Countries with developed and consolidated democracies
- Cluster3: Countries with higher socio-economic development
- Cluster4.1: Countries with high GNI within cluster 4
- Cluster4.2: Countries with low GNI within cluster 4
- Countries without data

* Cluster 4. Countries with relatively good level political situation but very low socio-economic

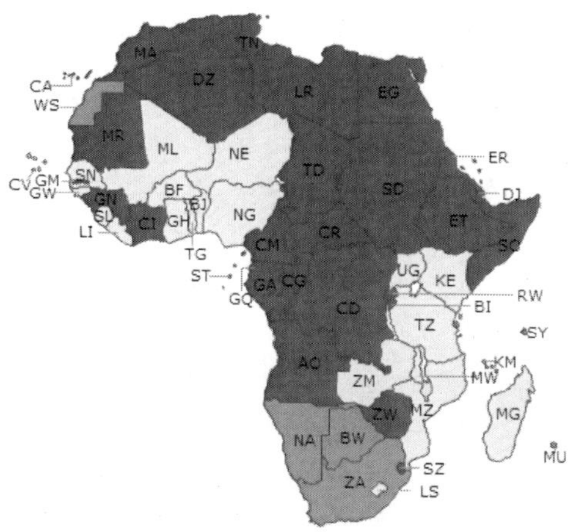

Map 2: Clustering of African countries according to the socio-economic and political development

- Cluster1: Countries socially and economically disadvantaged
- Cluster2: Countries with developed and consolidated democracies
- Cluster3: Countries with higher socio-economic development
- Cluster4.1: Countries with high GNI within cluster 4
- Cluster4.2: Countries with low GNI within cluster 4
- Countries without data

* Cluster 4: Countries with relatively good level political situation but very low socio-economic

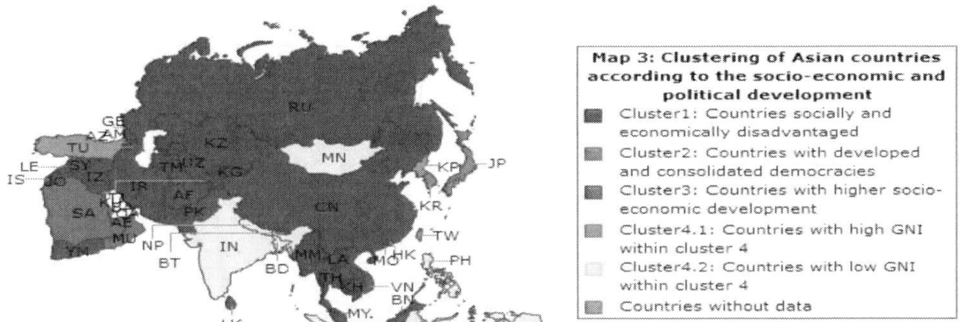

* Cluster 4: Countries with relatively good level political situation but very low socio-economic

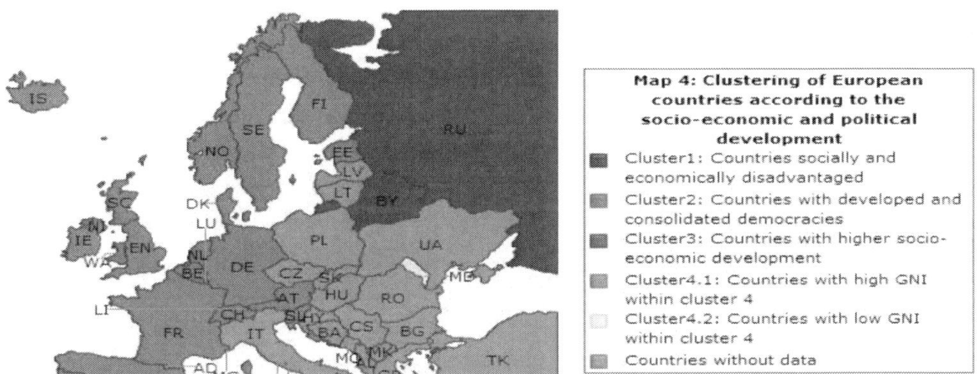

* Cluster 4: Countries with relatively good level political situation but very low socio-economic

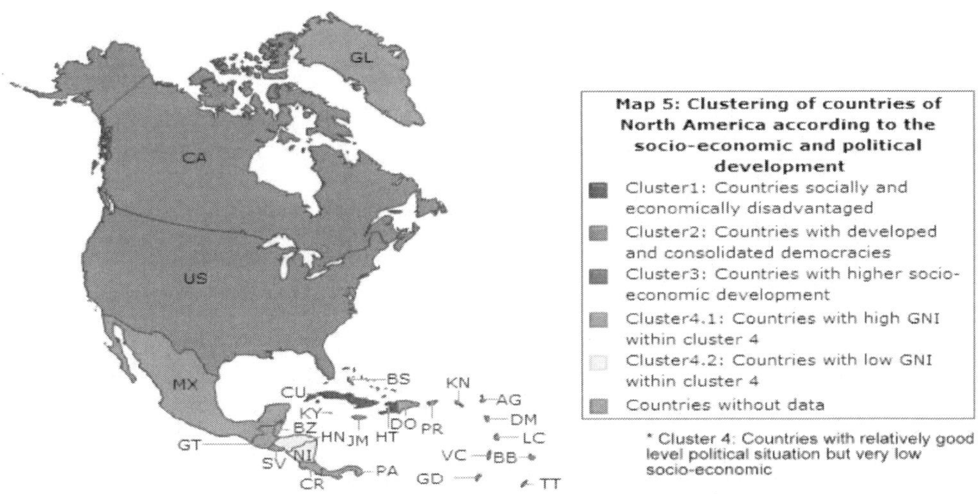

* Cluster 4: Countries with relatively good level political situation but very low socio-economic

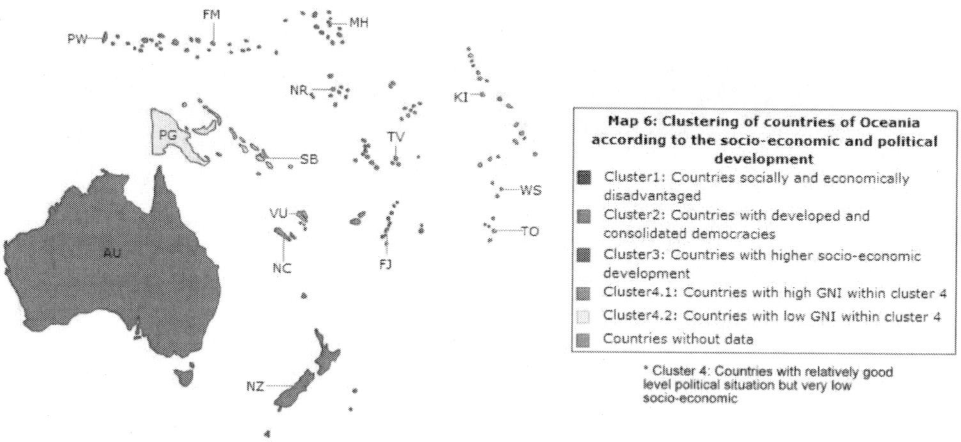

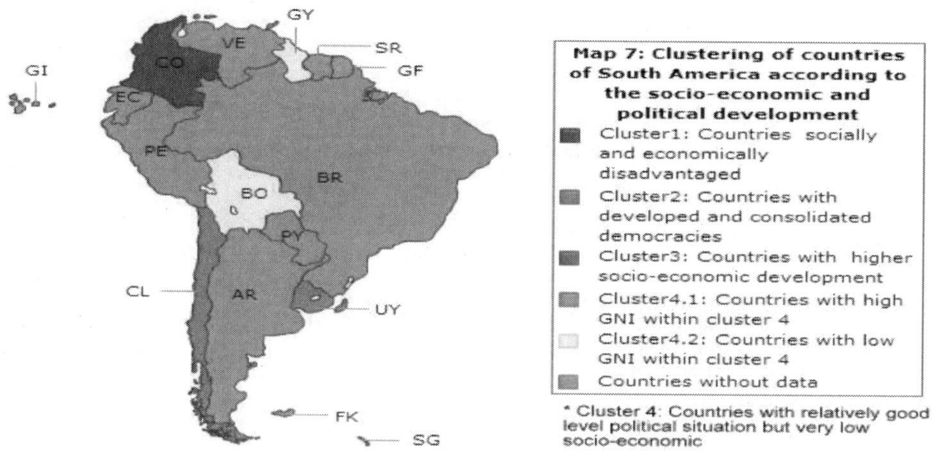

CONCLUSION

Factor analysis indicated that the six variables considered as the main determinants of development are integrated into two basic factors of development namely the socioeconomic factor and the political factor. The socioeconomic factor comprises the level of income per capita, the degree of human development, the level of perceived corruption and the extent of government effectiveness. The political factor comprises the range of political rights and the extent of civil liberties. Following this distinction of the two factors of development, countries are classified into four main distinct groups: The first comprises those countries associated with low values of the socioeconomic factor and low values of the political factor. Countries included in this group should pay balanced efforts towards their socioeconomic and political transformation in order to develop. The second group comprises those countries associated with high values of the socioeconomic factor and high values of the political factor. Countries belonging to this group seem to fulfill the conditions that guarantee their long-run overall development. These two groups of countries seem to confirm the prevailing hypothesis that socioeconomic and political development are positively correlated (Needler,

1968). In fact until the mid-1970s only highly developed economies enjoyed political democracy[6]. That is, it was accepted that economic development generates political development and vice versa. Later, however, it was realized that growth might have and negative effects on democracy. It is the destabilizing growth hypothesis that was proposed by Paldam (1998)[7].

The remaining two groups of countries seem to contradict the above common hypothesis. As we have shown, the third group comprises 9 countries associated with high values of the socioeconomic factor and low values of the political factor. For these countries their high levels of socioeconomic development are not compatible with respective high levels of political development. A "deficit" of political development seems to exist in this case. As a result it could be argued that the high levels of socioeconomic development of these countries are not long-run guaranteed or sustainable. The "deficit" of political development inhibits their long-run overall development prospects. As a result, a primary objective of these countries is the adoption of policies that promote their political development. The forth group is a very large group comprising 81 countries. This is a very heterogeneous group, mainly as far as its socioeconomic determinants, characterized by low values of the socioeconomic factor and relatively high values of the political factor. As we have already pointed out, in this group of countries the low level of socioeconomic development seems to be the basic factor inhibiting their long-run development. The primary objective of these countries is the adoption of policies that promote their socioeconomic development. Not ignoring of course that the political institutions of these countries might also require to be promoted.

Considering that the first two groups of countries seem to confirm the prevailing hypothesis that socioeconomic and political development are positively associated while the last two groups of countries seem to contradict this hypothesis, we investigate the relationship between the two factors of development taking all countries together. As it was expected, the correlation between each one of the variables comprising the level of political development and each one of the variables comprising the level of socioeconomic development is found to be moderate ($r<0.7$)[8]. As a result, the prevailing hypothesis of the positive correlation between the two factors cannot be empirically confirmed, at least completely and at least in the specific form of model specification.

Our cluster analysis has revealed that the largest dissimilarities or divergences exist between the third and the forth group of countries, while the smallest ones between the first and the forth group. Moreover, the analysis has shown that the score of each basic factor of development (i.e., the socioeconomic and the political one), differs significantly across the clusters. However, it has been established that the variable contributing more to the differentiation of clusters seems to be the political development.

In summary, the above empirical work has highlighted that the level of socioeconomic development and the level of political development are the most important dimensions that determine the overall long-run developmental patterns worldwide. The basic outcome of our empirical analysis is that in order to increase the level of overall development, not only economic but also social and political efforts should be undertaken. In some countries,

---

[6] For a review of the theory explaining this relationship between development and democracy, see Romer (1994).

[7] Some empirical work indicates that democracies do not appear to show different growth performance than non-democracies (Alesina, Özler, Roubini and Swayel, 1992). Most empirical work on this subject, however, investigates the relationship between political instability and economic growth.

[8] See Rontos, Salvati and Vavouras (2013b).

emphasis should be given to their socioeconomic development (countries belonging to group 4), in some to their political development (countries belonging to group 3), and in some countries to both dimensions of development, socioeconomic and political (countries belonging to group 1). The main conclusion of the above analysis is that not all countries should follow identical strategies in order to increase their overall long-run development levels. In line of the above analysis we argue that a high overall level of development is achieved and maintained in the long-run only when the socioeconomic development is associated with the consolidation of democracy. Rising incomes is therefore a necessary but not a sufficient condition to increase overall development levels, unless it is associated with the improvement of the other socioeconomic determinants of development as well as with the consolidation of democracy.

References

Alesina, A., Özler, S., Roubini, N. & Swayel, P. (1992). *Political instability and economic growth*, NBER Working Paper No 4173, September.

De Vaal, A. & Ebben, W. (2011). Institutions and the relations between corruption and economic growth. *Review of Development Economics*, vol. *15*, No. 1, 108-123.

Freedom House (2010). *Freedom in the world 2010. Global erosion and freedom.*

Freedom House (2013). *Freedom in the world 2013. Democratic breakthroughs in the balance.*

Huntington, S. P. (1968). *Political order in changing societies.* New Haven, Connecticut: Yale University Press.

Kaufmann, D., Kraay, A. & Mastruzzi, M. (2010).*The worldwide governance indicators: Methodology and analytical issues.* World Bank, Policy Research Working Paper No. 5430.

Kaufmann, D., Kraay, A. & Mastruzzi, M. (2009). *Governance matters VIII: Aggregate and individual governance indicators 1996-2008.* Policy Research Working Paper No. 4978, World bank.

Lalountas, D. A., Manolas, G. A. & Vavouras, I. S. (2011). Corruption, globalization and development: How are these three phenomena related?. *Journal of Policy Modeling*, vol. *33*, 636-648.

Lambsdorff, J. G. (2007). *The institutional economics of corruption and reform.* Cambridge, UK: Cambridge University Press.

Lederman, D., Loayza, N. V. & Soares, R. R. (2005). Accountability and corruption: Political institutions matter. *Economics & Politics*, vol. *17*, No. 1, 1-35.

Leff, N. (1964). Economic development through bureaucratic corruption. *The American Behavioral Scientist*, vol. *8*, 8-14.

Martinez-Vazquez, J., Arze del Granado, J. & Boex, J. (2007). *Fighting corruption in the public sector.* Contributions to economic analysis *284*. Amsterdam: Elsevier.

Needler, M. C. (1968). Political development and socioeconomic development: The case of Latin America. *The American Political Science Review*, vol. *62*, No. 3, 889-897.

OECD (1996). Ethics in the public service: Current issues and practice. *Public Management Occasional Papers* No. 14, Paris.

Paldam, M. (2002). The cross-country pattern of corruption. Economics, culture and the seesaw dynamics. *European Journal of Political Economy*, vol. *18*, 215-240.

Paldam, M. (1998). Does economic growth lead to political stability? in Borner, S. and Paldam, M. (eds.), *The political dimensions of growth: IEA Conference Volume 119*, Macmillan, 171-190.

Roemer, J. E. (1994). On the relationship between economic and political democracy. *Economic Design*, vol. *1*, 15-39.

Rontos, K. & Vavouras, I. (2013). Socioeconomic and political development: Their measurement and connections. *Global Journal of Human Social Science*, vol. *13*, issue 5, 51-65.

Rontos, K., Salvati, L. & Vavouras, I. (2013a). Corruption in the world: Its economic, political and geographic determinants and their interactions. *Journal of Regional and Socioeconomic Issues*, vol. *3*, issue 2, June 2013, 5-26.

Rontos, K., Salvati, L. & Vavouras, I. (2013b). Socioeconomic and political dimensions of development worldwide. *Sociology and Criminology*, vol.*1*, issue 1, August 2013, 2-8.

Tanzi, V. (1998). Corruption around the world: Causes, consequences, scope and cures. *IMF Working Paper*, No. 63.

Transparency International (2011). *Frequently asked questions about corruption*, http://www.transparency.org/news_room/faq/corruption_ faq#faqcorr1.

Transparency International (2010). *Corruption perceptions index.*

Transparency International (2008). *Poverty and corruption.* Working Paper No. 2/2008.

Treisman, D. (2000). The causes of corruption: A cross-national study. *Journal of Public Economics*, vol. *76*, 399-457.

UNDP (2009). *Human development report 2009: Overcoming barriers: Human mobility and development.* New York: Palgrave.

UNDP (2010). *Human development report 2010: The real wealth of nations: Pathways to human development*. Palgrave Macmillan, New York.

World Bank (2010a). *World development indicators database*, 15 December.

World Bank (2010b). The worldwide governance indicators, 2009 update. Aggregate indicators of governance 1996-2009. www.govindicators.org.

World Bank (1997). *World development report 1997.* Washington D.C.: Oxford University Press.

Zhang, Y., Cao, L. & Vaughn, M. S. (2009). Social support and corruption: Structural determinants of corruption in the world. *Australian and New Zealand Journal of Criminology*, vol. *42*, 204-217.

In: Towards a Society with a More Fair Economy
Editors: J. A. Filipe, N. Nagopoulos, K. Rontos et al.
ISBN: 978-1-63482-900-7

Chapter 3

ENDOGENOUS GROWTH, SOCIAL ECONOMY AND SOCIAL ENTERPRISES AS A MEANS OF REVERSING THE TRADITIONAL MODEL OF REGIONAL DEVELOPMENT

Nikos Nagopoulos** *and Kostas Rontos
University of Aegean, Mytilene, Greece

ABSTRACT

The new regional planning forms of endogenous growth and social development promote a different approach to resolve the structural and social problems in modern societies taking into account the social cohesion, social trust and active participation. In this context, focusing our interest on the role of local production systems and local labor markets, we examine the importance of the contribution of scientific and research institutions, as well as of social enterprises to the re-planning of priorities for regional social development in specific sectors of social policy, social economy and innovation. Finally, in the current paper, we analyze new systems of corporate social and environmental responsibility and different forms of social enterprises as an alternative business model.

Keywords: Endogenous Growth, Regional Development, Local Production Systems, Social Enterprises

3.1. INTRODUCTION

The success of a model of reorganization of the economic and social fabric, which is affected in times of recession and labour market deregulation, depends on the redesigning of the intergovernmental policy framework of the organization, as well as on the operation of the

* Corresponding author: Email: n.nagopoulos@soc.aegean.gr.

state at the regional level. This new framework should clearly define its political priorities within the Regions by exploring the social base in the selection and implementation of the objectives, at all levels of political and socioeconomic development. These changes require, in principle, the basic adjustment of the economic mechanism and economic policy in a democratic society and intergovernmental framework, with active participation of citizens in local communities[1].

In the shift of the political and economic context, the concept of development is built mainly by endogenous forces and resources that follow a widely legitimized intergovernmental goal and strategic financial planning. In this view, the discussion concerns the endogenous growth where social solidarity is inscribed not as an abstract concept but rather as a fundamental constitutive and programmatic principle. Within the same context, the reorganization of entrepreneurship through forms of social and solidarity economy acquires new content in social relationships that are established in political and economic life.

3.2. Concept, Objectives and Strategies of Regional Development

3.2.1. Basic Theoretical Dimensions of Regional Development

Regional Development studies the spatial dimension of growth and development; that is, it explores economic, social, environmental and other human behaviours in space.

Therefore, the relevant science (Regional Science) aims to study the distribution of income, production rates and wages in space; that is, it measures regional disparities, forms of homogeneous regions, explores criteria, rules and planning process activities and proposes mitigation measures of regional disparities. For this reason, regional/local analysis aims to compare regions or to compare a region with a wider geographical context (e.g. a country); that is, it is interested in comparing two regions and their development rather than in comparing the development of a single region.

In this sense, regional development is interested in understanding how income as well as resources and wealth between regions are distributed in contrast with the national development that is interested more in understanding an overall increase of them. Nevertheless, this differentiation in approaching development often brings in conflict objectives of national policy (increase) with those of regional/local policy (distribution).

The problem is exacerbated as regional analysis and policy (generally, the dimension of space) has been neglected by research and decision-making until recently, and the emphasis has been placed on national development and diachronic evolution (time dimension). To this problem have contributed dominant economic theories, such as Neoclassical theory, with the exception of German Economic Thought (Thunen, 1826, Weber 1909), Keynesian paradigms and, finally, regional models, and more particularly Growth Poles Theory (Perroux, 1955).

More specifically, Neoclassical theory postulates that seamless mobility of population and activities are desirable and necessary for the operation of the economic system. Neoclassical theory generally accepts that - in long run, with the smooth operation of the free market mechanism - the excellent geographic distribution of the population is achieved

[1] See G Argeitis: Constraints, objectives and key features of an alternative economic policy INE GSEE, 2012.

without any further intervention. With the theory that Keynes developed in 1935 (Keynes, 1955), both the potential of a perfect competition and all classic economic edifice on which their views on regional balance were based are refuted. However, some later Keynesian models adopt the approach that migration flows are more likely to be a balancing factor that can reduce regional disparities. Furthermore, theories of regional science, and, more particularly, growth poles theory, have favoured the creation of large concentrations of population and activities, whereas, approaches opposite to the aforementioned views - such as the Marxist one - did not show any interest in regional inequalities in population (Palloix C., 1978, Madel E., 1963).

Under the influence of the views that prevailed in the main schools of scientific thought, which have ultimately neglected the variable "space" as an autonomous dimension in the study of socio-economic phenomena, the lack of attention to regional dimension of social/economic phenomena is apparently justified.

3.2.2. The Reality and the Role of the European Union (EU) in Taking into Serious Consideration Regional Development

In practice, neither has the balance of classic view (i.e., the optimization of population distribution and activities in the area) been achieved nor has the diffusion of development in polar process ever occurred. On the contrary, there have been huge imbalances in population distribution and activities that created saturation problems in the (rich) host regions and deforestation in the (poor) regions of origin.

The reality has shown that the accumulation of population and activities in a region lead secondarily to an increased demand in developed regions which eventually leads to the introduction of new (supporting) activities (services, etc.) to them, a fact that exacerbates accumulation and uneven distribution of economic activities. As a result, the degree of employment resources is differentiated by region, then regional incomes are differentiated and, finally, regional inequality is expanded. Furthermore, although favoured areas are developed economies, they present significant problems with saturation, overpopulation and dysfunctions due to over-accumulation of activities (negative external economies).

This failure of theoretical approaches has contributed to systematic scientific study of space and the acquisition of "regional consciousness" by leading actors and citizens, thus the defence of "local and regional interests" has been strengthened. At the same time, the EU has contributed to consolidating the need to exercise regional policy by establishing a "Europe of Regions", setting up and strengthening regions through the ERDF (European Regional Development Fund). To document and support regional policy, the EU has set up a regional information system (database REGION, etc.) and has identified homogeneous regions by introducing, not only the physical space of Europe but the economic, social and demographic space as well.

In Greece a serious attempt for the country's regional development was made in the early 1980s, when appropriate development laws were introduced, but it was abandoned due to budgetary reasons in the middle of the same decade. It is a reality that fiscal problems in countries have as a victim, among others, regional and social policy, as other needs are considered more vital and require an immediate solution. Such tactics increases of course social and regional inequalities, as the abandonment of social and regional policy exacerbates the disadvantage of weaker regions and/or population groups that the crisis itself brings about.

3.2.3. Choosing a Regional Development Strategy

At the same time, within the context of alternative approaches to regional local development, the model of Bottom-up Development was emerging – either as endogenous growth or integrated or local development - as opposed to that of Top-down Development that had been established by then.

On the one hand, polarization has been a strategic issue for regional development. Two-Polar Growth Strategy concentrates on promoting dynamic industries in selected places, usually urban centers, with natural and acquired that are in favour of local development. At this stage, the pole drains resources from their surrounding region. The model presupposes the development of the pole at this first stage, which is spread out to the rest region at a second stage (Papadaskalopoulos, 1990).

On the other hand, in Bottom-Up development all local factors (local administration, enterprises, local initiative and entrepreneurship) are the basic tools of the development procedure. Furthermore, the so-called - comprehensive development is achieved; that is, the utilization of local advantages and the development of all spatial units of each region, in contrast with the development of a pole. In addition, in Bottom-Up development local authorities and the inhabitants of each region choose the type and pace of development they wish.

Moreover, there are more advantages in using Bottom-Up development. Whereas the goals of regional policy are not promoted sufficiently by central planning, they are promoted more easily by the model of Bottom-Up development. Such goals are the following:

- curb population;
- stimulation of employment;
- resource utilization;
- rise in living standards;
- stimulation of residents' psychology from participation;
- achievement of social cohesion, social trust and participation, that is, enhancement of social capital;
- scaling up social services to citizens of local communities; and
- development respecting and preserving cultural values of local communities.

Another good question is: "Which strategy and its corresponding pattern are predominant? Is the strategy of Top-down Development and the polar pattern that is connected with this kind of development or is the strategy of Bottom-up Development and the endogenous growth model that is associated with this?" Of course, the answer depends on the socio-economic characteristics of the country and its international orientations. Generally, a long-term development strategy should be based on the combination of both patterns that would alternate depending on economic times and the political orientations of the country. For example, while endogenous growth is required in times of crisis (structural changes, recession, unemployment, etc.), the polar model has increased growth potential in times of economic growth.

More specifically, polarization in times of crisis leads to a rapid decline in promotional polar "industries" that are in demand (activities in general), resulting in a reduction in production and employment, which have a big impact on the economy of the surrounding region. On the contrary, in periods of crisis - and despite the fact that it faces increased competition from newly industrialized countries in a globalized economy - endogenous growth reduces the consequences of crisis because of the relative (albeit selective) area of proficiency it achieves and the higher degree of integration of the region's productive fabric, shielding the region from the centripetal force of the poles. Moreover, it reduces the effects of competition from newly industrialized countries that emerge in the internationalization of markets.

Finally, one of the main means of this strategy is to enhance the transportation system so that the geographical, economic and social isolation is eliminated, thus helping remote and island regions face the economic crisis. In conclusion, the model of Bottom-up Development is appropriate to current and future conditions prevalent worldwide and more so in Greece, and nowadays it looks like a prospect out of the crisis and a protective shield.

3.3. Endogenous Growth, Local Production Systems and Social Economy

3.3.1. The Role of Local Production Systems and Local Labor Markets

At this point, we should note the importance of local production systems, as determining factors of regional policy planning and enhanced forms of social development, in accordance with the terms set by the social economy. This happens because local production systems and local labour markets are related to spatial distribution, structure and development of methods to determine the limits of economic activity. The emphasis on geographical aspects of the market facilitates the extraction of reliable scientific research results, documentation and empirical applications and the exercise of effective and targeted policy. Moreover, micro-economic approaches – from a spatial dimension point of view – to social events and behaviours are particularly compatible with the needs of regional and local development[2].

The usefulness of locality of labour markets for the study and implementation of policies is evident, regardless of probable non-identification of the administrative boundaries of regions and functional spatial field of labour markets, which, in this case, are determined by changes in the patterns of movement of employees. In each case, measurement, evaluation and investigation of the size of local labour markets and broader demographic trends contribute to attempting an interpretation of the degree of expansion, as the above discussion demonstrates a diversified labour division.

This segmentation in the workplace is directly related to financial and professional categorizations and to rapid social and professional mobility. The professional structure of employment at a regional level is often more appropriate from a research point of view

[2] Efstratoglou A.: *Local labor markets and employment services*, 2005, ed. by INE / GSEE, Athens, and Efstratoglou A.: *Local labor markets in Greece*, 2006, ed. by INE / GSEE, Athens.

because it reveals the social and technical features of labour division in a more effective way. This privileged research field in an environment for endogenous development is enhanced by administrative and operational determination of spatial dimension of labour markets and opens up a framework of a comprehensive policy planning by implementing operational action plans based on upgraded partnerships and networking at the local level. Social economy offers substantial enhancement in the local productive fabric at this level too.

Thus, the spatial dimension of the markets, by itself and beyond the prevailing globalized standards, requires an intergovernmental framework in which both local markets and active citizens who get involved in local communities in various ways can participate in and co-decide on critical objectives and perspectives of local development. It should be also noted that local labour markets combined with the quality of networks and employment services offered are increasingly becoming the central pillar of the development process at the national and mainly at the regional level[3]. At the same time, we should highlight the importance of regional and local dimension that focuses on a different allocation of collaborations and responsibilities, depending on the case. More particularly, these synergies are performed in a more efficient and controlled manner within "local homogeneous zones at small geographical scale" as "Micro-Planning".[4] In this way, a framework of social reforms and governance becomes necessary so that new policies of endogenous social development can be implemented with management tools that address and resolve problems and that are adapted to local realities.

3.3.2. The Dynamics of Social Economy

The recent financial crisis that has struck mainly the southern European countries has confirmed the aforementioned and has highlighted the bottlenecks and limits of the top-down model of development and economic growth that has prevailed over the past decades, which has been based on temporary profitability, exploitation of natural resources with incalculable environmental consequences and on enormous social and regional inequalities.

To a large extent, even the issues of financial equilibrium, swelling and weakness of public debt management and deregulation of the labour market in these countries demonstrate that there has been no alternative basis of social and economic policy through the prospect of a new form of social development.

The new development model, that is, the bottom-up model of development, adjusts the development objectives and enhances participatory governance systems. As discussed above, its objectives and mode of operation show that this model places emphasis on social economy that has already been implemented successfully in many European regions.

Similar initiatives to shift the growth model are supported by the Committee of the Regions, which recognizes and reinforces the importance of supporting social economy and social enterprises, as a means of improving working conditions and sustainability of

[3] Robolis, S. (Paper presented 2004), Regional-Local Development and Employment, Kozani.

[4] Papadaskalopoulos A., Christofakis M: "Micro-development planning and local endogenous growth. The case of Western Attica with emphasis on Thriassion Plane" (2011), in Rondos K. (ed.), *Issues of regional planning and spatial analysis: Methods, tools and support systems*, Benos.

employment.[5] However, the Commission's contribution to the scientific conceptualization and political determination of the new development model is based more on principles and less on an absolutely narrow and strictly defined regulatory framework. These principles are recommended as common both to most Member States, apart from the diversity of political, economic and social options, as well as to social entrepreneurs' capacity for innovation. Consequently, concerning this particular content that may be acquired by the new economic policy, it is up to the individual strategy that the Regions develop within them in an endogenous environment of "smart growth"[6]

In any case and at the level of principles, the contribution of social economy should be underlined as a key factor in achieving the objectives related to the eurozone economic growth[7], employment, the European social model (which is a combination of sustainable economic growth and continuous improvement of living conditions and labour), economic, social, territorial and environmental cohesion and (technological, social, administrative and environmental) innovation.

This alternative and supplementary economic activity is registered as an integral part of the European social model and plays a crucial role in the objectives of the European policy for social development, employment, social cohesion, new entrepreneurship and social administration. It also connects economic and social players by consolidating partnerships with the public sector, private enterprises and associations so that greater consistency is achieved, while helping enterprises gain a local access to a globalized economy.

Social economy - that is, the non-profit economic activity of small and medium-sized producers, which ensures fair prices, reasonable profit and decent income for farmers - has a lot of potential growth in the Regions of our country and, indeed, immediately. The increase in unemployment and poverty in Europe has already resulted, *inter alia*, the emergence of new social enterprises that combat social exclusion and innovators, as compensation for coverage of new needs, especially in view of the inability of the states to design effective policies[8], mainly those that are related to local development, the integration of the long-term unemployed and the fight against social exclusion.

It should be noted that Social economy enterprises are characterized by its members' strong personal involvement in the management of the enterprise and the absence of seeking profits in order to remunerate shareholders' capital. Social economy enterprises represent 2 million enterprises (i.e., 10% of all European businesses) and employ over 11 million paid employees (the equivalent of 6% of the EU working population): of these, 70% are employed in non-profit organizations, 26% in cooperatives and 3% in mutual insurance services. Social economy enterprises are present in almost every sector of the economy, such as banking, insurance, agriculture, craft, various commercial services, and health and social services etc.

[5] In the "European platform against poverty and social exclusion", 2008, the Committee of the Regions notes in Chapter "Social Economy, Social Innovation and Experimentation" that it welcomes the contribution of social economy, volunteering and corporate social responsibility in terms of added value they bring to the Regions.

[6] Landabaso M. 2012. Research and innovation strategies for smart specialisation. United Nations Economic Commission for Europe-Building Strategies for Regions of Innovation, Salle VII, Palais des Nations, Geneva.

[7] There is reference to the principles that are indicated in the revised texts of the Treaty of Lisbon (2009), too.

[8] "Social economy" as purposeful and necessary strategic orientation was formed in the Conference of Ministers of Social Affairs of the Member States of the OECD in June 1998. The core of the orientation that Conference provided is the regulation of the economic environment of social systems.

3.3.3. But How Is Social Economy (S.E.) Defined?

These activities take into account the overall social development and cohesion in local communities by giving priority to people's need and employment. The basic principle underlying the activities of S.E. is the principle of democratic organization, whereas the economic basis of this cooperation is based on the features of a new mixed economy that can ensure effective benefits if the existing welfare institutions and processes of exercising social policy are modernized in depth[9].

It should be noted that alternative and supplementary economic activity is nowadays an integral part of the European social model and plays a crucial role in the objectives of the policy on social development, employment, and social cohesion. Social economy includes cooperatives, mutual security funds, non-profit organizations of institutions and social enterprises, provides a wide range of products and services throughout Europe and creates new jobs. The EU policy in this area aims to create a favourable regulatory environment for social enterprises in order to grow together with other businesses.

Furthermore, social economy enterprises benefit from the actions planned under the Small Business Act for Europe - approved by the Commission to support all SMEs in June 2008 – thus, they can meet the challenges arising from globalization and rapid technological changes of the global economic recession[10]. Regardless of the legal status of the agencies that make up social solidarity economic interventions, Social Economy organizations create jobs according to the principles of social solidarity (employment integration of social groups that are excluded from the labour market), whereas in many cases they provide public services.

Nevertheless, they are mainly characterized by their objectives through a different administration style and management that continuously combine the public interest, economic performance and democratic operation, as well as adherence to values defined in the principles of the Social Economy Charter (broad social base, sustainable development, quality and stability of jobs and adoption of collective criteria for allocating profits).

3.3.4. Social Enterprises As an Alternative Business Model

Social enterprises are voluntary small scale systems of infrastructure and low-level interest and, therefore, their consistency and reliability are based on partners' will and self-commitment, without high interest and profit. A social enterprise refers to an economic and commercial activity that takes into account primarily the public interest, whereas it is often expressed with a high level of social innovation.

At the same time, the mode of production of goods or services seeks a social objective, such as: the fight against social marginalization and exclusion from the labour market, through social and professional integration of disadvantaged and low-skilled individuals.

---

[9] A. Giddens "State and Civil Society", 1996, Center for Women's Studies and Research (KGME in Greek): *Institutional formations and social realm: The role of NGOs and civil society in policy making at national and European leve*l, ed. by KGME, Athens, 2005.

[10] *EU* "Guide to Research and Innovation Strategies for Smart Specialisation (RIS 3)", 2012; Eu "RIS3 National Assessment: Greece – Clusters Smart specialisation as a means to foster economic renewal", 2012; Ortega-Argilés, R., (2013). Smart specialization: economic transformation strategy. Department of Global Economics and Management, Faculty of Business and Economics, University of Groningen, The Netherlands.

The mode of organization of social enterprises obeys to principles of participation and social justice and applies to entities with special status (cooperatives, foundations, associations, societies) and social enterprises in the form of private companies, seeking to develop sustainable jobs and enhance local social services. The establishment of collective systems plays crucial role in the success of social entrepreneurship and social enterprises; these systems are the following:

- local quality pacts;
- local exchange systems;
- networks of ethical fair-trade agreements operating under agreed price;
- social institutions, such as social excellence; and
- systems of corporate social and environmental responsibility.

Furthermore, the development of market policies related to the clientele expansion and the implementation of policies of flexible competitiveness, which are based on social demand and quality, are very important for the success of certain forms of social enterprises.

Social enterprises get involved in "smart growth"[11] through social innovation, responding to needs yet to be satisfied and taking into account environmental and social consequences of their activities. The greatest part of the surplus of social enterprises is designed for achieving sustainable development objectives and, in accordance with the conditions for ensuring social cohesion, and contributes to attaining the objectives of "Europe 2020[12]" and social and economic changes. These changes require wider voluntary and social participation, managerial autonomy and independence as well as the defense and the implementation of principles of solidarity and responsibility to do business.

This alternative business model can be the counterpart to the conventional market model in terms of attaining social objectives. Nowadays, the term "social economy is used in two ways: (a) as a term referring to businesses operating under specific legal form, whatever the object of their action, and whose profit does not result from investment capital; and (b) as a term referring only to enterprises of community action, regardless of its legal form, where the profit (if any) is reinvested in the enterprise business in order to better achieve its objectives.

The specificity of social enterprise is that it combines entrepreneurship and social objectives in a mixture of economic and social activities that differentiates it both from a classical enterprise and the traditional forms of non-profit organizations. These (social) enterprises can create additional employment because they cover new needs that derive from social changes, such as: demographic trends, aging population, high rates of female employment, large numbers of single-parent families. Furthermore, having innovation as a feature, social enterprises have expanded on new fields such as: neighbourhood services, restructure of troubled neighbourhoods, aid of the elderly and people with disabilities, professional and vocational integration of people with low educational level, as well as on commerce, ethics and solidarity funding etc. In this way, social economy also aims to fulfill the objectives of social policy or employment policy, while innovation of social enterprises is

[11] *EC (2010)* Regional Policy contributing to smart growth in Europe 2020, *SEC, 1183.*

[12] Bjorn Hacker, Till Van Treeck (2010 December), "The Reformed Stability and Growth Pact, the Europe 2020 Strategy and the European Semester". INTERNATIONAL POLICY ANALYSIS.

often associated with the utilization of social entrepreneurs' ingenuity to meet social needs in new ways, needs which are not met by the market or the public sector.

CONCLUSION

In conclusion, the exercise of regional policy has now more tools and theoretical approaches to interpret regional/local issues which, however, remain complex. Their study requires not only time and consideration of the circumstances that prevail in each period but also of the space, which is not "idle", as considered in the past; it is rather of a dynamic character, it affects and is affected by socio-economic phenomena.

Therefore, the solution of regional problems and the reduction in regional disparities often lay in mobilizing local social forces to utilize business opportunities and get involved in social and general activities that combine performance and equitable distribution in ways that local communities themselves decide upon.

Furthermore, the economic and social significance of social economy enterprises is growing to meet new social needs that arise, along with the positive impact they have on job creation, housing, and social services for vulnerable groups in local societies, especially in degraded areas. Thus, social economy also serves to achieve the objectives of social policy and employment. To this direction, in most European countries, the specificity to administer these policies has led to new expectations for the provision of services of general benefit more effectively, together with the potential of the state.

In conclusion, special attention should be paid for supporting and further publicizing local examples that combine economic activities in the services sector (e.g. tourist activities) with the primary sector or for strengthening the interrelationship of local branches of the economy, so that local consumption can be maximized. To this direction, there seems to be significant room for intervention in the employment field, especially for those who are outside the labour market, through the use of local experience (mainly drawing on existing cooperative units and cooperatives) and other initiatives. In this way, the endogenous approach to development objectives and social economy can be the subject of collective development activities, which will rely on the European social acquis (solidarity, equality, etc.), along with the benefits that will be brought to active citizens and local communities themselves.

REFERENCES

Argeitis, G. (2012). Constraints, objectives and key features of an alternative economic policy *INE GSEE.*

Bjorn Hacker, Till Van Treeck. (2010, December). "The Reformed. Stability and Growth Pact, the Europe 2020 Strategy and the European Semester". *International policy analysis.*

Center for Women's Studies and Research (KGME in Greek, 2005). *Institutional formations and social realm: The role of NGOs and civil society in policy making at national and European leve*l, ed. by KGME, Athens.

EU. (2012). "Guide to Research and Innovation Strategies for Smart Specialisation (RIS 3)".

EU. (2012). "National Assessment : Greece – Clusters Smart specialisation as a means to foster economic renewal RIS3 ".

EC. (2010). Regional Policy contributing to smart growth in Europe 2020, SEC 1183.

European platform against poverty and social exclusion. (2008).

Efstratoglou, A. (2005). *Local labor markets and employment services*, ed. by INE / GSEE, Athens.

Efstratoglou, A. (2006). *Local labor markets in Greece*, ed. by INE / GSEE, Athens.

Giddens, A. (1996). "State and Civil Society".

Landabaso, M. (2012). "Research and innovation strategies for smart specialisation" United Nations Economic Commission for Europe-Building Strategies for Regions of Innovation, Salle VII, Palais des Nations, Geneva.

OECD (1998 June). Paper in "Conference of Ministers of Social Affairs of the Member States of the OECD in June 1998.

Ortega-Argilés, R. (2013). Smart specialization: economic transformation strategy. Department of Global Economics and Management, Faculty of Business and Economics, University of Groningen, The Netherlands.

Reform Treaty of Lisbon. (2009).

Robolis, S. (2004). (Paper presented) Regional-Local Development and Employment, Kozani.

Papadaskalopoulos, A. & Christofakis, M. (2011). "Micro-development planning and local endogenous growth. The case of Western Attica with emphasis on Thriassion Plane" in Rondos K. (ed.) *Issues of regional planning and spatial analysis: Methods, tools and support systems*, Benos.

In: Towards a Society with a More Fair Economy
Editors: J. A. Filipe, N. Nagopoulos, K. Rontos et al.
ISBN: 978-1-63482-900-7

Chapter 4

CORPORATE SOCIAL RESPONSIBILITY: A THEORETICAL AND LEGAL BACKGROUND

Nikolaos Bloskas[*]
Department of Sociology, University of Aegean, Mytilene, Greece

ABSTRACT

Corporate Social Responsibility (CSR) is a business behavior linked with a number of other terms and definitions regarding the concept of social responsibility. Its implementations are quite vast and sometimes contradictive, especially under the context of the financial crisis and the recession that followed. The main goal of this research is to examine the wider concept of CSR regarding its theoretical and legal background, bureaucratization forms and relationship with legitimacy. This article comprises the theoretical level of CSR, which includes a number of thematics based on the governing framework of this new form of sustainable social development.

Keywords: Corporate Social Responsibility, Social Responsibility, Bureaucratization, Sustainable Social Development, Legitimation

1. INTRODUCTION

Corporate Social Responsibility (CSR) is a business behavior linked with a number of other terms and definitions regarding the concept of social responsibility. Its implementations are quite vast and sometimes contradictive, especially under the context of the financial crisis and the recession that followed.

The main goal of this research is to examine the wider concept of CSR regarding its theoretical and legal background. The main questions posed as research hypotheses are:

What is the role of certification in CSR regarding the wider concept of social responsibility and its bureaucratization?

[*] Corresponding Author: Email: socm11002@soc.aegean.gr

How do CSR and legitimation correlate?

In order for these questions to be answered this research comprises 2 levels: theory and an interview analysis. The theoretical level includes 6 thematics, which will be based on the governing framework of CSR.

In the first chapter there will be an analysis of the weberian theory contrasting CSR and emphasizing in the wider organization and implementation of CSR through bureaucracy. Then there will be an examination regarding the Marxist analysis of the surrounding global environment, which eventually is the framework for the CSR conduct. The following chapter addresses the issue of social policy and the welfare state and their reorganization through the neoliberal doctrine in accordance with the role of CSR. Special emphasis will be given on how EU, affected by the wider global developments, promotes CSR as a social policy instrument towards sustainable and social development. After all that, the legal perspective of CSR will be put on the table. At first there will be a focus on the relationship between CSR voluntarism and law, which will be followed by a chapter about legitimation, a concept analyzed by Habermas.

2. CSR As a Bureaucratic Structure

CSR is not just a term, but also a relationship between the economy and society. Classical sociology provides the tools for understanding this relationship in depth through the weberian theory and the homonymous work of *Economy and Society*. Emphasis is given to the discourse between these two parts, focusing on the individual actors and institutions forged by the wider societal context. A major concept of the weberian theory is individualism as a starting point of an analysis. Individuals form organized groups within which they orchestrate and plan their actions. As a result, definitions and practices are grounded neither as norms, as it happens with the modern CSR concept, nor as an aftereffect of the materialistic perspective of the Marxist theory, but rather occur by the set of interactions of the societal actors (Weber 1978: 313 – 316).

This context is analyzed historically as it passes through different stages. The most characteristic example is that of the Protestant Ethic (Calvinism) and its importance as a factor in the establishment of capitalism and its development as expressed today. In direct contrast with Marx, the emphasis is given to how a religious dogma, through its set of principles (rationality, accumulation, thrift) affected the economy, thus setting the ground for the needed capital accumulation to enable capitalistic expansion. As a result of the Protestant Ethic, the spirit of capitalism was inevitably linked with the instrumental type of rationality (calculation of means and ends)[1], which was grounded as a fundamental economic principle of modern capitalism and a dominant societal norm (Weber [1930] 1992: 8 – 11).

However CSR seem to differ from this, characterizing *value rationalization*, which has not yet been acclaimed as a virtue in any economic action, as it is in direct contrast with it, especially regarding the pursuit of profit. The value rationalization is not based in calculation, but rather derives from some societal values. At this historical point the dominant value system is definitely affected by the debate on social responsibility and CSR. As in the case of Calvinism, these newfound values, with the right preconditions, spark profound changes to

[1] According to Weber there are four: *instrumental, value, emotional, traditional*.

the social structure, thus altering the correlations between society and economy as it did with the Protestant Ethic (Boeddeling 2012).

As for the individuals, it is they who constitute the institutions within which society operates. In CSR this seems to apply to its both dimensions, internal and external. When individuals are organized into groups they create communities and societies, within which a culture is developed. In a business this works both ways, whilst there is the clear motive of profit, there is also a culture that defines the company and characterizes its actions and profile. From this perspective the pressure for the establishment of CSR does not come solely from consumers and public opinion, but also from the employees and the set of interactions between the organization itself and the surrounding external environment, whether it is local, national or global (Culler 2010).

Business, independent third party certification systems of CSR, multinational enterprises and all modern organizations, all function under the same regime, that of bureaucracy. Bureaucracy is nothing more than an established rational structure and result of the prevalence of instrumental rationality. As a structure it is responsible for carrying the community actions and values (social responsibility in this case) to rational and acceptable social actions, in accordance with the wider societal correlations of power (CSR) (Weber et. al. 1998: 227 – 229).

Bureaucracy as a social structure is everywhere, penetrating vertically all social structures, being linked with the organization of corporate groups, regardless of their values and goals. Every organization is forced to adapt to these conditions if it is to succeed and fulfill its purposes. From the moment that a bureaucratic structure is born it is very difficult, almost impossible to destroy it, regardless its implementation and its malfunctions (Weber 1947: 333 -334).

3. A Marxist Analysis of the Surrounding Global Economic Environment of CSR

CSR is term that is found and applied mostly in businesses. However there is also considerable debate about the implementation and the social parameters of the concept. From the traditional Marxist point of view, it can be argued that CSR is defined solely by the wider set of relationships between labor and capital. Special emphasis is also giver to crises, where capitalism as a system, and its major components, such as trade, industries and institutions, become completely disoriented and grind to a standstill due to some inner contradictions (Marx-Engels, [1848] 1965: 36). Economy, reflecting the production, is the base from which everything else evolves. Any change to that, fundamentally changes the structure of the whole society (Antonopoulou, 2008: 80-83). Traditional-orthodox Marxist theories cannot be examined separately from the economic system. As a result, definitions and terms such as CSR cannot be perceived sui generis as norms, but rather as misleading expressions of propagandistic ideas of the wider capitalistic ideology, which expanded through globalization and within which capitalistic expansionism is being manifested. CSR and other similar definitions are just materialistic phenomena and nothing more, without any moral or ethical cause and purpose (Akbas 2012). On the other hand, isolating fragments of Marxist thought can provide a less radical and more usable theoretical result for this case, but much more contradictory. The ideals of communism described by Marx and Engels can easily be traced in the concept of sustainable development, being however in direct contrast with the wider context of capitalism (profit). This also explains the difficulties for the establishment of social responsibility in a free market economy, where profit is an end itself (Hu 2008).

From another Marxist point of view it can be argued that concepts such as CSR are interpretations of the inner contradictions of the capitalist system itself: The combined need both for profit and balanced development, under expansionary dynamics and the reproduction of capitalism (World Association for Political Economy 2008). With the described objective, CSR functions in an instrumental way, providing an extra tool towards the exploitation and deception of the consumers. Companies do not care about social responsibility, only about their competitiveness. CSR provides a means to improve their reputation by pretending to put aside profit in favor of sensible social issues (Zaharia and Grundey 2011). In this guise, CSR does not represent a challenge to business organization, but rather constitutes a deeper embedment of the already established capitalistic social relationships, resulting in an opening of the wider social life to the rules of the market. Therefore CSR is not viewed as a driving force for change, but rather a result of the accumulated social and financial capital and its reorganization by new global developments (Hanlon 2006: 157). Emerging from traditional Marxism, neo-Marxist inclines to the view that international economic relations are the key driver for the corporate and entrepreneurial behavior (Wallerstein 1979). According to Hardt and Negri capitalism has been able to successfully integrate, social, economic and political power, thus reorganizing the status quo by weakening the national States to a new balance of power shared between global organizations, enterprises, nations and corporations. As a result a new set of actors, definitions and equilibrium were forged not only in economy, but also culturally, due to some rising ethical values that comprise the backbone of this new supranational world power known as *Empire* (Hardt and Negri 2000: 18).

4. CSR As a Trait of a New Social Policy under Development

The global market and its economic environment are of the upmost importance for the formulation of the welfare state and social policy. Social policy is a jurisdiction that requires organization. During the golden years of Keynesianism and New Deal, the implementation of weberian bureaucracy seemed dominant. However, after the rise of neoliberalism, through the governments of Reagan and Thatcher, this whole pattern shifted. Social policy and the welfare state felt into decay and declined, due to their extensive bureaucratic structures, their size and cost, and inability to stimulate competitiveness and the development of the free market. As a result the bureaucratic structures became more flexible, with emerging new forms of social policy taking the lead (Bloskas 2011).

With the rise of neoliberalism a new era began. Despite the welfare state model, the market doctrine became dominant and dictated the terms of a new social policy, which by definition was oriented towards liberalization. Social policy was stigmatized by the invasion of privatization and its reorganization with new standards set by the free market need for effectiveness, flexibility and low cost. This new technocratic perspective requires methodological tools for the constant supervision of the relationship between cost and efficiency, which seems to be the main criterion for the new policy making. As a result, a number of independent third parties were formed as tools of supervision, through various standardizations such as quality control (ISO) etc. These standardizations are crucial for a free market economy, providing the necessary tools for the market's professed self regulation (Markantonatou 2011). CSR standards of social responsibility on the other hand, just like ISO, are issued under a specific methodology, from similar independent third parties for the exact same reasons (Castka et al. 2004)

Social policy however does not stand alone. On the contrary, it is defined by the model of welfare state within which it is applied. These models are ideal notions that provide only a methodological tool for study. In reality the variations are numerous. The basic models according to Adersen (1989) are the liberal, the conservative and the Scandinavian. The first (USA, UK) is characterized by minimal state interventionism in accordance with the free market. The second one (Germany, France) accepts free market but provides adequate social benefits. The last one has the strongest welfare state with catholic social benefits and services. In practice, the more liberal the economic policy and the welfare state is, the more extensive is the participation in CSR policies from its government and corporations (Lim, Tsutsui 2012).

Interesting for CSR is the case of the Japanese welfare state, which is described as a hybrid between the conservative and the liberal models. Within it, catholic benefits are provided through private welfare plans (Andersen 1997). Special emphasis is given to big corporations who provide catholic welfare and social policy programs of their own to their employees. This relationship, apart from the fact that it is being stretched in a capitalistic context, still retains some elements of the pre-modern solidarity and community relations, with corporations and employees sharing a special bond of commitment to each other. (Odaka 2002). As a result in such cases, CSR implementations despite having shown considerable increase are considered a formality and a fashion due to the already increased social responsibility of the domestic corporations which are viewed not only as businesses, but also as social institutions (Demise 2006).

This situation matches the concept of corporate philanthropy, a term that poses corporate oriented initiatives as substitutes for the welfare state, with corporations attending philanthropic endeavors, programs etc (for example Russia). However this situation does not correspond to the principles set by CSR. CSR does not aim to replace the welfare state, but rather to enhance it with voluntary private actions (Godfrey 2005).

5. CSR as a European Policy Instrument for Social Policy and Development

Corporate Social Responsibility has clear implications for the EU's institutional framework, as an instrument for social policy. The whole concept of CSR in the European Union began in March 2000 with the Summit of the European Council for the ratification of the Lisbon Strategy. As a result, CSR was integrated as a part of the Lisbon Treaty: *to make*

Europe the most competitive and dynamic knowledge-based economy in the world, capable of sustainable economic growth with more and better jobs and greater social cohesion by 2010[2].

Special emphasis was given to sustainable growth and employment in environmental issues and social integration by *investing in people and developing an active and dynamic welfare state*[3]. The conclusions of the Lisbon process were confirmed and underlined further through the European Social Agenda at the European Council of Nice. There, for the first time CSR linked enterprises and local social services (NGO's and Local Governments), as a means to stimulate the empowerment of the whole concept through developmental partnerships[4].

After a year, in July 2001, the Commission presented the Green Paper for the *Promotion of a European framework for Corporate Social Responsibility*, always in the light of the goals set in Lisbon. In this paper, great importance was given to the ability of enterprises to adjust in the local business climate and society. The main goal is social development through entrepreneurship innovations. Continuing, a matter of special emphasis is that of consultation with the other social agencies, focusing on the creation of partnerships rather than just cooperations (COM(2001) 366). Accordingly, with the white paper on European Governance, partnerships are not just desirable, but necessary for the integration of enterprises into their local communities, whilst improving the business climate for the better utilization of their innovations (COM(2001) 428).

In addition to the institutional and legislative level, there have also been some initiatives to promote the implementation of CSR in Europe. The most important is the creation of a central European network for CSR, including all the national ones (CSR Europe and CSR Hellas respectively)[5]. From its creation, by the then President of the European Commission Jacques Delors, the goal of CSR Europe has been to help enterprises integrate CSR into their daily functions and transactions[6]. Apart from this, there have also been some actions to inform European public opinion and enterprises. NGO's and other actors set as goal the promotion of social cohesion in the European market by 2004, which was characterized as the *Year for Corporate Social Responsibility*. In a similar context, the *European Campaign for CSR 2005* was mounted, and sponsored a number of conferences in various European cities with the first one being held in Athens (Papagiannakis 2003: 250 – 251).

As for future plans in the field of CSR, they can be summarized in the renewed strategy of the European Commission for the period 2011 – 2014. According to the strategy, enterprises *should have in place a process to integrate social, environmental, ethical and human rights concerns into their business operations and core strategy in close collaboration with their stakeholders*. In order to accomplish this, the European Commission issued an action agenda, covering 8 areas. New elements of vital importance are enhancing the visibility of CSR, and the dissemination of its good practices. The establishment of both an award and a reward for socially responsible businesses and the adoption of other European

---

[2] <<European Dialogue>>, http://www.csreurope.org/pages/en/european_dialogue.html (last access: 26/5/2012).

[3] <<The Lisbon strategy: a more competitive Europe, with more and better jobs>>, http://www.europarl.europa.eu/highlights/en/1001.html (last access: 26/5/2012).

[4] << Presidency Conclusions of the European Council of Nice 7, 8 and December 9, 2000>>, www.parliament.cy/parliamentgr/101/conclusion_nice.pdf (last access: 25/5/2012).

[5] <<The European business network for CSR>>, http://www.csreurope.org/pages/en/ about_us.html (last access: 26/5/2012).

[6] <<CSR EUROPE>>, http://www.csrhellas.org/portal/index.php?option=ozo_ content&perform=view&id=198&Itemid=154&lang=EN (last access: 26/5/2012).

and global approaches to CSR (ILO, OECD, UN Global Compact, UN Guiding Principles on Business and Human Rights, ISO 26000 Guidance Standard on Social Responsibility). At the same time, special attention is being given to national and sub – national policy making for CSR, and its integration into education and training. There will also be full disclosure about enterprises and their progress towards social and environmental responsibility by improving and developing a short protocol to guide the development of regulation initiatives[7].

6. CSR As Soft Law and Matters of Legislation

With the development and expansion of the free market, the overall role of the modern State has shifted and declined. As a result the State has lost, consciously and unconsciously, part of its regulatory power and breadth. From this new reality, new perspectives in law and sociology have been formed. Traditional State regulation interventionism has been reduced to the supervision and the promotion of the various systems of control. The only possible legislation of CSR can be found in the set of standards that governments issue as a mean to stimulate the promotion of social responsibility (Williams, Aguilera 2008).

Such is the case of the issued principles of CSR. According to the OECD, the implementation of these guidelines is wider. While businesses are not forced to implement them, this is not the case for the member states in which they operate. These guidelines are binding commitments for each OECD member in accordance with the *Decision of the OECD Council on the OECD Guidelines for Multinational Enterprises*. In practice some of these even end up being legislated as general rules for entrepreneurial activity by national parliaments (OECD 2011). However that is the exception and not the rule. The reality follows the example of soft law, which aims to influence, rather than enforce or dictate the behavior of corporations, offering more flexible approaches (Croquet et al. 2009).

CSR at a theoretical level is the norm of social responsibility. The point of interest is to examine how it is manifested and applied. This implementation, regardless of its size and form depends heavily on legislation (Eijsbout 2011: 21 - 23). The relationship between CSR and law has engendered much academic controversy, due to the fact that CSR is not legislated, but rather depends on business voluntarism. However there is an undeniable link between these two contradictory concepts (Gjolberg 2011). Soft law, despite the lack of direct regulatory power, can sometimes lead to gradual legislation of corporate values in the wider context of sustainability (Dom 2012). Responsibility for the enforcement of this regulatory stimulation and wider supervision of the CSR concept, lies with NGOS and Governments, through the various public private partnership structures (Bloomfield 2006).

Soft law or not, the legislation of CSR is a crucial matter under discussion. According to EU: *Corporate social responsibility should nevertheless not be seen as a substitute to regulation or legislation concerning social rights or environmental standards, including the development of new appropriate legislation. In countries where such regulations do not exist, efforts should focus on putting the proper regulatory or legislative framework in place in order to define a level playing field on the basis of which socially responsible practices can be developed* (EU 2001: COM(2001) 366).

[7] <<2011 – New European Policy on CSR>> http://www.csrhellas.org/portal/index.php? option=ozo_content&perform=view&id=1750&Itemid=214&lang=EN (last access: 4/6/2012).

Beside the actually legislation of CSR, its implementation is quite strict. One of the factors for the rise of CSR is global diffusion as a result of the new economic reality, where law is substantially replaced by voluntarism. In this guise, voluntarism represents and reprises the anti-legislation trend, within which corporations avoid legal standards, through a less biding set of regulations and principles (Meyer 2010). As a result, matters of CSR such as human rights, environmental protection, fundamental labor rights and social responsibility are mostly encountered in international law. International law is the field where the global enterprises are in practice accountable. Albeit, the prevalence of soft law and its guidelines towards hard law and binding treaties, international law, despite its fragmentation and pliability is one of the few means of supervising globally and holistically the actions of multinational corporations, even if it is indirectly (Banlekas 2004).

7. CSR and Legitimacy

The implementation of soft law, despite its benefits, raises questions about democracy and legitimacy, especially in the cases of multi-national corporations. The EU makes extensive use of soft law for its structure, having the benefit of its less hierarchical networks for the decision making process. The same goes for CSR and all modern organizations and institutions (Morth 2004: 3-4).

At this point it is interesting to see how CSR can be interpreted through the theories of Habermars about legitimation. The main theme of legitimation is how governing structures retain their legal authority to govern while lacking the ability to demonstrate that they are still functioning, fulfilling the tasks for which they were constituted (Habermas 1973). Legitimation is shaped through *publicity*, the mode of expression to public opinion. This however creates an especially chaotic context about the social spheres (public and private) and their correlation. (Habermars 1991: 6). The use of mass media provides an essential tool for the shaping of public opinion for every organization that wants to legitimize itself and increase its appeal to the public (Habermas 1962: 16 -19).

Social responsibility however cannot be excluded as an essential part of public dialogue, whatever its true motives might be. It is one of the most important regulatory principles in the public discourse and the most acceptable rule between individuals, the forces of market and the government. (Penning 2007: 394 – 395).

NGOs have a special role to play in this new situation. Legitimation is not only essential for the political elite, but also for various economic actors such as businesses, enterprises and multi-national corporations. NGOs, through public private partnerships, are deployed in a constant interaction both with the corporations and with civil society. Therefore, they are necessary partners for entrepreneurial activity in general, as they are seen as representatives of public aspirations. The framework of this cooperation is CSR. The new multi-dimensional relationships between these actors are formed to a large extent by the corporation's views about social responsibility (Baur 2011).

In this context CSR is considered as a new form of legitimacy, within which business engages in a discourse with the rest of the society and its actors (Kuznetsov, Kuznetsova 2012). This perspective is emphasized in the organizational standards of a corporation. Legitimacy regarding CSR is perceived as an acceptance of societal values and norms by the companies. When a disparity occurs, legitimacy is threatened and diminished. Legitimacy is posed as a modern social contract between business and society. Beside the acceptance of the terms, in order to be fully functional and essential, another prerequisite is necessary: full disclosure and visibility (Cuganesan 2007).

Things become complicated when the enterprise under discussion is a multi-national corporation that is active in a host country. These companies have to adjust and apply CSR, if they decide to, in both the home market, as well as the host country. However, due to the differing perspectives on social responsibility, a number of issues can be raised about the legitimacy of these companies regarding their actions and policies in the developing countries (Barkemeyer 2007).

Legitimacy, however, is also linked to negative connotations. In this context CSR is nothing more than an advertising trick, being reduced merely to the marketing need for a friendlier public image (Farache 2013). After all, CSR, over time, has been vastly exploited for this purpose. This has resulted in an aura of negativity surrounding the term, and consequent rising skepticism about the whole concept of social responsibility. However, the fact still remains that the main purpose of CSR is to introduce an alternative socioeconomic activity in the context of sustainability, addressed mainly to small and medium sized enterprises (Theofilou, Jerofejeva 2010).

CONCLUSION

From its very inception, the concept of CSR has been the subject of debates, discourses and analyses. The governing framework for CSR is imported from outside Greece, more specifically from formal global institutions such as EU, promoting it as a social development instrument.

Regarding the first research hypothesis about the role of certification in CSR, the concept of social responsibility and its bureaucratization, the answer is quite complex. CSR is by definition not certificated. The organizations that issue these <<certifications>> do nothing more than quantify/measure some specific entrepreneurial aspects relate to socially responsible behavior. These standards began as necessary for the self regulation of the market and soon became a part of the free market itself, thus becoming a necessity for every entrepreneurial activity. Some of these certifications have even passed into legislation through Regulations in all EU member states (for example HACCP: Hazard Analysis Critical Control Points). As a result, these certifications became obligatory, bound by fixed bureaucratic procedures and methodologies regarding their measurements. CSR however is not mandatory. On the contrary, it is left to the discretion of the enterprise implementing it to find the mode of its expression. That expression is by definition external and organized. As a result of this organization there is an indirect bureaucratization, especially in cases were CSR is orchestrated formally from a specific department as an entrepreneurial policy. However, if social responsibility is expressed through some standards and specific methodology, then it will become just another routine procedure.

The second research hypothesis is about the relationship between legitimacy and CSR. This concept is by definition linked with large companies and corporations, which, due to their size and impact on the local communities, are forced to develop socially responsible activities through CSR. Whilst there is a clear link between CSR and legitimation, it can be argued that CSR is a little evasive on this point. CSR does not have the direct effect on sales that marketing does, and regardless of the purpose of its implementation it seems to be linked with a philosophy of social responsibility. CSR is not just a marketing tool, but an organized policy and strategy. Marketing is the tool for promoting CSR and CSR is the tool for making the concept of social responsibility more understandable to the consumers and the general public through a friendlier entrepreneurial profile.

Closing, CSR is linked with the entrepreneurial activity itself and with perceptions of it by public opinion. CSR has many definitions and even more modes of implementation. However, the fact that there is an undeniable obligation of the enterprises towards a more social behavior, dictates a turning point towards a more responsible type of entrepreneurship.

REFERENCES

Adersen, E., (1990). *The three Worlds of Welfare Capitalism*. Cambridge: Polity Press.

Adersen, E., (1997). "Hybrid or Unique?: the Japanese Welfare State Between Europe and America". *Journal of European Social Policy* Vol. 7. No. 3. Pp 179-189.

Akbas, E. K., (2012). *A Sociological Study of Corporate Social Responsibility: A Marxist Perspective*. Ankara: Middle East Technical University.

Antonopoulou, M., (2008). *The Classics of Sociology*. Athens: Savalas.

Markantonatou, M., (2011). "State and New Public Management: Deregulation and welfare through the Enterprise Governance, Good Practices and ISO-Modeling". *Thesis*, Vol. 116, July-September.

Banlekas, I., (2004). "Corporate Social Responsibility in International Law". *Boston University International Law Journal* Vol. 22. Issue 2. Pp 309-347.

Barkemeyer, R., (2007). 'Legitimacy as a Key Driver and Determinant of CSR in Developing Countries', paper for the *Marie Curie Summer School on Earth System Governance*, Amsterdam, 28 May-06 June.

Baur, D., (2011). *NGOs as Legitimate Partners of Corporations: A Political Conceptualization*. Springer: Issues in Business Ethics 36.

Bloskas, N., Chatzi, A., Spandonidou, E., (2013). "Social Development Through Corporate Social Responsibility and Social Responsibility: The Case of Lesvos in Greece". *International journal of euro mediterranean studies*. DOI 10.1007/s40321-013-0010-3.

Bloomfield, P., (2006). "The Challenging Business of Long-Term Public-Private Partnerships: Reflections on Local Experience". *Public Administration Review* Vol. 66, No. 3. Pp. 400-411.

Boeddeling, J., (2012). "Corporate social responsibility: A perspective from Weberian economic sociology". Diskussionpapiere, Wirtschaftwissenschaftliche Fakultat. Universitat Witten, Herdecke, No 22/2011, http://hdl.handle.net/10419/56042.

Castka P., Bamber C. J., Bamber, D. J., (2004). "Integrating corporate social responsibility (CSR) into ISO management systems – in search of a feasible CSR management system framework". *The TQM Magazine*, Vol. 16. Issue 3. Pp 216 – 224.

Culler, C., (2010). "Good Works: Assessing the Relationship Between the Organizational Culture, Corporate Responsibility Programs, and Weberian Theory". *International Journal of Arts and Sciences* Vol. 3. No 13. Pp 357 -374.

Cuganesan, S., Ward, L., Guthrie, G., (2007). 'Legitimacy Theory: A Story of Reporting Social and Environmental Matters within the Australian Food and Beverage Industry', paper presented for the *5th Asian Pacific Interdisciplinary Research in Accounting (APIRA) Conference,* Auckland, New Zealand, 8 - 10 July.

Croquet, N., Hameed, A., Yalkin, T. R., (2009). 'Corporate Social Responsibility in the European Union'. A research brief prepared by *Oxford Pro Bono Publico* for Pr. John Ruggie, UN's Secretary General of 'SPSG', viewed 18 January 2013, <http://www.law.ox.ac.uk/opbp/projects.php>.

Demise, N., (2006). 'CSR in Japan: A historical perspective', paper for *the Eighth World Congress of the International Federation of Scholarly Association of Management,* Berlin, 28-30 September.

Eijsbout, J., (2011). *Corporate responsibility, beyond voluntarism Regularity options to reinforce the license to operate*. Maastricht: Oce Business Services.

Farache, F., (2013). "Scepticism in CSR advertisement". *Journal of Language and Communication in Business*. Vol. 29, viewed 19 January 2013 <http://download2.hermes.asb.dk/archive/download/Hermes-49-2-farache.pdf>.

Gjolberg, M., (2011) "Explaining Regulatory Preferences: CSR, Soft Law, or Hard Law? Insights from a Survey of Nordic Pioneers in CSR". *Business and Politics* Vo. 13. Issue 2. Article 4.

Godfrey, P. C., (2005). "The Relationship Between Corporate Philanthropy and Shareholder Wealth: A Risk Management Perspective". *Acad Manage Rev.* Vol. 30. No. 4. Pp 777-798.

Habermas, J., (1991). *The Structural Transformation of the Public Sphere An Inquiry of a Category of Bourgeois Society*. Massachusetts: MIT Press.

Habermas, J., (1973). "What Does A Crisis Mean Today? Legitimation Problems in Late Capitalism". Social Research. Vol. 40. No. 4. Pp. 643-667.

Habermas, J., (1962). *The structural transformation of the public sphere*. Massachusetts: MIT Press.

Hanlon, G., (2006). Rethinking Corporate Social Responsibility and the Role of the Firm – On the Denial of Politics. In: Burchell J., Cook J., Hanlon G. *Shaping knowledge through dialogue: stakeholder dialogue and organisational learning*. Brussels: European Academy of Business in Society, pp 156 – 172.

Hardt, M., Negri A., (2000). *The Empire*. Boston: Harvard University Press.

Kuznetsov, A., Kuznetsova O., (2012). "Business Legitimacy and the Margins of Corporate Social Responsibility in the Russian Context". *International Studies of Management and Organization* Vo. 42. No. 3. Pp 35 - 48.

Lim, A., Tsutsui, K., (2012). "Globalization and Commitment in Corporate Social Responsibility: Cross-National Analyses of Institutional and Political-Economy Effects". *American Sociological Review* Vo. 77 No. Pp 169-198.

Marx – Engels (1965). *Manifesto of the Communist Party*, Athens: Papakostas.

Meyer, J. W., (2010). "World Society, Institutional Theories, and the Actor". *Annual review of Sociology* Vol. 36, Pp 1-20.

Morth, U., (2004). *Soft Law in Governance and Regulation An Interdisciplinary Analysis*. Massachusetts: Edgar Elgar Publishing.

Odaka, K., (2002). 'The Evolution of Social Policy in Japan', paper for the *WBI*. Stock. Washington: The World Bank, viewed 13 February 2013, <http://web.worldbank.org/WBSITE/EXTERNAL/WBI/0,,contentMDK:20177915~menuPK:556286~pagePK:209023~piPK:207535~theSitePK:213799~isCURL:Y,00.html>.

Theofilou, A., Jerofejeva, A., (2010). 'Measuring Levels of Skepticism Towards Corporate Social Responsibility (CSR) Activities', paper for the Corporate Responsibility Research Conference, Marseille 15-17 September.

Wallerstein, I., (1979) *The Capitalist World-Economy*. New York: Cambridge University Press.

Williams, C. A., Aguilera, R. V., (2009). "Corporate Social Responsibility in a Comparative Perspective". *The Oxford Handbook of Corporate Social Responsibility*. DOI: 10.1093/oxfordhb/9780199211593.003.0020.

Weber, M., [1930] (1992). *The Protestant Ethic and the Spirit of Capitalism*. New York – London: Routledge.

Weber, M., (1978). *Economy and Society Volume 1*. University of California Press.

Weber, M., Gerth H. H., Mills W. C., (1998). *From Max Weber: essays in sociology*. London: Routledge.

Weber, M., (1947). *The Theory of Social and Economic Organization*. New York: Free Press.

Yonghong, Hu., (2008). 'Marxist Vision of Sustainable Development and Corporate Social Responsibility', paper for the *3nd Forum of the World Association for Political Economy*. Langfang City, Hebei Province, China, 24-25 May.

Zaharia, R. M., Grundey, D., (2011). "Corporate Social Responsibility in the Context of Financial Crisis: A Comparison Between Romania and Lithuania" *Corporate Social Responsibility* Vol. XIII. No 29. Pp 195-206.

"The Lisbon strategy: a more competitive Europe, with more and better jobs", http://www.europarl.europa.eu/highlights/en/1001.html (last access: 26/5/2012).

"Presidency Conclusionsof the European Council of Nice 7, 8 and December 9, 2000", www.parliament.cy/parliamentgr/101/conclusion_nice.pdf (last access: 25/5/2012).

"The European business network for CSR",http://www.csreurope.org/pages/en/about_us.html (last access: 26/5/2012).

"CSR EUROPE", http://www.csrhellas.org/portal/index.php?option=ozo__content&perform=view&id=198&Itemid=154&lang=EN (last access: 26/5/2012).

"011 – New European Policy on CSR", http://www.csrhellas.org/_portal/index.php?option=ozo_content&perform=view&id=1750&Itemid=214&lang=EN (last access: 4/6/2012).

In: Towards a Society with a More Fair Economy
Editors: J. A. Filipe, N. Nagopoulos, K. Rontos et al.
ISBN: 978-1-63482-900-7

Chapter 5

THE EMERGENCE OF CSR IN GREECE AT LOCAL LEVEL: SYNERGIES BETWEEN SMEs AND LOCAL AUTHORITIES

Miltiadis Stampoulis[1*] and Vassiliki Dimitriou[2]
[1]Department of Educational and Social Policy,
University of Macedonia, Thessaloniki, Greece
[2]Regional Economist, MS

ABSTRACT

The subject of this thesis arose from the fact that both businesses and government are interested in rendering communities better places to live and work. Given that a great part of recent literature focuses on business and societal drivers of corporate social responsibility (CSR), this paper examines the role that the local government can play in promoting CSR within the business community - particularly within SMEs - during the deep recession that has followed the debt crisis and austerity measures imposed by the Memorandum.

When implemented piecemeal, occasionally and selectively during the period of economic crisis, CSR loses its dynamics. It is the local authority that can build up strong interpersonal relationships and successful local networking thus creating the optimal conditions for CSR to flourish and thereby enhance competitiveness of SMEs. Moreover, the paper draws on evidence from the Municipality of Athens in Greece, which implements the project "Development and Dissemination of Corporate Social Responsibility in the territorial limits of the City of Athens". This project is expected to contribute to the consolidation of CSR in local businesses and partly address the problem of inadequate public resources through private voluntary initiative. The example of the Municipality of Athens demonstrates that, by intervening in CSR, local authorities can become effective mechanisms for the achievement of social objectives they set.

Keywords: CSR, Local Authorities - Government, Voluntary Initiatives, Local Networking

* Corresponding Author, Email: staboulismiltos@gmail.com.

1. INTRODUCTION

Businesses have always been living organisms, whose actions and behaviour have had an impact on the people and societies within which they operate. This impact can be traced at a financial, employment, social and environmental level.

Today we are experiencing various new conditions such as globalisation & market liberalisation, rapid in communication technologies, pluralism of information, increase of consumer influence, diversification in citizens' needs and expectations, fundamental changes in the global community and, at the same time, weakening of the role of the state. These conditions configure a new social, political and economic context that highlights more than ever the complex role of the enterprise, as well as the dynamic interdependence between society and businesses. This relationship is primarily 'economic' as profit is the principal aim of any business, however , in order for it to obtain a social base and have a long-term and sustainable perspective, it has to develop a substantially social and environmental character .

At the same time, the global financial crisis makes it more and more imperative to achieve sustainable development, i.e., combining economic efficiency with social contribution and environmental awareness . Therefore, businesses are now challenged to operate on the principal that entrepreneurship is inextricably related to "doing good" so any business activity should address every single aspect of life and the environment in which it grows and evolves.

Thus, it is not surprising that Corporate Social Responsibility (CSR) has appeared over the last two decades as key item on European political agendas with Denmark, France, the UK and the Netherlands. When voluntary approaches are inadequate, CSR has been identified as an important public policy issue for implementing regulatory approaches and fiscal instruments.

Zadek, a pioneer among authors identifying government roles, describes the integration of governments in the CSR context as a new stage in the development of CSR and defines this as the "third CSR generation" where the newly emerging protagonist role of governments is promoting CSR.

Governments have the opportunity and the responsibility to assume a leadership role in setting conditions that promote sustainability and creating the appropriate environment in which businesses can thrive. (Albareda et al., 2008).

However, the role that the local government can play in promoting CSR within the business community has not yet been clarified. This is particularly to SMEs which need further motivation, encouragement and support in order to adopt CSR strategies due to the fact that they lack adequate knowledge and show little interest in social responsibility issues.

The question that arises is the following: What is the purpose of the local government being involved in a field of action which, until recently , had only the central government or/and specialized agencies (of public or private character) carry out projects for promoting CSR actions? Is it the current fiscal and economic crisis that renders it essential for the local government to undertake initiatives in order to mobilize business voluntary action to leverage additional resources which will meet the ever-increasing social needs expressed by local communities and help them reach sustainable development?

2. Local Sustainable Development, CSR and SMEs

2.1. Sustainable Development and CSR: Two Interrelated Concepts

Corporate Social Responsibility (CSR) has developed at international and European level in recent years as a means for sustainable development and sustainable business operation due to a series of conditions and processes that have taken place worldwide.

CSR is a reference point in order to balance the economic, social and environmental impact of business activity while increasing value for all stakeholders such as employees, shareholders, associates, suppliers, investors, consumers, communities within which businesses operate, etc. Moreover, the CSR concept affects the way a business entity seeks and implements the idea of sustainable development, which is based on three pillars: the economic, the social and the environmental pillar.

Indeed, CSR is more relevant than ever now that international negative factors have rendered business competitiveness vulnerable to assessments based not only on purely quantitative and economic criteria, but also on criteria related to the way major social problems (e.g. unemployment, pollution) are being approached. The need for businesses to contribute to the restructuring effort of the crisis-affected economies is imperative. Businesses are not responsible for all human suffering in the world, nor do they have the power and mechanisms to deal with every single problem. However, they do possess the expertise, the qualified staff, the financial resources and the organisational structure required in order to contribute to addressing various aspects of social, environmental and economic problems that directly affect the society and the economy. (Porter & Kramer, 2006).

CSR is the mechanism by which businesses operate tackle social, economic and environmental issues while differentiating themselves from competition. The CSR strategy serves the principles of sustainable development while creating benefits for the society, the environment and the business itself (Eklington, 1994). Besides, sustainable development is a key-concept in the 21st century and a major challenge for the entire humanity.

But for the business itself the adoption of CSR practices can bring forward multiple benefits as in a constantly increasing competitive environment the image and reputation of businesses that are socially and environmentally responsible get particular importance which differentiates them from businesses that pollute immeasurably and do not follow any social policy in their internal and external business environment.

The first reference to Social Corporate Responsibility was recorded in 1993 by the then President of the European Commission, Jacques Delors, who called upon European businesses to participate in the fight against social exclusion. This appeal resulted in high mobilisation and development of European business networks (COM, 2001, 366).

Some years later, in March 2000, the Lisbon European Council launched a call for the implementation of best practices by businesses in terms of lifelong learning, labour organisation, provision of equal opportunities in the workplace, social inclusion of vulnerable groups and sustainable development.

In July 2001 the European Commission issued the Green Paper on promoting a European framework for Corporate Social Responsibility (CSR). This was the first organized effort to acknowledging the contribution of CSR to the Lisbon strategic goal for an EU capable of sustainable economic growth with more and better jobs as well as greater social cohesion. Therefore, CSR is recognized in the Green Paper as a tool to achieve the Lisbon Strategy goal, in other words to build up a dynamic, competitive and cohesive economy with knowledge as its primary variable (Vaxevanidou, 2008).

In July 2002 the European Commission adopted an extremely important Communication on **"Corporate Social Responsibility: A Business Contribution to Sustainable Development"** following the public consultation launched with the Green Paper.

Later, in February 2005, the European Commission issued the Revised Lisbon Strategy which placed emphasis on promoting sustainable development and employment. Also, at the Spring Council in March 2005 it was ascertained that voluntary business activities in the form of social responsibility practices can play a significant role in ensuring sustainable development, innovation and competitiveness in Europe.

In January 2011 BUSINESSEUROPE[1] presented a Position Paper on "European Strategy for Corporate Social Responsibility 2011-2014", which constituted a reference point for the effectiveness of the European Commission CSR approach.

The most recent development in the European Commission concerns the European Parliament Resolution (8 June, 2011) on the *external dimension of social policy, promotion of labour & social standard and European Corporate Social Responsibility at a mainly European level* . The specific Resolution confirms the non-binding nature of CSR. In addition, it urges the EU to incorporate a "social clause" in accordance with other internationally agreed and recognized standards on all external trade agreements of the EU (for example, ILO core labour standards). In particular, the above Resolution recalled to the fact that the European Union aims at rendering Europe a pole of Excellence on CSR as well as promoting the external policies applied by the Commission (Vaxevanidou, 2011).

From all mentioned above it becomes clear that, through CSR, the business community can contribute significantly to achieving the key-objectives of the "Europe 2020" Strategy for smart, sustainable and inclusive growth. CSR offers a set of values laying the foundations to achieving at the same time more social cohesion and a sustainable economic system.

2.2. CSR and Small & Medium-sized Enterprises

The business size is one of the primary factors that correlate with the extent of CSR actions and the high likelihood of adopting social and environmental culture on the part of businesses (Andrew et al., 1989; Cowen et al., 1987; Huang et al., 2000). Undoubtedly, large businesses have greater visibility as to their actions and the impact thereof, since they attract more public attention and address an increased market share. At the same time, though, they are more exposed to criticism and pressures from society, consumers and shareholders so as to demonstrate environmentally and socially responsible behaviour. It is not a coincidence that large businesses publicise far more systematically their financial data as well as annual reports and activity reports concerning their actions on the environment and society, often seizing the opportunity to capitalize on them for for self-promoting purposes.

[1] BUSINESSEUROPE is the Union of Industrial and Employers' Federations of Europe, which operates under the Social Affairs Committee (SAC) and has integrated Corporate Social Responsibility in its field of action.

On the opposite side, SMEs are considered by many to face particular inherent limitations. Bramwell et al. (1996) characteristically point out that "SMEs lack resources that would allow them to maintain a close relationship with developments as well as their similar involvement in issues of sustainable development". Additionally, as noted by Simpsons et al. (2004), SMEs consider the adoption of environmentally responsible practices to be a financial burden that is difficult to pass on to the purchaser. Consequently, their business interests , which are clearly a priority to them in comparison to environmental issues, are being adversely affected. Implementing CSR practices costs and it is this cost that constitutes the main deterring factor for businesses, let alone in a period of recession and uncertainty (Fernández-Feijóo, 2009).

Moreover, even when SMEs are active in the field of CSR, their actions focus only one of the two CSR dimensions (either internal or external social responsibility) and are conducted in a non-systematic and informal way.Also, it quite often happens that businesses are not actually aware of the fact that they are implementing actions of social responsibility (CEFRE,2004).

However, CSR promoters in recent years have focused significantly on enabling SMEs to integrate social responsibility practices in their business operation.

Vives (2006) argues that SMEs exhibit a strong feeling of attachment to the region in which they operate and are quite concerned about the future of this. On the basis of this view studies conducted for the Inter-American Development Bank (Kantis et al., 2002, 2004) confirm that SMEs exhibit a relative awareness of measures and actions targeting the environment and local society.

Besides, the relationships that family businesses form with their suppliers, distributors and other partners are, in general, stronger and last longer (Lyman, 1991). Moreover, the small number of employees fosters harmonious relationships and higher trust in management who, in turn, show more concern in regard to their problems, needs, etc.

At the same time, the vast majority of European businesses fall into the category of SMEs. Thus, one realizes that it is necessary to provide guidance on sustainable and competitive operation; that is the reason why in recent years the European policy has fuelled interest in the field of CSR. As a factor of economic and social cohesion, growth and employment, SMEs should be gradually led to a healthy level of competitiveness.

For developing countries integration in the global economy through economic liberalisation, deregulation, and democratisation is regarded as the best way to overcome poverty and inequality. Crucial to this process is the development of a vibrant private sector in which SMEs play a central part. Although CSR as a term and business concept has been mainly associated with larger companies in the heads of many, CSR is not irrelevant to or not practised by SMEs. For example, early pioneers of social accounting included Ben & Jerry's (now part of Unilever), The Body Shop (no longer an SME) and the UK fair-trade Company Traidcraft (United Nations International Development Organisation, 2002). Of course, for a large proportion of SMEs the CSR process is likely to remain informal and intuitive, even if they do not know or use the term themselves (this is the so-called "silent CSR").

Because of the lower complexity and their owner's powerful role the owner, SMEs often handle their impact on society in a more informal way than that of large businesses. In fact, many SMEs are already implementing socially and environmentally responsible practices without being familiar with CSR as a concept or without communicating their activities (Ebner & Baumgartner, 2008).

As already mentioned, significant factors for the development of a socially responsible corporate profile are the owner's personality, family business culture and spirit of charity. However, even more important than the above is the external environment in which the business operates - the external environment being determined by the location of installation, the type of business, the evolution in consumption patterns, the wider CSR context (Berger-Douce, 2009). The same applies to SMEs and the social responsibility of micro-entrepreneurship – known also as micro-Business Community Responsibility; this is often related to the sensitivities of the civil society, even though there is not sufficient amount of research in this subcategory of businesses to adequately identify their social and environmental profile (Campin, 2013).

One study which focused on environmental performance indicators as opposed to policies and processes did not find the expected differences between small and large enterprises (United Nations International Development Organisation, 2002). Certainly, some aspects of SME behaviour can be seen as examples of 'silent Corporate Social Responsibility':

- SMEs are less internationally mobile than transnational companies; therefore, they take a longer-term view of investment in an individual locality.
- Some family-owned companies exhibit strong religious/charity approaches.
- SMEs have more links to the local civil and cultural environment and may be more aware of local risks and emerging issues than internationally managed businesses.

Briefly, the findings of the research on SMEs and CSR in Europe are the following:

- SME policies and practices are generally more developed in relation to environmental impact than to social and economic one . This reflects the higher degree of environmental public policy, public awareness and international standardisation of certification and auditing processes.
- SMEs tend to prioritize CSR issues and focus on one or two key issues rather than cover the broad mix that larger businesses are able to deal with.
- SMEs tend to focus to a greater extent on local issues and programmes.
- SMEs tend to be more active in terms of CSR when there are greater networks of relations, high focus on quality and links with foreign countries
- Most SMEs are already taking some measures to meet their social responsibility, often without consciously having a CSR strategy.

3. The CSR Implementation Framework in Greece

3.1. History of CSR – CSR Promoters

In Greece CSR is a relatively new concept and is admittedly in its 'infancy' stage compared to the European reality as Greece has been slow at joining the countries that are implementing CSR in an organized way. Essentially, the first actions to promote CSR began in 2001 among entrepreneurs, organisations and the state. Similarly, academic research is just taking its first steps in terms of CSR, a fact that partially restricts the scientific substantiation of the CSR institution in the Greek reality.

In order to understand the level of development of the culture of corporate responsibility in Greece, it is appropriate to make a brief reference to the main CSR promotion institutions and organisations at national level.

The **Hellenic Network for CSR** (EDEKE) is a non-profit business association based in Athens, which was founded in June 2000 by a group of 3 business entities and 13 major firms. Forerunner of the creation of EDEKE is considered to be the co-signing of the Declaration on the establishment of the "Hellenic Network for Social Cohesion" as a result of an event organized at the initiative of an executive member of the European Network (EBNSC) for the creation of a respective Network in Greece.

In 2000 the Network became a National Partner Organisation of CSR Europe and the following year the Network changed its name to "Hellenic Network for Corporate Social Responsibility" (CSR Hellas). The main mission of EDEKE (CSR Hellas) is to raise the awareness of more and more businesses of the integration of CSR strategies in their activities, which will contribute effectively to the harmonious coexistence of entrepreneurial success and social sensitivity. Members of the Network today are some of the largest Greek businesses which are sensitive to issues relating to society and the environment and prove it in practice by implementing respective practices. Today (September 2014), the EDEKE members amount to 117 businesses and 7 business associations (www.csrhellas.org).

The Hellenic Federation of Enterprises (SEV), one of the three founding members of the Hellenic Network for Corporate Social Responsibility, has included in its mission statement the modern concept of "corporate citizenship" and the importance of social sensitivity for businesses that wish to play an active role vis-à-vis the challenges and changes occurring in the global society. To this end the SEV General Assembly of 2005 adopted the **"Charter of Rights and Obligations of Businesses",** by which Greek businesses declare their voluntary commitment to recognizing and "honouring" their obligations while claiming for their rights at the same time. One of the key factors of business ethics, on which the Charter is based, is the belief in the obligation to respond to the demands of society and implement social responsibility policies (www.sev.org.gr).

The **Global Compact Network Hellas** for CSR was established in 2008 with the participation of 70 businesses of all sizes. Aiming at the widest dissemination of the Global Compact principles, national networks have been established in all the countries of Europe. In our country, the organisation that coordinates the activities of Global Compact Network Hellas is the Hellenic Network for Corporate Social Responsibility (www.globalcompactnet work hellas.gr).

The **Hellenic Business Ethics Institute** (EBEN GR) is a non-profit organisation founded in 2005. As member of the European Ethics Network it aims to promote the principles of business ethics, CSR and Corporate Governance in the private and public sector, academia and voluntary organisations. The EBEN GR aspires to play an important role in business, providing support to organisations and professionals in order to implement a new management style by means of consultancy, research tools, training and dissemination of good practices (www.eben.gr).

EuroCharity, the reference point for CSR and the Green Economy, created the first CSR e-Guide in Greek and in English in 2006. The e-guide, which is posted on www.eurocharity.gr and www.eurocharity.com for foreign readers, serves the purpose of fully informing the public by communicating and promoting activities, programmes and initiatives of businesses, organisations, NGOs, the media and professionals on issues related to CSR.

The **Quality Net Foundation** is also a non-profit organisation that promotes social responsibility with a view to developing partnership schemes to meet social needs. Its financial resources derive exclusively from sponsorships of businesses which are socially aware of its programmes and from money raised from services provided . The entire generated revenue goes to support the operation of programmes and further development of services. (www.qualitynet.gr).

The **Great Place to Work Institute** is an institution of research and study of the factors that render an organisation an ideal working environment. It is an international firm for research, consultancy and training services which helps organisations to identify, create and sustain great working environments by cultivating a culture based on trust. The organisation, with offices in 45 countries on all 6 continents, has been operating in Greece since 2004. Every year it conducts research based on the responses of more than 10 million workers representing more than 5,500 enterprises and organisations of various sizes, sectors and structures – from the 45 host countries. These measurements are the basis of the methodology used by the Great Place to Work Institute for providing counselling to companies and organisations on how to create a great workplace, which will consolidate them among the best firms to attract and maintain appropriate human resources (www.greatplacetowork.gr).

3.2. The Impact of Economic Crisis on the Institution of CSR

The crisis contributed to the rapid reduction of phenomena where CSR used to function mainly as a tool for marketing and public relations because consumers have now developed a suspicion and distrust due to the so-called “corporate hypocrisy” (Klára, 2011; Quelch & Jocz, 2009). Quelch & Jocz emphasize the fact that consumers tend to adopt a favourable attitude to brands or companies with specific positive social actions. Furthermore, CSR offers ways of boosting the desired business competitiveness, while finding solutions to social problems which could not be achieved by only political means.

Especially in Greece, where the impact of the crisis is particularly pronounced, the need to reform the country’s development model is even more imperative and the contribution of enterprises to meeting constantly increasing social needs has become even more essential. The effort to bring the country back to a course of growth requires mutual trust among society, businesses and the public sector. In this context, it is not surprising that significant partnership schemes have developed among multiple organisations, businesses and local governments while businesses with strong CSR commitment seem to have their social profiles partially shield against the effects of consumers and local societies’ distrust.

On the other hand, the view that CSR is a "redundant” flexible expense has become common belief nowadays since businesses, and particularly SMEs, are being faced with serious liquidity problems, and even have to struggle for survival .

Indeed, today **with the economic and social crisis still in full swing,** there are several cases of related programmes having to be cut off **by reason of cost**, under the drastic measures taken by many businesses to reduce costs and enhance liquidity. The argument in all these cases is that it is not possible to allocate resources for social purposes when even in the business itself many employees are running the risk of losing their jobs.

In general, the recession has led to the prevalent tendency of reducing the budgets for CSR initiatives, especially at a time when demand for these very actions has increased considerably. Amid crisis, therefore, businesses adopt a more conservative and defensive strategy (Ellis & Bastin, 2011; Harwood, Humby & Harwood, 2011; Yelkikalan & Köse, 2012). Njoroge (2009) finds out that, due to the crisis, the CSR initiatives or policies, mainly in their social dimension, decrease in number and range, are postponed or even cancelled.

Similarly, there are concerns with regard to integration of Corporate Social Responsibility in the production process . The adoption of the so-called 'ethical' supply chain has an extra cost for the company, which cost today has either to be cut down or inevitably be passed on to the price of products and services. Needless to say that this is considered by many to represent a competitive disadvantage at a time when – due to the crisis and prevailing insecurity - the consumer is not willing to pay even one more cent for any product.

According to Dra Fernández-Feijoo, in periods of crisis CSR poses a threat for f the survival of businesses and, therefore, such a strategy is not expected at times of uncertainty. However, basing the decision to implement CSR on costs incurred is a major mistake in long-term strategic planning. In addition, excessive use of corporate sponsorship having marketing purposes as the ultimate goal can change the positive perception that consumers may initially have of the business. Nevertheless, there can be made some observations so that the negative perception can be turned into an opportunity for those businesses who take the step to either introduce, or continue with CSR implementation. This new perspective, which is absolutely necessary for the aforementioned turnaround, is based on the hypothesis that CSR is a management tool under constant renovation to last throughout time. To move towards this goal the development of models to manage CSR tools is necessary. Specifically, there are a set of common issues which can be redirected to convert the perspective of implementing CSR models from a threat into an opportunity in periods of crisis (Figure 1):

Hence CSR is said to offer solutions and outlets that businesses really need in periods of crisis . Specifically, CSR processes require innovation, comfortable atmosphere, stakeholder participation, corporate strategy, market view, investors' confidence and, above all, deep internal reflection.

Source: Fernández -Feijoo Souto B., (2009) "Crisis and Corporate Social Responsibility: Threat or Opportunity?

Figure 1. CSR implementation process and crisis periods_necessities.

3.3. National Strategy for Corporate Social Responsibility (CSR) for the Period 2014-2020

There is currently intense mobility at international level in the field of drafting or even improving Draft National Strategies of Corporate Social Responsibility. In Europe the mobility is more pronounced as - at the same time - a pertaining Directive is adopted "on disclosure of non-financial information"[2].

In this context, and on the initiative of the General Secretariat of Commerce, Greece joins the rest of the European countries that have an action plan for Corporate Social Responsibility. Specifically, in December 2013 an appropriate Working Group, established by a Ministerial Decision, drafted the Action Plan / Strategy Greece for Corporate Social Responsibility, whose public consultation closed on 22.09.2014.

The background of the National Strategy for CSR also includes setting the goals of the Ministry of Development and Competitiveness until 2020 as part of the 'Europe 2020' Strategy and the National Reform Framework:

- Setting employment rate target to 70% for the age group 20-64 .
- Decreasing by 450,000 individuals the number of citizens at risk of poverty and/or social exclusion.
- Decreasing by 100,000 individuals the number of children and young people (0-17) at risk of poverty.
- Meeting immediate needs as well as designing effective and sustainable long-term services of social protection, thus creating a "social safety net".

Therefore, the aim of the National Strategy for CSR is to create a comprehensive framework for action for the consolidation, dissemination and application of CSR principles in Greece for the period 2014-2020. In this context, the National CSR Strategy aspires to create a stable framework for cooperation among stakeholders that will contribute to the development of strategies, policies and CSR activities within the context of an integrated approach for development and social cohesion.

More specifically, the Integrated National CSR Strategy includes three main axes:

(a) POLICIES AND STANDARDS for promoting CSR that can be implemented by public bodies:

- Providing information on the concept and necessity of CSR
- Strengthening the potential of businesses to implement CSR
- Supporting and enhancing transparency procedures in business transactions
- Supporting development and implementation of CSR actions in supply chains, branding / labelling
- Communicating dissemination and rewarding of CSR actions

[2] Proposal for a Directive of the European Parliament and of the Council amending Directives 78/660 / EEC and 83/349 / EEC on disclosure of non-financial information and information about the diversity by some large companies and groups.

- Socially Responsible Public Procurements.

(b) MEASURES AND TOOLS of public policy to facilitate the implementation of CSR policies and activities by businesses. Such measures may be:

- Legislative (laws, directives)
- Economic (taxes, subsidies),
- Informative (awareness raising campaigns, educational activities)
- Networking (creating stakeholder networks)
- Hybrid (combination of the above tools/measures), which is the most common.

(c) CSR IMPLEMENTATION FIELDS in line with national priorities, which may concern the following:

- human resources (skills development and training of personnel, protection of labour rights, health and safety, work and life balance)
- business leadership (enhancement of CSR business culture, building up public trust and transparency with stakeholders)
- the market (development of products and services integrating CSR principles, implementation of CSR principles in the supply chain)
- the natural environment (improvement of energy footprint, integration of environmental criteria),
- the social environment (development of good relations with local communities, support of social groups in need).

A particularly important objective of the National Strategy for CSR is to expand its expertise to businesses.

The effective dissemination of the National CSR Strategy requires the substantial involvement of the Regions in the implementation of policies and the use of the tools provided for in this plan. At the same time, it is imperative that local needs be prioritised in order to allow concentration of forces to areas where benefits and positive impact will bring relief or even resolve problems.

In every case it is noted that what determines the decentralized character along the development of CSR actions by public bodies is the integrated approach to CSR and participatory processes in the design, implementation and monitoring process of the national CSR strategy. Specifically, besides the Central Government (Ministries) and Regions, the public bodies that have a say in the implementation of the Plan adapting the general objectives of the Plan to their strategy and the specific environment they operate in are the following:

- Municipalities
- Public enterprises (legal entities under private law)
- Public organisations (legal entities under public law)
- Business bodies (e.g. professional chambers, trade unions, business associations)
- Universities

Thus, it is clear that the Action Plan / Strategy of Greece for Corporate Social Responsibility is based on a holistic approach towards both the planning and implementation of interventions for promoting social responsibility in the country and **includs local government as a required level of involvement and cooperation**.

4. CSR and the Small and Medium Dimension of the Greek Economy

4.1. Recording the Current Situation

More recent data are provided by the longitudinal survey of the Institute of Communication on CSR and responsible consumption, which has been conducted simultaneously in more than 25 countries since 2004 in cooperation with the international organisation GlobeScan and the Panteion University of Athens (www.instofcom.gr). The main conclusions drawn from the recent representative survey of 2013 are as follows:

In 2013 34.2% of Greek consumers rewarded a socially responsible company (either through purchase of a product or through positive comments expressed about this company) while 19.6% thought to do so. The conscious act of rewarding and the corresponding consideration of such an act (53.8%) noted a significant increase compared to the results of the CSR survey conducted in 2012 (8%).

Similarly, 38.3% of Greek consumers "punished" a socially responsible company in 2013 (either by refusing to purchase a product or through negative comments expressed about this company) while 18.9% thought to do so.

A significant increase was also recorded in the number of rather "conscious consumers" (14% in 2013 vs 5.1% in 2012) whereas there was a reduction in the number of 'impulsive consumers' (19.8% in 2013 from 24.7% in 2012).

The above data indicate that the behaviour patterns of Greek citizens-consumers change - the main trend being the growing demand for safe and healthy products, environmentally-friendly products and products produced by socially and environmentally responsible means.

Consequently, this demonstrates the necessity for the enterprise to provide the consumer with high-quality products at the lowest possible price and always offer the same high standards.

Yet, it is widely accepted that Corporate Responsibility is no longer a 'peripheral' activity for businesses. Still, though, according to findings of Communication Consultants specialised in the field of CSR, it seems that in Greece businesses have not come to an absolute action model; therefore, in many cases it still happens that sporadic donations or charities are called CSR programmes. This can be partly explained by the fact that most enterprises are small and/or family businesses and their corporate responsibility is equated with the owner's philanthropic (Analytis, 2007).

This is confirmed by the few studies conducted in the business community. Such a survey was conducted in 2006 by the Laboratory of New Technologies in Communication, Education and Mass Media of the University of Athens, initiated by the Hellenic Network for

Corporate Social Responsibility[3]. Involving 300 SMEs of the wider Athens region, the survey led to the following conclusions: First, it was established that the sampled businesses are sufficiently aware of the concept of Corporate Social Responsibility and undertake such actions, but, at the same time, there is a need for further information and initiatives aiming at exploiting the full potential and benefits for the firms and the community deriving from the implementation of CSR actions.

Regarding the extent of adherence to CSR practices among SMEs in Greece, 35% of small and medium entrepreneurs themselves believe that such practices are adopted in moderation, whereas 53% believe that CSR practices are adopted little or very little -thus recognising that the level of adherence is low. SMEs consider that they follow CSR practices to a moderate or low degree for a number of reasons -the most significant ones being financial cost, lack of time and insufficient information. With regard to the cost, in particular, it is noted that it clearly affects corporate decisions although in most cases it is not a deterring factor, or at least not the main factor to be considered; it is in combination with the above mentioned parameters that it limits the scope of CSR practices. As for incentives, the overall results of the study are once again compatible with the priority of intra-corporate CSR practices; the most important incentives - with a slight differentiation to the degree of importance - are considered to be business promotion, sectoral competition, improvement of relationships within the business environment and employees' requests.

At the same time, a strong role is attributed to both the indirect benefits of CSR activities and the positive corporate image which is created to the recipients of products and services; a conclusion which also stems directly from the results and may constitute a dynamic pole of interest within the context of a communication strategy for the dissemination of the CSR .

With regard to the fields of CSR actions, the survey highlighted as most important the field of human resources, followed by the fields of the market and the environment. The most widely implemented social responsibility actions relate to actions concerning equal opportunities for the staff, followed by human resource training actions and the provision of additional benefits (e.g. healthcare services, financial facilities, etc.). Actions of cultural and sporting character generally directed towards society are implemented to a much smaller extent than other forms of social responsibility actions. In Greece although there is a significant number of businesses and organisations demonstrating substantial progress in integrating CSR into their business practice, there is still a need to raise the awareness among businesses, expand their knowledge on CSR and achieve wider participation (CSR Action Plan). In an effort to identify problems and weaknesses as well as opportunities that characterize the CSR setting in Greece, indicative is the following SWOT analysis.

4.2. Factors Affecting the Extent of Adoption of CSR Practices by Smes in Greece

As indicated in the Action Plan/Strategy Plan of Greece for Corporate Social Responsibility, the Greek economy is based on very small, small and medium enterprises, which constitute the vast majority of businesses in the country. These businesses experience

[3] Available on the website: http://www.csrhellas.org/csr_last2/portal/images/stories/files /SURVEY_ RESULTS_gr. pdf

the effects of changes in the global economy more intensely and have difficulty adapting to the new international trends and changes. This has consequences not only on their growth and competitiveness, but also on their viability, thus affecting their degree of engagement in CSR issues.

Evaluation of the and Weaknesses of CSR in Greece

STRENGHTS	**WEAKNESSES**
• Existence of legislation related to CSR issues. • Possibility to finance businesses to undertake CSR activities (focusing on SMEs) through the National Strategic Reference Framework (NSRF). • Enhanced capacity for autonomous decision-making of the regions in terms of strategy and economic policy. • Establishment of institutions that promote cooperation between state administration and private initiative in support of innovation and sustainable development. • Non-profit organisations (e.g. CSR Hellas) and academia (e.g. Athens University of Economics and Business/ OPA) with extensive expertise and research / teaching experience in the field of CSR.	• Lack of national strategy at national, regional or local level renders the enhancement of corporate CSR activities fragmental. • Lack of citizen-awareness of the CSR concept and its benefits in a business and social environment. • Limited information, expertise and specialized knowledge in public administration in order to allow the development, implementation, monitoring and evaluation of the impact of public CSR policies. • Lack of incentives (financial and fiscal) for businesses to undertake CSR activities based on a national CSR policy. • Absence of a separate administrative unit for the development, implementation, monitoring and evaluation of a national CSR strategy. • Lack of tools and mechanisms for supporting businesses to undertake CSR activities.
OPPORTUNITIES	**THREATS**
• Growing importance of CSR at European level (new EU policy on CSR, Action Plan 2011-14) increases the need for harmonisation of national and European policy. • CSR can provide the theoretical and practical basis for innovation and new entrepreneurship in the setting of overcoming the current economic crisis. • CSR can be a differentiating factor for export-oriented businesses as a strategic response to domestic economic crisis.	• The current economic crisis may lead to difficulties even greater than those encountered by businesses (especially SMEs) when undertaking CSR initiatives and actions; thus, setting CSR in low priority. • Fiscal consolidation efforts could worsen the allocation of adequate financial resources for the implementation of public CSR activities in the context of the national CSR strategy.

• CSR can support the entry of businesses (especially SMEs) to international supply chains. • Businesses can respond more effectively to new international consumer trends (e.g. environmental and social awareness, client participation in the financing and development of products, demand for transparency in business practices, etc.)	• The promotion of CSR in the context of a national strategy for businesses can be seen as an attempt to conceal adverse business practices (e.g. "greenwashing" phenomenon).

Source: Working document on the draft national strategy of Greece for the Corporate Social Responsibility, 2014

Furthermore, intrinsic parameters affecting the degree of adoption of CSR practices relate to the following:

- inadequate to non-existent knowledge and ability of most SMEs to respond to the complex economic environment.
- lack of information upon benefits of CSR to SMEs and the collective business representative bodies (e.g. Chambers); this limits the adoption of a modern model of responsible entrepreneurship.
- inadequate human resources for dealing with drafting a business CSR plan.

Besides, even in supply chains of large businesses where the majority of associated firms are SMEs, the implementation of CSR encounters difficulties and obstacles. Finally, recognizing the role of the public sector and, especially, public companies in promoting CSR activities poses challenges. In this context, the integration of CSR into the business strategy and operating practices is a crucial parameter for reinforcing national economy and achieving objectives set at a European level.

5. Promoting CSR through Collaborative Schemes between the Local Government and SMEs - The Example of the City of Athens

Most businesses operate within communities and it is at this local level that they seek to achieve social performance. Moreover, local governments understand better the needs of their communities; as a result, they can have a multiplier effect. CSR offers an opportunity for municipal local authorities to share their social objectives with private organisations and engage them in the dialogue to jointly achieve sustainability goals.

The findings of numerous studies indicate that *municipalities have not harnessed the opportunities to engage the private sector in achieving a common good.*

The Government's sustainability goals overlap with CSR goals. This overlapping area or "common ground" presents opportunities for greater government intervention. There are several reasons why local governments should be interested in CSR. Firstly, many of the sustainable development goals are similar to the CSR goals of corporations. Secondly, CSR efforts include public benefits that impact local communities governed by municipalities.

Thirdly, public interest in sustainability and CSR is high making it politically attractive to include linkages between CSR and social sustainability (Mathias, 2005).

Over the last decade, national, regional and local governments have joined other stakeholders in assuming a relevant role as CSR drivers , working together with intergovernmental organisations and recognizing that public policies are a key factor for raising greater CSR awareness.

A typical example is that of the Dutch government, which has long provided a framework for urban policy (grotestedenbeleid) encouraging municipalities to collaborate with a range of partners, including businesses. More recently, the Dutch government stated that it would follow a more 'personalised approach', that is bringing parties together, developing and disseminating know-how and, above all, promoting transparency so that stakeholders can fully perceive the concept of corporate social responsibility (Moon, 2004).

In Greece the involvement of local government is in its early steps. However, what clearly determines the decentralized character of CSR actions taken by public bodies is the integrated approach to CSR - promoted through the National Action Plan for CSR - and the participatory practices in designing, implementing and monitoring the national CSR strategy.

The local government as a key institution of public nature can take initiatives and coordinate actions and programmes aimed at promoting CSR actions in the business community.

In this context, the City of Athens took the truly innovative initiative to implement the project "Development and Dissemination of Corporate Social Responsibility in the territorial limits of the City of Athens", by which they expect to contribute to the consolidation of CSR in local businesses and to partly address the problem of inadequate public resources through private voluntary initiative in order to meet the high social and environmental needs.

Specifically, the project is designed to implement a range of varied and interdependent actions that aim at activating private enterprises and business networks operating in the City of Athens (regardless of the place of their registered office) as well as executives of private businesses (managers and top executives), who implement or will implement CSR activities in the City of Athens in areas that indicatively concern:

- ⇨ liaison and cooperation among private businesses, social services and structures of the City of Athens in order to promote a framework for drawing sponsorship packages
- ⇨ liaison, networking and cooperation between private businesses and the City in the field of tourism by promoting actions that improve the tourist city model and enhance visiting traffic
- ⇨ liaison, networking and cooperation between private businesses and the City in the field of environment by promoting actions that improve the environmentally friendly image of the city
- ⇨ liaison and collaboration between private businesses and social enterprises.

The project implementation of a total budget of 2,100,000 €, has been assigned to four (4) appropriate **partnership schemes** comprising organisations representing businesses or NGOs.

The **individual strategic goals** of the project focus on the liaison and cooperation of private businesses and networks with services and structures in the City of Athens, in order to:

- develop sponsorship packages for covering the gaps between needs and supply by offering help to individuals and groups of citizens in need
- develop actions that improve the tourist city model and enhance visiting traffic to the benefit of the local economy
- implement actions that improve the environmentally friendly image of the city of Athens.

Considering the above goals, **a set of multidimensional measures** was selected aiming at supporting businesses, networks and executives for the implementation of Corporate Social Responsibility actions by SMEs and large businesses.

➡ **actions for providing information and raising awareness** of target groups and specific audiences (Ministries, Local Authorities, social bodies, organisations representing workers, etc.)

➡ **actions for providng counselling and information** with the aim of creating a mechanism of Collective Informing and Individual Counselling-Support that will promote liaison, networking and cooperation of businesses/ executives and the City of Athens and provide essential counselling to implement CSR actions

➡ **training actions** aiming at training entrepreneurs and business executives on issues of CSR implementation

➡ **networking activities** aiming at creating a wider network to promote CSR at the local level and transfer experience of "successful CSR practices' from abroad

➡ **implementation of pilot applications** to the areas of social welfare, tourism and the environment in the City of Athens.

The **target groups of the project** are schematically classified into three broad categories and include a number of specialized subclasses.

1. The first category comprises the target groups that are directly benefited:
   - o Private businesses and networks that do business in the City of Athens. These are stakeholders from the immediate external environment of the business and are directly involved with each business and develop strategic relationships for CSR purposes.
   - o Private businesses that will actually implement strategies and actions for corporate social responsibility
   - o Executives (directors and officers) of private businesses that have implemented or will implement CSR activities in the City of Athens
2. In the second category fall the agencies to whom the project is indirectly targeted. These agencies implement policies of the City of Athens and act as intermediaries providing services of the first target group to the citizens of Athens. In other words, the City of Athens, and individual bodies of the local authorities, NGOs.

3. The third category comprises people who are positively affected - either directly or indirectly - by procedures/ actions of businesses and by policies of the City of Athens.

The **expected results** of the project relate to:

- ✓ *Establishing a stable framework for cooperation among the major industry bodies - businesses of the City of Athens and municipal services.* The aim is to implement a modern model of corporate social responsibility that will contribute to the activation of businesses and staff for the benefit of the Athenian community.
- ✓ *Strengthening social accountability of local businesses.* Through the project there will be advisory services and training provided that shall contribute to improving the social image of the Athenian businesses and to upgrading the skills of employees to become more socially responsible.
- ✓ *Strengthening environmental protection and improvement of the visiting traffic in the City of Athens.* Through the action plan there will be CSR activities for the protection of the environment. Also, advice will be provided upon actions of corporate social responsibility, green business issues and production of environmentally friendly goods and services.
- ✓ *Strengthening the media and tourism promotion of Athens through CSR actions.* This will contribute to upgrading the tourism image and, as a consequence , the tourism product of the city.
- ✓ *Strengthening social cohesion within the City of Athens with the contribution of entrepreneurial bodies and businesse*s. By implementing CSR actions they can help bridge the gaps in social services and meet the needs of socially vulnerable citizens.
- ✓ *Transferring know-how and best CSR practices* from foreign organisations (businesses, Chambers, industry bodies, etc...).
- ✓ *Increasing participation of businesses of the City of Athens in implementing CSR actions.* This can be achieved by encouraging businesses operating within the municipality to cooperate with the authorities and legal entities of the City of Athens for the promotion of CSR actions.
- ✓ *Upgrading the image and reputation of businesses operating within the City of Athens* with regard to their social orientation and support of socially vulnerable groups.
- ✓ *Standardisation, pilot implementation and dissemination of CSR actions* that can be potentially applied by interested businesses in the future and supported by industry bodies and legal entities of the City of Athens.

Although the results from the implementation of this project are not know yet, it goes without saying that it is an ambitious and mainly innovative project for the Greek reality., This is the first time that a local authority body has ever taken the initiative to "initiate" SMEs to the CSR concept and practices, not only in theory, but also by involving them in the actual implementation through pilot interventions. Emphasis will be placed on key areas where the necessity of social responsibility and activation emerges, taking into account the social needs of the local community (housing, spatial planning &environmental problems, local development priorities, etc.). The local government of the Municipality of Athens are more aware of these problems than anybody else.

CONCLUSION

The implementation of CSR among small businesses has the potential to contribute to their growth recovery and create sustainable jobs. It is necessary to give priority to the new generation of entrepreneurs, who will contribute to the country's exit from the crisis and will enhance domestic competition with their original ideas. In this context, we should further enrich business education on issues of socially responsible entrepreneurship and promote or update special financing tools for entrepreneurs - particularly young entrepreneurs. In this way they will acquire adequate knowledge in order to design their own business plan for implementing CSR actions. It is also very important that there be a special privileged status and an attractive incentive system for entrepreneurs, which will encourage them to join the process of integrating CSR into their activities.

Especially for self-employed entrepreneurs or very small businesses there should be special care such as supportive mechanisms, so that they are not isolated due to their limited capabilities.

However, the transition of businesses to CSR is not an easy task at all, especially when historically opposed practices and attitudes have been consolidated. Corporate irresponsibility (e.g. use of illegal, undeclared and uninsured labour, tax evasion, social insurance contribution payment avoidance, etc.) has become for some entrepreneurs a key element of competitiveness within the context of the collapsing development model.

In that context, adopting CSR activities secures the following **preconditions:**

- identify areas where governments and businesses can work together to achieve common social objectives and determine an effective role for local governments within the process
- identify small actions in areas such as human resources, supply chain, community, or environment that can foster SMEs motivation and engagement.

In the past decade governments have become increasingly proactive in promoting CSR through their public policies. In recent times companies have seen increased government involvement in the business sector—partially due to the global financial crisis—and this trend is expected to continue in the future. Having this in mind, it is likely that governmental promotion of corporate responsibility and good governance will continue to grow in the coming years.

What poses a challenge for governments is to find a way to design and implement public policies that will generate leadership and partnership-based innovation; and even further seeking to maximize the benefits of these innovations by ensuring their systematic acceptance and application within the wider business community.

In promoting CSR public authorities have a range of policy levers to use: legal instruments; economic and financial instruments; information instruments; partnering instruments. They can also serve as examples and provide best practices, using their own organisational style to demonstrate the effectiveness of CSR approaches.

Several such examples come from France where the local government adopt CSR practices within organisations in order to improve their public image. . The action plan drafting for local authorities usually consists of two levels: a) obtaining the relevant certificates and b) using rating systems of environmental and social performance (Millénaire3, 2010).

In conclusion, today that the small and medium size of the South European economy is called to come up with the local government and face the increasingly growing pressures of civil society collectivities, CSR is emerging as an alternative for dealing with consequences of the current economic crisis. CSR can become a useful tool both for SMEs - that desperately seek to assure their viability in a difficult and highly demanding environment in terms of social and environmental awareness - and local authorities that have to cope with the high social needs and environmental problems, having, though, fewer financial and intangible resources available to them.

As long as it comes to a success, the example of the City of Athens could attribute added value to any institutional intervention aiming at consolidating the role of local government in the promotion and diffusion of CSR in the business community.

References

Non-Greek References

Albareda, L., Lozano, J.M., Tencati, A., Midttun, A., Perrini, F., (2008). "The Changing Role of Governments in Corporate Social Responsibility: Drivers and Responses". *Business Ethics: A European Review*, Volume 17 Number.

Andrew, B.H., Gul, F.A., Guthrie, J.E., Teoh, H.Y., (1989). "A Note on corporate social disclosure practice in developing countries: The case of Malaysia and Singapore", *British Accounting Review.*

Berger-Douce, S., (2009). "Profils de créateur et stratégie d'engagement sociétal". *Actes du 4ème congrès de RIODD* (Lille, 25-26 juin 2009).

Bramwell, B. et al. (1996). Sustainable Tourism Management: Principles and Practise, *University Press*, Tilburg, The Netherlands.

Campin, S., Barraket, J., Luke, B., (2013). "Micro-Business Community Responsibility in Australia: Approaches, Motivations and Barriers" *Journal of Business Ethics*, July 2013, Volume 115, Issue 3, pp 489-513.

Cowen, S.S., Ferreri, L.B., Parker, L.D., (1987). "The impact of corporate characteristics on social responsibility disclosure: a typology and frequently based analysis", *Accounting, Organisations and Society.*

Ebner, D., Baumgartner, RJ., (2006). "The Relationship Between Sustainable Development and Corporate Social Responsibility". www.crrconference.org [17 September 2007].

Elkington, J., (1994). Towards the Sustainable Corporation: Win-Win-Win Business Strategies for Sustainable Development. *California Management Review.*

Ellis, L., Bastin, C., (2011). "Corporate Social Responsibility in Times of Recession: Changing Discourses and Implications for Policy and Practice". *Corporate Social Responsibility and Environmental Management.*

Fernández-Feijoo Souto .B., (2009). "Crisis and Corporate Social Responsibility: Threat or Opportunity?. *International Journal of Economic Sciences and Applied Research*, Vol.2, No.1.

Harwood, I., Humby, S., Harwood, A., (2011). "On the Resilience of Corporate Social Responsibility". *European Management Journal*, 283-290.

Huang, C., Yatim, N., Yusoff, H., (2000). "Voluntary disclosure of financial information: The Malaysian Evidence.", *BRC Journal*, Universiti Teknologi MARA.

Kantis, H., Ishida, M., Komori, M., (2002). "Entrepreneurship in Emerging Economies: The Creation and Development of New Firms in Latin American and East Asia.", *D.C.: Inter-American Development Bank*, Washington.

Kantis, H., Angelelli, P., Koening, V., (2004). "Developing Entrepreneurship: Experience in Latin American and Worldwide", *D.C.: Inter-American Development Bank*, Washington.

Klára, P., (2011). The Impact of Recession on the Implementation of Corporate Social Responsibility in Companies. *Journal of Competitiveness.*

Lyman, A.R., (1991). "Customer service: Does ownership make a difference?", *Family Business Review*, IV (3).

Mathias, A., (2005). "Corporate Social Responsibility and Social Sustainability: A Role for Local Government". *Simon Fraser University.*

Moon, J., (2004). "Government as a driver of corporate social responsibility: the UK in comparative perspective", *International Centre for Corporate Social Responsibility Research Paper* No. 20-2004, Nottingham, UK: Nottingham University Business School.

Njoroje, J., (2009). "Effects of the Global Financial Crisis on Corporate Social Responsibility in Multinational Companies in Kenya". *Covalence Intern Analyst Papers.*

Porter, M. E., Kramer, M. R., (2006). "Strategy & Society: The Link Between Competitive Advantage and CSR". *Harvard Business Review.*

Quelch, J. A., Jocz, K. E., (2009). "Can Corporate Social Responsibility. Leader to Leader".

Simpson, M., Taylor, N., Barker, K., (2004). "Environmental responsibility in SMEs: Does it deliver competitive advantage?", *Business Strategy and the Environment.*

Vives, A., (2006). "Social and environmental responsibility in small and medium enterprises in Latin America", *The Journal of Corporate Citizenship.*

Yelkikalan, N., Köse, C., (2012). The Effects of the Financial Crisis on Corporate Social Responsibility. *International Journal of Business and Social Science.*

Greek References

Vaxevanidou, M., (2008). "Corporate social responsibility: contribution to sustainable development and to effective management of European businesses" *«SPOUDAI»*, Vol. 58, No 1-2, (2008). University of Piraeus pp. 91-114.

Vaxevanidou, M., (2011). *"Corporate Social Responsibility"*. Athens: Ath. Stamoulis Editions.

Analytis, N., (2007). Paper on the presentation of the results of the research conducted by the Institute of Communication on *"Corporate Social Responsibility and Responsible Consumption-CSR 2007"*, 24 April, Athens.

Internet Sources

CEFRE (2004). "Guidelines for the dissemination of corporate social responsibility among small and medium-sized businesses", Research conducted by CERFE on behalf of the European Commission-DG Employment and Social Affairs, http://www.csr-romania.ro/media /8_wp_18.pdf.

Laboratory of New Technologies in Communication, Education and the Media, Department of Communication and Media - University of Athens (2006). Research on Corporate Social Responsibility in SMEs - Report of results, http://www.csrhellas.org /csr_last2/portal/images/stories/files /SURVEY_RESULTS_gr.pdf.

European Commission (2001). 'Green Paper - Promoting a European Framework for Corporate Social Responsibility", European Commission, COM (2001) 366 final, 18.07.2001, Brussels, http://www.fgi.org.gr /uploads/ largefiles/COM2001% 20_prasini Vivlos.pdf.

Working Paper on the draft national strategy of Corporate Social Responsibility of Greece (Draft v0.14), 28 July 2014, http://www.opengov.gr/ypoian/?p=5188.

United Nations International Development Organisation, Corporate Social Responsibility: Implications for Small and Medium Enterprises in Developing Countries, Vienna (2002). http://imuna.org/sites/default/files/Implications%20for%20Small%20and%20 Medium%20Enterprises %20in%20Developing%20Countries.pdf

Millénaire3, (2010). "La Responsabilité Sociale des Entreprises (RSE): un bref état des lieux", http://www.millenaire3.com/uploads/tx_ressm3/La_Responsabilite_Societale_des_Entreprises_02.pdf

www.instofcom.gr
www.greatplacetowork.gr
www.qualitynet.gr
www.eurocharity.gr
www.eben.gr
www.globalcompactnetworkhellas.gr
www.sev.org.gr
www.csrhellas.org

In: Towards a Society with a More Fair Economy ISBN: 978-1-63482-900-7
Editors: J. A. Filipe, N. Nagopoulos, K. Rontos et al.

Chapter 6

Environmental Education, Environmental Policy and Socioeconomic - Sustainable Development

Niki Psoma
University of Aegean, Mytilene, Greece

Abstract

Chapter 6 investigates the link between environmental education and sustainable development. This present article provides a concise and comprehensive view of the concept of environmental education and sustainable development the author analyses the basic characteristics of environmental education, the precursors of educational movements before environmental education and the popular milestone in its history and its relationship with the European Union. Furthermore, the author analyses the good practices with respect to the inclusion of environmental education in the formal school curriculum and its use as a tool of environmental policy. Subsequently, the concepts of sustainability and sustainable development are introduced and analyzed regarding their connection with environmental education. These concepts are the implement that will promote the necessary environmental knowledge and will provide all of us with skills for critical evaluation and for active participation in making environmental decisions.

1.1. Introduction

Environmental issues are multidimensional. People of tomorrow must have clear values, critical thinking and the ability to act collectively in order to solve environmental issues.

Environmental education was born in the light of the necessity to address the ecological crisis. This is about the process which "will help people to gain knowledge of the environment and, above all, become capable and determined, be willing to work individually and collectively, achieve and maintain a dynamic balance between the quality of life and the quality of the environment" (Flogaiti, 2006).

Recognizing the value of education, which will make students capable of giving their own meaning to the concept of sustainability, Environmental Education appears for the very first time in 1947 and in the 60s is firstly connected education with society. Then, it follows a series of milestones on the evolutionary path. Nowadays, the main objective of the European Union is that Environmental Education no longer takes place on a voluntary basis at schools, and instead become part of the official curriculum, with due respect to the particularities of each country's educational system.

1.2. The Concept of Environmental Education and Its Characteristics

Environmental education was developed during the decades 1960-1970, within the framework of reflection that highlighted the environmental movement. The modern environmental movement, apart from environmental awareness, challenged the system of social values, which until then was based on an anthropocentric concept, according to which man was above the environment (Tsampoykoy – Skanavi, 2004:78). So, it was found that environmental problems had a social dimension and it was deemed necessary updating and raising awareness of the public and the development of a system of values for environmental issues as well. In the wider context of this reflection, the Environmental Education was born, which after a series of international meetings, conferences, conventions held by international organizations emerged as an educational proposal. Therefore, the modern environmental movement broadened the boundaries and the concept of E.E, which turned to education of citizens, aiming to change attitudes, perceptions and behaviors.

According to the first definition given in Nevada in the 1970s "environmental education is the process of recognizing values and clarifying concepts in order to develop skills and attitudes necessary to understand and appreciate the interrelatedness among men, his culture and his biophysical surroundings. E.E also entails practice in decision-making and self-formulation of a code of behaviour about issues concerning environmental quality" (IUNC, 1970).

1.3. Precursors Educational Movements Before E.E.

The term "environmental education", appears for the very first time in 1947 in the book of Paul & Percival Goodman, Communitas. However, a series of educational movements which already pre-existed, carry all those elements that will provide the basis to form E.E. (Gavrilakis Sofoulis, 2005: 54). The 1960s, does not constitute a milestone when education and society connected for the first time. On the contrary, it is a milestone in an evolutionary process, which had begun at least two centuries ago. During that time, the environmental movements in society fuelled a series of educational currents, which are expressed in different ways and terminology, depending on the spirit of the season (Flogaiti, 2006: 27). The most important precursors of educational movements for the environment that developed in the late 19th and early 20th century were the following:

- The "Progressive Movement in Education" developed in America and Europe with leading exponents Dewey, Rug, etc., with a focus on education and society interconnection. Many features, such as active participation in learning, holistic approach, etc. are present in E.E. (Tsampoykoy - Skanavi, 2004: 78-79, Papadimitriou, 1998: 21).
- The "Study of Nature" and the "Rural Education ", with main exponents Muir and Millis, were educational movements that had focused on student engagement with nature. Their purpose was the understanding and appreciation of beauty and magnificence of nature (Skanavi, 2004 -Tsampoykoy: 79; Papadimitriou, 1998: 22-26).
- The "Education for Conservation" linked to the movement for the conservation of nature and natural resources. Developed as a reaction to disasters from soil erosion and flooding of the 1930s (Tsampoykoy - Skanavi, 2004: 79. Papadimitriou, 1998: 26-30).
- The "Education out of School" refers to educational activities outside the classroom. The main purpose here was the direct contact with the natural environment and the acquisition of experience from this. Supporters of this movement were the Sharp and Smith. Their basic idea was the return to nature as a reaction to urbanization (Tsampoykoy - Skanavi, 2004: 79. Papadimitriou, 1998: 30-3).
- The "Field Study" used the environment as a laboratory for learning in various fields more efficient. Field studies had a great tradition in Great Britain (Tsampoykoy - Skanavi, 2004: 80, Papadimitriou, 1998: 32).

1.4. Popular Milestones in the History of Environmental Education Internationally

Initially, E.E was oriented to developing educational techniques specific to the issues and the problems of the environment. Soon, however, it was found that in order to be able to contribute effectively and tackle the ecological crisis, it should broaden its limitations. Namely, it should no longer be seen as "education of specialists" and be transformed into "civic education". At the same time, the threat of ecological disaster prompted schools to include in their educational curriculum courses related to the environment. No matter how important these courses were, the transmission of knowledge was fragmentary.

In 1968 was held in Paris, under the aegis of UNESCO, the Conference on the Biosphere. There, it was formulated the request for the development of teaching materials related to the study of the environment. Two years later, in 1970, in Nevada, USA was held the first international meeting on environmental education, where was formulated the first widely accepted definition of E.E. (which was cited at the beginning of this chapter) (IUNC, 1970).

The necessity of E.E. was recognized by the international community at the Stockholm Conference in 1972, organized under the aegis of the United Nations. This Conference is considered to be not only a milestone for the development of international environmental problems, but also for the establishment of E.E. as a course of action for addressing environmental degradation. As a result of this Conference, emerged the "Declaration on the Human Environment". In addition, the Stockholm Conference led to the establishment of the

United Nations Environment Programme (UNEP). This program, hereupon, and with the cooperation of UNESCO created the International Environmental Education Programme (IEER) (Tsampoykoy- Skanavi, 2004: 82).

In 1975 convened in Belgrade the first international meeting for E.E., the International Conference on environmental education, which was attended by 65 countries. The Declaration of the Conference, also known as the "Charter of Belgrade", is a landmark for E.E. and the first global manifesto that promotes its rejuvenating aspect (Papadimitriou, 1998: 50).

After the Belgrade Conference, a series of meetings took place in different parts of the globe, which prepared the ground for the Conference – milestone of Tbilisi. The latter was held in 1977 in Georgia with the participation of representatives from 68 countries as well as representatives of NGOs. In Tbilisi Conference, the final objectives, goals, features and content of E.E. were established (Papadimitriou, 1998: 54) and the following definition was given: « *Environmental education is a process aimed at developing a world population that is aware of and concerned about the total environment and its associated problems, and which has the knowledge, attitudes, motivations, commitments, and skills to work individually and collectively toward solutions of current problems and the prevention of new ones.* » (UNESCO, 1978).

Ten years after the Conference in Tbilisi, in 1987, and while the environmental problems multiplied, the public begins to become sensitized. The "green" parties and environmental groups are in their prime. Then, the International Conference on environmental education and training was held in Moscow. This Conference, having certified the environmental dead-end, presented an international strategy for education and training and introduced the term of «sustainable development» (Tsampoykoy - Skanavi, 2004: 85).

In 1992, was held in Rio, Brazil the International Conference on environment and development, under the aegis of the United Nations. The outcome of the Rio Conference, known as Agenda 21 refers to education and its redefinition towards sustainable development, the promotion of public awareness and training (chapter 36 of Agenda) (Tsampoykoy - Skanavi2004: 87). In the same year was organized in Toronto of Canada the International Conference on Education and Communication for Environment and Development (ECOED), by UNEP, UNESCO and the ICC (International Chamber of Commerce). This Conference discusses the educational part of the Rio recommendations and is mainly preoccupied with the educational part of the Rio recommendations. The E.E. is recognized as an essential tool for the achievement of sustainable development. As mentioned, education should serve the needs of sustainable development by the citizens, in order to improve productivity, encourage technological progress and promote cultural conditions that lead to social and economic change (Chaleplis, 2008).

In 1997 was held in Thessaloniki a Conference on E.E. entitled "Environment and Society: Education and Public Awareness for Sustainability". What has been pointed out, was that teachers are deprived of environmental education and thus in schoolchildren environmental education is either completely absent or incomplete. The finding of serious mistakes in the course of E.E., created a tendency for deletion of the term "Environmental Education" and its replacement with the term "Education for Sustainable Development" (Knapp, 2000).

The ultimate milestone in the evolution of E.E. internationally, is the Summit for sustainable development held in Johannesburg in 2002. Governments and other participants gathered to discuss the major challenges facing the world today in order to identify the best ways of implementation of Agenda 21. This summit reaffirmed sustainable development as the key element of international interest and gave new impetus to global action so as to protect the environment. Furthermore, governments agreed on a series of specific commitments in order to achieve more effective implementation of the objectives of sustainable development. The two official documents adopted by governments was the Johannesburg Declaration and the Implementation Plan (Tsampoykoy - Skanavi, 2004: 89-90). The matter for regret of the summit is that although the E.E. is essential for the achievement of those objectives that were set, it seemed to be entirely missing from the discussions.

1.5. European Union and Environmental Education

As reported in detail in the previous chapter, the European Union (that time EEU), since its foundation showed an interest towards the protection of the environment. The importance of balance between economic growth and quality of life, highlighted particularly at the Paris Summit, and it was recognized that education is the most effective means for the protection of the environment.

The first essential step towards decision making on issues for the E.E. took place in 1971 with the Declaration of the Committee of Ministers of the Council of Europe. There, the value of E.E. was officially recognized in the preparation of the European citizen who will gain knowledge about environmental protection. In a similar framework was initiated and the Declaration of the Ministers of Education in 1988, in which it was agreed to develop action for the promotion of E.E.. All Member States committed themselves to promote the E.E. in all sectors of education (Katsikis & Zachariou, 2005: 262).

The meeting held in Dublin in 1990 set a new dimension in environmental protection: that of sustainable development, which will be discussed in detail in a separate chapter. The declaration looks forward to a new action programme for the environment (the 5th), whose objective is the diffusion of E.E. in the Curricula of all European countries up to 2000 (Tsampoykoy – Skanavi, 2004: 213). In addition, teaching ecological lessons should be associated with the direct social and natural environment of students so that the latter seeing the environmental issue in its actual dimensions should be more willing to develop environmental initiatives.

For the promotion of E.E. at European level, several programs and at various levels are funded. The problems identified in the International Conference on E.E. in 2000, in Greece, were that the integration of the education systems of European countries is being made far too slowly. This is due to many reasons such as incomplete or inadequate training of teachers, lack of educational material, lack of finance etc. (Papadimitriou, 1998). The main objective of EU is that E.E. will no longer take place on a voluntary basis in schools, and to become part of the official curriculum, with due respect to the particularities of each country's education system.

1.6. Good Practices for the Integration of E.E. in the Formal School

The USA is the country that played a decisive role in the emergence of E.E. movement and its global acceptance as well. Regarding the promotion of E.E. made several attempts to integrate it as a legitimate part of the official curriculum and **America** was the first country that established a federal law for this purpose. This law, approved by the Congress and published in October 1970, when even the remaining countries still did their first steps in this area.

However, this law did not find the expected support but gave incentive to those interested to develop their own initiatives towards this direction. In 1971, the US National Association for E.E was founded and contributed to the creation of educational material (Tsampoykoy – Skanavi, 2004: 208. Papadimitriou, 1998: 44)

In **Britain**, the contemporary movement for the E.E. began with the Conference at Keele in 1965. There met people who were close to countryside, and teachers of Geography, Biology and Agricultural Studies to discuss issues related to nature. At this Conference, the term E. E was used for the first time in Britain. In 1968 the Council and the Company for the E.E. wereestablished (Papadimitriou, 1998: 44-45).

A typical example is **Germany**, which raised before 1970 the concept of "environment" as a basic necessity for the educational system in the country stressing at the same time the need to orient schools towards an environmental education (Georgopoulos, 2005: 264). And in **France**, with the circular of the Ministry of Education in 1972, the need for an education that promotes the issues regarding the environment was stressed, while the centers to be acquainted with the environment were established in 1977. Finally, in **Norway**, in 1971 becomes mandatory the teaching courses on the environment and in 1974 the E.E was included in secondary school educational curricula (Papadimitriou, 1998: 46-47).

The above mentioned countries were those that first linked the notion of the environment with that of education, and made the first attempts to integrate E.E. in school curricula. Unlike those, countries like Poland, Denmark and Greece have set some guidelines as national action plans but not before the 1990s.

1.7. Environmental Education As a Tool of Environmental Policy

The institutionalization of environmental education could be regarded as an environmental policy tool since it is aimed at understanding from the students' aspect the relationship between humans and natural environment, their awareness of the problems associated with it and the adoption of positive attitudes. Thus, the ultimate goal of environmental education is to create environmentally sensitive citizens.

1.8. ENVIRONMENTAL EDUCATION AND SUSTAINABLE DEVELOPMENT

The term “sustainable development” or “sustainability” is widely used in the 1980s. However, the link between environment and development begins several years before and becomes the subject of international discussions from the 60s-70s (Papadimitriou, 1998). This is the period of time when scientific communities and environmental movements highlight the enormous environmental problems that emerged as a result of industrial civilization. The ecological crisis surfaces the dullness of the value system of the Western world. It is a system of economic development (capitalist or socialist) based on greed. At the same time, the environmental awareness begins to spread within society and discussions about environmental limits of growth are at the epicentre of international concern.

Undoubtedly, taking the evolution of E.E. into consideration, we realize that it grew beyond all expectations. Maybe it was supported by international and regional institutions, national organizations and NGOs but dynamically promoted mainly from the base (Flogaiti 2006: 133).

The heyday of E.E. can be seen by the great mobility that characterizes the area at international level. Various national and international scientific associations and teachers' organizations have been exclusively recommended to E.E. and parallel institutions have been established in many countries that support the theory and practice. There is no country, at least in the developed world, that has not somehow incorporated E.E. in the educational system and there is no country that does not have to a greater or lesser extent green curricula at school as well. (Flogaiti 2006: 135).

1.8.1. Sustainable Development - The Answer to the Dead-End of the Development

The first intergovernmental conference in Stockholm in 1972 under the aegis of the United Nations on “the human environment” was crucial. The Conference postulated the opinions concerning social problems of economic growth and built the foundations for the adoption of environmental policies development. Yet, it had to determine the exact meaning of development. So, in this period the concept of growth takes various forms. It becomes negative development, eco-development, zero growth (Flogaiti, 2006). In the late 1970s the international organizations IUCN, UNEP and WWF establish the “global strategy for the environment” (the IUCN/UNEP/WWF/1980) and suggest the term "sustainable development" as they wanted to show that these concepts complement one another.

What is next, in the 1983 World Commission on environment and development or the Brundtland Committee which was set up by the UN with a view to formulating policy strategies that will bridge the concept of development with that of the environment. In 1987 the Commission publishes a report titled "our common future". In this report, sustainable development is presented as the most appropriate development policy. The next step takes place in the 1992 UN Conference in Rio de Janeiro under the theme "Environment and development". The outcome of this conference is "Agenda 21" which was signed by 108 heads of State (Flogaiti, 2006). "Agenda 21" is an action plan for the achievement of sustainable development in the 21st century. The same text describes the conceptual framework, the tools and the process that will lead to sustainable development and the above mentioned Conference recommended the "United Nations Commission for sustainable development" being responsible to monitor this programme of action.

The adoption of sustainable development as a central international policy is confirmed at the World Summit under the theme "sustainable development", which took place in Johannesburg in 2002. During the Conference the results of the Rio Conference were assessed and the further elaboration and adoption policies were discussed as well.

As Flogaiti notes down, none of the titles of three major conferences "human environment", "Environment and Development" and "sustainable development", understands the processes and the evolution of the concept of sustainability (Flogaiti, 2006: 81).

1.8.2. The Concept of Sustainable Development

The concept of sustainability, although internationally accepted when first introduced, it was disputed by both the supporters of growth and organisations to that advocated the protection of the environment. Supporters of environment faced with scepticism the acceptance of sustainable development from the business, industrial and political world considering that this is a ploy to appease the reactions about the environmental disaster while they will keep the same political economy by sacrificing the environment at the altar of profit. The business world faced with the same incredulity the prospect of a sustainable development arguing that the planet does not face any ecological crisis and all these are findings of scientists and environmental movements in their effort to promote their interests (Flogaiti, 2006). In spite of these disputes, the road to sustainable development had already opened.

Over the years, there were several definitions for sustainability. The dominants and commonly acceptable is that of the Brundtland Commission, ""Sustainable development is development that meets the needs of the present without compromising the ability of future generations to meet their own needs" (WCED 1987: 43) and the second is that of organizations, UNEP and WWF IUNC that defines sustainable development as "improving the quality of human life within the carrying capacity of supporting ecosystems " (the 1991 IUCNetal.: 10).

Both definitions encapsulate the meaning of economy, society and the environment, which are the three dimensions of sustainable development. According to UNESCO (2005) the social dimension of sustainability involves the understanding of the concept of democracy, cooperation, participation and dialogue as necessary tools for resolving disputes and the common path towards development. The concept of the economy refers to the redefinition of human needs and consumption on the basis of social justice and protection of the environment. Finally, the environmental dimension in the concept of sustainable development involves awareness of the need for conservation of biodiversity and the sustainable use of natural resources (Liarakoy, Flogaiti, 2007). The necessary condition for sustainability, identifies the relationship of the three dimensions mentioned above as a relationship of interdependence and equivalence.

1.8.3. Models of Sustainable Development

Based on the environmental ideology, Orr and Ress (Orr, 1992, Ress, 1990 in Papadimitriou, 1998: 126) distinguished between two structural models for sustainable development: the technological and ecocentric (Papadimitriou, 1998). These two models present different policies in order to achieve sustainability. The technological model presents sustainability through the existing development policy remodeling some aspects and enriching others. This model supports the use of technology, the search for substitutes for natural resources, the imposition of taxes in order to achieve sustainability. (Papadimitriou, 1998). So, the technological model approximates the meaning of sustainability from the perspective of an alternative lifestyle. Basically it is a mild form of sustainability that draws its ideology from the modern environmentalism (Flogaiti, 2006).

Ress (1990 in Papadimitriou, 1998: 127) distinguishes four trends of technological approaches of sustainability. The first includes the cynics and opportunists. To this group belong people who on the pretext of environmental protection aim to make profit. The second trend describes the technological response and setting. In this group are those who argue that the use of technology can solve environmental problems while at the same time it can contribute to economic growth. The third trend refers to the restructuring of economic growth. In this case sustainability is achieved by restricting the use of natural resources and the imposition of taxes. Finally, the fourth model of technology trend for sustainable development refers to growth with equality which means that economic growth becomes the means of lifting the inequality. Economic growth in this case means reallocation of resources between poor and rich countries (Papadimitriou, 1998).

On the contrary, the technological model for sustainability is the ecocentric. It is an ideology that promotes to a post-modern world (Flogaiti, 2006). The ecocentric model refers to the change of the value system of the man himself and that of societies, in human awareness as part of the world and not something separate, shifts the meaning of quality of life from consumerism to improve human relationships and finally raise a holistic perception of the world.

Orr (1992, in Papadimitriou, 1998: 129) by contrasting the two above models of sustainable development argues that their differentiation lies in the fact that the first seeks the development through the existing financial system while the second looks in a post-modern world that will ostracize all features of society that were the causes of not only environmental but also of other plagues of mankind. Nevertheless, he argues that the two models can co-exist in a period of time as well as he recognizes the technological model as the transition period for the passage to ecocentric (Papadimitriou, 1998).

1.8.4. Education and Sustainable Development

Education for sustainable development did not come from inside the educational community but emerged through discussions of international organisations for the protection of the environment and economic development.

The first UN Conference under the theme "human environment" which introduced the term "sustainable development", highlighted the contribution of teachers to achieve social change that is necessary for sustainable development. What is next, the Conference in Rio de Janeiro where as already mentioned is Agenda 21 with the strategic actions that will lead to sustainable development. Chapter 36 titled "Promotion of education, Public Awareness and training'' refers to a broader concept of education for both the formal and informal education as a tool for promoting the concept of sustainability (Papadimitriou, 1998). What follows are several important conferences of international organizations where the concept of sustainability is an important dimension of education and gradually the term "Education for Sustainable Development" begins to be used.

Education is no longer considered to be a goal in itself but a means, an important tool for the achievement of sustainable development. Sterling notes: "a society that considers that there is an urgent need for change towards a more social, economic, ecological basis should reassess the organisation of training as a primary means of reproduction of social values" (Huckle & Sterling, 1997). Reorganisation of education in the context of sustainable development means change in its principles, objectives, content, and methodology.

The framework of the principles governing education for sustainable development as expressed by UNESCO are summarized in recognition of the diversity of human experience, recognition and interaction with the different, the importance of dialogue for coexistence and resolve disputes, the promotion of the values of respect and dignity in your personal and professional life, faith of human capacities, recognition of the "local" knowledge for the protection of fauna and flora, support practices and traditions that contribute to sustainability, recognition of the different cultural approaches of nature, society, the world and last the support of the local dialect as a vector of interaction and cultural identity (Liarakoy, Flogaiti, 2007).

The objectives of education for sustainable development focuses on information, awareness, changing values, attitudes and skills, in the development and adoption of appropriate behaviours. (Tsampoykoy - Skanavi, 2004). The desideratum is a well-informed citizen, socially and environmentally aware who will support a democratic and safe environment, within which he/she operates according to sustainable patterns of production and consumption.

In relation to the content of education for sustainable development, that stems from within the sphere of society, economy and environment that all three are dimensions of sustainability. Regarding the economic dimension, poverty reduction, collective responsibility and accountability for the protection of the environment and justice are under discussion. As to the dimension of society that includes human rights, peace and human security, interculturalism, gender equality and health. And last but not least, concerning the environment, the content of education that refers to the right management of natural resources, the growth of agriculture and the sustainable urbanization (Liarakoy, Flogaiti, 2007).

In relation to the teaching approaches, traditional forms of learning do not seem to meet the needs of high-quality learning that requires the education for sustainable development. Therefore, it is proposed a new model of educational process where the holistic and multidisciplinary approach to knowledge, action and development critical thinking lead to the development of attitudes and skills that are specific to the characteristics of sustainable development (Tsampoykoy-Skanavi, 2004).

Specifically, the holistic approach refers to the concept of sustainability as something that is diffused throughout the curriculum and not as a separate discipline. The interdisciplinary approach describes the input from all disciplines such as language and mathematics for understanding and cultivating the concept of sustainability. In addition, the learning is not only based on the transmission of knowledge but also in an approach where students are exploring together, gather information, make hypotheses, take decisions critically and ultimately act so as to solve a problem. This model of experiential learning is considered to be the most suitable for the formation of sustainable society citizens.

Though, all of the above describe the reorientation of formal education towards a sustainable lifestyle. However, as has already been reported in the Rio Conference the role of both formal and non-formal education for sustainable development was highlighted. In this context, non-governmental organizations, the state, the community itself are all invited to organise and offer their members the relevant educational opportunities.

Finally, in all international conferences after the Rio de Janeiro Conference, there is an intense discussion about a lifelong education in order to achieve sustainable development. Formal education refers to a specific, limited period of human life where it is not possible to obtain all the assets for a sustainable lifestyle. Therefore, education should extend outside the confines of the school, in daily life, in the neighbourhood, at work. For this reason it is proposed the concept of learning for sustainable development as more representative (Liarakoy, Flogaiti, 2007).

1.8.5. The Relationship of Environmental Education and Education for Sustainable Development

From the first discussions on sustainable development, environmental education was considered as a suitable training ground for its realisation. Environmental education, as was demarcated during the 70s, did not differ in its objectives, content and methodology with the kind of education for sustainable development, as presented by the international organisations, conferences and declarations. However, although the principles of environmental education did not differ from those of education for sustainability, during the 1970s environmental education mainly negotiated matters related to the natural environment and less issues concerning society and economy (Papadimitriou, 1998: 145).

Over the years, were expressed doubts as to the relationship of environmental education and education for sustainable development, resulting in four different approaches (Liarakoy, Flogaiti, 2007).

The first approach refers to the integration of education for sustainable development in environmental education. The concept of sustainability is enriching environmental education and comes to connect the environment with development. In the second approach, environmental education is the one that is included in the sustainable education. In this sustainable education point of view, it occurs as a broader context, a puzzle. One of its pieces is environmental education, another is cross-cultural education and any other form of training comes to fill in the puzzle of sustainability, an objective image of the worldwide community of the 21st century.

The third perspective describes environmental education and education for sustainable development as two different subjects that partly overlap. Supporters of this view see the two concepts as non-identical but complementary. They consider the remarkable results of the application of the influenced effectively the context of environmental education for sustainability. Additionally, they support the view that environmental education during the 70s was orientated on issues relating to pollution and this had as a result to affect the subsequent topics and to cut down on issues concerning the environmental protection.

The fourth and final perspective for the relationship of these two fields is summarized in terms that education for sustainable development is the evolution of environmental education. It is the same education but it adapts to the data of the new era.

According to theorists, environmental education followed an evolutionary path of three different periods. In the 1960s the emphasis was placed on the nature and the man and not only was not considered part of the system but also was the main cause of its destruction. In the 80s the emphasis was placed on the concept of the environment where man belongs as well. At the same time, solving environmental problems is treated with more optimism. Last, in the 90s the concern for the environment is enriched even further and new concerns bring new ideas. The environment is no longer only natural but also social and economic. Then, environmental education followed a similar evolutionary path which is an indispensable part of environmental concerns. (Liarakoy, Flogaiti, 2007). So, in our ages, we tend to discuss an education with definite orientation towards sustainability.

1.8.6. Historical Review of the Sustainable Development

From the preceding analysis, it was clear that sustainable development was brought to the fore as a necessary and unique treaty of reconciliation of human activity with nature. The 1980s marked the end of a culture where the environment was in the service of mankind. The new orientation is an egalitarian relationship of human interaction with nature. The term sustainable development, as identified by the international organizations and conferences, encompass the principles, content, process of achieving this kind of relationship.

The adoption of a technocratic model of sustainable development or otherwise of a mild form of sustainable development certainly leads to an alternative lifestyle. Though the technology is sufficient to resolve the "controversies" of man with his own nature and with the environment as it is considered to be enough for the restoration of their relationship.

The alternative route is the ecocentric model of sustainable development. It is a more time-consuming and laborious process for both the man himself and the society. The characterization of laborious refers to the need for a reorientation of the value system of human society. After all, how easy it is for someone who until recently identified quality of life with economic criteria to obey to his nature and to turn in fellow man?

The adoption of the ecocentric model for sustainable development involves reorientation and change in the value system of human society. Education, as a means of reproduction of social values will be used to achieve the new objective. Nevertheless, up to now, its organisation does not seem to serve the new needs. Thus, this change will start from education. As Sterling notes: "Education should be at the epicentre of this effort to change society, both as a subject and as a means" (Huckle & Sterling, 1997).

International organizations identify the wider context of sustainable development education and talk about lifelong learning, formal and informal education. Therefore, education for sustainability is not a process completed in the narrow context of school. It is a process that lasts throughout the human lifespan and apart from the school, it can take place at home, in the workplace, neighbourhood, community.

The part that is about formal education, education for sustainable development is considered to be part of environmental education by some environmental theorists. For others environmental education is placed under the umbrella of education for sustainability. A third view would argue that these are two different subjects with some common characteristics. While a fourth point of view will deal with education for sustainable development as the evolution of environmental education.

Anyone studying the principles, features, content and methodology of education for sustainable development as expressed by the international organisations, forms the impression of an ideal process. The UN General Assembly in December 2002 declared the decade 2005-2014 as the "Decade of education for sustainable development" and UNESCO undertakes the development of an international plan to implement (Liarakoy, Flogaiti, 2007).

The E.E is a radical form of education for sustainable development which is projected by international organisations, scientific and intellect decision-makers as the new educational stream who will act as a transforming agent in education and society (Flogaiti 2006: 257).

Its wide field, if supported, is the means that will promote the necessary environmental knowledge and will provide all of us with skills for critical evaluation and for active participation in environmental decision-making.

CONCLUSION

To conclude this chapter, we observe that the European Union's concern for the environment and the formulation of a common environmental policy is a result of long-term efforts. *Despite the fact that the European Community had as its primary goal the elimination of technical obstacles regarding the free transportation of products, it developed an extensive environmental policy which sets rules and boundaries that restrict market freedoms.*

Environmental education was the fruit of searches and reflections, devotees and sensitive active citizens on subjects related to Humans, Culture and the Environment, that had as their starting point the environmental movement of the 1960s, and now has conquered in actuality a highly critical position, as it is regarded as one of the most effective solutions to a wide range of environmental problems.

The school environment, indisputably, is not an exclusive source of knowledge, but is in fact along with the family of one of the most important institutions that contribute substantially to shaping attitudes and behaviours. Therefore, the school with proper planning and strengthening the environmental dimension of education can cultivate in pupils positive attitudes towards the environment and formulate, ultimately, environmentally responsible citizens, as required by the modern reality (Chaleplis, 2008).

Nowadays, Environmental Education, either as a self-contained institution or within the wider conceptual framework of Education for Sustainability and Sustainable Development, responds with clarity and completeness to Environmental, Educational and Pedagogical challenges of the present and the future.

E.E stands for Environmental Education throughout the text.

REFERENCES

Flogaiti Ev. (2006). Education for the environment and sustainability, Ellinika Grammata, Athens.

IUNC. (1970). International Working Meeting on Environmental Education in the School Curriculum, Carson City, Nevada, USA.

Knapp, D. (2000). "The Thessaloniki Declaration: A Wake- Up Call for Environmental Education?", *Journal of Environmental Education*, *31* (3) 32-39.

UNESCO. (1978). Final Report Intergovernmetal Conference on Environmental Education, UNESCO- UNEP, Tbilisi, **ΕΣΣΔ**, 14-26 October 1977, UNESCO ED/MD/49, Paris.

2.3. Cooperation As a Strategy to Get Wealth Effective Results

Cooperation may represent a way for the human race to develop strategies to get better results from an activity. In reference to what happens in the commons area, it can be said that this kind of problem may be integrated in the very well-known problem that results from the traditional formal question of the "dilemma of the prisoner" that is relevant in the Game Theory analysis.

This problem can be posed in a Game Theory for situations in which two players, for instance, have a dominant strategy which requires the solution of the game to have a dominant strategy equilibrium. This equilibrium is stable and players will not change their choices. The solution that this kind problem implies is a total payoff only results if the players had some form of cooperation between them. In such a situation, players will choose the dominant strategy (which in the case of the natural resource exploitation, for example, will always be the strategy of non-conservation) and they will not have incentives to use it efficiently and conserve the resource.

Players are compelled to choose this strategy because they are functioning in competitive conditions. Therefore, this puts a player in a situation that represents a dilemma with ethical boundaries. On one side, a player really thinks that it is important to have a proper management policy for the use of a resource in the long term but by the other side he is compelled to have an egoistic and myopic view of the resource use and exploits it too much relative to the ideal inter-temporal production level.

A situation of open access and freedom of use without rules creates a situation of tragedy (...). Ruin is the destination towards which all men rush, each pursuing his own best interest in a society that believes in the freedom of the commons. Freedom in a commons brings ruin to all (Hardin, 1968).

The problem of over-exploitation has long been argued for good practices from a preserving approach stand point and from cooperation and processes of decision making by resource management institutions. This may contribute to solving some of the multiple problems in the ethical area of commons. Therefore, to solve the problem of maintaining the biodiversity and the preservation and related ethical issues in this area, it is necessary to pose questions about how to use the environment and the Earth's resources and how to treat other species, plant or animal.

This may bring the possibility of developing projects by exploiting while at same time preserving Nature, for example, conducting nature tourism instead of killing animals or destroying trees.

In the Azores, Portugal, the example of using whales as tourism projects is an interesting case of how to use nature for good instead of killing the whales for consumption as was done in the past or even today where specific communities use whales for "scientific purposes" (!?).

This problem raises a central question in resources economics when resources are exploited. What should be the level of the inter-temporal discount rate, that is, the time preference rate? This discount rate is used to evaluate projects. In this sense, the rate highlights the relation between present and future consumption. It gives an idea about the way present generation gives importance to the resources left to the future generations and their level of welfare.

Although cooperation is an important and constant phenomenon in nature in many situations, human cooperation may represent an important way to manage resources and bring the participants better global results for the present and for the future. The cooperation for many other species with regard to the scale and range of cooperative activities may be represented maybe at a lower scale as it is fundamental for some species to get food and crucial for their survival as well in many known situations.

The differences among the ways humans and non-humans use cooperation as a strategy may require analysing different conditions and an enormous set of situations in which cooperation is relevant as an appropriate strategy. For our purposes, the importance in this study is to see how the strategies are employed to maintain cooperation and control free-riders, and how humans may use it as a strength to keep communities aggregated and unified to face difficulties that arise during crises which some developed countries are facing today.

Cooperative behaviours may produce immediate results but sometimes the long term results are even more effective and important. However, many people often prefer short-term benefits for themselves in their self-interest rather than the long term benefits from cooperation and the greater good for the group where all may benefit, which makes it is necessary to create rules for that purpose.

In many situations, to promote effective cooperation and avoid free-riding, it is important that a set of enforcement mechanisms are used, which leads to higher levels of cooperation and effective involvement of the group participants. This may involve common practices among unrelated individuals and in large groups (see Melis and Semmann, 2010).

Besides, cooperation may also be seen to develop activities that bring added value. For example, cooperation in agriculture or when a house is built in a small community where people help each other brings significant advantages that have to be taken into account.

It is important that governments and public agencies create conditions for the better use of resources for the common good and where effective exploitation of resources benefits a large number of people. Public policies have to promote conditions for sustainable use and support new challenges to develop new trends in human behaviour.

2.4. Learning from the Experience on Previous Projects. Cooperation Advantages

There are many projects around the world where experience has shown how populations have benefited many times from cooperation.

Cooperation, when players are committed and effectively involved, brings very interesting results that are real in many parts of the world and in several eras of history. Now is time to work on this. Individuals are facing critical problems and the outlook for the future is not optimistic. Solutions may be found in the creation of associations and common projects involving different agents with complementary capabilities.

Prof. Ostrom has stated that traditional systems, like market and state, work well in some situations but not in all and explained how alternative ways of managing resources may often contribute to bring wealth to many individuals.

The problem has been discussed for many situations in developing countries but the conclusions may be derived from developed countries during these difficult times of transition. During difficult times, simple solutions may be found but people now have to face a new relationship within a community framework. Often people are embarrassed by their situation because in developed countries poverty is often embarrassing. However, with rising poverty, cooperation in communities must grow as well to provide specific results of increasing wealth through common projects from cooperation. In real world experience, several cases can be presented to develop projects using cooperation. Different communities may have specific problems considering their different cultural situations but they face a common set of problems.

There are many examples of cooperative advantages given by Prof. Ostrom (see for example, Ostrom, 1990; Ostrom, 1999; Ostrom, 2000; Ostrom and Ostrom, 1977; Ostrom et al, 1999; Ostrom et al, 2002). Many other cases may be presented to show the benefits of cooperation. For example, it can be shown that there are some cooperation advantages on a small scale. For agriculture, for instance, often the resources may be better managed at a community level on a small scale. For some kind of cultures and several situations, small farmers can work together more effectively if they aid each other to plant and harvest together. Sometimes cooperation can be seen as a powerful method in the organization of agriculture practices. This kind of cooperation is not the only way to manage resources efficiently, but often it is a powerful way. It may be seen for managing forests or pasture lands. Some local communities in the past, and also in particular today, where people in the community have their own sheep or goat or other livestock when there is a different person taking turns pasturing each day. Such an example shows that cooperation results in a stronger way to improve efficiency in the community. It is time to create new conditions for new real communities in which wealth may be generated like the one presented here.

Another example may be given for little villages where migration took people from the countryside to coastal zones in the past.

Now, it is possible again to bring the population back to these "lost" areas in several ways. Providing incentives for people to come back by developing projects to attract people through, for example, local tourism projects and by providing incentives for people to stay by developing commercial infrastructures with restaurants and hostels with nature tourism activities in the area, depending on the region's attractions. This is true for many places in the European Mediterranean regions. In these regions there are many possible ways of cooperating at several levels, including cooperation among local authorities and local companies and families by organizing structures to become successful. At the tourism level, some additional observations can be considered. In many regions it is possible to exploit their attractive natural scenery and historical heritage for enjoyment in a sustainable basis while preserving it. The cooperation between national and regional authorities is essential and coordinated efforts on a local scale by companies and agencies are also vital. The existing regional structures and the cultural features are often under exploited even though they have great potentials for developing sustainable tourism through cooperative local organizational and community structures. However, sometimes there is not enough coordination among local agents themselves and with local and national authorities to develop integrated strategies in developing tourism products for the region, including integrated and diversified offers for tourism products and price coordination and joint actions to find chain added value for economic agents in the region (see Filipe, 2014).

3. The Collaborative Commons

3.1. First Considerations

Historically, new situations emerge in societies and paradigms change. Currently, new economic trends are coming which bring a new reality to the global world. This new situation brings new challenges and new ways of dealing with these economic changes. In Rifkin's (2014) "The Zero Marginal Cost Society" example of the internet shows how the spontaneous economic movements inside the system may profoundly change the run of capitalism. In "The Zero Marginal Cost Society", Rifkin (2014) describes a situation in which the "emerging 'internet of things' is speeding people to an era of nearly free goods and services, precipitating the meteoric rise of a global Collaborative Commons and the eclipse of capitalism".

The traditional vision for production in the past centuries shows how difficult it is to make significant changes involving the fundamental capitalistic system. Several experiences have resulted as alternatives but usually on a small scale basis. However, the system seems to fail and many are arguing the need of its reformulation. Besides, some practices are working on a larger scale. Cooperation and coordination seem to have successively more importance and influence in the management of the production system.

3.2. A New Production Mode Stream

Examples of 'commons-based peer production' are given in studies by Benkler 2002, 2006 or Rifkin 2014. Benkler's research focuses on commons-based approaches to managing resources in networked environments. He invented the term 'commons-based peer production' (Benkler, 2002) to describe collaborative efforts based on sharing information, such as free and open source software and Wikipedia[1]. He uses the examples of Wikipedia, Slashdot, the Open Directory Project, and Google to reveal fundamental characteristics of commons-based peer production, distinguishing it from the property - and contract - based modes of firms and markets. He also uses the term 'networked information economy' to describe a "system of production, distribution, and consumption of information goods characterized by decentralized individual action carried out through widely distributed, nonmarket means that do not depend on market strategies" (Benker, 2006).

Commons-based peer production represents a new model of socio-economic production in which the creative energy of a large number of people is coordinated (usually with the aid of the Internet) into large, meaningful projects mostly without traditional hierarchical organization. These projects are often, but not always, conceived without financial compensation for contributors. Benkler (2006) examines the ways in which information technology permits extensive forms of collaboration that have potentially transformative consequences for the economy and society. Benkler contrasts commons-based peer production (based on sharing resources among widely distributed individuals who cooperate

[1] The paper's title "Coase's Penguin, or Linux and the Nature of the Firm" refers to Ronald Coase, who originated the transaction costs theory of the firm that provides the methodological template for the positive analysis of peer production offered in the paper, and "Penguin" to the Linux mascot.

with each other) with firm production (in which tasks are delegated based on a central decision-making process) and market-based production (in which tagging different prices to different tasks serves as an incentive to anyone interested in performing a task). He refers to peer production as being a subset of commons-based production practices. It refers to a production process that depends on individual action that is self-selected and decentralized. YouTube and Facebook, for example, are based on peer production.

Tapscott and Williams (2006)[2] suggest an incentive mechanism behind common-based peer production. "People participate in peer production communities for a wide range of intrinsic and self-interested reasons... basically, people who participate in peer production communities love it. They feel passionate about their particular area of expertise and revel in creating something new or better".

Following this idea, Rifkin (2014) argues that the capitalist era is passing - not quickly, but inevitably. The rising 'internet of things' is giving rise to a new economic system - the Collaborative Commons - that will transform people's way of life. Rifkin exposes a paradox at the core of capitalism that has impelled it to a very high stage but is now passing away - the inherent entrepreneurial dynamism of competitive markets that drives productivity up and marginal costs down, enabling businesses to reduce the price of their goods and services in order to win over consumers and market share.

The central point defended by Rifkin (2014) is that if the marginal cost of producing each additional item falls close to zero, then everything gets a tendency to become almost free. In the pursuit of profit, businesses will have irrevocably undermined their own margins: capitalism will have destroyed itself. Rising in its place, Rifkin argues that there will be a civilisation based on a new and more fulfilling communitarianism, free of the hang-ups that have characterised the materialistic individualism of the late capitalist age.

Rifkin (2014) defends that the Collaborative Commons is the first new economic paradigm to take root since the advent of capitalism - and its antagonist socialism. The Collaborative Commons is already transforming the way people organize their economic life, with profound implications for the future of the capitalist market.

The trigger for this great economic transformation is known as Zero Marginal Cost[3].

Ironically, Rifkin says that while economists have always welcomed a reduction in marginal cost, they never anticipated the possibility of a technological revolution that might bring marginal costs to near zero, making goods and services priceless, nearly free and abundant, and no longer subject to market forces. He argues that a formidable new technology infrastructure - the Internet of things (IoT) is emerging with the potential of pushing large segments of economic life to near zero marginal cost in the years ahead. Rifkin describes how the Communication Internet is converging with a nascent Energy Internet and Logistics Internet to create a new technology platform that connects everything and everyone. Billions of sensors are being attached to natural resources, production lines, the electricity grid, logistics networks, recycling flows, and implanted in homes, offices, stores, vehicles, and even human beings, feeding Big Data into an IoT global neural network.

---

[2] According to the authors, Wikinomics is based on four ideas: Openness, Peering, Sharing, and Acting Globally. Wiki is a web application which allows people to add, modify, or delete content in collaboration with others.

[3] Marginal cost is the cost of producing an additional unit of a good or service after fixed costs have been absorbed. Businesses have always sought new technologies that could increase productivity and reduce the marginal cost of producing and distributing goods and services, in order to lower their prices, win over consumers and market share, and return profits to their investors.

Rifkin (2004) enrols the evidences of collaborative commons benefits. Prosumers[4] can connect to the network and use Big Data, analytics, and algorithms to accelerate efficiency, dramatically increase productivity, and lower the marginal cost of producing and sharing a wide range of products and services to near zero, just like they now do with information goods. They can now produce and share their own music via file sharing services, their own videos on YouTube, their own knowledge on Wikipedia, their own news on social media, and even their own free e-books on the Internet. The plummeting of marginal costs is spawning a hybrid economy - part capitalist market and part Collaborative Commons - with far reaching implications for society. Hundreds of millions of people are already transferring parts of their economic lives to the global Collaborative Commons. Prosumers are plugging into the fledgling IoT and making and sharing their own information, entertainment, green energy, and 3D-printed products at near zero marginal cost. They are also sharing cars, homes, clothes and other items via social media sites, rentals, redistribution clubs, and cooperatives at low or near zero marginal cost. Students are enrolling in free massive open online courses (MOOCs) that operate at near zero marginal cost. Social entrepreneurs are even bypassing the banking establishment and using crowd funding to finance start up businesses as well as creating alternative currencies in the fledgling sharing economy.

In this new world, social capital is as important as financial capital, access trumps ownership, sustainability supersedes consumerism, cooperation ousts competition, and "exchange value" in the capitalist marketplace is increasingly replaced by "sharable value" on the Collaborative Commons.

Rifkin concludes that capitalism will remain, in an increasingly streamlined role, primarily as an aggregator of network services and solutions, allowing it to flourish as a powerful niche player in the coming era. Rifkin says that people are now entering a world beyond markets where we are learning how to live together in an increasingly interdependent global Collaborative Commons.

3.3. New Trends

The new world viewed by Rafkin (2014) brings the new spontaneous organization of societies in a very cooperative virtual world. This vision shows the perspective of mass production with zero marginal costs, in the future. For example, Rifkin anticipates that by 2030, there will be more than 100 trillion sensors connecting the human and natural environment in a global distributed intelligent network. Besides, he argues that the bulk of the energy we use to heat our homes and run our appliances, power our businesses, drive our vehicles, and operate every part of the global economy which will be generated at near zero marginal cost and be nearly free in the coming decades. That is already the case for several million early adopters who have already transformed their homes and businesses into micro-power plants to harvest renewable energy on-site.

This shows in fact a tremendous improvement in productivity and welfare enhancement. However, nowadays countries are facing a problem of unemployment and a set of strong imbalances. So the new economic performances will depend on integrating new innovations, including organizational and logistic, with society trends on the system's balances.

[4] Proactive consumers.

It is impossible to dissociate the new role of technology with the level of employment and with the level of population structure as well as the way factories perform based on the new intensive processes and technology. The new arrangements for society´s development need to integrate constantly the different stages of technology improvements, the collaborative commons and the societal structures.

Considerable reflections are needed about the present evolution of societies but reality shows that drastic changes are going on and that it is clear that they have to integrate the future social and organizational system with its structure.

4. THE CONTRIBUTION OF ANTI-COMMONS THEORY TO CHANGE BEHAVIOURS

Anti-commons framework has been used to study several economic situations in which underuse of resources happens.

Anti-commons theory has appeared representing the idea of an excessive partition of property rights. This theory has appeared in the 80's of last century, introduced by Michelman (1982). In the last years of the 20th Century several ideas about this new problem around property rights have emerged in which too many rights of exclusion and a reduced level of utilization of the resource are present. Many examples have been given in the areas of pharmaceutics, intellectual property, or natural resources, for example.

When Michelman (1982) presented the notion of "anti-commons", he defined it as "a type of property in which everyone always has rights respecting the objects in the regime, and no one, consequently, is ever privileged to use any of them except as particularly authorized by others".

Considering the anti-commons concept, Buchanan and Yoon (2000) wrote that the anti-commons concept helps to explain how and why potential economic value may disappear into the "black hole" of resource underutilization.

The description of the "anti-commons" settings provides evidence of the lack of efficiency in several situations in which each one of several owners with property rights over a given resource has no effective rights to simply use the resource (and also, each one has the right to exclude other agents from its utilization) or to use it properly.

If property rights are too dispersed and complementary factors owners are unable to come up with efficient agreements, a "tragedy of the anti-commons" may happen (Heller, 1998; Bergstrom, 2010). Heller (2008) presents many examples of anti-commons in diverse legal fields in many countries around the world. Although Heller (2008) views are considerably powerful in the debate of many legal, social and economic situations, they have been the object of many criticisms (see for example Claeys, 2011; or Epstein, 2011). Heller (2008) himself notes that anti-commons theory is now well established, but empirical studies have yet to catch up. Heller states that there is a free market paradox: usually, private ownership creates wealth, but too much ownership has the opposite effect – it creates gridlock. When too many people own pieces of one thing, cooperation breaks down, wealth disappears and everybody loses.

The discussion around this is urgent and needs to find some kind of solutions which can overcome these situations. Maybe sometimes new legislation by governments are needed to overcome these obstacles to solve this kind of problems. For example, for several years - let's say 5 years - during which a piece of land is not being used, someone may request to use it, paying a rent to owners (or state) but always with the understanding that the space becomes available if demanded by the owners to use it. A state agency would intermediate this kind of processes. These processes would add value and would allow the poor people or people without livelihoods to find ways to work and have an income, not penalizing others and bringing value to society.

Analyzing projects through the anti-commons framework allows us to understand how some interesting economic projects inhibited by bureaucracy cannot be developed and prevent integrated development of some areas where investment could bring sustainable regional development in less developed areas.

Bureaucracy has been studied through the anti-commons framework. Buchanan and Yoon (2000) have presented diverse bureaucratic situations in which anti-commons theory can be applied. The analysis permits theorizing about the inconveniences of complex administrative procedures. The reality shows that bureaucracy prevents creation of value and this reduces the welfare of communities by reducing the creation of value from economic projects, and the ability to improve the quality of life, jobs creation and the communities' progress.

As discussed previously, many situations have been studied. Coelho et al. (2009) and Filipe et al. (2011, 2012b), for example, have proposed the study of the aquaculture sector in Portugal to show how bureaucracy prevents value creation for projects in this sector. Also Filipe (2014) in the tourism area and Lamelas and Filipe (2014) in an elderly nursing home project approval, for example, show how bureaucracy in other sectors negatively impacts the creation of value. A society can become more progressive from a more sustainable level of administrative processes that can improve the well-being of the population (job creation, profitable projects, earned revenue of the communities, increasing taxes, etc.).

5. Considerations for the Future

As stated in Filipe (2011), many countries are facing severe financial and debt problems as well as high unemployment rates, long term low economic growth rates and low inflation rates. The crisis scenario is creating significant economic, social and political problems.

There are severe difficulties generated by the policies that governments are currently implementing, particularly in some European Countries. Many regions and many families as well as many companies in many countries in Europe are dealing with severe economic and social problems.

A new model for these societies may be discussed that consider the factors below.

- Many projects of social responsibility are being developed by involving communities to create value and organize structures from which families may live from.
- People are reducing costs by sharing resources.
- Community projects are developed to enhance new value through shared resources.
- Internet is allowing access to products with lower price.

- Internet is allowing resources to be shared and products to be created with zero marginal costs.
- Internet allows improvement in knowledge without significant costs.
- Reduction in the levels of bureaucracy is needed.

Several difficulties have to be considered:

- There are many macroeconomic unbalances.
- Growth is based on monetary Added Value.
- Company profits are the support of new investments and employment.
- The world population keeps growing and unemployment is growing as well.
- The international worldwide environment is exhausted: economically, politically and socially.

The supportive arguments of a new era for humanity show the enormous potentials for human accomplishments. However, there is also a fundamental need for a reorganization of a country's structures, for a societal reorganization, for a new vision of economic orientation and an economic system redefinition. The adjustments have to be made gradually and supported with production adjustments and by government directives.

The social and economic predictions, for the short and medium terms, are not positive considering the current situation: social, political, economic macrostructures, national and local organizations, and the way society is structured, including the internal method of organization.

A profound reflection is needed and a structural change is urgent. It is essential that decision makers reflect on practices of a conscience need for a more balanced world consistent with environmental perspectives and economic practices that are crucial for the future development of societies.

For the future, new stages for development are crucial, based on new ways of organizing central, regional and local structures of public administrations as well as changes needed for markets, companies, and a way of regulating the markets and resources.

Conclusion

The current situation that many countries face shows that new strategies are needed. The evidences show that new solutions have to be created. The governments can look for solutions and negotiate common policies to obtain global results. However, the problems are cumulative from several decades ago and will increase in the future and the solutions are not easily found. Policies have been delayed for too long and politicians have contributed to the problems. Out dated solutions may not be the best solutions. Cooperative policies by governments and by regional and local organizations may be established on a consensus basis and a global solution may be sought. Additionally, collaborative commons have appeared supporting a new basis for economic development.

Cooperation may allow certain kinds of social and economic problems to be solved through either the spontaneous or an induced cooperation where cooperative political strategies may ease the process. New ways of micro economic cooperation need to be implemented by considering new changes in the regional and international macro-economic situation.

References

[1] Benkler's (2002), Coase's Penguin, or Linux and the Nature of the Firm, *112 YALE L.J.* 369.

[2] Benkler, Y. (2006), *The Wealth of Networks: How Social Production Transforms Markets and Freedom*. New Haven, Conn: Yale University Press.

[3] *Brundtland Report/Our Common Future (1987)*, Oxford: Oxford University Press.

[4] Buchanan and Yoon (2000), Symmetric Tragedies: Commons and Anticommons, *Journal of Law and Economics*, 43 (1), pp. 1-13.

[5] Coelho, M., Filipe, J. A. and Ferreira, M. A. M. (2009), *Coastal development and bureaucracy: Aquaculture in Portugal. The possible emergence of an 'anti-commons tragedy'*. 3rd Congress of Nature Management and Conservation. Proceedings.

[6] Coelho, M., Filipe, J. A. and Ferreira, M. A. M. (2009), *Tragedies on Natural Resources: a Commons and Anti-Commons Approach*. School of Economics and Management. Technical University of Lisbon. Department of Economics. WP 21/2009/DE/SOCIUS. Working Paper.

[7] Filipe, J. A. (2006), *O Drama dos Recursos Comuns. Um caso de Aplicação da Teoria dos Jogos aos Comuns da Pesca. Estudo da Cooperação aplicada à pesca da sardinha nas Divisões VIIIc e IXa do ICES*. PhD Thesis presented at ISCTE. Lisboa.

[8] Filipe, J. A. (2009), A Note on the Drama of the Commons. How to deal with an old problem in natural resources: the resources overexploitation, *International Journal of Academic Research*. 1 (2), pp. 158-161.

[9] Filipe, J. A. (2011), Socio-Economics in Transition Times: A Reflection on Cooperation as a Strategy to Promote Wealth, *International Journal of Latest Trends in Finance and Economic Sciences*, 1 (3).

[10] Filipe, J. A. (2014), Tourism Destinations: A Methodological Discussion on Commons and Anti-commons. The "Ammaia" Project's Locale Impact. *International Journal of Latest Trends in Finance and Economic Sciences*, 4 (2).

[11] Filipe, J. A., Coelho, M., Ferreira, M. A. M. (2007), *O Drama dos Recursos Comuns. À Procura de Soluções para os Ecossistemas em Perigo*. Sílabo. Lisboa.

[12] Filipe, J. A., Ferreira, M. A. M., Coelho, M., e Yordanova, D. (2011), Aquaculture Procedures in Portugal and Bulgaria. Anti-commons and Bureaucracy. *International Journal of Academic Research*. 3(2), Part II, pp. 540-544.

[13] Filipe, J. A., Ferreira, M. A. M., Coelho, M., Pedro, M. I. (2012a), Cooperation on Stocks Recover, *International Journal of Latest Trends in Finance and Economic Sciences*, 2 (1).

[14] Filipe, J. A., Ferreira, M. A. M., Coelho, M., Pedro, M. I. (2012b), Fisheries Problems and Bureaucracy in Aquaculture. An Anti-Commons View, In: *Emerging Issues in the Natural and Applied Sciences*, 2(1), 51-64.

[15] Filipe, J. A., Coelho, M., Ferreira, M. A. M. (2013a), Entrepreneurship Obstacles: Bureaucracy and Administrative Procedures. An "Anti-Commons Tragedy" Emergence in The Portuguese Aquaculture Sector?, *Journal of Applied Management and Investments*, 2(2).

[16] Filipe, J. A., Coelho, M., Ferreira, M. A. M., Mutharasu, S., Figueredo, I., Yordanova, D. (2013b), Corporate Social Responsibility: An International Study: The Case of CGD (Portugal), Vale (Brazil), TechnoLogica (Bulgaria) and IndianOil (India). *International Journal of Latest Trends in Finance and Economic Sciences*, 3(1).

[17] Hardin (1968), The Tragedy of the Commons, *Science*, 162, pp. 124-148.

[18] Melis, A. P. and Semmann, D. (2010), How is human cooperation different? *Philosophical Transactions of the Royal Society B: Biological Sciences* 365 (1553). pp. 2663–2674.

[19] Ostrom, E. (1990), *Governing the Commons: The Evolution of Institutions for Collective Action.* Cambridge University Press.

[20] Ostrom, E. (2000), Collective Action and the Evolution of Social Norms, *Journal of Economic Perspectives*, 14.

[21] Ostrom, E. and Ostrom, V. (1977), A theory of institutional analysis of common pool problems, In: G. Hardin and J. Baden, eds., *Managing the commons*, W. H. Freeman, San Francisco.

[22] Ostrom, E., Burger, J., Field, C., Norgaard, R. B., and Policansky, D. (1999), Revisiting the commons: local lessons, global challenges, *Science*, 284.

[23] Ostrom, E., Lam, W. F., Pradhan, P., and Shivakoti, G. (2011), *Improving Irrigation in Asia: Sustainable Performance of an Innovative Intervention in Nepal*, Cheltenham, UK: Edward Elgar.

[24] Ostrom, E., Dietz T., Dolšak, N., Stern, P. C., Stonich, S., and Weber, E. (Editors) (2002), *The Drama of the Commons, Committee on the Human Dimensions of Global Change*, National Academy Press Washington, DC: National Research Council.

[25] Rifkin, J. (2014). *The Zero Marginal Cost Society: The Internet of Things, the Collaborative Commons, and the Eclipse of Capitalism*, Palgrave Macmillan.

[26] Tapscott, D. and Williams, A. D. (2006), *Wikinomics: How Mass Collaboration Changes Everything*, Portfolio.

[27] Schlager, E. and Ostrom, E. (1992), Property-Rights Regimes and Natural Resources: A Conceptual Analysis, *Land Economics*, 68(3), pp 249-262.

[28] Vollan B. and Ostrom E. (2010), Cooperation and the Commons. *Science*, 330 (6006), pp. 923-924.

In: Towards a Society with a More Fair Economy
Editors: J. A. Filipe, N. Nagopoulos, K. Rontos et al.
ISBN: 978-1-63482-900-7

Chapter 8

MEDITERRANEAN, REGION, DEVELOPMENT: THREE KEY WORDS AND A BRIEF COMMENTARY

Luca Salvati[*]
Consiglio per la Ricerca in Agricoltura e l'analisi dell'economia Agraria (CRA), Rome, Italy

ABSTRACT

Urbanization is one of the main expressions of human societies. The present study proposes a review of the development – urbanization nexus in post-war southern Europe. In the Mediterranean region, developing an overall assessment of urban cultures is particularly difficult and challenging at the same time due to the multifaceted conflicts and intense exchanges from three different continents.

By rejecting a unique model for Mediterranean urbanization, our findings reveal that the Mediterranean region results as heterogeneous in some aspects (i.e., morphology and economic function), but quite similar in social dynamics and behaviors. The article finally discusses on the individual dynamics of the Mediterranean countries which have played a key role in the economic development of the whole region.

Keywords: Urban Growth, Socio-Spatial Patterns, Sustainable Development, Southern Europe

INTRODUCTION

Taken as a paradigmatic and metaphorical example of a disadvantaged region in Europe with persisting economic disparities and traditional socio-spatial structures, the Mediterranean space was the privileged subject of a number of theoretical and empirical studies that rethinking the recent development path of southern Europe through the use of both quantitative and narrative tools (Minca, 2004). Site-specific peculiarities and the structural

[*] Corresponding author: E-mail: bayes00@yahoo.it.

divergence with northern counterparts were extensively analyzed and interpreted as factors limiting the socioeconomic convergence of Mediterranean countries towards the wealthier European countries (Leontidou, 1993). Elusive definitions, ambiguous boundaries, variegated land-use structures, different cultures, peculiar morphological and socio-spatial forms and a relatively static economic base, among others, make the analysis of Mediterranean urbanization really tricky (Giaccaria and Mina, 2010).

The awareness of being still dependent on interpretative faults makes the search for definitions of typical elements of the Mediterranean - such as cities, landscapes or economic structures - a quite evanescent issue (Muscarà, 1998). At the same time, Conti and Segre (1998) stressed the importance of unifying definitions for Mediterranean geographies avoiding 'acts of faith' in the existence of a geographical scale identifying homogeneous boundaries defined through linear approaches (Miani, 1998).

In this context, Mediterranean urbanities emerge as a rather flexible phenomenon, whose territorial extension and implications vary according to the adopted point of view (Minca, 2003). This awareness, however, should not limit the analysis of Mediterranean urban and regional issues; it should indeed stimulate more efforts on critical definitions, cartographic representations, geographical metaphors (Minca, 2004). Based on these premises, the objective of this paper is to represent an homage to a line of interpretation different from the dominant paradigm developed mainly in the 1990s – albeit in a thoughtful and somewhat critical approach.

The line of thought that sees Pace (1996, 2002), Leontidou (1990, 1993, 1995, 1996) and Minca (2003, 200) as the most critical voices to the reductionist approach, stimulates a thorough reflection on the necessity of making judgments on the 'Mediterranean periphery' based on post-modern thinking, rejecting 'convergence' and 'stadial' interpretations of Mediterranean economic backwardness (Longhi and Musolesi, 2007), accepting a critical review of the culture-economy dichotomy and opening up to other components (e.g. territorial, environmental) of the development debate (Fuschi, 2008).

In this light, renewed interpretations - despite the undoubted transition of several southern regions to 'northern' and 'western' models - retain much of their applicability in the context of socio-demographic transitions still observed in southern Europe and, more generally, in the Mediterranean basin (Gargiulo Morelli and Salvati, 2010).

The Mediterranean 'Weak' Thought

A way to make this strategic vision operative is to recall the definition of the 'Mediterranean boundaries' provided by Minca (2004):

> "We could think about the Mediterranean area as a sort of nebula consisting of a series of virtual networks that connect information, people, services and goods with a number of places and nodes, which in turn interact with this (supposed ephemeral) dimension in a seemingly unpredictable way to measure and interpret spatial and temporal complexity".

The critical reference is centered on overly schematic approaches and positivist interpretations of the relationship between society and territory, not necessarily limited to the anodyne vision given by official statistical data (Leontidou, 1995).

The criticism on the economic 'scale of production' also affects the scale of interpretation of Mediterranean urbanization, allowing to recognize that

> "Ambiguity and poetic geometry of the Mediterranean represent its wealth and strength, instead of weakness and inconsistency that the vision produced by the statistics that count in the hierarchical division of the planet seems to implicitly attribute to this area with the result of marginalization and disclosure (...)" (Minca, 2004).

Mediterranean spaces should not be interpreted as 'weak' and poorly performing, just because hardly interpretable through the spatial logic of binary inclusion/exclusion and the reading of linear-type maps, documents and statistics (Leontidou, 1996).

The risk of 'cultural' marginalization in the mainstream urban discourse is lurking, being supported by quantitative approaches proposed by a 'reductionist' perspective (Giaccaria and Minca, 2010). Such approaches definitely produce partial interpretations of Mediterranean geographies and societies, based on potentially comparable elements with those proposed by a 'northern' literature on urban systems (Cori and Lemmi, 2001). By contrast, latent social phenomena, sometimes difficult to reveal through purely quantitative approaches, consolidate their importance. Reflecting on critical definitions applied to the Mediterranean region, intended as a people, economies and institutions melting pot is thus straightforward. Following Minca (2004), the concept of 'border' contrasts the choice of the horizon as a fundamental reference chosen to talk about 'our' sea, contrasting the arid statistical figures, in search of qualitative answers and narrative interpretations.

On the other hand, this reflection is not denying the awareness of quantitative approaches based on comparative procedures and objective methodologies in shedding light on the complexity of southern territories. But, at the end of each statistical exercise, we continue looking for narratives, metaphors, horizons, because statistics are not entirely satisfied with the thirst for knowledge of the many latent factors - so difficult to define and quantify - still playing a role in the Mediterranean region (Farinelli, 1998). By realizing that much has been written on the Mediterranean geography, we welcome gladly the invitation not to write on the Mediterranean region but to confront it with metaphors and discourses potentially free from spaces rigidly determined. The prudential clause proposed by Matvejevic (1996) cannot be questioned: the Mediterranean has been already narrated, his story already written. But our sea continues to exceed all the literature about him.

A Claim for Mediterranean Speeches

The Mediterranean Sea is the sea of loneliness, says Matvejevic (1998), and its discursive and, at the same time, cumulative discovery continues to involve scholars, stimulating analyses and narratives, interpretations and reflections. To speak about the Mediterranean one must imagine the land and the sea, rather than defining them in axiomatic or cartographical terms. In this effort we should abandon the stiffness of deterministic constructs, reducing the lure of some functionalist discourses, to read the heterotopic space as an utopia in progress, a late modernity which is based on a fascinating game that produces spatial order and, at the same time, the conditions for the deconstruction of that order (Kourlourios, 2003).

In some way, it indicates a space without measurements, with no limits, no boundaries, an horizon that is approaching and moving away from the observer's point of view. Just thinking about the sea as heterotopia, you can give substance to a definition not distorted by deterministic and functionalistic thinking (Minca, 2003).

For this reason, a renewed Mediterranean geography can only begin from the sea, a 'liquid plain' (following the evocative definition provided by Braudel (1987) and Farinelli (1998)) that connects land and balances the uneven topography of the countries that surround it. Sea is seen as a means of communication, but also a friction to trade and as a consolidator of cultural differences and economic disparities, such as those existing between the north and south shores. The sea is expressed with the heterotopia that explains "the co-existence on its banks of totalitarianism and resistance, of rationality beyond the 'reasonable', of 'local' issues intermixed with 'global' issues, and all that is in the middle, and the difference between identity and the inexhaustible thrust towards progress" (Autori Vari, 1995).

Speaking about the Mediterranean, most of the urban geography literature focuses on the analysis of coastal areas seen as an opportunity for settlement and as a result of public policy planning (Giannakourou, 2005). From the ecological point of view, if you look at the Mediterranean bio-geographical area and especially the olive tree areal, it can be assumed that there are homogeneous environments that can be found into a zone less than 200 km from the coast line. From the socioeconomic point of view Braudel's vision of a 'Greater Mediterranean' is challenging: fuzzy boundaries, determined by men instead of climate regimes and vegetation attributes, with no limits and barriers (Fuschi, 2008).

Pace (1996) reminds us, that the main protagonist of the development of the region is man. Taken as a product of the joint action of climate and landscape, local communities produce kinds of 'Mediterranean life styles', seen as an easy simulacrum of literary descriptions for all-times narrative, trivializing southern spaces as for the production of sun, bucolic landscapes valued for balance and harmony, full of wisdom and tranquility. Matvejevic (1998) is responsible for an open critique of this view, emphasizing the non-existence of a cultural identity, and inviting to grasp more attention to the uneven differences among people and culture rather than to enhance the 'rarely similar and never identical' social traits of the region. The Mediterranean is heterogeneity and not harmonization, gradients (never as dense as elsewhere) and not concentration: exclusion and inclusion processes are continuously facing in the same spaces (Troin, 1997).

The analysis of territorial gradients brings to mind the concept of fracture of an homogeneity condition sought but, perhaps, never been found.

An element of rupture in this (supposed homogeneous) territory is the one provided by the urban hierarchy, which interrupts a similarity of agricultural and forest landscapes, with lack in infrastructures and less populated (Ribeiro, 1972). A 'scale jump', which is initially demographic and economic, shapes the socio-spatial structure reflecting a polarized landscape in conflict with the surrounding areas. In this sense the Mediterranean urban footprint appears as the prototype of a 'geography of the fracture' (Kayser, 1996), which distinguishes spaces with the economic strength of advanced manufacturing, the industrial and commercial power of relatively few cities from the weakness of rural landscapes dedicated to agriculture and livestock (Muscarà, 1986).

This traditional view may fit also with the most recent picture offered by poly-centric models (Hall, 1997, 2001; Sassen, 2001), reinvigorating the metaphor of the 'fracture' proposed by Kayser.

The rift in the economy refers to the international position of countries that gravitate towards the Mediterranean basin: their role in the global economic systems, the acute territorial disparities, the unresolved environmental issues, exacerbate social gaps in a context of increased political instability and economic crisis, reproducing even today, ten years after the entry into the new millennium, a peripheral condition for the whole region (Viganoni, 2007). It prevails in the countries of the southern shore and still haunts some regions of the northern shore, in a process of 'lacking convergence' towards models considered, from various points of view, economically dynamic, socially cohesive and environmentally sustainable (Gargiulo Morelli and Salvati, 2010).

Fifteen years ago, King et al. (2001) reflected on the definition of a semi-peripheral Mediterranean zone characterized by political, economic and social instability, secularism and religious traditionalism. These classifications can still be applied, without substantial differences with the past, to a number of Mediterranean countries. The reasons for this classification have been clarified by the same authors, which depicts the majority of the Mediterranean countries as “stacking in the middle [between a northern centre and a southern periphery] (...), they have to run at high speed to maintain the same position, sometimes failing”. This constraint highlights the need to restructure themes, interpretation and practical tools to understand a complex territorial system like the Mediterranean region. In view of the undoubted economic changes, but also the impact of the single currency and the persistence of European development policies that have focused on the 'late periphery', we note that the distance of these countries with the north is still pronounced (Talia, 1998).

Structural backwardness and the peripheral position in the global arena reflect in local uncertainties and in a regional crisis that goes beyond the boundaries of the economic domain.

The unstable, degraded, deprived Mediterranean cities are the main signal for crisis supposedly lacking of that intelligence that could allow to plan, promote, innovate and compete globally, contrary to a sort ‘imperviousness to change’ (Leontidou, 1993). Despite being important places in the regional market, these areas seem to struggle following virtuous trajectories, incardinated indeed into societal and economic structures somewhat archaic, unable to face the competition with the new world advancing rapidly. We can thus speak about a crisis for the whole Mediterranean region? We can speak about the crisis of whole regions and cities, which in some way represent the most developed exponents of the Mediterranean territories? Or maybe, paraphrasing Latouche (2000), it would be better to focus on the 'regions of the crisis', the crisis of democracy consolidated by a crisis in citizenship, public participation, collective individualism embedded in a progressive loss of ethic values and conceptual referents (Salvatori, 2008). This will produce contexts reflected in those 'cathartic' landscapes of the Mediterranean periphery, along the 'new' fringes that are dispersed in a no-place landscape.

The 'Mediterranean Delay': Rhetoric and Material Conditions

The alleged delay of the Mediterranean societies has been long discussed. Many scholars have questioned the (not metaphorical) meaning of delay, replacing this concept with other terms such as 'other modernity': a modernity condition that does not lend itself to be assessed and quantified with the rule typical of northern countries. Scholars have also introduced the evocative notion of 'resistance to modernity' (Leontidou, 1995), which stems from a critique to the dominant Anglo-American culture, expressed in an identity-veiled impatience with rules and objectives imposed by northern countries – e.g. through European Community decisions- intervening deeply in the national political and social debates of southern European countries. Leontidou (1996) wonders if "the ambiguous forms of post-modernism were not perhaps already dominant in the Mediterranean cities well before the Anglo-Saxon academy and the post-Fordist flexible accumulation identified and bordered the 'spaces of the future'?"

The weakness of the positivist definition of 'territorial delay' emerges from the above mentioned studies. Minca (2004) states that the Mediterranean lends very little to the '*reductio ad unum* of mechanistic metaphors embedded in the positivist brand, while calling upon scholars on the themes of narrative space , boundaries , horizons , suggesting criticism of the language and the schematic scale - global and polarized - condemning the Mediterranean discourse to a fallback position.

In addition to definitions, even the most objective measures may show a weakness when applied to the Mediterranean region. Leontidou (1990) regarded as inappropriate the statistical classifications imported from the 'global north' to be directly applied to the southern context, thus calling back the core of a traditional Anglo-American literature interpreting Mediterranean societies as framed, governed by informal relationships based on pre-capitalistic transactions, signal of social delay and deferring the required development. These stereotypes are born from the models of 'Nordic' or 'Atlantic' urban development, which regurgitate as 'abnormal' any deviation from the trajectory predicted by the model itself. On the other hand, the result of this model was also highlighted by Farinelli (1998), which contrasts the rational northern models to a Mediterranean framework that works even contrary to the territorial logic that drives the modern capitalist state, where urbanization has usually been interpreted as an expression of the various stages of the industrial revolution.

Going beyond the ordered patterns of European spaces and identity, we need to focus the concepts that may contribute to reinterpret the condition of Mediterranean periphery. This does not mean the search for other definitions, measurements and standards, but it obliges us to put back the centrality of the Mediterranean into the cultural debate and the political agenda (Kourliouros, 2003). In fact, the Mediterranean has, in part, regained the role of social and cultural bridge between Europe, Africa and the Middle East in the last decade. The economic scenarios and the geo-political uncertainty, have contributed to the redefinition of this (supposedly lost) centrality.

Some regions, especially those most open to trade, have sometimes formulated a competitive proposal for their re-emergence in the international context. By reducing the economic polarization and the socio-political gap with northern Europe, coastal areas, more traditionally suited to international competition, seem to have found, through the most varied formulas and experiences, a new dimension of attractiveness (Vicari-Haddock, 2004).

It remains, however, the weakness of many southern regional economic systems. Many of the limits set in the 1990s are valid still today.

The loss of centrality, observed since the sixteenth century, is derived from the progressive shift of commercial, social and cultural networks towards the northern countries assuming the control of the global economic system. This happened first with the colonial phase, and subsequently with the industrial revolution, and finally with the post-industrial economy and the globalization of markets.

This framework resulted in the Mediterranean locked societies with significant examples of convergence and vitality provided by the coastal urban systems (e.g. Albanese, 2008). At the same time, the rapid growth of the population moved the demographic engine of the Mediterranean from the northern side to the southern side (Fuschi, 2008). Peri-urban areas, coastlines, flat spaces, were the areas of population growth, in Italy as in Israel, in Spain as in Turkey, in Greece as in Morocco. Population growth has placed the north Mediterranean region in front of new decisive issues, both in the management of large flows of migrant population and in the massive socio-environmental implications of this exodus.

As a consequence, the environmental issues related to the massive and spontaneous urbanization (e.g. wastewater management, soil waste recycling, water, soil and air pollution), combined with those dictated by a rapid transformation of agricultural land into man-made space to sprawl (compaction and contamination of fertile soils, groundwater pollution, water scarcity and drought, unsustainable intensive farming, land fragmentation, loss of the cultural elements of the landscape), creating vulnerable areas where different impacts lead to dangerous spirals towards self-powered deforestation, desertification and the irreversible degradation of natural capital.

Social and cultural changes, preferences and tastes, lifestyles and consumption patterns, invest southern countries in very different forms, but the basic elements of this change intersect with an array of deeper thought, combining and permeating societies and cultures beyond religions, political influences of the individual states and local factors. Two interpretative keys may be sought in the works of Camus and Gramsci in the light proposed respectively by Cassano (1996) and Leontidou (1995).

Despite these thoughts stem from very different contexts, they seem to be shared in the Mediterranean narrative where freedom is reflective of society and individualism intermingled with the pervasiveness of the family control, which maintains and strengthens the cohesion of a society seemingly on the verge of disintegration.

Combined with the demographic transition and the undeniable cultural changes, the shift of the economy towards (more or less advanced) services is another trait of the recent evolution of the southern socioeconomic systems.

This transformation is not just peculiar to the Mediterranean basin. A question of what direction is taking the economic structure of southern European is challenging, focusing on the importance of the advanced tertiary sector - which is increasingly viewed as a proxy for dynamic, competitive regions.

The experience of the 1990s demonstrated that the economic 'big push', and especially the industrial growth, was only partially observed in southern urban systems (Autori Vari, 1995). A typical trait of the Mediterranean cities can be outlined in their partial outsourcing and 'non-advanced' economic structure, the partial failure of economic development policies towards modernization, competitiveness, the revitalization of the Central Business District, as well as the development of cultural tourism and business (Scott, 2001). The 'impermeability' of the Mediterranean society to cultural innovations was regarded as the main factor determining locked societies and stagnating economies.

In varying degrees between the north and the south, between the east and the west, Mediterranean societies tend to retain lifestyles and patterns of behavior, some of which relate a tradition that is not always the best in terms of social ethics and occasionally results in organized crime or fundamentalist intolerance (Pace, 1996).

CONCLUSION

Twenty years later the seminal study from Leontidou (1990), what has changed in this picture? Which cities have really started an evolutionary path towards the re-appropriation of an international role? How many have maintained their regional niche? Questions that deserve a full debate by re-thinking the contributions of Leontidou and Minca. Just to provide a paradigmatic example from the economic side, the role of spontaneous activities is going to lose the importance observed in the past. Although the informal economy is an identity trait of developing countries, the Mediterranean 'alternative' to this phenomenon offers very different outcomes compared with those observed in the poorest countries.

Mediterranean spontaneity expresses, in fact, a duality based - on the one hand - on the widespread recognition of the role of the market and the capital and- on the other hand - on the non-recognition of the state power to regulate these dynamics. This process hinges on the role of the family, often pervasive, not only in rural areas but also in urban areas, where opportunities for informal activities, primarily (but not exclusively) aimed at low-skilled labor proliferate in an environment not necessarily degraded and deprived. In fact, the informal sector development does not allow the emergence of a strong middle class. In such contexts, late industrialization highlights the absence of a 'bourgeois hegemony', but above all the heterogeneity, versatility and diversity of Mediterranean societies (Corna Pellegrini, 1998).

In conclusion, Mediterranean social geographies push us to interpret differently the role of the informal economy from the classic ideal type, rejecting 'the reason without reasonability', the 'rationality without wisdom' (Cassano, 1996). Informal economy has been in the past the way to the survival of many people, already secured by the achievement of a sufficient level of development and the presence of market mechanisms.

To the contrary, nowadays the incipient promotion of some social strata dominates the Mediterranean scene: the protagonist is sometimes the middle class, whose demographic weight increases, and that obviously cannot be drawn exclusively from the economic satisfaction of the free market. Somehow, the informal economy was seen as a response to market failures or a strategy to overcome the *laissez-faire*, strategy of the public sector, uncaring youth and female unemployment, educational and infrastructural gaps and consolidating income inequalities. The lack in salary adjustment, especially in some sectors of employment and mainly in the major urban areas - where a large segment of the population is most exposed to the risk of poverty - reinforces the picture.

From the side of the small and medium enterprise, the motivations are diametrically opposed, but yet equally shared. Excessive labor costs, wage rigidity, difficulty in finding qualified workers, but also a limited contractual flexibility and job constraints are important elements that justify the use of informal employment.

The circle is finally closed considering the social background of the two actors, proletariat and petty bourgeoisie. Acting in view of a partial redistribution of income, informal occupations are not recognized as a non-value: both actors consider them a replacement mechanism and thus are so pervasive to the action of the state.

The basis of social control that allows a similar contamination remains the supremacy of family status, the fronting of the particular interest to the common good. It is difficult to predict if the gap between divergent interests will be long-term compatible, especially in post-industrial economies where urban competitiveness is high.

Rediscovering limits and opportunities of Mediterranean socioeconomic systems, starting from the most competitive areas, such as the cities, is thus a necessary step in the take-home research and policy exercise for the next 'summer holiday'.

REFERENCES

Autori, V., (1995). *Mediterraneo. Citta', territorio, economie alle soglie del XXI secolo*. Roma: Cresme and Fonspa, Credito Fondiario e Industriale.

Albanese, V., (2008). Il ruolo di un grande evento nella riqualificazione delle città portuali. Il caso di Valencia. *Bollettino della Società Geografica Italiana*, 2008, Serie XIII, vol. I, p. 949-963.

Braudel, F., (1987). Il *Mediterraneo*. Milano: Bompiani.

Cassano, F., (1996). Il *pensiero meridiano*, Bari: Laterza.

Conti, S., Segre, A., (1998). *Mediterranean geographies*. Roma: Geo – Italy 3. Società Geografica Italiana and CNR – Italian Committee for International Geographical Union.

Cori, B., lemmi, E., (2001). *La regione mediterranea. Sviluppo e cambiamento*. Bologna: Patron.

Corna pellegrini Giacomo (1998), An attemptable classification of the Mediterranean cities. In: VALLAT, Colette (Ed.). *Petites et grandes villes du Bassin Méditerranéen – Études autour de l'œuvre d'Etienne Dalmasso*. Roma: Collection de l'Ecole Française de Rome n. 246, pp. 563-575.

Farinelli, F., (1998). Il Mediterraneo, la differenza, il differimento. *Geotema*, 12, p. 57-62.

Fuschi, Marina. Il *Mediterraneo. Geografia della complessità*. Milano: Franco Angeli.

Gargiulo Morelli, Vittorio and Salvati, Luca (2010). *Ad hoc urban sprawl in the Mediterranean city: Dispersing a compact tradition?* Roma: Aracne.

Giannakourou, G., (2005). Transforming spatial planning policy in Mediterranean countries. Europeanization and domestic change. *European Planning Studies*, 13(2), p. 253-264.

Giaccaria, P., Minca, C., (2010). The Mediterranean alternative. *Progress in Human Geography*, in press.

Hall, P., (1997). Modelling the post-industrial city. *Futures*, 29(4/5), p. 311-322.

Hall, P., (2001). *The polycentric city*. London, Earthscan.

Hall, P., Pain, K., (2006). *The polycentric metropolis. Learning from mega-city regions in Europe*. London: Earthscan.

Kayser, B., (1996). Il *Mediterraneo. Geografia della frattura*. Milano: Jaca Book.

King, R., De Mas, P., Beck, J., (2001). *Geography, environment and development in the Mediterranean*. Brighton: Sussex Academic Press.

Kourliouros, E., (2003). Reflections on the economic-noneconomic debate: a radical geographical perspective from the European south. *Antipode*, 35 (4), p. 781-799.

Latouche, S., (2000). *La sfida di Minerva*. Torino: Bollati Boringhieri.

Leontidou, L., (1985). Urban land rights and working-class consciousness in peripheral societies. *International Journal of Urban and Regional Research*, 9(4), p. 533-556.

Leontidou, L., (1990). *The Mediterranean city in transition*. Cambridge: Cambridge University Press.

Leontidou, L., (1993). Postmodernism and the City: Mediterranean versions. *Urban Studies*, 30, p. 949-965.

Leontidou, L., (1995). Repolarization in the Mediterranean: Spanish and Greek cities in neoliberal Europe. *European Planning Studies*, 3(2), p. 155-172.

Leontidou, L., (1996). Alternatives to modernism in (Southern) urban theory: Exploring in-between spaces. *International Journal of Urban and Regional Research*, 20(2), p. 180-197.

Longhi, C., Musolesi, A., (2007). European cities in the process of economic integration: towards structural convergence. *Annals of Regional Science*, 41, p. 333-351.

Matvejevic, P., (1996). *Mediterraneo. Un nuovo breviario*. Milano: Garzanti.

Matvejevic, P., (1998). Il *Mediterraneo e l'Europa*. Milano: Garzanti.

Miani, F., (1998). La dimensione urbana per l'integrazione mediterraneo-europea. *Geotema*, 12, p. 68-73.

Minca, C., (2003). Critical peripheries. *Environment and Planning D, Society and Space*, 21, p. 160-168.

Minca, Claudio (Ed.) (2004). *Orizzonte mediterraneo*. Padova: Cedam.

Muscarà, C., (1986). *Megalopoli Mediterranea*. Milano: Franco Angeli.

Muscarà, L., (1998). Mediterraneo ed Europa: identità culturali e chiusure territoriali. *Geotema*, 12, p. 74-80.

Pace, Giuseppe (Ed.) (1996). *Sviluppo economico e urbano delle città mediterranee*. Napoli: Istituto Italiano per gli Studi Filosofici.

Pace, Giuseppe (2002). Ways of thinking and looking at the Mediterranean city. < http://mpra.ub.uni-muenchen.de/10511/> [accessed April 2014]

Ribeiro, O., (1972). *Il Mediterraneo. Ambiente e tradizione*. Milano: Mursia.

Salvatori, Franco (Ed.) (2008). *Il Mediterraneo delle città. Scambi, confronti, culture, rappresentazioni*. Roma: Viella.

Sassen, S., (2001). *La città globale*. Roma: Il Mulino.

Scott, A., (2001). *Global city-regions. Trends, theory, policy*. Oxford: Oxford University Press.

Talia, I., (1998). *Competizione globale tra città. I casi di Napoli, Palermo e Bari*. Napoli: Liguori.

Troin, J.-F., (1997). *Le metropoli del mediterraneo. Città di frontiera, città cerniera*. Milano: Jaca Book.

Vicari Haddock, S., (2004). *La città contemporanea*. Bologna: Il Mulino.

Viganoni, L., (2007). *Il mezzogiorno delle città – Tra Europa e Mediterraneo*. Milano: Franco Angeli.

diamonds, sulphur, coal, oil, natural gas, and even sand and gravel over the past century than over all earlier centuries put together. He says that the pace continues to accelerate, so that today the world annually produces and consumes nearly all mineral commodities at record rates. As these resources are finite, the problem of their exhaustion can be predicted, although technological innovation enables their reutilization and a greater efficiency on their exploitation and use as well as reproduce them in specific cases. The example of the oil problem is raised in this chapter by considering its importance to most motor vehicles depending on it.

The effective stocks of natural resources may eventually be expanded by technological developments and motor vehicles may continue to use this kind of energy or be converted to use another kind.

The big question is the discussion on the efficiency, on costs and on the environment. The improvement in living standards in the last centuries, particularly in the few last decades, shows how energy and transport vehicles have become important for humanity and - of course - the question of what kind of energy will be used is very relevant to the debate.

Now humanity has reached the beginning of a new stage of development. Environmental and ecological attitudes have changed and so have the criteria and conditions for businesses - see for instance Hardin (1968), Filipe, Coelho and Ferreira (2006), Ferreira, Filipe and Chavaglia (2014). Companies and governments seem to be concerned about pollution and the negative effects on the Earth and human welfare standards - on this subject see Kunstler (2006). There are very important changes coming up fast in the way of living and in balancing the resources of the planet – see Filipe, Coelho and Ferreira (2006). Conventional sources of energy are exploited at a very fast rate and will be exhausted in the near future, maybe within just a few decades under normal conditions. Also, new kinds of energy are being discovered and prepared for future use.

Although innovation increases productivity from natural resources, for example, increasing the gas mileage of cars, recycling the resources and reducing the waste in their extraction and processing, the real dilemma is that new efficient and interesting alternatives are being developed for the future. Even though innovation affects the potential output of natural resources, a methodological discussion may be raised to consider the possibility of dismantling or recycling the motorcars by considering how new ways of energy propulsion may be used.

The world is moving forward to a new era of energy source. Many of the non-renewable resources are often considered to be over-exploited and conventional sources of energy such as oil, gas and coal, that have been civilization's source of fuel in the last centuries, will disappear soon if the same course is maintained. Possibly firstly oil, then gas and lastly coal. As a result, new opportunities for businesses are springing up, as well as globally, associated with using alternative sources of energy.

Environmental problems have emerged from using the wrong kind of resources - see Filipe, Coelho and Ferreira (2006). The demand for inputs by industries has increased greatly in the last two centuries to satisfy the demand because of either the strong growing world population or from supporting the higher standard of life for a large part of the world population. All the wastes produced for many decades must be overcome and it is important to knowhow to recycle old equipment into useful devices whenever possible – see Ferreira, Filipe and Coelho (2008) and Ferreira et al. (2008).

In: Towards a Society with a More Fair Economy
Editors: J. A. Filipe, N. Nagopoulos, K. Rontos et al.
ISBN: 978-1-63482-900

Chapter 9

A QUEUE MODEL FOR IDLE MOTORCARS MANAGEMENT CONSIDERING AN ENERGY SOURCES' NEW SCENARIO

***Manuel Alberto M. Ferreira*[1,*],**
***José António Filipe*[1,1] *and Manuel Coelho*[2,2]**
[1]ISCTE-IUL, Department of Mathematics, Lisboa, Portugal
[2]ISEG-UTL, Department of Economics, Lisboa, Portugal

ABSTRACT

A queue system with infinite servers at which customers arrive according to a Poisson process at rate λ is considered in this study. With this tool a model is built to analyse a situation in which motorcars arrive at the system after getting idled, and considering a scarce conventional energy state, leaving it as soon as they are recycled or dismantled. Both situations are modelled with the same purpose. The model allows a conclusion to be drawn that when the rate of dismantling and recycling of motorcars is greater than the rate at which they become idle, the system has a tendency to balance. The time spent in dismantling or recycling each idle motorcar plays a central role in this hazard rate function model.

INTRODUCTION

Natural resources have been used continuously for a long time ago. Tilton (2001) stat that human kind has consumed more aluminium, copper, iron and steel, phosphate roc

* Manuel Alberto M. Ferreira: ISCTE-IUL, Department of Mathematics, Av. das Forças Armadas, 1649-02 Lisboa, Portugal. E-mail: manuel.ferreira@iscte.pt.
[1] José António Filipe: ISCTE-IUL, Department of Mathematics, Av. das Forças Armadas, 1649-026, Lisbo Portugal. E-mail: jose.filipe@iscte.pt.
[2] Manuel Coelho: ISEG-UTL, Department of Economics, Rua do Quelhas, nº 6, 1200-781, Lisboa, Portugal. I mail: coelho@iseg.utl.pt.

Many new problems may emerge and it is important to know how quickly changes may happen as societies today develop new sources of energy to create a new economy and a reorganized society.

The aim of this chapter is to show that motorcars which use oil may have alternative uses when this conventional source of energy is replaced by other kinds; or they may simply be dismantled. The model presented here uses infinite servers queues to consider that too many motorcars will become idle if the conventional energy source is replaced by alternative sources, as such renewable ones.

The rate at which the recycling and dismantling actions are performed in this analysis is essential and relevant in the service hazard rate function - see Ross (1983).

This chapter is based on the work presented in Ferreira, Filipe and Coelho (2008), Ferreira et al. (2008) and Ferreira et al. (2011).

"Non-Renewable" Natural Resources and Renewable Natural Resources Incoming: The Development of New Energy Alternative Cars

The effective stocks of a natural resource may not be reduced significantly (and even in some cases can be increased) if diverse forms of improving exploitation and utilization are considered, namely by considering technological innovations, and facilitating the recycling through the use of new techniques within the technological changes context, or the (partial) substitutability with some other resources. In some cases, artificial production can be considered as in the case of artificial oil substitutes.

The use of renewable energy sources are growing fast in several types of businesses. In the auto industry, for example, there are new sources of power from electric or hydrogen energy. Some of these new sources are mentioned below. There are other alternatives and other sources already in use. However, the ones considered are presented here.

Many alternative sources of energy for cars have been tried in the past years and new models using these new sources of energy are already being produced. One must not forget that the conventional model is the norm and so there are large obstacles to alternative new models. For example, the use of electric energy for cars has been tried on vehicles in the past. In the early 1900s, the most common way to fuel a vehicle was by using electric energy. There were more electric than gasoline-powered vehicles. As the production of gasoline becomes cheaper, electric vehicles went out of production. Meanwhile, gasoline prices and pollution have increased considerably in the last decades and recently the idea of electric cars has made a comeback. Some manufacturers such as Tesla Motors have found efficient methods to produce electric cars to make them affordable to consumers as well as reliable to drive. There are diverse benefits from electric cars such as zero-emission, a quiet ride, ease of use and a lower cost of ownership, for example. Since the end of the last decade, new models of electric cars have been produced as an alternative to the conventional cars and with diverse brands.

There are also vehicles powered by hydrogen. Hydrogen vehicles use hydrogen as their primary source of power. Hydrogen can either be used in the combustion process (hydrogen burned in the engine); or in the fuel-conversion process (hydrogen is converted to electrical energy which powers the electric motor). The best part of using hydrogen is that the by-product of using it is water.

Hydrogen fuel has already been used in space rockets, submarines, cars, buses, or motorcycles. For instance, BMW, Chevrolet or Honda have models using the hydrogen source of power.

Still hybrid vehicles use two or more power sources for locomotion. Hybrid-electric vehicles use both gasoline and electricity for internal combustion and powering electric motor. The world's first commercially mass-produced hybrid vehicle was the Toyota Prius. Cadillac, Chevrolet, Chrysler, Ford or Honda are examples of companies that have launched hybrid vehicles.

There have been reports of a growing trend of many electric car enthusiasts converting their vehicle's petrol-fueled engine to electric motor. Such conversion is a result of the rising high price of oil. However, this has not been widespread because of the technical knowledge required for conversion.

The possibilities discussed show that alternative fuels for cars appear promising.

THE MODEL

In the $M|G|\infty$ queue – see Takács (1962) and Ferreira (1995) - customers arrive according to a Poisson process at rate λ and each one receives a service where the length is a positive random variable with the distribution function $G(.)$ and a mean value α. There are infinite servers, that is, when a customer arrives it always finds an available server. The service of a customer is independent from other customers' services and from the arrival process. An important parameter is the traffic intensity, called $\rho = \lambda\alpha$. The $M|G|\infty$ queue has neither losses nor waiting. Note that there is no queue in the usual sense of the word.

The question for this study is whether the customers are the motor cars that become idle. The arrival rate is the rate at which the motor cars become idle. The service time for each one is the time that goes from the instant they get idle to the instant they become either recycled or dismantled.

Call $N(t)$ the number of occupied servers (or the number of customers being served) at instant t, in a $M|G|\infty$ system. From Ferreira (1995), $p_{0n}(t) = P[N(t) = n|N(0) = 0]$, $n = 0,1,2,\ldots$, is given by:

$$p_{0n}(t) = \frac{\left(\lambda\int_0^t [1 - G(v)]dv\right)^n}{n!} e^{-\lambda\int_0^t [1-G(v)]dv}, \quad n = 0,1,2,\ldots \tag{1}$$

So, the transient distribution, when the system is initially empty, is Poisson with mean $\lambda\int_0^t [1 - G(v)]dv$.

The stationary distribution is the limit distribution:

$$\lim_{t\to\infty} p_{0n}(t) = \frac{\rho^n}{n!} e^{-\rho}, \quad n = 0,1,2,... \tag{2}$$

This queue system, as in any other, has a sequence of busy periods and idle periods. A busy period begins when a customer arrives at the system and finds it empty. Be $p_{1'n} = P[N(t) = n | N(0) = 1']$, $n = 0,1,2,...$, meaning $N(0) = 1'$ is the time origin at the instant at which a customer arrives at the system, moving the number of customers from 0 to 1. That is a busy period begins, at $t \geq 0$ possibly - see Ferreira (1995):

- The customer that arrives at the initial instant either abandons the queue system with probability $G(t)$, or goes on being served, with probability $1 - G(t)$;
- The other servers, that were unoccupied at the time origin, either go on unoccupied or occupied with 1,2,... customers, with the probabilities $p_{0n}(t)$, $n = 0,1,2,...$. Both subsystems, the one with the initial customer and the one the servers initially unoccupied, are independent. So

$$\begin{gathered} p_{1'0}(t) = p_{00}(t) G(t) \\ p_{1'n}(t) = p_{0n}(t) G(t) + p_{0n-1}(t)(1 - G(t)), \; n = 1,2,... \end{gathered} \tag{3}$$

It is easy to check that

$$\lim_{t\to\infty} p_{1'n}(t) = \frac{\rho^n}{n!} e^{-\rho}, \quad n = 0,1,2,... \tag{4}$$

Calling the service time hazard rate function $h(t)$, according to [19]:

$$h(t) = \frac{g(t)}{1 - G(t)} \tag{5}$$

where $g(.)$ is the density associated with $G(.)$. The service time hazard rate function is the rate at which the services end. For the situation under study in this chapter, it is the rate at which the motorcars become either recycled or dismantled.

Proposition 1

If $G(t) < 1$, $t > 0$ continuous and differentiable and

$$h(t) \geq \lambda, \quad t > 0 \tag{6}$$

$p_{1'0}(t)$ is non - decreasing.

Dem

It is enough to note, according to (5), that $\frac{d}{dt}p_{1'0}(t) = p_{00}(t)\big(1 - G(t)\big)\big(h(t) - \lambda G(t)\big)$.■

Obs

- If the rate at which the services end is lesser or equal than the customers' arrival rate, $p_{1'0}(t)$ is non- decreasing.
- For the M|M|∞ system, exponential service times, $h(t) = {}^{1}/_{\alpha}$ and (6) is equivalent to

$$\rho \leq 1 \tag{7}$$

Equation (6) shows that if either the recycling or the dismantling rate is greater or equal than the rate at which the motorcars become idle, the probability that the system is empty at instant *t*, meaning it that there is no idle motorcars, does not decrease with *t*. So the system has a tendency to become balanced as far as time goes on.

Denoting $\mu(1',t)$ and $\mu(0,t)$ the distributions given by (3) and (1) mean values, respectively,

$$\mu(1',t) = \sum_{n=1}^{\infty} n p_{1'n}(t) = \sum_{n=1}^{\infty} n G(t) p_{00}(t) + \sum_{n=1}^{\infty} n p_{0n-1}(t)(1 - G(t)) =$$

$$G(t)\mu(0,t) + (1 - G(t))\sum_{j=0}^{\infty}(j+1)p_{0j}(t) = \mu(0,t) + (1 - G(t)),$$

Resulting in

$$\mu(1',t) = 1 - G(t) + \lambda\int_0^t [1 - G(v)]dv \tag{8}$$

Proposition 2

If $G(t) < 1, t > 0$ continuous and differentiable and

$$h(t) \leq \lambda, \quad t > 0 \tag{9}$$

$\mu(1',t)$ is non - decreasing.

Dem

It is enough to note, according to (5), that $\frac{d}{dt}\mu(1',t) = (1-G(t))(\lambda - h(t))$. ■

Obs

- If the rate at which the services end is lesser or equal than the customer's arrivals rate, $\mu(1',t)$ is non-decreasing.
- For the M|M|∞ system (9) is equivalent to

$$\rho \geq 1 \tag{10}$$

Equation (9) shows that if either the recycling or the dismantling rate is lesser or equal than the rate at which the motorcars become idle, the mean number of motor cars in the system does not decrease with time. This means that the system has a propensity to become unbalanced as far as time goes on.

Note that for exponential service times considered in both criteria, the condition $\rho \leq 1$ guarantees the system will balance.

Cost-Benefit Analysis

In the previous section it is seen how important is the role of $h(t)$ and λ to monitor the way the system of recycling and dismantling motor cars is managed. To perform a cost-benefit analysis based on the previous model presented, further consider p as the probability, or percentage, of the motorcars arrival for recycling being $1\text{-}p$ to be the same as the dismantling. Call $h_i(t), c_i(t)$ and $b_i(t), i = 1,2$ the hazard rate function, the mean cost and the mean benefit, respectively for recycling when $i = 1$ and for dismantling when $i = 2$.

So the total cost per unit of time for motor cars recycling and dismantling is:

$$C(t) = pc_1(t)\lambda + (1-p)c_2(t)\lambda \tag{11}$$

and the benefit per unit of time resulting from recycling and dismantling is:

$$B(t) = b_1(t)h_1(t) + b_2(t)h_2(t). \tag{12}$$

From an economic point of view, for it to be quite extreme, it must be $B(t) > C(t)$ for any t. So recycling is advantageous if

$$b_1(t) > \max\left\{\frac{pc_1(t)\lambda + (1-p)c_2(t)\lambda - b_2(t)h_2(t)}{h_1(t)}, 0\right\}. \tag{13}$$

If $G_1(t)$ and $G_2(t)$ are both exponential, with means α_1 and α_2, respectively, (13) becomes

$$b_1(t) > \max\left\{(pc_1(t) + (1-p)c_2(t))\rho_1 - \frac{\alpha_1 b_2(t)}{\alpha_2}, 0\right\}, \tag{14}$$

with $\rho_1 = \lambda\alpha_1$.

Dismantling is advantageous if

$$b_2(t) > \max\left\{\frac{pc_1(t)\,\lambda + (1-p)c_2(t)\,\lambda - b_1(t)h_1(t)}{h_2(t)}, 0\right\}. \tag{15}$$

If $G_1(t)$ and $G_2(t)$ are both exponential, with means α_1 and α_2, respectively, (15) becomes

$$b_2(t) > \max\left\{(pc_1(t) + (1-p)c_2(t))\rho_2 - \frac{\alpha_2 b_1(t)}{\alpha_1}, 0\right\}, \tag{16}$$

with $\rho_2 = \lambda\alpha_2$.

In a more global approach and more realistic and not so extreme, consider a period of time with length *T*. Then it must be $\int_0^T B(t)dt > \int_0^T (T)dt$. It is not so simple to deal analytically with this expression as in the former situation. But, considering that $b_1(t)$ and $b_2(t)$ are both constant in $[0, T]$ with values b_1 and b_2, respectively, it is obtained

– Recycling is advantageous if

$$b_1 > \max\left\{\frac{\lambda[pC_1^T + (1-p)C_2^T] - b_2 \ln\frac{1-G_2(0)}{1-G_2(T)}}{\ln\frac{1-G_1(0)}{1-G_1(T)}}, 0\right\} \tag{17}$$

– Dismantling is advantageous if

$$b_2 > \max\left\{\frac{\lambda[pC_1^T + (1-p)C_2^T] - b_2 \ln\frac{1-G_1(0)}{1-G_1(T)}}{\ln\frac{1-G_2(0)}{1-G_2(T)}}, 0\right\} \tag{18}$$

where $C_i^T = \int_0^T c_i(t)dt, i = 1{,}2$.

Conclusion

To apply this model and obtain useful conclusions, it is important to check if the customer's arrival occurs according to a Poisson process - see for instance Kelly (1979). In this kind of problem this is easily accepted, in general, due to the huge quantity of motorcars where owners certainly will look for these services. It is essential to estimate λ and *h(t)* to get specific conclusive results about the system from available data. A correct estimate of λ will depend also on the arrival process to follow the Poisson process. Certainly the way to decide the λ mean estimate for a given period of time is easy since the arrival rate will depend on time. Also, it is clear that with very large populations, such as the ones dealt with in these situations, the estimation of $h(t)$ is in general technically complicated. Then the best solution is to estimate $h(t)$ directly instead of estimating the service time distribution first followed by the consequent computation of $h(t)$. For exponential service times all this is particularly easy since in this case $h(t)$ does not depend on t.

From the cost-benefit analysis performed, based on this model, the conclusion is that there are minimum benefits above which, from an economic point of view, both dismantling and recycling are advantageous. And the most advantageous is the one for which this minimum benefit is the least. That is, in a broader perspective, an activity is more efficient if it corresponds to a lower minimum level for the minimum advantageous benefit.

For the results presented above, the situation of negative individual benefits is excluded because of individual self-interest. In fact, the minimum benefits above which, from an economic point of view, both dismantling and recycling are advantageous are positive according to the restrictions considered. Also, if restrictions are not considered, the possibility of not being positive is admissible. This situation reflects the possibility of an individual self-sacrificing to favour the collective benefit.

The model presented here contributes to a better understanding of this kind of problems. It may be applied, with modifications, for example to study other social economic and financial problems such as unemployment (Ferreira et al., 2011), health (Ferreira, 2014a; 2014b), pensions' funds (Ferreira et al., 2012) or investment projects (Ferreira et al., 2011). An interesting application is to repair systems, concerning technical and economic features, which are considered in Ferreira (2003), Ferreira (2013), Ferreira, Andrade and Filipe (2009), Ferreira, Filipe and Coelho (2008) and Ferreira, Filipe and Coelho (2014).

REFERENCES

DOI:10.4028/www.scientific.net/AMR.1036.1043.

Ferreira, M. A. M. (1995). *Comportamento Transeunte e Período de Ocupação de Sistemas de Filas de Espera sem Espera*. PhD Thesis discussed in ISCTE, Lisboa.

Ferreira, M. A. M. (2003). *A two echelons repair system modelled through infinite servers queues*. Proceedings of the 21st International Conference Mathematical Methods in Economics 2003, 75-80.

Ferreira, M. A. M. (2013). Modelling and differential costs evaluation of a two echelons repair system through infinite servers nodes queuing networks. *Applied Mathematical Sciences* 7, 112, 5567-5576.DOI:10. 12988/ams.2013.38478.

Ferreira, M. A. M. (2014a). *The pandemic period length modelled through queue systems*. Proceedings of the International Conference Quantitative Methods in Economics (Multiple Criteria Decision Making XVII), 43-47. Virt, Slovakia.

Ferreira, M. A. M. (2014b). $M|G|\infty$ queue system in the pandemic period study. *Applied Mathematical Sciences* 8, 73, 3641-3646. DOI:10. 12988/ams.2014.45328.

Ferreira, M. A. M., Andrade, M., Filipe, J. A., Coelho, M. (2011). Statistical queuing theory with some applications. *International Journal of Latest Trends in Finance and Economic Sciences*, 1, 4,190-195.

Ferreira, M. A. M., Andrade, M., Filipe, J. A., Selvarasu, A. (2009). The management of a two echelons repair system using queuing networks with infinite servers queues. *Annamalai International Journal of Business and Research*, 1, 32-37.

Ferreira, M. A. M., Andrade, M., J. A. Filipe (2009). Networks of queues with infinite servers in each node Applied to the management of a two echelons repair system. *China-US Business Review*, 8, 8, 39-45.

Ferreira, M. A. M., Andrade, M., J. A. Filipe (2012). Studying pensions funds through an infinite servers nodes network: a theoretical problem. *Journal of Physics: Conference Series* 394, 1, Article number 012035. DOI: 10.1088/1742-6596/394/1/012035.

Ferreira, M. A. M., Filipe, J. A., Chavaglia, J. (2014). Nanotechnology and processes the nano-photovoltaic panels. *Advanced Materials Research*, 837, 694-698. DOI:10.4028/www.scientific.net/AMR. 837.694.

Ferreira, M. A. M., Filipe, J. A., Coelho, M. (2008). A queue model for motor vehicles dismantling and recycling in a scarce energy ambience. *APLIMAT - Journal of Applied Mathematics*, 1, 1, 337-343.

Ferreira, M. A. M., Filipe, J. A., Coelho, M. (2014). Performance and differential costs analysis in a two echelons repair system with infinite servers queues. *Advanced Materials Research*, 1036, 1043-1048.

Ferreira, M. A. M., Filipe, J. A., Coelho, M., Andrade, M. (2008). *An infinite servers model for motor vehicles dismantling and recycling in a scarce energy ambience*. Proceedings of the International Conference Quantitative Methods in Economics (Multiple Criteria Decision Making XIV), 178-186. High Tatras, Slovakia.

Filipe, J. A., Coelho, M, Ferreira, M. A. M. (2006). *O Drama dos Recursos Comuns - À Procura de Soluções para os Ecossistemas em Perigo*. Edições Sílabo, Lisboa.

Hardin, G. (1968). The Tragedy of the Commons. *Science*, 162, 124-148.

Kelly, F. P. (1979). *Reversibility and Stochastic Networks*. John Wiley and Sons, New York.

Kunstler, J. H. (2006). *O Fim do Petróleo - O Grande Desafio do Século XXI*. Editorial Bizâncio, Lisboa.

Ross, S. (1983). *Stochastic Processes*. John Wiley and Sons, New York.

Takács, L. (1962). *An Introduction to Queueing Theory*. Oxford University Press, New York.

Tilton, J. E. (2001), Depletion and the Long-Run Availability of Mineral Commodities. In: *Mining, Minerals and Sustainable Development*. Vol. 14, March, International Institute for Environment and Development.

In: Towards a Society with a More Fair Economy
Editors: J. A. Filipe, N. Nagopoulos, K. Rontos et al.
ISBN: 978-1-63482-900-7

Chapter 10

EXPLORING ENVIRONMENTAL CONVERGENCE IN COMPLEX SOCIO-ECOLOGICAL SYSTEMS: A BRIEF COMMENTARY

Luca Salvati*

Consiglio per la Ricerca in Agricoltura e l'analisi dell'economia agraria (CRA), Rome, Italy

ABSTRACT

Processes leading to regional and local convergence in territorial and environmental issues have been reviewed in this paper through a literature analysis. Providing empirical evidence on this emerging phenomenon, recent studies on convergence in territorial variables encompass the single disciplines (economics, sociology, geography, planning). Convergence issues require an integrated view to be correctly understood and monitored over time. Assessing regional convergence in territorial and environmental phenomena contributes to clarify, for example, the evolution of complex processes of environmental degradation and its main socioeconomic drivers. Beta and sigma convergence concepts were introduced using various geographical scales of analysis. The use of homogeneous spatial scales from ecological, economic, and institutional perspectives were debated to underline implications for both research and policy. The causes of territorial convergence were then disentangled according to the economic characteristics of the studied area, and the implications this process has in land resource depletion were finally discussed.

Keywords: Environmental quality, convergence, geographical scale, policy implication

---

* Corresponding Author: Email: luca.salvati@entecra.it.

1. Introduction

Sustainable development involves important aspects of social, economic, and ecological relevance (Antle and Heidebrink, 1995; Steer, 1998). Several countries have undergone continuous economic growth over the last fifty years paying a cost in terms of reduced environmental quality and natural resource depletion (e.g. Aldy 2006, Ezcurra 2007).

The neoclassical growth model predicts the convergence phenomenon (Quah, 1996) which applies to poor economies that tend to grow faster than rich ones. This notion was generalised through the concept of 'conditional convergence' (Sala-i-Martin, 1996, 2002) which applies when the growth rate of an economy is positively related to the distance between the economy's level of income and its own steady-state (Barro and Sala-i-Martin, 2004). The two concepts coincide if a group of countries or regions tends to converge to the same steady-state (e.g. Mainardi, 2007). One way to test the convergence hypothesis is to check whether systems with similar characteristics (e.g. systems which are likely to converge to the same steady state) converge in an absolute sense. The convergence issue is a traditional research theme for growth economics, but it represents a meaningful concept in political matters, too.

Studies on regional convergence in territorial and environmental variables are meaningful in this direction (Neumayer, 2001). They provide basic information useful to design policies contrasting environmental degradation, which is triggered by both biophysical and socioeconomic variables and shows complex, often unpredictable, dynamics (Thornes, 2004). A simple, explorative framework may provide clear outputs which could represent the basis for more detailed, sophisticated models (Aldy, 2006, 2007; Kolejka and Marek, 2006; Ezcurra et al., 2007; Camarero et al., 2008).

In the last years assessment has taken place and evidence found in the convergence of demographic variables, life quality indicators, environmental governance and policy formulation among countries and/or regions (see Salvati et al., 2008a and references therein). By contrast, convergence in human pressure on the environment has less frequently assessed (see Neumayer, 2001; Aldy, 2006; Ezcurra, 2007 and references therein), especially in variables concerning the degradation/depletion of land resources (see the discussion in Salvati and Zitti, 2008b). In a context of climate change and increasing anthropogenic pressure on the ecosystem, filling this gap is meaningful as research on regional convergence in territorial variables provides crucial information to orient policies towards multi-scale and multi-domain applications (e.g. Salvati et al., 2008). For example, convergence in a given socio-environmental process may indicate that policy strategies carried out at different spatial scales with the objective to reduce disparities among countries (or regions) are effective (Neumayer 2001).

An in-depth investigation of the interactions between biophysical patterns and socioeconomic factors is required to delineate environmental degradation and the evolution of its main drivers (e.g. Salvati and Zitti 2008a). In such a context, (i) moving from cross-country to single-country studies mitigates the problems associated with data comparison from different countries (Vincent 1997), and (ii) focusing on scale issues allows to empirically analyse environmental phenomena whose knowledge may be influenced by the scale of observation, because they generally depend on drivers acting at different scales. The Environmental Kuznets Curve (EKC) supports the hypothesis that environmental quality

REFERENCES

Abdelgalil, E. A., Cohen, S. I., (2001). Policy modelling of the trade-off between agricultural development and land degradation: The Sudan case, *Journal of Policy Modelling*, Vol. 23, pp. 847-874.

Aldy, J. E., (2006). Per capita carbon dioxide emission: convergence or divergence?, *Environmental and Resource Economics*, Vol. 33, pp. 533-555.

Aldy, J. E., (2007). Divergence in State-Level Per Capita Carbon Dioxide Emissions, *Land Economics*, Vol. 83, pp. 353-369.

Antle, J. M., Heidebrink, G., (1995). Environment and Development: Theory and International Evidence, *Economic Development and Cultural Change*, Vol. 43, pp. 603-625.

Arbia, G., Paelinck, J. H. P., (2003). Economic convergence or divergence? Modelling the interregional dynamics of EU regions 1985-1999, *Geographical Systems*, 5, 1-24.

Arrow, K., Bolin, B., Costanza, R., Dasgupta, P., Folke, C., Holling, C. S., Jansson, B.-O., Levin, S., Mäler, K.-G., Perrings, C., Pimentel, D., (1995). Economic Growth, Carrying Capacity, and the Environment, *Science*, Vol. 268, pp. 520-521.

Baldazzi, B., Corrado, H.-C., Ferruzza, A., (1998). The quality of life in some local metropolitan labour markets in Italy, *Social Indicators Research*, Vol. 44, pp. 71-95.

Barro, R. J., Sala-i-Martin, X., (2004). *Economic growth*. Cambridge, Massachusetts: MIT Press.

Bimonte, S., Punzo, L. F., (2003). *Environmental policy options in the multi-regimes framework*, Quaderni n. 389, Dipartimento di Economia Pubblica, Università degli Studi di Siena.

Camarero, M., Picazo-Tadeo, A. J., Tamarit, C., (2008). Is the environmental performance of industrialized countries converging? A 'SURE' approach to testing for convergence, *Ecological Economics*, in press.

Castles, I., Henderson, D., (2003). The IPCC emission scenarios: an economic-statistical critique, *Energy and Environment*, Vol. 14, pp. 159-185.

Ciscar, J. C., Soria, A., (2000). Economic convergence and climate policy, *Energy Policy*, Vol. 28, pp. 749-761.

Dumanski, J., Pettapiece, W. W., McGregor, R. J., (1998). Relevance of scale dependent approaches for integrating biophysical and socio-economic information and development of agroecological indicators. *Nutrient Cycling in Agroecosystems*, 50, 13-22.

Ezcurra, R., (2007). Is there cross-country convergence in carbon dioxide emissions? *Energy Policy*, 35, 1363-1372.

Ezcurra, R., Pascual, P., Rapun, M., (2007). The spatial distribution of income inequality in the European Union, *Environment and Planning* A, Vol. 39, pp. 869-890.

Galeotti, M., (2007). Economic growth and the quality of the environment: taking stock, *Environment, Development and Sustainability*, Vol. 9, pp. 427-454.

Ibanez, J., Martinez Valderrama, J., Puigdefabregas, J., (2008). Assessing desertification risk using system stability condition analysis. *Ecological Modelling*, 213, 180-190.

Kok, K., Patel, M., Rothman, D. S., De Groot, R., (2004). *Multi-scale scenario development within Medaction.* In: P. Gagliardo, ed. Desertification: actors, research, policies. Società Geografica Italiana, Studi e Ricerche, no. 14, Rome.

Kolejka, J., Marek, D., (2006). *Sustainable land use convergence in border area of central Europe.* In: Environmental Security and Sustainable Land Use: With special reference to Central Asia. Springer Netherlands, pp. 183-198.

Mainardi, S., (2007). Resource exploitation and cross-region growth trajectories: nonparametric estimates for Chile, *Journal of Environmental Management*, Vol. 85, pp. 27-43.

Merrett, S., (2004). The potential role for economic instruments in drought management, *Irrigation and Drainage*, Vol. 53, pp. 375-384.

Mukherjee, S., Kathuria, V., (2006). Is economic growth sustainable? Environmental quality of Indian states after 1991, *International Journal of Sustainable Development*, Vol. 9, pp. 38-60.

Neumayer, E., (2001). Improvement without convergence: pressure on the environment in European union countries, *Journal of Common Market Structure*, 39, 927-937.

Papyrakis, E., Gerlagh, R., (2007). Resource abundance and economic growth in the United States, *European Economic Review*, Vol. 51, pp. 1011-1039.

Quah, D. T., (1996) Empirics for economic growth and convergence, *European Economic Review*, Vol. 40, pp. 1353-1375.

Rubio, J. L., Bochet, E., (1998). Desertification indicators as diagnosis criteria for desertification risk assessment in Europe. *Journal of Arid Environment* 39, 113-120.

Sala-i-Martin, X., (2002). *15 Years of new growth economics: What have we learnt?* Columbia University, Department of Economics, Discussion Paper Series, No. 0102-47.

Sala-i-Martin, X., (1996). Regional cohesion: evidence and theories of regional growth and convergence. *European Economic Review*, 40, 1325-1352.

Salvati L., Zitti, M., Ceccarelli, T., (2008), Integrating economic and environmental indicators in the assessment of desertification risk: A case study, *Applied Ecological and Environmental Research*, 6, 129-138.

Salvati, L., Zitti, M., (2005). Land degradation in the Mediterranean basin: linking bio-physical and economic factors into an ecological perspective, *Biota*, Vol. 5, pp. 67-77.

Salvati, L., Zitti, M., (2008a). Regional convergence of environmental variables: Empirical evidences from land degradation, *Ecological Economics*, in press.

Salvati, L., Zitti, M., (2008b). Natural resource depletion and the economic performance of local districts: suggestions from a within-country analysis, *International Journal of Sustainable Development and World Ecology*, accepted for publication.

Salvati, L., Zitti, M., (2007). Territorial disparities, natural resource distribution, and land degradation: a case study in southern Europe, *Geojournal*, Vol. 70, pp. 185-194.

Salvati, L., Zitti, M., (2008c). Assessing the impact of ecological and economic factors on land degradation vulnerability through multiway analysis, *Ecological Indicators*, in press.

Salvati, L., Zitti, M., (2008d). Sustainability and weighting of ecological and economic indicators: Exploring the importance of various components of a synthetic index, *Ecological Economics*, forthcoming.

Slottje, D., Nieswiadomy, M., Redfearn, M., (2001), Economic inequality and the environment, *Environmental Modelling & Software*, Vol. 16, pp. 183-194.

Steer, A., (1998). Making development sustainable, *Advances in Geo-ecology*, Vol. 31, pp. 857-865.

Tanrivermis, H., (2003). Agricultural land use change and sustainable use of land resources in the Mediterranean region of Turkey. *Journal of Arid Environment*, 54, 553-564.

Thornes, J. B., (2004). *Stability and instability in the management of Mediterranean desertification,* In: J. Wainwright and M. Mulligan (eds.) Environmental modelling: finding simplicity in complexity, pp. 303-315. Wiley, Chichester.

Vincent, J. R., (1997). Testing for Environmental Kuznets curves within a developing country. *Environmental and Development Economics*, 2, 417-431.

Zuindeau, B., (2007). Territorial equity and sustainable development, *Environmental Values*, Vol. 16, pp. 253-268.

Case Studies Worldwide

In: Towards a Society with a More Fair Economy
Editors: J. A. Filipe, N. Nagopoulos, K. Rontos et al.
ISBN: 978-1-63482-900-7

Chapter 11

CASE STUDY: SOCIAL ECONOMY AND ENTREPRENEURSHIP: THE CASE OF GREECE (OR EVIDENCES FROM GREECE)

Kostas Rontos and Nikos Nagopoulos*
Department of Sociology, University of the Aegean,
Mytilene, Greece

ABSTRACT

Main goal of this article is to examine the various aspects of the role of social economy in regional development and the promotion of investments in social entrepreneurship. The article attempts to approach possibilities and successful actions to develop an institutional, regulatory, administrative and financial framework in Greece, which could promote different forms of social economy as well as the establishment and the operation of social enterprises. To this end, it is very important to examine integrated initiatives, partnerships, networks and operations taking place at local level, as a result of efficient regional planning for social entrepreneurship, as well as to implement actions in the field of social economy. An important issue is the specification of the criteria for the identification and verification of Social Cooperative Enterprises, which are trying to develop modern methods and Tools. Finally, the article enters into the debate, according to which local Councils, with an extended participation of local community organizations and market players, may develop thematic dialogues, utilize specific research material for social development and economic growth of regions and find ways to encourage labour market demand and establish social enterprises at a local level.

Keywords: Regional Development, Endogenous Growth, Social Solidarity

---

* Corresponding Author, Email: *n.nagopoulos@soc.*aegean.gr.

1. Introduction

The implementation of a new development model, based on the social economy and social entrepreneurship, involves all the local benefits (physical, social, economic resources) of the regions, with the simultaneous activation of all local actors (local authorities, institutional and non-governmental organizations, local businesses, human capital, etc.), in order to create a form of development with activities and cooperatives in crucial sectors of the local social economy (small enterprises, alternative forms of tourism, etc.).

An important success factor for the reversal of the traditional development model is the strengthening of "regional awareness" of the citizens of the region. This is achieved through better understanding of regional issues and broader support of local and regional interests.

To this end, the Greek crisis can be addressed through actions and successful practices at the regional level, with the development of new forms of social entrepreneurship.

2. Institutional Framework in Greece and Recent Legislation for Social Economy

As far as Greece is concerned, it is a common view that Social Economy is not a "distinct field" as deficit or the indeterminacy of political design to create a functional and flexible framework that provides policy, institutional and administrative support of initiatives. This is also confirmed by the fact that this sector does not appear in any of the official statistics as a separate category, something that also confirms that it is stereotypically often equated to charity.

And, of course, these stereotypes, negative or underlying, sometimes hinder the proper promotion of the sector and the development of partnerships with financial scope among agencies of social economy and private sector agencies. Thus, it remains an area that largely defines and conceptualizes itself in ad hoc initiatives and types of interventions that integrate the key features of social development primarily at regional and local level.

These are activities that integrate the whole grid of the activities of their interventions mostly in European Directives that are implemented through transnational shapes and partnerships and maintain operational and partly institutional legitimacy of European policies, or, at least, seek through them to identify these activities as integrated in social economy.

From the above, it becomes clear that knowledge and data that exist in this area are not only incomplete but also limited and scattered and do not fall into a single logical and political constitution so to be classified and researched with the same methodology; a substantial institutional consultation with civil society is not to be found either. It is truly astonishing that, whereas such initiatives – in addition to the benefits that have been discussed previously - help address serious problems, such as unemployment, marginalization, social exclusion and discrimination, domestic political reality has yet to lay seriously the foundations for an institutional treatment and a regulatory framework for the organization and operation of a sector, which - due to the institutional ambiguity[1] that surrounds it and the

[1] It should be noted that Law 2716/99 that is limited to Social Cooperatives Ltd provides a variety of supportive regulations such as: tax-exemption, potential concession for use of movable and immovable property by a public entity (NPDD in Greek), contracts of privileged status, preferential employment status for vulnerable

absence of favourable supporting framework - cannot achieve those returns that could have been predicted.

Thus, it is not surprising that many of these initiatives either exhaust their potential by being cancelled during the course, or face problems with renewal, public recognition and their linkage with broader production systems and organizations or state enterprises. However, Local Councils of Social Entrepreneurship have been established under the Community (EU) Initiatives, and partnerships and network operators at local level have been consolidated so that the social sector would be strengthened and the exclusion from the labour market of vulnerable groups would be fought against. Local Councils, with an extended participation of local community organizations and market players, may develop thematic dialogue, utilize specific research material for social development and economic growth of regions and think how to encourage labour market demand and establish social enterprises at a local level.

Certain criteria should be also specified: how to identify and verify social enterprises, how to develop modern methods and tools so that social enterprises are funded by and networked with public and private sectors and local authorities, as well as how to explore the potential that social enterprises are given contracts by public and private agencies.

Among others, historical, cultural and economic conditions explain why civil society has yet to find fertile ground in Greece. The very concept of cooperativism and its practice, which is the heart of social economy, has not been expanded particularly out of the agricultural sector, whereas a small share is held by cooperative banks that have created specific financing product of alternative micro-credit, through which small loans are provided to financially weak business persons and even a smaller share is held by health funds and cooperative manufacturing organizations.

Despite the flaws of the institutional framework within the context of Community Initiatives, local Councils of Social Entrepreneurship were established in 2005 to consolidate partnerships and networks of agencies at local level in order to strengthen the social sector and to fight against the exclusion of vulnerable groups from the labour market.

Local Councils with an enlarged participation of bodies of local society and market can develop thematic dialogue, make use of specific research material for social and economic development of regions,[2] and can both elaborate ways to stimulate demand in the labour market and establish social enterprises at local level.

It should be noted that the National Strategic Reference Framework 2007-2013[3] aims to strengthen regional planning for social entrepreneurship and to implement actions in social economy by financing integrated initiatives towards this direction. That is a reality that has made it imperative to develop institutional, regulatory, administrative and financial framework in our country so that social economy is promoted and the establishment and operation of social enterprises are facilitated.

A kind of Social Enterprise was established in Greece in 1999; this enterprise was in the legal form of cooperatives, retaining elements of multi-partnership and having heterogeneous

groups. Apart from the aforementioned, women's cooperatives and social enterprises of various legal forms that have been developed in our country for the last 15 years, either they are led to become idle or to close down, or simply to operate as nonprofit corporations or charities.

[2] See EC (2012) Eurostat regional yearbook 2012. Luxembourg, Office for Official Publications of the European Communities, Rontos K. (ed.) (2012): Regional planning Issues and spatial analysis. Methods, tools and support systems, Benos, Athens, Petrakos G/ Psycharis G. (2004): Regional Development in Greece, Athens, Kritiki.

[3] NSRF: 2007-2013

partners such as Social Cooperatives Limited (Koi.SPE, in Greek), in accordance with Article 12 of Law 2716/1999. These enterprises integrated in work people suffering from chronic and severe mental disorders. There were also enterprises established in the legal form of agricultural cooperatives to develop agrotourism activities, mainly by women.

Depending on their specific purpose, Social Cooperative Enterprises (Koi.S.Ep. in Greek) are divided in the following three categories:

a) Social Cooperative Enterprises of Integration, which involve the integration of economic and social life of people belonging to vulnerable groups. Social Cooperatives Limited (Koi.SPE, in Greek) are included here;
b) Social Cooperative Enterprises of Social Care, which relate to the production and supply of products and services, social welfare and health care to specific vulnerable groups; and
c) Social Cooperative Enterprises of Collective and Productive Purpose, which relate to the production of products and services to meet the needs of the collectivity (culture, environment, ecology, education, public utilities, utilization of local products, preserving traditional activities and professions, and other) that promote local and collective interest and employment, as well as to strengthen social cohesion through economic and social development initiatives.

Twelve years after the implementation of Law 2716/1999, the Social Cooperative Enterprises (Koin.S.Ep) were established as the agency of social economy, with the new Law 4019/2011. They are a civil partnership with a social purpose and have a statutory commercial license. Members of the Koin.S.Ep. can be either natural persons or natural persons and legal entities that participate in them with a vote, regardless of the number of cooperative shares they hold. It has been regulated so that the Koin.S.Ep. may cooperate with each other having as an object, for example, the exchange of services or the implementation of programmes funded by national, European or international organizations, in accordance with the statutory purposes. The Koin.S.Ep. can collaborate by creating joint ventures and cooperatives, associations, and European cooperatives or European groups. It should be noted that the profits of the Social Cooperative Enterprise are not distributed to its members, unless those members are employees of this enterprise. The profits are allocated annually by 5% to create a reserve; they are allotted by up to 35% to employees of the enterprise as a productivity incentive, as defined in its statute, and the rest is for the activities of the enterprise and the creation of new jobs.

The resources of the Koin.S.Ep. consist of the enterprise's capital, donations of third parties, revenues from the utilization of its property, income from its business activities, from funds granted by the Public Investment Programme, the European Union, international or national organizations or Local Authorities of 1st and 2nd grade, income from other programmes, capital from endowments, donations and concessions to use assets and any other income from development activities.

Both Koin.S.Ep.and Koi.SPE have access to funding from the Social Economy Fund, which has been established by the joint decision of the Ministers of Finances, Development, Competitiveness and Shipping, and Labour and Social Security, as well as by the National Fund for Entrepreneurship and Development. Further, they can be embedded in programmes that support entrepreneurship and in programmes of the National Organization for the

Employment of the Labour Force (OAED, in Greek) that support employment, as well as in any active employment policies.

3. Recommendations for the Development of Social Economy in the Greek Regions

As part of the assessment of findings and identification of good "bottom-up" practices so that decision-making centers are influenced, it is illustrated that in all policy proposals the focus on Regionalism as a privileged and living space of creation and operation of social enterprises has been pronounced.

The development of Social Economy could be achieved through the following policies:

- Enhancing the access to traditional and modern means and funding mechanisms, such as development laws in the Credit Guarantee Fund for Small and Very Small Enterprises (E.T.E.AN. S.A, in Greek) and Programmes to support entrepreneurship in SMEs;
- Mapping agencies and social partners of Social Economy and statistically monitoring the relevant activity;
- Classifying and documenting individual economic activities in the field;
- Implementing transactional mechanisms that can facilitate the consumption of services of Social Economy;
- Implementing Social Performance Clauses in public procurement; and, finally, by
- Intervening to enhance the recognition of the role of Social Economy in Regional Development.

On this basis, it should be noted that efforts to develop initiatives of Social Economy actors in Greece are found to be against significant institutional problems, including the inability to access traditional and modern instruments and financing mechanisms. Women's cooperatives, urban non-profit organizations of social (or quasi-social) purpose, urban cooperatives, cooperatives of Law 2716/99, NGOs with business activities, open and close their lifecycle without having met even the usual and conventional financing tools of a small business, using up free grants from European co-funded projects.

In order for any corporate action to be taken, the current economic conjuncture requires some kind of aid, either through state or through financial agencies. So today, while the state has developed corresponding tools for financial support (development laws for large enterprises, Guarantee Fund for Small and Very Small Enterprises, entrepreneurship support programs for SMEs, etc.) for almost all forms of formal business activities, nevertheless, no aid is provided in the field of Social Economy, because of its particular features.[4] Moreover, social enterprises face exclusion from the classical banking system, due to the fact that they fail in providing guarantees for their usually low returns of capital and their risky viability. In any case, there is a need to develop such new activities that will greatly contribute to meeting

[4] See Institute of Social Innovation: System of Social Control and Evaluation of Social Enterprises. Study in the frame of the project: Social Business Ability for the fighting of exclusion-From Solidarity to Market Success- of CIP Equal, 2004.

basic and critical local needs, by utilizing local capacity, and at the same time they will give space so that their initiatives will be fully fledged and the local community will participate in these activities.

Based on the aforementioned, the obstacles of financing social enterprises can be summarized as follows:

- Exclusion from the classical banking system due to: the charitable and non-profit character of social, a fact that leads partly in a risky viability of low returns on capital and failure in providing guarantees;
- Exclusion from co-funded programmes due to the lack of information about the availability of relevant programmes, the lack of expertise in drafting a proposal and the failure in meeting the expenses of their own participation;
- Lack of highly experienced management and expertise so that they can claim and use modern methods and tools for funding;
- Reservation to incur high risk venture (in terms of borrowing);
- Lack of business plan development to clearly determine and plan financing needs;

However, the need for financial instruments suitable for the specific needs of agencies being active in the field of Social Economy in Greece has been made explicit by agencies of implementation.[5]

After these mechanisms and methods have been examined and both the existing experience and other information and data[6] have been taken into consideration, the following financial tools and initiatives are suggested:

- A broader legal coverage and an integrated statutory function of principles at European and national level for social enterprises, foundations, mutual societies and associations;
- On the basis of the legal status, clear regulatory definition of partnerships that may be operating legally as social enterprises;
- A complete mapping of agencies and social partners involved in social economy at the regional level;
- Classification and documentation of individual economic activities and promotion of representative bodies in the public consultation;
- A visible and distinct presence of social economy in official statistics;
- Criteria for determining how to do social business and how to promote investments in social entrepreneurship;
- In the effort to fight against poverty and social exclusion, support of social economy should be used as a tool for active inclusion, by facilitating access to funding programmes of the European Union in this field;[7]

---

[5] See Community Initiative EQUAL (Development Partnerships [DPs] and National Thematic Network) under both the 1st and the 2nd cycle of implementation. The Community Initiative EQUAL, through EQUAL Development Partnerships and the National Thematic Network (ETHD in Greek) for Social Economy, has contributed decisively to identifying the funding problems that social enterprises face and, through its actions, promotes alternative mechanisms and funding methods.

[6] Op. cit.

- Search for a facility framework for the development of solidarity investment funds;
- Support for the development of small enterprises in social economy based on the European Progress Microfinance Facility;
- Expansion of microcredit on vulnerable groups and facilitation of the creation of innovative social enterprises;
- Facilitation practices for trade agreements to entities, such as small and medium-sized social enterprises and voluntary community organizations, regardless of the legal form they use when hiring people;
- Configuration of a special loan of limited amount that fully meets the requirement for guarantees of security mechanism (TEMPE in Greek) and fully covers of its cost (interest free loan);
- Implementation of a transactional mechanism that facilitates consumption services of Social Economy through payment vouchers, aiming, on the one hand, at the widespread use of these services, and, on the other hand, addressing the problem of financing Social Economy agencies;
- Implementation of "social clause execution" in public procurement through the development of a Local Cooperation Agreement. In particular, the involvement of social enterprises in public procurement and services, through the operation of local partnerships expressed by tripartite Territorial Pacts for Employment and Social Economy (Administration - Contractors - Social Enterprise), is suggested;
- Interventions to enhance recognition of the contribution of forms of social economy and "do business intelligently and differently" in regional development.

4. Good Practices of Social Entrepreneurship in Disadvantaged Regions: The Northern Aegean Sea Example

Despite these problems in Greece and in some Regions, particularly in the North Aegean Region for instance,[8] a characteristic example of business development that belong to Social Economy sector are cooperatives (those of women mostly) that are mainly active in rural areas and their members are involved in the production process of the enterprise.

These are non-formal cooperative enterprises whose members, without necessarily owing the same business or farm, participate in the cooperative enterprise as employees, reaping reward from this work and dividend tax on distributed profits. This last feature makes these cooperatives distinct from other rural and urban ones, whose members sell their products through these cooperatives or obtain raw materials from them. Cooperatives of this type have been operating more than about three decades providing employment opportunity for women in rural and often deprived areas.

Nevertheless, these enterprises had been operating out of necessity – due to the absence, until recently, of a specific institutional framework - as classical cooperatives. For these

[7] EC (2004) *Joint Report on social exclusion*. Luxembourg, Office for Official Publications of the European Communities, EC (2007) *Cohesion policy 2007-13: Commentaries and official texts*. Luxembourg, Office for Official Publications of the European Communities.

[8] See Spilanis, I. 2013. Strategy for Insular Area and Development Planning 2014-2020. NGANP, Laboratory of Local and Insular Development University of the Aegean. 1st National Development Conference 2014-20, Athens, 04/04/13.

aspects to be considered and to be had in account when CSR is studied. This study discusses the implications of CSR for economic development, environmental sustainability and social welfare in five countries.

Keywords: Social Responsibility, Sustainable Development, Environmental Sustainability, Caixa Geral de Depósitos, TechnoLogica, Vale, Indian Oil, COCOMAT

11.2.1. Introduction

According to a basic principle of modern programmatic strategic planning businesses as productive-economic entities along with the profit seek to attain, to involve and to retain other elements that determine any form of social organization. In this sense, the efficiency of entrepreneurship in a given organizational environment serves apart from efficiency and sustainability, basic social needs and aspirations, so that firms become organizations of individuals interacting and constitute the most numerous groups on a social level corresponding to systems of coordinated and organized action.

High level of specialization – which characterizes the structure and coordination of organizations – as opposed to diffused and volatile relations among unorganized individuals, makes each organization a sociological unit of significance comparable to a biological organism (J. March & H. Simon: 1993, pp. 79-106). The simplistic and reductive practice of these entrepreneurship forms that ignore the complex issues of best management practices and satisfaction of the workforce has equated objectives with short-term profitability and simply tried to impose the adaptation of the human factor on the imperatives of technological rationality.

Initially, radical changes in the process of mass production aiming at maximizing profit did not only remained indifferent in new forms of human misery, due to the acceleration of production factors, but also unprepared to follow new developments in the field of technology, information and their impact on society, labor relations and the environment, which demand a reconfiguration of relations within organizational business structures. In this way, the openness of enterprises was in the service of an economic theory which placed emphasis on increasing business efficiency through a uniquely maximizing entrepreneurial process, without giving particular importance to the fact that decision-making process as a collective activity serves as a balancing mechanism for both participants in organizational structures and the broader social and environmental conditions. For example, issues related to workplace discrimination and the quality of working life, as well as abusive practices of many enterprises, contributed to a growing exacerbation of problems. Furthermore, prolonged exploitation of natural resources, incalculable environmental consequences, as well as enormous social and regional disparities increased skepticism on the unimpeded growth and the unregulated sector of entrepreneurial activity.

In view of all these dangers, there has been a need to redefine the concept of business profit so to minimize any negative consequences on social cohesion and the preservation of ecological balance. Considering this, Corporate Social Responsibility (CSR) got a very relevant role in the organizations and nowadays is important enough to make that organizations put very challenging objectives in this area. Many companies feel, in fact, a strong need of commitment with society and environmental concerns. This can happen when a company seeks to reconcile various stakeholders' demands and needs, while achieving a balance acceptable by all sides (employees, local communities, customers, suppliers, public authorities, competitors and society as a whole) (COM (2001) 366, (2002) 347, COM (2011) 681). The European Commission encourages enterprises to voluntarily incorporate social, environmental and ethical concerns into their business operations and core strategy in collaboration with their stakeholders.

11.2.2. Theoretical Background

The Concept of Corporate Social Responsibility

Aguinis (2011:855) defines Corporate Social Responsibility as "context-specific organizational actions and policies that take into account stakeholders' expectations and the triple bottom line of economic, social, and environmental performance." Corporate social responsibility is the continuing dedication to a responsible business, behaving in ethical premises and contributing to economic development, improving the life quality of workers, of their families and of local communities, aiming to have a positive contribution for the society as a whole. The organization must be active and lead to the economic, technological and human development. To that extent, its performance requires full respect for human rights, investment in personal enhancement, environmental protection, combating corruption, compliance with social norms and respect for ethical values and principles of the society in which it operates. In fact, companies are today much concerned with the image they have in the public opinion. When organizations commit with social responsibility, they intend to behave ethically, feel, a strong need of commitment with society and environmental concerns and intend to make business considering communities' interests.

If an organization intends to be socially responsible, many presumptions have to be considered and, parallel with all stages of decision-making procedure, ecological, social, ethical or even cultural concerns have to be taken in account. In this direction Social Responsibility consists of four components: the economic, legal, ethical and discretionary expectations of a society towards the local entrepreneurs and their business, with the enterprises usually choosing a particular layer to focus on. On the other hand, CSR remains consistent, thus sharing the same values with Sustainable Development and its implementation (Ebner and Baumgartner, 2006).

Sustainable Development entered the domain of public dialogue through the famous Brundtland Report which describes it as a "development that meets the needs of the present without compromising the ability of future generations to meet their own needs". From then on a new developmental perspective was born. Economic growth should be balanced with social and environmental criteria by aiming at including a number of goals such as the reduction of poverty, better resource management, social justice etc (United Nations 1987).

Since the inception of CSR various debates and practical examples have produced valuable insights into the concept. Each definition analyzes basic perspectives about CSR under a different aspect that, at the time, dominated public discussion about social responsibility (Rahman 2011). These perspectives can be categorized as: environmental protection; the relations between businesses and society; the relationships between stakeholders, employees and managers; and the impact of integrating CSR into business activity (Dahlsrud 2006). Besides these, there are also some underlying fundamental concepts at the core of each CSR definition, such as social investment, transparency and trust, public expectations about the wider social role of businesses, voluntarism and self interest (Asocio 2004). CSR has four main drivers: market, social, governmental, and globalization (Moon, 2007).

Linked with CSR in the academic literature and business practice, there are also other terms expediting a specific dimension of CSR. It has been estimated that, in Europe alone, there are over 50 different modules and over 40 labels for CSR, beside the synonyms and the multiplicity of the aligned terms that define the relationship between business and society (Visser 2005: 33 – 38, Melo Neto & Froes, 2001). For example, there are also corporate citizenship, corporate philanthropy and responsible business behavior, community development, community affairs, community relations, global citizenship and corporate social marketing. These, despite shared objectives as implemented, each set their own standards, theory and background (Marrewijk 2003).

CSR and Economic Development

CSR as a term refers to a new form of behavior encompassing moral, ethical and societal obligations. CSR is not enforced but rather depends on the commitment of the specific enterprise to an alternative set of principles besides profit. These principles, residing at the core of every implementation of CSR, are not sui generis; on the contrary, they are based on a slate of specific globally shared values expressed as *guidelines* by international accepted institutions, within which CSR is promoted and established (Wang 2008).

Within this spectrum, CSR guidelines are not solely derived from an abstract conceptual framework of CSR, but rather are products of its combination with the particular institutional context of social responsibility. Guidelines, as a term, came into the spotlight, and were established, through the OECD Declaration: *Guidelines for Multi National Enterprises* (OECD 2008).

It is no coincidence that one of the most important steps for promoting CSR was the UN Global Compact, a strategic policy initiative for businesses. Global Compact was launched in July 2000 as a practical framework for the development, implementation, and disclosure of sustainability policies and corporate practices, all designed to help and advance sustainable models of growth. By adopting it, business can ensure that economic development proceeds so its benefits are shared between economies and societies. For those businesses deciding to answer the call, there are a number of obligations about their operations and strategies, which used to be fulfilled in accordance with the ten universally accepted principles covering the areas of human rights, labor, environment and anti-corruption, which were developed in 2000[1]. According to these principles, businesses must, support the protection of human rights, ensuring that they are not abused. Also they must uphold freedom of association and the effective recognition of the right to collective bargaining (syndicates etc). Key concepts are:

[1] <<Overview of the UN Global Compact>>, http://www.unglobalcompact.org/ AboutTheGC/index.html (last access: 3/6/2012).

the elimination of all forms of forced, compulsory and child labor, and discrimination in respect of employment.

At the same time, the fight against corruption in all its forms (extortion, bribery etc) is of great importance. If a company accepts these terms its chief executive signs a commitment. This commitment is supposed to ensure that all the above principles will be integrated into the company's daily function and business culture, as well as the annual report of Global Compact. Today there are over 8,700 corporate participants and other stakeholders from over 130 countries, making it the largest voluntary corporate responsibility initiative[2].

In addition to these guidelines the implementation of social responsibility and CSR is ultimately based on the formulation of specific codes of conduct, rather than objective criteria. The formulation of these codes, practically, is not based only on guidelines, but mainly in the volunteering and discretion of the enterprise that issue them.

CSR and Environmental Sustainability

The environment also plays a major role; businesses must develop environmental friendly technologies and precautionary approaches to these kinds of challenges by promoting greater environmental responsibility (Kroetz, 1999). In this direction environmental accounting is the record of environmental assets. Paiva (2003) defines it as the activity of identifying data and records of environmental events, processing and generating information that assists the user serving as a parameter in his decision making. The role of environmental accounting is to provide regular information to internal and external users about the environmental events that caused changes in the assets of the respective entity, measured in currency.

For Ferreira (2003), the development of environmental accounting results from the need to provide information tailored to the needs of environmental management. The author states that the environmental accounting does not refer to a new accounting, but a set of information to report fairly, in economic terms, the actions of an entity that alters its assets. This set of information is no other accounts but a specialization. This is a new base and a new system of recognition and measurement of costs, including externalities.

For Bergamini Jr. (1999), environmental accounting aims the registration of the company's transactions that impact on the environment and their effects that affect or should affect the economic and financial position of the business, ensuring that costs, environmental assets and liabilities are accounted in accordance with generally accepted accounting principles or in its absence, with the generally accepted accounting practices and environmental performance and with the wide transparency that users of accounting information need.

For the Environmental Reporting Guidelines cited by Tinoco and Kraemer (2004), environmental accounting is a framework that quantitatively estimates the environmental conservation efforts in monetary terms. It is also a significant technique that may indicate the state of environmental conservation to stakeholders. This accounting is more ambitious than the traditional, since it aims to know the negative externalities and record, measure, assess and disclose all environmental events.

[2] <<Corporate Sustainability in The World Economy>>, http://www.unglobalcompact.org/docs/ news_events/ 8.1/GC_brochure_FINAL.pdf (last access: 1/6/2012).

Environmental event is any entity's interaction with the environment that generates economic consequences of present or future, in view of the regulatory standards or social responsibility that is subject to a specific company. Examples of environmental events have been spending on development or acquisition of technologies, machinery and antipollution equipment; search for waste reduction, employee training methods of clean production and the laws, raising revenue, as a consequence of materials recovery (recycling), among many others.

Tinoco and Kraemer (2004) list events and environmental impacts related to operational activities of various sectors that affect the assets and business continuity, quality of life, fauna, flora, rivers and seas, and that therefore shall be subject to registration, collection, measurement, evaluation and dissemination by the accounts, highlighting in particular:

- Coal Mining: causes impacts on the environment evidenced in the atmosphere, soil and surface water and groundwater.
- Steel: Degradation of water quality, which requires local water-dealing, construction of landfills, air pollution, pollution emissions from power plants, especially particulate matter, release of oils and greases, organic loading, soluble manganese, ammonia, etc. involving investments to control them.
- Other activities that also deserve mention: the production of lime, cane sugar, pulp and paper production and the oil industry.

According to Tinoco and Kraemer (2004), several advantages related to the use of accounting in the environmental focus may be pointed, such as:

- Measurement and allocation environmental costs, allowing a continuum of planning applications;
- Measurement of environmental liabilities;
- Intensive use of explanatory notes and environmental performance indicators;
- Being able to accurately verify the reductions in resources such as water, energy, soil and other potential physical environment;
- Making decisions based on the costs and benefits recorded in their own environmental accounting;
- Providing information and statements about the effectiveness and economic feasibility of the environmental actions;
- Publishing the social and environmental issues, creating transparency and social interest;
- Constant corrections of environmental actions, reducing the level of aggression against nature in the manufacture of products and services essential to the population,
- Quality data analysis and interpretation by both internal and external audiences, allowing an evaluation of the quality of environmental management of the entity.

The concept of sustainable development has emerged from studies of the United Nations on climate change in the early 1970s, as a response to the concern of humankind, given the environmental and social crisis that has befallen the world since the second half century. This concept, which seeks to reconcile the need for economic development of society to promote social development and respect for the environment, today is a vital topic on the agenda for discussion on a variety of organizations, and with different levels of organization society, as in discussions on the development of cities and regions, current day-to-day society. Follows a short presentation of the evolution of the concept since its inception to the present.

The year 1968, according to Camargo (2003) was the first serious sign of popular discontent with the model of industrial capitalism towards the end of its cycle, with the outbreak of student protest in the chain, started in Paris in May 1968, rising Berkeley, Berlin and Rio de Janeiro.

Breaking the walls of the economics bastion, environmentalism came to question the economic rationality in terms of its own criteria. More specifically, the new debate shows that, compared to several problems and dilemmas that industrial development poses, the solution or the way to overcome them may not require a new jolt, but the adoption of restrictive measures to increase economic production, which raises the idea of ecological rationality as the basic principle and limiting the economic rationality and self development.

The Club of Rome, an entity formed by intellectuals and businessmen, who were not environmentalists, was an initiative that grew out of discussions regarding the preservation of natural resources of the planet. He produced the first scientific studies about environmental preservation, which were presented between 1972 and 1974, and that related to four major issues that should be resolved in order to reach sustainability: control of population growth, control of industrial growth, lack of production food, and depletion of natural resources (Campbell, 2002).

Development and environment have merged on the concept of eco-development, which in the early 80's was supplanted by the concept of sustainable development that has been adopted as the official expression in UN documents, IUCN (International Union for Conservation of Nature) and WWF (World Wild Fund for Nature).

CSR and Social Welfare

A key concept for CSR is that of social justice and legitimacy, which motivates socially responsible behavior as a business practice. Social justice is expressed through a number of principles which are linked with cooperative activity and are not encountered in any other economic action.

Cooperative activity, social economy and CSR are close by definition, sharing the same set of values that distinguish them from wider and more usual profit-centered economic activities. Sustainability is the main platform, within which a number of values such as quality services, distribution of profits and measurement of the societal and environmental needs, are developed. Terms such as social economy, alternative entrepreneurship and social responsibility do not differ conceptually from each other, but remain consistent throughout their usage in alternative socio-economic discourse grounded on the same principles and focused on a different kind of development; social development; a development that utilizes inner societal relations and networks, as well as their interaction with other institutions. CSR is increasingly used as a framework for private sector involvement in poverty alleviation (Holliday et al., 2002; WBCSD, 2001).

Social economy and social entrepreneurship are just two of the terms used to describe the social development implementation of entrepreneurial activity. CSR, on the other hand, provides a certification that some of these values are integrated into the core of the business planning. However, this reassurance is not needed with cooperatives, as their very foundations are a result of the integration of community values in the modern economic context.

Despite their common conceptual ground, this does not mean that these terms are congruent. It can be argued that CSR expresses a standardization of the principles set by social development, towards a more business friendly set of values. That does not negate the fact that both terms are pioneers in social development. In the same time the pursuit of profit in general can be compatible with the adoption of principles of entrepreneurship that ensure a number of standards such as the quality of products, the position of workers and the wider social and environmental objectives (Nagopoulos, Rontos, Pantazidou, 2013).

Corporate Social Responsibility has clear implications for the EU's institutional framework, both as an instrument for social policy and of local development[3]. In July 2001, the Commission presented the Green Paper for the Promotion of a European framework for Corporate Social Responsibility, always in the light of the goals set in Lisbon. In this paper, great importance was given to the ability of enterprises to adjust to the local business climate and society. The main goal is social development through entrepreneurial innovations that would strengthen employment growth. Special emphasis is placed on consultation with the other social agencies, focusing on the creation of actual partnerships rather than just ephemeral cooperations (COM(2001) 366).

Accordingly, with the white paper on European Governance, partnerships are not just desirable, but necessary for the integration of enterprises into their local communities, whilst improving the business climate for the better utilization of their innovations (COM(2001) 428). Beside the institutional level, companies need to integrate CSR in their business core as a strategy for creating a positive image promoting the company in the communities and society as a whole, thus contributing to the collective welfare of the society.

In recent years, companies have increased the role of Corporate Social Responsibility in their activities. Progressively an increasing number of companies show to be concerned about their performance on this subject and about reaching their objectives involving CSR. The effectiveness of investment ventures does not contradict social welfare and inclusively enlarges the importance of the concept of collective profit. In this way, CSR has also become part of the same strategic business planning. Companies shall have self-regulating mechanisms to monitor responsibilities and to guarantee that ethical standards and international norms are assured.

The attempted change in the entrepreneurial goals of Corporate Social Responsibility is associated to the finding that the effectiveness of investment ventures does not contradict social welfare; on the contrary, it contributes to the concept of collective profit in it. In this way, CSR has also become part of the same strategic business planning. Over the time it has become conspicuous that socially responsible activity is limited neither to philanthropic activities nor the acceptance of legal obligations within the context of entrepreneurial business correctness; it is to satisfy all critical factors inside, such as human resources, labor relations and a range of factors related to consumers of products and services, suppliers, shareholders and the local community itself as a whole.

---

[3] <<European Dialogue>>, http://www.csreurope.org/pages/en/european_dialogue.html (last access: 26/5/2012).

Within this context and with a view to redefining key priorities, there has been a need to move towards an extended nature of the business beyond the idea of a purely economic entity and gradually incorporating an array of responsibilities towards society, confirming its socially responsible role and the fact that is constitutes an integral part of the society in which it operates.

Over the years, the concept of Corporate Social Responsibility has gained great importance, and its integration in the entrepreneurial policy is getting more and more necessary. Businesses have gradually realized that their increased productivity is connected with social responsibility shown by contributing to local, social and economic development and quality of life. Focusing on changes related to the infrastructure of enterprises concerns activities that take place within the company and contribute to proper management and human resource development, satisfaction on the part of management and employees with increased rights of participation, information and negotiation. Another important factor is the provision of a healthy and safe working environment that ensures the prevention of occupational accidents, equal opportunities and the harmonization of work and family life.

At the same time, fair recruitment procedures are ensured, as well as reward systems are developed that provide facilities for staff and their families, along with those required by law. Moreover, company training and professional development of staff is a major concern of a socially responsible company, so that employees maintain or improve the level of their skills whose immediate effect is a better performance. Moreover, as far as the impact on external environment is concerned, actions have been developed that go over beyond the boundaries of the enterprise, such as local communities, suppliers, customers, NGOs and the environment (Kyriakopoulos, 2004: 73).

The implementation of quality systems in the production process, credibility towards consumers in connection with investment in research and social development creates stability and trust relations, as most products are now adapted to some identified social needs. Moreover, the company can develop synergies with local communities and actively participate in designing development prospects relevant to business (chambers, associations), social (civil society) and natural environment (environmental associations). Participation in all of these sectors highlights the social profile of the company, its reputation and ultimately offers multiple benefits both for it and society in general.

11.2.3. Case Studies in Five Countries

Social Responsibility conceptualization is associated with the idea of companies deciding, in a voluntary base, to contribute for a fair society and a cleaner environment. In this framework the purpose of this chapter is to emphasize the perspective of the concept of corporate social responsibility. It is intended to analyze the strengths and weaknesses of the development of measures of social responsibility in this area and to observe examples of companies in five different countries, which have integrated crucial Principles of CSR: Caixa Geral de Depósitos (Portugal), Vale (Brazil), TechnoLogica (Bulgaria), Indian Oil (India) and COCOMAT (Greece). These are important companies concerned with the development of CSR activities and have some very interesting results in this area.

1. Portugal: CGD

Companies in Portugal have a long tradition in social intervention which remounts to the century XV and the foundation of the Mercies. Recently environmental concerns have contributed to the important performance and developments in CSR area in some important Portuguese companies. The development of many companies' strategies move across the CSR objectives.

In 2009, the Caixa Geral de Depósitos (from now on "Caixa" or "CGD") joined the United Nations Environmental Programme for the Financial Sector (UNEP FI) and became the first Portuguese bank to join this program. Since 1991, when it was created, the UNEP FI works the themes of sustainability in the financial sector with the aim of promoting good practices in the international financial institutions. This program reflects the recognition by the United Nations concerning the role of this sector in promoting sustainable development in that the processes of financial intermediation have repercussions in investment programs and, indirectly, in the allocation of natural resources. Sustainable Development is aimed at rational utilization of natural resources while maintaining capacity for renewal and ecological stability and respect for inter-generational solidarity.

According to the Brundtland Report (1987), sustainable development is one that meets present needs without compromising the ability of future generations to meet their needs. The accent on the issue of environmental sustainability and eliminating poverty are key aspects of this new vision, which is raising the banner of growth with quality of life based on three pillars: economy, society and environment, combined with the issues of governance. This adherence to the Program highlights Caixa concerns with the long term and confirmed its activity in supporting environmental sustainability. The basis is the conviction that the principles of Sustainable Development will form the basis of guidelines for future development. According to Mr. Faria de Oliveira, President of CGD, the times where structural changes are the ethical, environmental and social have been gaining weight. There are conditions to innovate and develop a better society and that membership of the UNEP-FI is a public commitment to sustainable development.

Note that this commitment of CGD with environmental sustainability and Corporate Social Responsibility in general seems to be, according to the statements of those responsible, the "genetic code" of the company / group. Built in 1880, the Caixa Económica Portuguesa, as then called, revealed at once their social concerns being intended to receive the savings of the less wealthy and providing a "nest egg" in the long term. By 1885, with the reform, Caixa Nacional de Aposentações (National Fund for Retirement) was born. After, Caixa was going to be established as Caixa Geral de Depósitos e Instituições de Previdência. In the Estado Novo regime, Caixa became a key institution in the operations of agricultural credit and industrial and in 1969 assumed a central role in housing loans. All these aspects permit to understand the role that public authorities were successively assigning to the Caixa Group, the largest institution of public nature on the financial sector.

According to the Office of Historical Heritage (Gabinete do Património Histórico) of CGD - "From the History of the institution over 133 years, Caixa served various aspects of Portuguese society, having had in mind the moral principle of social intervention." The great values that guide the work of Caixa and are the basis of its performance in terms of Social Responsibility is appreciable in the Code of Conduct issued by the institution and designated in the Good Government report. The commitment of Caixa is immediately identifiable, if we hold fast to its mission.

CGD's Mission is:

- Consolidating its position as a Group structuring the Portuguese financial system, distinguished by strong accountability and relevance of its contribution to economic development and to strengthen the competitiveness, innovation and internationalization of Portuguese companies;
- The stability and soundness of the financial system;
- As market leader, finding a balanced development between profitability, growth and financial strength, always within a prudent risk management.
- In this context, the Group's strategic priorities defined for the three years 2008-2010 included:
- The development of a human resources policy based on the pillars of Values and Culture of Enterprise, Knowledge, Communication and Performance;
- The supporting of the cultural and social development, promoting sustainability and being a reference to the Good Government in Portugal.
- There is a set of clearly identifiable concerns about the wishes that pursue social responsibility. These guidelines are then translated into 19 management priorities that include, among others:
- To boost the performance at the cultural level, and promote social sustainability;
- Proactive in developing best practice governance and ethical conduct.

The Code of Conduct establishes the rules and principles of professional conduct, being that the CGD staff on business principles of ethics, accuracy, truth, transparency, stability and security in relationships with customers. Caixa has adopted the principles of Good Governance and public sector undertakings (Council of Ministers Resolution 49/2007) and undertook initiatives for compliance including preparation of an annual business plan (JEE, 2011) continuing to implement their mission and objectives of company as well as a report of compliance with these objectives and integrating sustainability analysis in the economic, social and environmental.

Caixa 2010, Zero Carbon Strategy

By the end of the twentieth century humanity faces the challenge of climate change and overuse of natural resources, issues that dominate the UN agenda. This has promoted a fundamental discussion about a new development model. As we saw, according to the Brundtland Report this new model is identified with a development that meets present needs without compromising the ability of future generations to meet their own needs, ie, the Sustainable Development.

The scientific evidence of the phenomenon of climate change (refer to the reports of the IPCCIntergovernmental Panel on Climate Change): disasters, suggest a range of impacts that are not only environmental but also economic and social. The impacts are being felt in politics, markets and quality of life, affecting employees and customers of Caixa, worldwide.

So, to combat this we must build an economy with lower emissions of GHG (greenhouse gases) per unit of wealth created. For the EU this may represent, in the spirit of post-Kyoto negotiations a 20% reduction in emissions in 2020, compared with 1990 levels, or even 30% if accompanied by other developed countries. According to the negotiation of the G8 summit of June 2007 the reduction is expected to reach 50% by 2050 (U.S. listed.). It's clear that this new reality changes the logic of economic decision imposing new requirements for investment and risk management, while encouraging new markets (such as renewable energy) and adding new financial solutions. Caixa sees this and recognizes this as an opportunity.

In this line, promoted by Caixa since 2007, the program Caixa Zero Carbon is a strategic program that aims to help reduce the environmental impact of its activities while it induces good practices among its employees, customers and society in general. These are ambitious objectives involving:

- More knowledge about the carbon footprint / emission levels of the activities of Caixa to allow the setting of reduction goals;
- More economic and energy efficiency, including through the adoption of measures to gain the use of renewable energy,
- Monitoring and evaluation of performance at this level;
- And new business development to strengthen the group's position in the domestic market - with new solutions to support and incentives to customers of cash to change their energy bill, support for demonstration projects in the fields of energy efficiency and promoting education and literacy carbon to employees and customers.

This action, through a course of action and dissemination, consistent and coherent, around climate change to help differentiate the profile of Social Responsibility, Caixa intends to improve the reputation of its brand.

The Caixa Zero Carbon Program 2010 implements the strategy acting on five axes:

a) Information - Case reports on carbon reductions
b) Internal Action - Caixa reduces energy consumption and carbon emissions
c) Compensation - Caixa offsets carbon emissions inevitable
d) Market - Caixa promotes low carbon business
e) Communication - Communicate through Caixa Carbono Zero

The Projects

Central Solar Térmica (Thermal Solar Central)

One of the most visible projects to the reduction of CO2 emissions was the installation of solar panels on the roof of the headquarters building of CGD, transforming this building, located in Lisbon, in a huge Central Solar Thermal. The installation of one hundred and fifty of solar collectors on the roof (1 600 m2) of the headquarters building at Avenida Joao XXI, allows the production of energy used to heat water for air conditioning systems and plumbing. In total, there is a saving of more than 1 million kWh of electricity per year (about 5% of global consumption).

The plant has a system for monitoring the energy produced, allowing to analyze the performance of the facility, and outlining a possible expansion of the use of solar energy to other buildings in Caixa.

The Thermal Solar Central CGD, along with other energy efficiency measures already implemented, results in electricity savings equivalent to annual consumption of about 2,000 people, thus preventing the annual emission of more than 1,700 tonnes of CO2. This office building has a Certificate of Energy and the Ambient Air Quality, issued by ADENE-Energy Agency, with the highest A^+ rating.The policy of energy saving is extensible to the network of agencies that is being gradually equipped with PV.

Dia a Dia Carbono Zero (Day to Day Zero Carbon)

Along with new technology and with the direct participation of employees, Caixa has been producing a kind of guide on best environmental practices to adopt in our daily lives, whether at work or at home, which is available (PDF) in the site of Caixa. The mission of awareness extends to the general public through the production of the TV show “O Planeta Agradece” (The Planet Appreciates), an item on the radio and a “blogue”. This program is part of the Caixa Zero

Carbon Program 2010, and aims to promote behaviours that help Caixa to reduce her own emissions. Simultaneously, it is to be replicated in a larger universe, to help the country meet its international commitments in this matter. Day by Day Zero Carbon is a program involving customers and employees around the world in combating climate change.

Floresta Caixa (Caixa Forest)

Of vital importance to the planet as CO2 sinks, the forests have, also, been addressed in the program. The forests are a major renewable resource of Europe and the most important component of nature within EU. In Portugal (occupying nearly 40% of the country) forest constitute constitutes an important area of activity that involves more than 150 thousand workers. Forests are also essential in promoting biodiversity, protection against soil erosion, correction of water regimes and air quality. It is therefore essential to promote effective forest management as a way to preserve and foster an important renewable resource, while contributing to meeting the emission limits set for Portugal under the Kyoto Protocol.

The program FLORESTA CAIXA represents a set of initiatives aimed to contribute to the construction of a new forest in Portugal. These are developed in partnership with some major environmental groups and linked to the stakeholders in the sector such as QUERCUS and ANEFA (National Association of Business - Agriculture, Forestry and the Environment).

The actions that the program will materialize: recovery of areas burned and the creation of sustainable forests with preservation of native species. It includes several projects for forestation and raising awareness of the importance of the forest.

Environmental Awareness

In the field of the *FOREST ENVIRONMENTAL AWARENESS - CAIXA* includes initiatives aimed to promote the adoption of appropriate environmental behaviour. In addition to the above set of actions we can cite the sponsorship of the Conference of Al Gore in our country and Portugal's edition of the book "An Inconvenient Truth." In the "lounge" area of the headquarters of Caixa there are several brochures available on forests and on the theme of climate change. Shares of Christmas "for a better future" call attention in this court, to the importance of forest preservation… and for indigenous species to be preserved. It also counts the support measures to forestation with children and young people from schools, participation of employees and their families.

Cartão Caixa Carbono Zero (Caixa Card Zero Carbon) -Cartão Caixa Carbono Zero (Caixa Card Zero Carbon)

One of the recent innovations in this field gives the name of Caixa Card Zero Carbon (the card that embedded in nature, according to advertising copy CGD) and represents another step in implementing the strategy of CGD in combating Climate Change. It is a card truly innovative, unique of its kind in Portugal. Integrated in the Program Caixa Zero Carbon 2010 (Market axis), this Caixa Card Zero Carbon intended to be a means of encouraging a lifestyle of low carbon and allows its user to offset emissions that cannot avoid.

The Card provides special conditions in the purchase of goods and services with greater energy efficiency and better environmental performance, providing a solution that simultaneously reduces emissions, preserving the planet, and provides a significant financial savings for its user. Presents a set of features that make it attractive for the user, in particular, on favourable terms involving the return of annuities according to their original use and the amounts reached in the transactions, the flexibility of the conditions and terms of payment and in consideration of an interest rate of operations truly competitive.

Caixa Card Zero Carbon is a genuine product of low carbon, in which key elements were designed to minimize the effects of climate change. Firstly because it is a credit card made from recycled material, free of chlorine and that fosters communication by electronic means, thus thought to cause minimal effects on climate. By contributing to projects that absorb or prevent CO2, the card offers a portfolio of carbon credits to offset unavoidable emissions permits, making the day-to-day more "user-friendly" environment. In choosing this card, customers have access to special discounts on the purchase of goods and services more energy efficient, including a cash-back program that offers them carbon credits to offset emissions. The Card gives therefore CO2 credits, which means that the amount accumulated in the cash-back program is channelled to projects that absorb or prevent carbon dioxide. Emissions from the production and distribution of the card are quantified and compensated.

To that extent, it can be said that the name Card Zero Carbon is justified-it is a card with no effect on climate. *Tapada Nacional de Mafra* is the first project to benefit from funds provided by the Card Box Carbon Zero. This is an area of 50 hectares, which is strongly affected by the fires of 2003. Integrating project in forest area, the Card came enable the proper management of this area, with special attention to newly installed stands and processes of natural regeneration. It is intended to ensure sustainable forestry, fire protection and enhancement of biodiversity. The project ensured the monitoring of the action over 30 years. The project includes the development and implementation of a management plan that will allow carbon sequestration of a total of about 3000 tons. CO2 equivalent (CO2e).

The recent innovation in this area is called Cash Carbon Calculator. Installed at the site of the institution allows the user to calculate their carbon footprint quantifying the emissions associated with daily life from issues that relate to two key areas: housing (domestic consumption) and mobility (use of means of transport).

Supporting Scientific Research

Along with these actions that directly target the environmental, Caixa is integrating its activities in the promotion of scientific research as central to the evolution of knowledge and change attitudes and mentalities. The role of education is central to sustainable development. Hence: Firstly, and according to the desideratum of increasing the financial literacy of potential users, Caixa has created mechanisms that are simple, practical and accessible, to encourage savings. This has created a financial education program, called Positive Balance, with access to the Net (www.saldopositivo.cgd.pt) to customers and non-customers. The contents are useful application in the daily management of the family budget, and include suggestions for energy saving approach of diagnostic tools to prevent financial indebtedness, financial products etc.

For young people there is a Program – *Ciclo da Poupança* (*Cycle of Savings*) which points to the need for savings and simple formulas to achieve them. It led in 2007 to a game with hundreds of agencies and students of 1st and 2nd cycles, on the celebrations of World Savings. Most interesting, the *Programa Nova Geração de Cientistas Polares* (*New Generation of Polar Scientists Programme*) results of a collaboration with the Portuguese for the International Polar Year. It assigns scholarships to young scientists for studies to focus on relevant issues of Climate Change and its effects (Biology, Physics of the Atmosphere, etc.) on Antarctica Region. Simultaneously, Portuguese started a major campaign in Antarctica with the participation of Portuguese scientists held until 2009, Nov. The Committee for the polar year, consisting of researchers from several universities in Portugal and its action promotes the integration of young scientists in the work of teams who are developing this area of science, creating critical mass and promoting the image of the Portuguese Science World.

The lectures "*Um Alerta Global para o Desenvolvimento Sustentável*" ("A Global Warning for Sustainable Development"): in this field, there are alerts for sustainable development by supporting a series of conferences in Culturgest promoting discussion of relevant issues and with the participation of some of the most significant researchers (with themes such as Climate Change, Human Rights, Sustainable Development and the Information Society, Architecture responsible).

A way that promotes the development of skills in the area still refers to the *Concurso de Design de Mobiliário com Materiais Reciclados* (Furniture Design Competition with Recycled Materials) that challenged the young people of Portuguese universities and polytechnics to display their talents, contributing to the development of proposals for Eco-Design and thereby furthering rows of recycling. And others:

- Publications (the magazine "Azul"),
- Renewable energy credit programs, with special conditions for acquisition and installation of equipment;
- My Energy Program, in partnership with EDP - integrated solution of micro-generation solar thermal, photovoltaic and wind power for small and medium consumers. Obviously that environmental sustainability should not be disconnected from the other two pillars of development: economic and social. We do not want to enlarge this communication, but we would like to stress the importance of Caixa's solidarity actions, as well as actions to support culture and sport of its employees and the Community, or their efforts on the transparency of information.

2. Bulgaria: TechnoLogica

In Bulgaria, companies are going through new realities and CSR is going as a new experience to implement a new attitude facing the new reality. TechnoLogica is enlarging its determination and motivation to go by new practices and come close to customers. TechnoLogica recognizes that social benefit is important to develop the company's strategy and shall be assumed in every action TechnoLogica undertakes.

TechnoLogica is one of the biggest Bulgarian software companies. TechnoLogica's business is to help companies and organizations to implement and to take advantage of new information technologies in their developments and projects. According to the last two CBN Bulgaria ICT Ranks™ TechnoLogica is the largest Bulgarian-owned software company. TechnoLogica has been active on the Bulgarian market since 1990. Today, the company has offices in Sofia, Plovdiv, Varna and Skop (Macedonia) and is a member of various business associations and chambers. The company Mission is:

In order to stay competitive as the provider of technology transfer services, TechnoLogica follows a target oriented policy of innovation by anticipatory implementation, adaptation and further development of new information technologies and building of technological software tools. TechnoLogica is an intellectual capital company, which actively participates in the development of the knowledge-based economy. Among the most recent acknowledgements of TechnoLogica's achievement in this area are the 2008 first prizes in the "Investor in Knowledge" category awarded by the Bulgarian Business Leaders Forum and in the "Knowledge Management" category in the annual HR awards of the Bulgarian Human Resources Management and Development Association.

Business ethics makes an integral part of TechnoLogica's corporate culture, because if the Company wants to be sought after as a valuable technological partner in the projects of its partners, its name must stand for a guarantee of high technological level and exceptional business ethics. The business of TechnoLogica as a technological partner requires that the Company be easily accepted by the other players in the field of information technologies.

The Business Ethics Certificate was awarded to TechnoLogica in the year of 2003. TechnoLogica does business that is socially responsible. The management of the Company recognizes social benefit as a touchstone of every action TechnoLogica undertakes. As a company that is dedicated to innovation, TechnoLogica considers social issues as providing challenges and opportunities.

Young People and Education Benefit Projects

TechnoLogica traditionally supports and consistently accomplishes the idea for close cooperation between business and the academic circles. The management realizes the necessity for the business to contribute to the quality education and professional fulfillment of the young people in Bulgaria as well as the benefits of such cooperation for TechnoLogica's strategy realization. TechnoLogica has long years of experience in cooperating with the academic circles. Yet in 1993 the first summer internship of students from the American University took place thanks to the initiative of TechnoLogica. The company has made donations to almost all universities of Bulgaria and aims at being a catalyst for a stable cooperation between business and education.

TechnoLogica participates actively in the Business Master Classes organized by the Bulgarian Business Leaders Forum (BBLF) with lecturers in the Information Technologies and Human Resources modules. The latest program of the company for the benefit of young people and education is being developed at the Faculty of Mathematics and Informatics (FMI) of the Sofia University "Kliment Ohridski". The program consists of several projects related not only to the students but also to their professors. At the TechnoLogica Education Centre for Professionals we regularly organize workshops for students from the Master's Programs at the FMI. It is already a tradition that certified practicing professors train the faculty professors and system administrators in the newest technologies free of charge. This is done in order to facilitate the process of implementing new technologies and also to provide resources for it. Following this trend a specialized free of charge training in Microsoft starts from academic year 2006/2007. This training is a part of the approved academic curriculum and is lead by certified professionals from TechnoLogica. TechnoLogica regularly accepts trainees from the faculty who get the opportunity to continue working at the company on full time employment agreements after the completion of their internship programs. In 2006 TechnoLogica announced a contest for "The Lecturer in a Subject in the Information Systems Field Best Appraised by the Students" with a prize fund amounting to 5 000 leva.

As a company specialized mainly in information systems development, by means of this annual award TechnoLogica expresses its gratitude and respect to the professors who have contributed to teaching the students useful knowledge that could later on be used in their practical work. Through direct voting on the FMI web site the students chose the three lecturers with the greatest contribution to their professional growth as IT specialists. A challenge to the young software specialists is also the contest called "Wings for Your Ideas" which aims at looking for new and original ideas for software products, instrumental tools and technologies.

The company will invest in the best ideas and will facilitate their actual implementation in all aspects and all the projects that have participated in the contest shall be published on a special web site and popularized among the companies in the IT sector. The authors of the ideas preserve their copyright over those ideas and all additional conditions for their implementation will be organized in the form of a contract. TechnoLogica was the first to respond to the charity campaign for an elevator for students with disabilities in the FMI building and donated 10% of the needed 100 000 leva. By doing so TechnoLogica hoped to give a good example of charity activities in the IT sector and also expected that the kids with disabilities will receive an equal start for education and professional fulfillment, just like their healthy peers.

At the end of 2006 the gathered amount comprised 50% of the sum necessary for building the elevator. The "Engineering Education – Solid and Working" program started at the end of 2003 as a model for bringing business and education closer and it develops successfully and gives good results for the students as well as for the production enterprises. Even then the initiators of the program forecasted the strong demand for engineers which already is a proven fact. The program started with the donation of a software with a trade price amounting to 2.5 million dollars – an act of support by the American corporation, software producer, SolidWorks. It encompasses six universities and numerous Bulgarian industrial enterprises, the donation thus being only a part of the initiative. The goals of the program are improving the quality of the engineering education, increasing the interest towards it and stimulating the joint practical developments of the universities and the enterprises.

Thus, simultaneously will increase the competitiveness of the Bulgarian companies and the opportunity for successful professional fulfillment of such specialist will arise. DiTra, the CAD/CAM center of TechnoLogica and official representative of Solid Works for Bulgaria and Macedonia, made an installation of the donated software, trained the lecturers and supplied studying materials. In April 2006 was published the new SolidWorks textbook –

"SolidWorks – User's Book. Functionality, Examples, Guidelines". It is sold on preferential prices to students. The industrial enterprises actively participate in the initiative by means of offering guest lecturers, workplaces and practical help.

Within the bounds of the initiative are carried out university days, seminars, job fairs, master classes as well as the student contest for working with SolidWorks. The student contest takes place in two categories - for best project done with SolidWorks as well as for speed, skillfulness and ability to work with the software. The contest finals take place at the annual meeting of the friends of SolidWorks where young engineers can demonstrate their abilities in front of potential employers. The winners receive the annual TechnoLogica scholarship. Almost all finalists from the contest find good jobs at prestigious Bulgarian companies. That was the main objective of TechnoLogica and the American software producer SolidWorks – to fill in the gap in the education of engineers and to establish a lasting connection and engagement between employers and students.

In the year 2006 another producer of software joined the program – Delcam, who offered licenses of the CAM system FeatureCam to the technical universities in Sofia, Varna, Rouse and Gabrovo. DiTra in its turn taught the professors how to work with the software. DiTra, as an official representative of SolidWorks for Bulgaria and Macedonia, annually maintains the working capacity of the installed software and right now the universities work with the latest actual version. As a result of the work and desire of all the participants in the program, the students at three different faculties of the Technical University in Sofia, as well as the Technical Universities in Varna, Rouse and Gabrovo and the University of Food Technologies in Plovdiv study and work with SolidWorks and SolidCAM, just like their colleagues at the Massachusetts Institute of Technology.

In the year 2006 DiTra opened a Laboratory for Assistance of Innovative Processes in Industry which has at its disposal the latest software tools. It is equipped with a high class machine for rapid prototyping of Stratasys and a 3D scanner. Apart from the advantage to the Bulgarian companies, the functioning of that laboratory is also related to the next big step in the "Engineering Education – Solid and Working" program and more precisely, its turning into a model for other similar laboratories at the Technical Universities in Bulgaria. Still in 2007 the University of Rousse "Angel Kanchev" became the first academic institution with a similar laboratory. Thus, the first step to the goal was made – for the Bulgarian Technical Universities to be promoters of the latest technologies and centers for their pilot application in the industry, as well as for the scientific potential of universities to meet the necessity projects of the industrial enterprises. That is a meeting which could bring many benefits to both parties.

Carting for Employees

The main resource in the software branch is the human capital. A spirit of innovation is one of the important criteria in the selection of personnel at TechnoLogica. The firm has created an atmosphere of creativity and it is a given that everyone working here is willing to be a professional and an innovator, and that these qualities must be stimulated. One very important quality that TechnoLogica is proud of is free communication. The management is not only open to innovative and daring ideas by everyone about anything, but it is also proactive in the process of conceiving of and formulating the ideas of its employees. At TechnoLogica, 15% of each employee's working time is dedicated to research and training. Most often it is used for collecting information about new technologies, and for analysis of their potential and applicability. Given the speed at which the field of information technologies has been developing, these require special attention and sufficient resources for up-to-date introductory training.

Appreciating the importance of high-quality training, in 1995 TechnoLogica created the first certified training centre for IT professionals in Bulgaria. Professionals there are educated on the basis of specifically designed training programs and backed up by the financial support of the world's software leaders, who certified all the tutors teaching in the programs. The facilitated access to teaching materials on new technologies provides an opportunity for constant and consistent learning on the part of the trainees. Internal training courses have also been developed on issues regarding the latest technologies and the technological tools owned by the company. These courses are modified for clients and also as an element of the technological transfer offered to them by TechnoLogica. What is of utmost importance to TechnoLogica is to work for the formation and development of professionals on an international level. TechnoLogica helps its young employees develop as valuable professionals through arranging for the sponsorship of their certification courses by the leading IT corporations. All employees receive financial support when they marry or have a child. It is a common practice that interest–free loans are provided to employees for the purchase of real estate property.

Community Benefit Projects

In 2007 on the occasion of the 50th anniversary of the National Polytechnic Museum TechnoLogica financed entirely the building of a new web site representing the activity and development of the museum and its branches. Following its strategy for supporting the Bulgarian cultural institutions, TechnoLogica also supported the National Polytechnic Museum in staging the "The Bulgarian Trace in Science" exhibition, prepared by the museum. So that the less popular facts from the Bulgarian scientific development, contained in the exhibition, could reach wider audience, TechnoLogica shall donate copies from "The Bulgarian Trace in Science" to different governmental and academic institutions. Through the financial aid granted by the company the new and revised edition of the book of Prof. Isaak Passi "Motives of Human Behavior" appeared on the book market at the end of 2006.

Still in 1993, TechnoLogica, absolutely free of charge, for the first time in Eastern Europe used multimedia kiosks for new quality service for the visitors of a public forum, namely the Technological Fair in Plovdiv. The kiosks were equipped with touch-sensitive screens, and provided information about the exhibiting firms, the location of their stands, the exhibition town and the sightseeing places in Plovdiv responding to visitor-entered criteria. TechnoLogica provided for free a similar kiosk to the National Historical Museum, so that children can search by themselves for the information they are interested in and get used to working with a computer. TechnoLogica also created the first compact disc presenting Bulgaria's historical and cultural heritage.

The multimedia presentation of the Bulgarian Army, provided by TechnoLogica at the celebration for NATO's headquarters in Mons, Belgium 30th anniversary called for a new look at Bulgaria. The CD, enhanced with a presentation of the Atlantic movement in Bulgaria, was the official present of the Bulgarian delegation for NATO's 50th anniversary in Washington DC. The project received high acclaim from the Pact's Management. TechnoLogica stimulates and promotes new modern methods of presenting Bulgaria and Bulgarian institutions to the world. The firm has created pro bono a number of websites for the Atlantic Club in Bulgaria, the Ministry of Internal Affairs, the first website of the Bulgarian Business Leaders Forum, to list but a few.

By donating software (HeRMeS) needed for building a database and releasing an Internet portal for potential employers, as well as for the supply and demand of human resources among the retired military, TechnoLogica referred to the problem of military retirees' social adaptation. The project aims to establish connections with HR managers, services assisting former military in their adaptation, and with training organizations. A project with a similar objective featured the launching of a new interactive forum in the web-site of the Employment Agency, which contains profiles of job seekers, registered in all employment bureaus in the country. The company developed that forum at a symbolic price with the sole aim to demonstrate the capacities of technologies and their use for the public.

On the eve of year 2000, the Company decided to donate the sources it had spared for equipping a gym for its employees to the "Dara" Christian National Mercy Association in Stara Zagora for supporting parentless children. Throughout 2006 the employees of TechnoLogica gathered clothes, toys and necessities and donated them to the children from the Medico-Social Care Centre in the town of Pernik. Apart from that all employees offered certain sums from their salaries and to every lev given by an employee the company added three more. The money was used for the purchase of new kitchen furniture for the Care Centre. During the Christmas and New Year holidays the team of TechnoLogica once again made a donation to the kids from the Care Center which was again multiplied by three. In 2007 the gathered amount will be used for the renovation of the sanitary premises at the Center. One of the kids prepared a Christmas card which TechnoLogica sent to all its clients and partners donating part of its circulation also to the needs of the Care Center.

Another charitable project in which TechnoLogica got involved was initiated by BAIT (The Bulgarian Association for Information Technologies) and the "Charity Doer" Foundation. The project is called "In the web" and the aim is to equip with computers and Internet connection the greatest possible number of centers for bringing up and educating parentless children. TechnoLogica participated in the campaign with a donation of color display monitors. At present around 350 kids have access to modern information technologies and make use of the vast amount of information offered in the Internet. Thanks to this stimulus more kids were motivated to make more efforts and act responsibly towards their duties. TechnoLogica actively participates in the work of six non-governmental organizations (BBLF being one of them) and invests significant resources in them - approximately 1.3% of its annual turnover and two man/months per year for supporting their activities.

3. Brazil: Vale

In Brazil, the basic needs of large segments of the population are still not being met. Issues related to survival, hunger, unemployment and social exclusion, among others, lead discussions about social responsibility of business to a lower level. In this sense, it is necessary an important debate on the corporate social action in Brazil.

The example of Vale in Brazil is presented to show important strategic policies carried out by companies dealing with social responsibility In Brazil, the corporate social responsibility is still a big challenge, since the actions of social responsibility have not contributed effectively to improve the living conditions of society and the transformation of existing social reality. This chapter emphasizes the perspective of environmental sustainability that underpins the more general concept of social responsibility. Besides, it is presented the case study of the company Vale, carrying out business in Brazil.

The company Vale is the second largest diversified mining company in the world in market value. World leader in the production and export of iron ore and pellets, and an important producer of nickel, copper concentrate, bauxite, alumina, potash, kaolin, manganese, ferroalloys and coal, the company has offices and operations in over 30 countries on five continents. Vale was the first Brazilian company to achieve the rating of investment grade and the first Brazilian company to trade its shares on Euronext (Paris).

The company has gained an enormous strength with the ore extraction in the Amazon, more specifically in the Carajas region, located in the southeastern state of Para Company, in its first year, produced 40 tons of iron ore, equivalent amount that is loaded per hour today. Vale has diverse activities within the mining sector.

The company operates in the segments below:

- Ferrous: iron ore and pellets, manganese and ferroalloys.
- Non-ferrous: kaolin, potash, copper and nickel.
- Logistics: Railroads, port terminals, coastal shipping and logistics solutions.
- Aluminum: Bauxite, alumina and aluminum.
- Energy: Eight hydroelectric dams, seven of which are already in operation.
- Coal.

Vale and Environmental Policy

According to the company report, the essence of its work is the search for a balance between socio-economic development of territories and maintaining the quality of natural resources, biodiversity and life.

To do so, Vale has made continuous investments in the management of environmental impacts of operations and research of new technologies that improve the environmental control systems. The guidelines that guide its actions are explained in the policy of sustainable development of Vale, a document that guides the process from decision making to the actions performed on the day to day operations.

Vale considers the respect for the environment a key component of its sustainability strategy, seeking to balance environmental protection and economic development. To come to this end, the company has an Environmental Policy, in which commitments to environmental aspects are clearly explained.

The company's main points of its environmental policy are as follows:

- Maintain an environmental management system, aiming to ensure that activities comply with applicable laws and standards set by the company, in the absence of specific legislation, Vale will implement the best measures of environmental protection and minimizing risk.
- Educate and train employees to act in an environmentally responsible, ensuring the implementation of environmental policy.

- Develop research and incorporate new technology for continuous improvement activities, aimed at reducing environmental impacts and consumption of energy and matter.
- Maintain ongoing dialogue with its employees and the community, aiming at improving environmental actions.
- Strive to their subsidiaries and affiliated companies to adopt practices consistent with this environmental policy.
- Request their products and services suppliers with proven environmental quality.

Vale policies, standards and environmental procedures are defined by the Department of Environment and Sustainable Development, which coordinates the Management System for Environmental Quality (SGQA) of the company, setting guidelines and targets, monitoring the development of environmental performance and providing tools for managing the environmental aspects related to the activities, products and services of Vale.

The Environmental Policy with the subsidiaries is still in process of discussion and alignment. In the context of the Management System of Environmental Quality are developed measures for monitoring, conservation, environmental protection and recovery which ensure the maintenance and recovery of ecosystems in which Vale operates.

The environmental management system is based on the guidelines ISO 14001 (International Organization for Standardization). Periodically, the operations are subject to external audits.

In recent years, important achievements were obtained in the rational use of water and energy, waste disposal and the awareness of people to environmental quality. Follows the environmental performance of the last three years. Vale is in fact aware that there are opportunities for improvement and is committed to the continuous improvement in building an environmentally friendly business model.

According to the report of the company, Vale has a great concern for environmental issues, and as a consequence there are significant investments in the environment. Its commitment is not limited to the environmental control systems that are required. The environmental aspect is an important component of the evaluation of new projects and decision-making investment for expansion of the company. Expenditures are monitored monthly and reported quarterly to the public opinion, and it counts with periodic financial audits.

The relationship with the various stakeholders is present in Vale environmental management. In each area where Vale acts, the company tries to be an agent of change, listening from outside and proposing alternatives and looks for integrating other social actors in the effort of finding solutions to environmental issues.

Most of the resources were allocated to three lines of expenditure:

- acquisition and implementation of environmental control equipment, aiming to improve performance in existing operations;
- maintaining environmental and geotechnical safety of dams and waste dumps;
- reforestation and rehabilitation of degraded areas, which form the program *Florestar Vale*.

Furthermore, the management system of environmental quality determines the development of effective monitoring, conservation, environmental protection and rehabilitation, aiming to ensure the maintenance and recovery of ecosystems in which Vale operates. The system is based on the guidelines of ISO 14001 (International Organization for Standardization) to which additional aspects were added making up the standard of environmental quality in Vale. Aiming to assess the management and guarantee the evolution of performance, multiple transactions are submitted periodically to internal and external audits.

Policies, standards and environmental procedures of a general nature are defined corporately, and management is under responsibility of operations and business areas.

Social Aspects

The quest to build a positive social, economic and environmental legacy in regions where Vale operates is one of the principles that underlie the Sustainable Development Policy of Vale.

Activities, especially mining, are limited to the lifetime of the mineral deposit and therefore the presence in a particular place, in general, is finite.

Along the mineral cycle, there is a challenge to Vale: to make that actions are catalyst for regional economic development based on regional competences, which can ensure the perpetuity of social welfare in equilibrium with the environment. In that search, Vale performs management actions that enhance the positive effects of the presence of Vale, reducing the social risks of operations and at the same time, contributing to strengthening the foundations for local development in the long run.

Vale invests in integration, in cooperation with public and social agents, to encourage:

- the hiring of local employees and suppliers;
- education for human development, for work and income generation;
- planning the use of taxes generated by the operations of the company;
- the diversification of local economies;
- the strengthening of institutions;
- environmental conservation and cultural heritage.

Thus, Vale tries to build social transparent networks, based on dialogue and permanent respect for the culture of each community. At the same time, tries to invest in management tools to foster the development of the territories. The intention is to build, considering society as a whole, the foundation for continuous improvement of quality of life.

Management of Local Development

Vale has several programs and tools, in different areas and regions of operation, to manage social and environmental impacts arising from the activities.

In the analysis of the feasibility of implementing projects, the methodology Front-End Loading (FEL) is adopted covering social, health, safety and environment, and economic and operational risks.

Furthermore, based on environmental, social and economic assessments, performed in the EIA/RIMA (Environmental Impact Assessment and Impact Report for the Environment), potential impacts of the presence of Vale are considered in the regions already in the phase of licensing and deployment projects.

These tools, together with the socioeconomic diagnoses made by Vale Foundation, conduct the Management Programs of Environmental and Socioeconomic Impacts, intending to find the mechanisms to avoid or minimize negative impacts and to maximize the positive impacts on the performance of Vale. These programs are implemented according to the needs of each project and consider the particularities of each region. Through these tools, it identifies the main impacts associated with the presence of mining. Among them stands out:

- **Direct economic impacts**
  Positive: Generation of Employment, Vocational Training, Increased taxes, Hiring of local products and services, investments in infrastructure.
  Negative: Environmental impacts such as dust and noise, interference with land use, risks of accidents.
- **Indirect economic impacts**
  Positive: increase the wages, benefit income making, Leverage of other economic sectors, suppliers attraction, development of local suppliers, attraction of investments from various spheres of public and private sectors.
  Negative: Pressure on infrastructure and public services, due to population increases; speculation in remote areas, due to the low housing supply and high demand; generation of economic leakage effects, due to the hiring of suppliers and employees of other regions, due to the lack of local businesses and experts.

Programs and Management Impact Practices

In order to leverage and maximize the positive outcomes of Vale in the territories, Vale works with structured programs considering the various relationships that Vale has set.

Qualification

Vale seeks to maximize the hiring of residents of the localities where it operates, especially in developing countries and remote areas.

Vale invests in professional training programs related to mining activities and other activities of the local economy. Through these programs, Vale aims to contribute to employment and income generation and diversification of the economy of the communities where it operates.

Relationship with Communities

At all stages of the company's ventures, from the start to the closing of operations, Vale counts with an Institutional relations and communications team. There are programs for establishing relationships with the communities that are based on a permanent and participatory dialogue between the community and Vale. Programs include visits to mining communities, meetings with leaders and participatory forums. In addition, it is intended to establish a direct and transparent dialogue with not only the community but also with the local government in order to build a harmonious relationship.

Relations with Traditional Communities

Vale gives special attention to the traditional communities in the localities where it operates. The basic guideline of the Interaction Program with Indigenous Communities is to ensure that the benefits generated by the project are enjoyed by the indigenous communities, respecting their cultural traditions in order to avoid, minimize or offset any adverse effects that the activity may stimulate.

Culture Appreciation

It is understood that anyone can contribute and participate in programs of recovery, revitalization and protection of cultural property. Projects are supported and agreements settled to the restoration of cultural and archaeological heritage of places where it operates. An example is the project of rescuing the language of the Kanak communities.

Besides these programs, implanted directly in the units, Vale Foundation works for the development of communities where Vale is present, helping to empower people and respecting local cultural identities through social programs structured.

Investment in Infrastructure

Over the past three years, the amount applied was approximately $169 million. There is a fall in the investment in infrastructures in 2008 due to the completion of current projects.

In the following years, southeastern Pará may have significant investments to remedy deficiencies in existing social infrastructure and prepare the region for a projected economic growth of 18% per year. To deal with these investments, the municipalities have counted with an ability of own investment which may have generated gross savings of $504 million between 2006 and 2010.

This is one of the main conclusions of the Integrated Socioeconomics Diagnostic of Southeastern Pará, a study made between 2006 and 2007, by Vale and Vale Foundation, under the auspices of Diagonal Urbana, a Brazilian consultant, specialized in integrated social management that counts with the participation of communities.

Although a significant structural deficit, the Southeast of Pará has great opportunities for sustainable development. After all, it is one of the richest regions of the world in natural resources and one of the major mineral provinces in the world. Since it has begun operations in the region, in the 80s, Vale has been supporting the development of the municipalities that are in its area of influence, while helping to preserve an area of 8 thousand km2 of native forest in *Mosaico* de *Carajás*.

Investments in infrastructure, urban sanitation, education and culture have contributed significantly to the development of the region. Even the company's growth over this period brought more opportunities for skills and employment for residents, more business for local suppliers and increase tax collection by government agencies, contributing to the local socioeconomic development.

Vale has currently 15 projects in the area and intended to make new investments, trying to reach the total value of U.S. $13 billion (from 2003 to 2010). To increase its presence and be more effective and socially responsible, Vale and its Foundation have decided that, first, it was necessary to know the region, understanding the present moment and projecting the future in the region.

Diagnostics marks only the beginning of the Plano de Gestão Integrada em Socioeconomia do Sudeste do Pará (an Integrated Management Plan for Socioeconomics of

Southeast of Pará), which also includes the steps of preparing and implementing the Action Plan. The Plan, which is already being prepared in 2007, determines what should be done in the investments area and how each party should participate. The action already implemented is a stage of implementation of improvements, including efforts to seek financing. "This is a powerful tool that allows Vale to contribute to the sustainable development in regions where it operates", according Vale Foundation. The Plan includes six municipalities (*Parauapebas, Canaã dos Carajás, Curionópolis, Marabá, Ourilândia do Norte and Tucumã*), and influences the Eldorado dos *Carajás*.

Health and Safety Activities and Policies

In 2007, Vale has continued to carry out the strategy for health and safety through various activities, among which are:

- Policy Review Health and Safety - the new text of the policy specifies the commitments and the basics of managing Health and Safety, which embody the value of respect for life.
- Elaboration of Requirements for Systemic Health and Safety - the standard defines what must be done to ensure the proper development of the organizational processes of Vale. These requirements stem from the Health and Safety Policy and its Principles. They are the ones that underlie the procedures, tools and performance indicators of health and safety management.
- Elaboration of Requirements for Critical Activities (RACs) - The requirements established for the execution of critical operational activities, with the purpose of preserving people's lives, ensuring the integrity and protect health in all areas of the company, so as in its subsidiaries and affiliates. The 10 activities of greater risk appetite for Vale are working at height, motor vehicles, mobile equipment, blocking and signalling, cargo handling, confined space, machine protection, slope stabilization, and detonated explosives and chemicals.
- Implementation of Information System Health and Safety - in order to improve the management and flow of information from Health and Safety, begins the deployment of a single information system for Vale in Brazil. The tool will support management decisions, according to the results of business areas.
- Membership in the Global Business Coalition on HIV / AIDS, Tuberculosis and Malaria - GBC (Global Business Coalition against HIV / AIDS, Tuberculosis and Malaria) - joins the group of more than 200 member companies of the GBC, an organization aimed at mobilizing resources for initiatives for combating and prevention of HIV / AIDS, tuberculosis and malaria.
- Event "Construction" - in June and July 2007, approximately 2.5 thousand leaders in Vale gathered in 19 cities of Brazil, to build together the foundations of a culture of prevention in health and safety.
- The new Health and Security Policy of Vale, released in March 2008, establishes the following commitments:
- To control all risks associated with activities, processes, facilities, products and services.
- To act proactively in managing risks to health and safety of persons and facilities.

- Meet the legal requirements of health and safety and to take voluntarily.
- To continuously improve the performance in health and safety through the improvement of activities, processes, products and services, focusing on the use of innovative solutions and developing people competences.
- To encourage the development of performance in health and safety service providers.
- To maintain communication channels with the communities where operate and other stakeholders, so as to remain always alert to the influence of its operations in the health and well-being of people.

Since 2006, the performance goal of workplace safety (accidents with remote and internal corporate standards) is tied to variable pay of employees. In 2007, the process changed so that in contemplating the health data. The set of actions already implemented and the beginning of the process of cultural transformation have already shown some results.

Between 2005 and 2007, various measures to improve management of health and safety are implemented, for example, setting targets covering issues of health and safety for all departments and the intensification of awareness campaigns.

Starting in 2007, a process of improvement of registration procedures and data collection on health and safety began. The standards of classification of accidents were implanted according to the rules Occupational Safety & Health Administration (OSHA), the Agency for Safety and Health at Work in the United States, and several initiatives for training and for employees awareness were held in order to standardize the recording of information.

With the implementation of this process, in 2007 some improvements were got.

Regarding the rate of accidents with lost time, a significant reduction was got over the period 2005 to 2007. This means that the accidents of greater severity were reduced. The perspective is that in the coming years, accident rates may continue to reduce, both because of the improvements implemented as because of the stability in the form of gathering and recording data. In this sense, the participation of Vale began in a working group of ICMM (SCHEBenchmarking) in order to align indicators of health and safety and occupational hygiene.

With regard to risk prevention and health guarantee, Vale maintains a rigorous system for identifying health risks in all its units. The goal is to use this information to the creation of specific programs that can be deployed, promoting an attitude of prevention by employees, relatives and the communities in which Vale operates. By the end of 2007, risks for the following diseases were identified:

- Occupational: musculoskeletal diseases, back pain, risk of hearing loss and pneumoconiosis.
- Endemic: intestinal parasites and diseases carried by animals, dengue, malaria, chagas diseases, yellow fever, hepatitis A and B, HIV / AIDS, leishmaniasis, and worms. Among the programs maintained by the company are: campaign to prevent sexually transmitted diseases - STD / AIDS, World Day to Combat AIDS, workshops on alcohol and smoking, and prevention campaigns against cancer and diabetes; support group for diabetics, hypertensives and people with cardiovascular risks; program of gym work, education program affective-sexual (Vale Youth - developed by Vale Foundation), aimed at young people from nearby communities in order to guide the sexual life and preventing the occurrence of sexually transmitted diseases;

campaigns of vaccination against influenza, and inspections to prevent and treat dengue and yellow fever. Besides these initiatives, Vale offers health plans to its employees and third parties as described in the job session and People Development.

Such efforts have earned public recognition. The Healthy Living Program, of Albras, won in 2005, the Social Value Award (jury of experts and jury) in the category "Quality of Working Environment" and, in 2007, Lennart Levi Award in the category "Poster Enterprises", VII Congress of Stress of ISMA (International Stress Management Association). Vale invested U.S. $25.2 million by the mid 2009.

According to the testimony of some local politicians, royalties would be a form of compensation to alleviate the problems acquired with the implementation of Vale projects in EPC. The royalties would also help to solve problems such as sanitation, health, etc., that are considered by municipalities as socially critical areas, which solutions would not be viable only with the transfers from state and from Union resources.

4. India: Indian Oil Corporation Limited (IOCL)

Indian Oil Corporation Limited (IOCL) or IndianOil is the largest commercial enterprise in India and the 125th highest ranked Fortune Global 500 Company in the country. For over five decades, IndianOil has been the leader in the petroleum business in the country with presence in downstream petroleum refining and marketing and upstream exploration and production. A visionary plan to diversify into petrochemicals, Gas marketing and globalization has enabled the company to grow as a diversified, transnational energy major company. Today, IndianOil has a presence in Sri Lanka, Mauritius and the Middle East. Its subsidiary IndianOil Mauritius is one of the major players in the petroleum business in Mauritius. In Sri Lanka, its subsidiary Lanka IOC has established itself as a benchmark for fuel retailing besides expansion into other related areas.

At IndianOil, corporate social responsibility (CSR) has been the cornerstone of success right from inception in the year 1964. The Corporation's objectives in this key performance area are enshrined in its Mission statement: "…To help to enrich the quality of life of the community and to preserve ecological balance and heritage through a strong environment conscience".

IndianOil has defined a set of core values for themselves – Care, Innovation, Passion and Trust – to guide the corporate in all they do. IOCL is able to claim all countrymen as their customers. That's why, they coined the phrase, "IndianOil – India Inspired", in their corporate campaigns. Public corporations like IndianOil are essentially organs of society deploying significant public resources. Therefore, they are aware of the need to work beyond financial considerations and put in that little extra to ensure that they are perceived not just as corporate behemoths that exist for profits, but as wholesome entities created for the good of the society and for improving the quality of life of the communities they serve as a constructive partner in the communities in which it operates, IndianOil has been taking concrete action to realize its social responsibility objectives, thereby building value for its shareholders and customers.

The Corporation respects human rights, values its employees, and invests in innovative technologies and solutions for sustainable energy flow and economic growth. In the past five decades, IndianOil has supported innumerable social and community initiatives in India. The company has performed by touching the lives of millions of people positively by supporting environmental and health-care projects and social, cultural and educational programmes. Besides focusing primarily on the welfare of economically and socially deprived sections of society, IndianOil also aims to develop techno-economically viable and environment-friendly products & services for the benefit of millions of its consumers, while at the same time intends to ensure the highest standards of safety and environment.

IOCL has had a task to prepare a 360 degree Media Campaign leverage IndianOil's CSR activities and to meet its marketing central goal. The problem perceived by IOCL as a large government owned company is that it takes a number of initiatives as part of its social responsibility program. However, it is not communicated to public at large. But, at a time when the new economy is in the forefront, IndianOil needs to project this aspect of the corporation for projecting a positive brand image and the same image can be leveraged to attain corporation's marketing objectives. The main objective of the company's CSR advertising campaign is to focus both on the core strength of the corporation as well as to create an emotional connection with public to enhance the image of the corporation and to leverage it to meet its marketing goals. Target consumers of the campaign are both male and female, general public, all India socio-economic classes. The advertising happens to be firstly in English language and further translated in various other official languages of India. In addition to print media, the campaign is inclusive of 360° branding proposal hoarding/ banner/ poster/ TV/ radio/ any other.

Indian Oil Corporation Limited (IOCL) is one of the top most leading Maharathna corporate companies spending the highest share of profit toward corporate social responsibility. The most successful CSR advertising campaigns of IndianOil are 'Empowering 40000 women, planting 1 million trees and having 16.572 billion investments on research and development for green fuel projects' and yet 'The smiles we multiply in the deprived society'.

5. Greece: COCO-MAT S.A.

Compared with other European and international standards, CSR has not been developed extensively in Greece. There are several companies in Greece that implement special CSR programmes. However, it is estimated that only 10% of Greek companies have a comprehensive strategy for CSR, while in Europe the same figures are at much higher levels. It could be said that social responsibility policies are mainly drawn upon high-turnover companies and multinational companies. There is a special department in these enterprises which is in charge and manages CSR issues. On the contrary, the integration of CSR principles in SMEs remains particularly restricted, as in these companies competitiveness is low, while basic priority is sustainability and short-term profit (Tzivara, 2007). In fact, as far as in what Greece is concerned, the limited implementation of CSR principles can be understood by the fact that fewer than 10% of companies operating in the Greek market are big enterprises, run by professional managers, prepare social accounts and have the ability to synchronize and adapt to changing conditions, thus resulting in a globalized economy environment.

The case study we are considering in this paper demonstrates that the pursuit of profit can and must be compatible with the adoption of principles of entrepreneurship that ensure the quality of products, the position of workers in the productive process and the wider social and environmental objectives. This company, COCO-MAT SA, integrates a CRS perspective in its business core as a strategy for creating an image and promoting the company in the communities and society as a whole, considering sustainable practices but also seeing this way as an approach to keep it ahead in the long term. COCOMAT SA is concerned with a set of ways of contributing to the collective welfare on the society, to the interests of the communities and to the environment. Finally, the study shows the importance of business ethics and the respective impact on organizational structure in companies as well as the importance of a set of items in the relationship with stakeholders, both internal and external, to the companies.

Social and Environmental Activities of the Company Sustainable Development

COCO-MAT S.A. is a Greek-Dutch company with franchise stores all around the world. The Athens branch was founded in 1989 and initially operated in the production of mattresses made of natural materials. Its brand name cognates from the word COCO, namely the coconut used in the production of mattresses in Greece for the first time, and from the word MAT, namely mattress. In 1992 the company headquarters moved to the Industrial Area of Xanthi (Northern Greece), which factory premises currently produce a wider range of products, such as mattresses, pillows, furniture and linens. The company employs approximately 220 people. From the very beginning, the company developed a quality policy and has been participating in the EFQM Business Excellence Model since 1997.

The policy of COCO-MAT SA is based on sustainable development and focuses on four main areas:

- the ecological quality products,
- customer satisfaction,
- employee satisfaction, and
- social contribution (COCO-MAT, 2009).

From very early, the company oriented itself towards social service in the 1990s, when the concept of Corporate Social Responsibility was still at a very early dissemination stage in Greece. From the very beginning, the social work practice included some social responsibility, aiming at focusing more on environmental protection, the promotion of equality, all at work and social care (C. Pantazidou, 2009). There is a separate sector of Corporate Social Responsibility (CSR) in the company, but the person responsible for the systematic practice of CorCSR) since 2001 is also Head of Totally Quality Management (TQM). The company has clearly specified to its employees and customers the values and rules of conduct related to Corporate Social Responsibility through presentations in order to develop a common vision.

Its participation in conferences or other collective initiatives (local, national, sectoral, etc.) relevant to the promotion of Corporate Social Responsibility is continuous, since it tries to remain informed and active in CSR practices. A very important element showing the company's awareness of social and environmental issues is that the COCO-MAT SA is an active member of the Greek Network for Corporate Social Responsibility and its activities are referred to the 'List of Best Practices for SMEs" Network for CSR. As discussed above, the company has encountered no obstacles in the implementation of corporate social responsibility (CSR). Instead, the benefits received and collected by COCO-MAT, while implementing such practices, have been clear from the outset: "The Company has served as an example for all companies and established close ties with its customers, after having satisfied their needs and demonstrated its respect for the environment and the values it stands for". Additional benefits are the satisfaction of the society, the recognition of the company as a model of social contribution, the increase of productivity, the reduction of costs and the confidence of its employees in it.

Company and Employees

Thus, there is a continuous effort on the part of Administration to provide growth prospects, ideal working conditions and shorter working hours. Additionally, employees receive a large number of privileges, such as continuing education, ability of staff to take an interest-free loan from the company of around 3,000 euro, encouragement to use the company's products that they themselves produce, buying them at special prices or with non-interest payments. Furthermore, it is important to recognize and reward personal achievements of staff in the form of salary bonuses, promotions and gifts, as well as by organizing events with a special award to employees with outstanding offer to the company.

What is important is the fact that employees in the company can express their views on labor issues affecting them through relevant forms, so that their views are taken into account in the formulation of the strategy and design of COCO-MAT SA. For people with "special needs" who are employed in the company, special facilities, such as a specific number of hours or days of work per week, are provided, depending on their needs and abilities. Additionally, this group of employees is encouraged to participate actively in the process of customer service. As far as education and training opportunities for workers of COCO-MAT SA are concerned, these are provided on an ongoing basis through organization of training seminars and encouragement for further academic education. Moreover, the company organizes special training courses which are monitored by the heads of departments, the managers of stores and all employees. Furthermore, the head of each department organizes hourly lessons once a month, so that employees are aware of the arising challenges and needs. Certification of improvements is controlled through the electronic database of the company.

Among the immediate priorities of the company COCO-MAT SA are the implementation of policies for the protection of human rights and their opposition to any form of discrimination in the workplace. The company management recognizes the diversity of people, so it does not use tight criteria in hiring new employees. "What is mainly examined are morals, personality, energy, environmental awareness and consistency of prospective employees, of course, without ignoring the qualifications of each candidate, such as education, knowledge, professional development and experience".

Therefore, the main company policy is to provide equal opportunities for all employees. It should be noted that COCO-MAT SA has accomplished a great and commendable first position: more than 40% of all employees are refugees from the former Soviet Union and Turkey, which proves the company's interest in vulnerable groups of foreigners in our country, helping to address racial, religious and ethnic discrimination. Concern for equal treatment of all citizens is also expressed by hiring people with "special abilities" and people from large families. It is characteristic that almost 10% of COCO-MAT SA employees are disabled. The management of the company has shown right from the beginning confidence in these individuals and has assigned them important responsibilities, so that a large proportion of these people have managed to reach high hierarchical positions.

Incorporations of Quality System

Moreover, since its first steps the company COCO-MAT SA has developed a policy with a focus on quality and participates in the EFQM Business Excellence Model since 1997. In addition, the company implements a Quality Management System and an Environmental Management System, which were designed and operated based on ISO 9001:2000 and ISO 14001 standards respectively. Within this context, the company is environment aware, so it implements various policies to reduce environmental effects. The common practice is not to use chemicals throughout the production process. The raw materials used in the products of COCO-MAT SA are natural ones, and their use for the production of environment - and human-friendly products is a matter of principle.

For example, some raw materials that are the basis for its products are:

- coconut (fibers that surround the coconut after suitable treatment are combined with natural rubber to create a resilient coconut),
- natural rubber (the sap of the tree, called HEVEA, after processing into a foamy layer of natural rubber),
- wool and cotton (coming from Thrace (Greece) and considered to be the best in terms of quality due to the unique climatic conditions and the composition of the subsoil),
- seaweed (used in order to offer additional iodine to people with asthma and respiratory problems),
- horsehair,
- linen,
- feather, and lately
- activated carbon.

Dedication to maintaining ecological balance is also evident by the fact that the purity percentage of the natural rubber produced in the company comes up to 96%, something which COCO-MAT SA boasts of as an exclusive feature. Furthermore, concern is expressed for the health of people by producing environment - and people-friendly products, including packaging. Even packaging materials used for the company's products are recyclable (transport of mattresses in cotton pouches) and are collected by the company upon delivery of products to the customer in order to recycle them. It should also be mentioned that the prospectus of the company "Delta" is now diffused 100% online, so that there is minimal environmental damage caused by printing brochures.

In 1998, COCO-MAT SA designed and implemented a programme aimed at using less plastic. Furthermore, the plastic that has already been used in the production process of the company is collected after its use and sent for recycling. The same happens with the paper used for the needs of production and administrative needs of the company. In addition, the company continued its campaign in order to ban the use of plastic by running a programme which title was "2004 without plastic." For this purpose, it proceeded to the replacement of plastic mattress case with fabric and to the transportation of furniture in wooden boxes. In addition, 100% cotton bags are now manufactured, which are distributed for free along with the list of COCO-MAT, and since 1998 until now almost 650,000 bags have been distributed.

Environmental Impact

The environmental impact of the operation of the central factory of COCO-MAT SA is continuously reduced to a minimum. For example, the wastewater of the factory is only those of the staff and the usual cleaning. In addition, the company operates the factory in the industrial area of Xanthi, in the industrial park E.T.V.A (Greek Bank of Industrial Development), where the infrastructure is such that it allows the company to produce without burdening the environment with industrial noise. Machinery company is certified with the CE mark and a special low-noise in operation by the level of noise allowed by existing laws. Moreover, the plant of the company has no chimneys to avoid polluting the environment. Finally, it is important to refer that COCO-MAT SA uses gas for its cars and factories.

Finally, of particular importance is the environmental awareness that COCO-MAT SA demonstrates, which is also reflected by its participation in relevant conferences and events, by its sponsorships to environmental organizations, etc. Typical examples of activities are tree planting activities organized from time to time and cleaning rivers and beaches. During the 20 years of its operation, the company has won major awards for its environmental awareness. In addition, the company ensures that the activities undertaken reflect social needs and expectations. Thus, it provides financial support for activities and programmes of the local community, by sponsoring sports' clubs, clubs in general and cultural events. Furthermore, it finances ecological activities, campaigns and people with special social needs, such as flood and fire victims, the elderly and refugees. In this project, the company collaborates with many local organizations, nongovernmental and other organizations.

CONCLUSION

Corporate social responsibility is a contradictory term and the subject of much discussion in relation to its contribution to economic development, environmental sustainability and social welfare. The dialogue about CSR covers many aspects and perspectives regarding its interpretation as a part of the wider concept of social responsibility, and its practical implementation in terms of business behavior. CSR presupposes the existence of an attitude and ethical and responsible corporate behaviour, a set of values, an entrepreneurial strategic posture; a relationship strategy, a strategy of institutional marketing; strategy valuation of the shares, a human resources strategy; a strategy to develop products/services, a strategy of integration into the community, a strategy of social development in the community should work as a promoter of individual and collective citizenship, as an exercise in ecological awareness and professional training as an exercise. It is these multiple aspects that constitute an integrated support to a responsibility that organizations must take, including to ensure their long-term operation.

Responsible corporate governance combined with sustainable development, is a modern and socially acceptable expression of a new organizational culture of enterprises. In this framework responsible corporate governance is at the heart of a company's strategic planning and contributes to the fulfilment of broader needs arising through the demands and the needs expressed by civil society. At the same time, the concept of financial and business benefits is re-identifies and the longterm profitability of the enterprises is ensured. In this way, the adoption of these principles refers to a variety of stakeholders who affect or create a new development model in accordance with the public interest (public bodies or bodies of local self-government). On the other hand, both employee and citizen groups are affected by this type of business activity that enhances the quality of life of local societies.

In practice, corporate social responsibility refers to the adoption of a model of business management in which the companies, being aware of their social commitment of co-responsibility in social and human development, hear, preserve and respect the interests of different parties, their stakeholders, incorporating different needs of the business planning and operating them through their decisions and activities. There is no doubt that this is a significant change because, a few decades ago, one had the idea that private companies should be accountable only to their shareholders and they should produce profits.

Social responsibility is certainly not just philanthropy, but can/should also include this activity. Increasingly, social responsibility, in general, and promoting environmental sustainability, in particular, carries out an operation more effective if integrated into the global perspective of business and relationship with their environs. Although much discussed, the concept is not yet finally stabilized. In any case the effort of researchers to differentiate the simple idea of charity has proved essential to its proper scope and understanding by companies and managers.

To all these difficulties of CSR implementation and spreading, bureaucratic crunches and weaknesses in creating organized structures of social and political debate should be added, factors that rather discourage the implementation and strengthening of CSR principles in the different countries. The lack of maturity level of CSR in most companies, which practically means not incorporating CSR activities in the applied strategy and corporate culture is often due to ignorance and lack of knowledge of both its existence and medium/long- term positive effects brought about by its implementation.

The purpose of this chapter was to emphasize the contribution of CSR in five companies in five different countries (Portugal, Brazil, Bulgaria India and Greece) to economic development, environmental sustainability and social welfare. Through the case studies of Caixa Geral de Depósitos, Vale, TechnoLogica, Indian Oil and COCOMAT it was intended to analyze the Companies with management strategy which believe in ethical and solidarity with their colleagues and with the Community share these processes as an important "capital".

In Portugal, companies have a long tradition in social intervention which remounts to the century XV and the foundation of the Mercies. Recently environmental concerns have contributed to the important performance and developments in CSR area in some important Portuguese companies. The development of many companies' strategies as Caixa Geral de Depósitos move across the CSR objectives.

In Brazil, the basic needs of large segments of the population are still not being met. Issues related to survival, hunger, unemployment and social exclusion, among others, lead discussions about social responsibility of business to a lower level. In this sense, it is necessary an important debate on the corporate social action in Brazil., and in the framework the Vale activities is a very important example and a good practice.

In Bulgaria, companies are going through new realities and CSR is going as a new experience to implement a new attitude facing the new reality. In this direction the case of TechnoLogica is very important to confirm this development.

In India, there is still a strong gap between Indian societal, environmental and -+business needs and current practices in the field of CSR. The Indian business begins to go into the international markets, what makes that becomes crucial that CSR philosophy develops to be integrated in the business goals for long-term sustainability in economic, social and environmental areas. The example of Indian Oil company is representative for the entrepreneurship development in this country.

Finally, Greece is a country with many small and medium-sized enterprises and with a small number of companies with activities in the field of CSR. The important case of COCO-MAT, SA was studied, working on the concept of CSR and dealing with the purpose of getting a positive impact on areas such as environment, consumers, employees or communities.

It is too early to evaluate the results of the implementation of such strategies. The impact of the conduct of social responsibility, especially in this aspect of environmental sustainability, can only be realized in a longer period.

REFERENCES

Aguinis, H. (2011). Organizational responsibility: Doing good and doing well. In S. Zedeck (Ed.), *APA handbook of industrial and organizational psychology* (Vol. *3*), 855-879. Washington, DC: American Psychological Association.

Asocio Policy Paper (2004). *Corporate Social Responsibility*.

Asongu, J. J. (2007). The History of Corporate Social Responsibility, *A Journal of Business and Public Policy*, *1*(2).

Baker, M. (2000). *Corporate Social Responsibility – What does it mean?* Retrieved on 23 March, 2009, from http:// www.mallembaker.net/ csr/definition.php.

Becker, B., et al. (1995). *Geografia e meio ambiente no Brasil*. 2. ed. São Paulo: Hucitec.

Becker, B. K. (1994). *Repensando a questão ambiental no Brasil a partir da Geografia Política*. In: Leal, M.C. et al. (org.) Saúde, ambiente e desenvolvimento. (vol. *I*) São Paulo: Hucitec.

Bergamini Júnior, S. (1999). Contabilidade e riscos ambientais. Revista do BNDES, *Rio de Janeiro*, v. *6*, n. 11, Jun..

Bezerra, M. C. L. & Bursztyn, M. (cood.). (2000). *Ciência e tecnologia para o desenvolvimento sustentável. Brasília*: Ministério do Meio Ambiente e dos Recursos Naturais Renováveis: Consórcio CDS/ UNB/ Abipti.

Brundtland Report. (1987). *Our Common Future*. Oxford: Oxford University Press.

Brüseke, F. J. (2003). *O problema do desenvolvimento sustentável*. In: Cavalcanti, Clóvis (org.). Desenvolvimento e natureza: estudos para uma sociedade sustentável. 4. ed. São Paulo: Cortez; Recife: Fundação Joaquim Nabuco.

Camargo, A. (2003). *Governança para o século 21*. In: Trigueiro, A. Meio ambiente no século 21: 21 especialistas falam da questão ambiental nas suas áreas de conhecimento. Rio de Janeiro: Sextante, 307-322.

Camargo, A., Capobianco, J. P. R. & Oliveira, J. A. P. (org.) (2004). *Meio ambiente Brasil: avanços e obstáculos* pós-Rio-92. 2 ed. rev. São Paulo: Estação Liberdade: Instituto Sociombiental; Rio de Janeiro: Fundação Getúlio Vargas.

Campbell, C. J. (2007). *Petroleum and people; Population and Environment* 24/3 November. 2002.

CECOA. (2004). *Responsabilidade Social das Empresas – Estado da Arte em Portugal*, 2004. Centro de Formação Profissional para o Comércio e Afins, Lisboa.

CGD. (2009). *133 Anos a construir O Futuro: Um Modelo sustentável*. Entrevista Fernando Faria de Oliveira – O Futuro Sempre Presente, Azul, *39*, 22-37.

Coelho, M, Filipe, J. A. & Ferreira, M. A. (2011). Environmental sustainability as a dimension of corporate social responsibility: The case of CGD – Caixa Geral Depósitos / Portugal, *International Journal of Academic Research*, Volume *3*. Issue 1. January 30.

COM. (2001). 366 Final Green Paper Promoting a European framework for Corporate Social Responsibility.

COM. (2002). 347 Communication From The Commission concerning Corporate Social Responsibility: A business contribution to Sustainable Development, http://eur-lex.europa.eu/LexUriServ/LexUriServ.do? uri=COM:2002 :0347:FIN:en:_PDF

COM (2011). 681 Comunicação Da Comissão Ao Parlamento Europeu, Ao Conselho, Ao Comité Económico E Social Europeu E Ao Comité Das Regiões - Responsabilidade social das empresas: uma nova estratégia da UE para o período de 2011-2014.http://eur-lex.europa.eu/LexUriServ/ LexUriServ.do? uri=COM:2011:0681:_FIN:PT:PDF.

Cox, M. J. (2008). Sustainable communication: A Study of Green Advertising and Audience Reception within the growing arena of Corporate Social Responsibility. Case Study: British Petroleum. *Earth & E-nvironment*, (*3*), 32-51. ISSN 1744-2893.

Crane, A., McWilliams, A., Matten, D., Moon, J. & Siegel, D. S. (2009). *The Oxford Handbook of Corporate Social Responsibility*. Oxford University Press, USA.

Crowther, D. & Capaldi, N. (2008). *The Ashgate research companion to Corporate Social Responsibility*. Ashgate. 288-402

Dahlsrud, A. (2006). *How corporate social responsibility is defined: an analysis of 37 definitions*, John Wiley & Sons,

Dawkins, J. (2004). Corporate Responsibility: The communication challenge. *Journal of Communication management*, *9* (2), 108-119.

DELOITTE (2003). *O Desafio do Desenvolvimento Sustentável nas Empresas Portuguesas, Management Solutions, Relatório*, Deloitte, Lisboa.

Ebner D & Baumgartner R. J. (2006). *The Relationship Between Sustainable Development and Corporate Social Responsibility*. www.crrconference. org[17 September 2007].

European Commission (2001). *GREEN PAPER - Promoting a European framework for Corporate Social Responsibility*, http://eur-lex.europa.eu/ LexUriServ/site/en/com/2001/ com2001_0366en01.pdf, accessed in 18/09/2010

Ferreira, A. C. S. (2003). *Contabilidade ambiental*. São Paulo: Atlas.

Filipe, J. A. (2009). *A note on the drama of the commons. how to deal with an old problem in natural resources: the resources overexploitation*, International Journal of Academic Research. Ijar: Azerbaijan.

Filipe, J. A., Coelho, M. F. & Ferreira, M. A. M. (2007). *O drama dos recursos comuns*. Sílabo: Lisboa.

Fukukawa, K. (Ed) (2009). *Structural Change in Corporate Society and CSR in Japan.* Corporate Social Responsibility in Asia Ch.2. Routledge International Business in Asia.

Furtado, C. (1992). *Brasil, a construção interrompida.* São Paulo: Paz e Terra.

Holliday, C., Schmidheiny, S. & Watts, P. (2002). *Walking the Talk: The business Case for Sustainable Development*, Greenleaf Publishing: Sheffield.

Hunnicutt, S. (2009). *Corporate Social Responsibility (Opposing Viewpoints).* Greenhaven Press.

James, D. (2002). *Consumer Activism and corporate Responsibility, Journal of Research for consumer* 3. Retrieved on 15 October, 2008, from http://www.Jrconsumers.com/ academic-articles/issue-3/James.pdf

Kinard, J., Smith, M. E., Kinard, B. R. (2003). Business executives` attitudes to social responsibility: past and present, *American Business Review*, *21* (2), 87-91.

KLD (2006). *The Corporate Social Ratings monitor.* Retrieved on 8 May, 2006. from http://www.Kld.com/research/socrates/index.html.

Kotler, P. & Lee, N. (2008). *Corporate Social Responsibility: Doing the Most Good for Your Company and Your Cause.* New Jersey: John Wiley and Sons.

KPMG. (2007). *Estudo da KPMG sobre a Publicação de Relatórios de Sustentabilidade em Portugal*, KPMG Advisory, Consultores de Gestão; BCSD Portugal; Informa, D&B.

Kroetz, C. E. S. (1999). Auditoria do balanço social. *Revista Brasileira de Contabilidade*, n. *116*, Mar/Abr.

Kyriakopoulos, O. (1/4/2004). *The new corporate culture of social Responsibility*, Oikonomikos Tachydromos, Athens.

Lee, S. (2009). *A case study for the Oxford - Achilles Working Group on Corporate Social Responsibility, Corporate Social Responsibility in India.* http://www.xjjz.co.uk/achilles/ downloads/research/India.pdf

Lichtenstein, D. R., Drumwright, M. E. & Braig, B. M. (2004). The effect of corporate social responsibility on customer donations to corporate-supported nonprofits. *Journal of Marketing*, *68* (4), 16-32.

Maignan, I. & Ferrell, O. C. (2004). Corporate social responsibility and marketing: An integrative framework. *Journal of the Academy of Marketing science*, *32* (1), 3-19.

Mallin, C. A. (2009). *Corporate Social Responsibility: A case study approach.* Edward Elgar Publishing, pp.192-287.

Manner, M. H. (2010). *Human Behavior and the Corporate Social Responsibility of Firm Leaders.* Nova Science Pub Inc. (Paperback).

March, J. G. & Simon H. (1993), *Organizations.* Oxford: Blackwell Publishers

Marrewijk van M. (2003). Concepts and definitions of CSR and corporate sustainability, *Journal of Business Ethics*, *44* (2/3).

May, S. K., Cheney, G. & Roper, J. (2007). *The debate over Corporate Social Responsibility.* Oxford University Press. 370-490

Melo Neto, F. & Froes, C. (2001). *Gestão da Responsabilidade Social Corporativa: O Caso Brasileiro*, Qualitymark, Rio de Janeiro

Mohr, L. A. & Webb, D. J. (2005). The Effects of Corporate Social Responsibility and Price on Consumer Responses. *The Journal of consumer Affairs*, *39* (1), 121-147.

Moon, J. (2007). The contribution of corporate social responsibility to sustainable development. *Sustainable Development*, *15*(5), 296-306.

Morsing, M. & Schultz, M. (2006). Corporate social responsibility communications: Stakeholder information, response and involvement strategies. *Business Ethics: A European Review*, *15* (4), 323-338.

Mullerat, R. (2009). *International Corporate Social Responsibility: The Role of Corporations in the Economic Order of the 21st Century*, Kluwer Law International, Alphen aan den Rijn.

Nagopoulos, N., Rontos, K. & Pantazidou C. (2013). Corporate Social Responsibility in Greece, *International Journal of Latest Trends in Finance and economic Sciences*, Volume *3*, No. 2

OECD (2001). «*The OECD Guidelines for multinational enterprises and Global Instrument for Corporate Social Responsibility*», Directorate for Financial, Fiscal and Enterprise Affairs, European Union.

OECD (2008). *OECD Declaration: Guidelines for Multi National Enterprises*.

Paiva, P. R. (2003). *Contabilidade ambiental*. São Paulo: Atlas.

Pantazidou, C. (2009). "*Corporate Social Responsibility. A Case study in Greece*" (2009). Master Thesis prepared within the framework of the Postgraduate Studies Programme of the Department of Sociology at the University of the Aegean with the title "Research in local social development and cohesion".

Pirsch, J., Gupta, S. & Landreth Grau, S. (2007). A framework for understanding corporate social responsibility programs as a continuum: An exploratory study. *Journal of Business Ethics,70*, 125-140.

Pomering, A. & Johnson, L. W. (2009). Advertising corporate social responsibility initiatives to communicate corporate image: Inhibiting scepticism to enhance persuasion, *Corporate Communications: An International Journal*, *14* (4), 420 – 439. Online since 1996.

Porter, M. E., Kramer, M. R. & Zadek, S. (2007). *Redefining corporate Social Responsibility*. Harvard Business Review.

Prout, J. (2006). Corporate responsibility in the global economy: a business case. *Society and Business Review*, *1* (2), 184-191.

Rahman, S. (2011). Evaluation of Definitions: Ten Dimensions of Corporate Social Responsibility. *World Review of Business Research*, Vol.*1*. No.1

Sachs, I. (2000). *Caminhos para o desenvolvimento sustentável*. Rio de Janeiro: Garamond.

Santos, R. (1980). *História econômica da Amazônia (1800-1920)*. São Paulo, T.A. Queiroz.

Sen, S., Bhattacharya, C. B. & Korschun, D. (2006). The role of corporate social responsibility in strengthening multiple stakeholder relationships. *Journal of the Academy of Marketing science*, *34* (2), 166.

Shrivastavan, P. & Roy, S. (2010). The Nature of socially responsible communication in Indian companies. Theory and practice ISSN 1648-0627 print/ISSN1822-4202 online.

Sri Urip (2010). *CSR Strategies CSR Strategies: Corporate Social Responsibility for a Competitive Edge in Emerging Markets*. John Wiley & Sons (Asia) Pte Ltd.

Tan, T. & Uncles, M. D. (2008). *Corporate social responsibility as an advertising Appeal*. ANZMAC.

TechnoLogica, http://www.technologica.com

Tinoco, J. E. P. (2004), *Balanço social*. São Paulo: Atlas.

Tinoco, J. E. P. & Kraemer, M. E. P. (2004). *Contabilidade e gestão ambiental*. São Paulo: Atlas.

Tzivara, M. – K. (2007). *«CSR: How Far Has Greece Gone? A Case Study: Piraeus Bank»*, Published Research Project, University of Westminster (MA), UK.

Vale, S. A. (2007). *Relatório de sustentabilidade*

Vale, S. A. (2008). *Relatório de sustentabilidade*

Visser, W. (2004). *Corporate Social Responsibility in developing Countries.*

Walter Leal Filho (2009). *'Professionals' Perspectives of Corporate Social Responsibility'.* Springer.

Wang, T. H. (2008). *The Effect of modified Collaborative Strategic Reading on EFL learners' Reading Comprehension.* Unpublished MA dissertation, National Changhua University of Education, Changhua, Taiwan.

WBCSD (2001). *The business case for sustainable development: Making a difference towards the Johannesburg Summit 2002 and Beyond*, World Business Council for Sustainable Developmet (WBCSD): Geneva, Switzerland.

Werther, W. B. & Chandler, D. (2006). *Strategic Corporate Social Responsibility. Stakeholder in a Global Environment.* SAGE Publications. Thousand Oaks. 151-356.

Windsor (2001). The future of corporate social responsibility. *International Journal of Organizational Analysis, 9* (3).

In: Towards a Society with a More Fair Economy
Editors: J. A. Filipe, N. Nagopoulos, K. Rontos et al.
ISBN: 978-1-63482-900-7

Chapter 13

CASE STUDY: ENVIRONMENTAL EDUCATION CENTERS IN GREECE

Niki Psoma
University of Aegean, Mytilene, Greece

ABSTRACT

This case study investigates the in depth institution of the environmental education centers (EECs) as it has been developed in Greece. More specifically, the case study examines the contribution of endogenous development and Local Agenda (the transfer of the principles of Agenda 21 at the local level) in the creation of EECs in areas of increased environmental interest. In addition, the following information regarding EECS is mentioned: aim, staffing, funding, infrastructure, operations, the environmental education programs conducted for students, training, education material, thematic networks, partnerships, evaluation, the course of creation of a network of EECs in Greece and the problems of their function.

INTRODUCTION

Environmental Education Centres were established and operated according to the logic of the endogenous development in areas of increased environmental interest, remote from urban centres. Thus, EECs created jobs in villages and at the same time gave incentives to residents of regions and local entities to establish and develop business activities in specific areas, enhancing the local economy.

However, for their creation, had preceded the contribution of Agenda 21, which stipulated the democratic and consensual procedures ensuring the active participation of citizens and their development of ecological consciousness and conveyed the principles of Agenda 21 at local level i.e., region, county and each district. This was the triggering event to establish and operate and in Greece, even as pilots, the first Environmental Education Centre.

11.3.1. The Contribution of Endogenous Development in the Creation of EECs

According to the article "The endogenous development and the social economy as an instrument for the inversion of the traditional model of regional development" (Rontos, Nagopoulos, 2013), in times of recession in order to restructure the economic and social fabric, the intergovernmental framework at the regional level is being reoriented. At the turning point of the political and economic framework, the concept of development is based mainly on endogenous forces and resources that follow a widely legitimized intergovernmental objective and a strategic financial planning.

Regional development studies the spatial dimension of development and evolution, exploring the economic, social, environmental and other human behaviors in space. The regional analysis aims to the comparison between two regions or one region with a broader geographical context (e.g. a country). To be more specific, it is interested in the comparison of two regions and their evolution and not to compare the development of a united region, often bringing into conflict the goals of national policy with those of the regional/local policy.

Reality (according to the above mentioned article) has shown that the accumulation of population and activities in an expanded area leads secondarily to the increase of demand, which eventually leads to the introduction of new activities (services, etc.). At the same time emerges the model of Bottom-up Development, achieving the so-called integrated development which means the utilization of local advantages and development of all spatial units of each region. In this manner, the transportation system is reinforced and the geographical, economic and social isolation of remote and island regions is eliminated and thus helping them to cope with the economic crisis.

Up to this point, it can be said that Environmental Education Centres were established and operated on the basis of the above mentioned rationale in areas of increased environmental interest, remote from urban centres. In this manner, they created job posts for public servants in villages while offered incentives to residents of areas (first phase) and in local bodies (afterwards) to create and develop entrepreneurial actions in specific areas, enhancing the local economy.

11.3.2. The Contribution of Local Agenda

Theterm «LocalAgenda 21» or «Action Plan 21» is relatively unknown in Greece. In 2002 the first implementation of Local Agenda 21 was completed in the Municipalities of Amarousion and Chalandri.

Agenda 21 is a text – action plan that records the decision taken in 1992 at the Rio Summit, which took place in the context of the World Conference on Environment and Development. It deals with the need for collective action in the 21st century, aiming to enhance the environment and improve people's living conditions (Gittins, 2005: 679). This text was a commitment between the Member-States of the UN to "green" policies.

The most important innovation of Agenda 21 consists of the definition of the procedures suggested as appropriate in order to achieve the objectives. It is about democratic and consensual procedures ensuring the active participation of citizens and the development of their environmental consciousness.

The Local Agenda is the transfer of the principles of Agenda 21 at local level i.e., Region, County and each district. In this manner, it transferred the value and application of Environmental Education in Europe with the Declaration of the European Parliament in 1993 (with the most distinguishable example that of Great Britain).

This triggered the establishment and operation in Greece, even as a pilot program, the first Environmental Education Center (EEC) in Kleitoria of Achaea in 1993. And we have to mention that this was the driving force for the creation of the first EEC, after the Ministry of Education had already signed a law since 1989. And that "maybe" because there was a specific community budget line for the implementation of Agenda 21 in Greece as well as for any other EU country (Georgopoulos, 2005: 43).

In conclusion, it can be said that Environmental Education has emerged as a necessity of the times as the relationship of human societies with nature because of the criticality of contemporary environmental and social problems had to be redefined. The educational policy of our country turned in this direction and aimed at the effectiveness of Environmental Education programs in relation to the solution of environmental problems through a series of pedagogical practices.

Environmental Education Centers are an indispensable part of this necessity. Through these, the educational system is facilitated in the investigation of environmental issues with a view to informing, sensitizing and activating students in critical ecological and environmental issues. In any case the impact that Environmental Education and the EECs have on educators is great, as many programs are now an indispensable part of their educational action.

It is certain that if the broad field of Environmental Education is supported, it can be the instrument that will promote our environmental knowledge and will equip us with the skills required for active participation in environmental decision making.

11.3.3. The Environmental Education Centers (EEC) in Greece

Before we start examining the EECs as environmental education structure, it is advisable to mention the format that they belong. We recall that the Environmental Education occurs in three forms: typical, non typical and atypical (Skanavi, 2004: 112). The typical Environmental Education is developed exclusively within the boundaries of the formal education system, from kindergarten up to tertiary education. A common feature is that their audience is already certain and has common characteristics such as age, level of education etc.

The non-typical Environmental Education aims to develop environmental concepts, skills, attitudes and environmental awareness. It usually takes place in various institutions but also in areas of natural beauty (such as museums, zoos, etc). It is addressed to everyone without assuming that the participants meet some criteria (e.g. income, age, etc.). It also includes broadcasts or special shows in the mass-media.

Finally, the atypical Environmental Education evolves throughout a person's lifetime. Each one of us can have an atypical education in environmental studies depending on his/her own desire, without any systematic presence in educational institutions. It is not directed at specific audiences and is based on goodwill and volunteerism of the individual.

When it comes to Environmental Education, as characteristically stated in the text of the Strategy of “Education for the Sustainable Development: 2005-2015”, a prerequisite for the achievement of education for sustainable development is the strengthening of formal education via its connection with the atypical education, which is more participatory, oriented to the learner and lifelong learning (Zachariou 2008: 2).

The Environmental Centers have a long-term course on examining environmental issues as they are associated with forerunner pedagogical mainstream and environmental movements for the protection of the environment. Their role in the promotion of issues relating to the environment and in the formulation of active citizens, in environmental terms, emerges as crucial to the foundation of the strategy for “education for sustainable development”.

The term "Environmental Centre" is very broad and covers a wide range of centers outside school, with different objectives, activities and organization, depending on the reasons of their establishment, the area they are located, the audience targeting, and so on. They are recognized as settings with pluralistic actions that can contribute to the promotion of the principles of environmental education since they can connect with the local community. They can also be connected with the typical and non-typical education, enhance the external environments as essential educational tools, promote lifelong learning and education, enhance the participation of local communities in their initiatives and actions and finally contribute to the creation of networks of communication and collaboration with local populations (Zachariou 2008: 3). Their importance in the promotion of Educational Issues concerning the Environment and Sustainable Development is reinforced by the recognition that the local community and the environment are now the most important fields of action.

Environmental Centers can be divided into: Nature Centers, Urban Environmental Study Centers, Centers of Environmental Education and Environmental Laboratories (Skanavi 2004: 38). In this direction the EECs are settings that beyond providing information and guidance can also provide citizens with regard to environmental issues. EECs are structured using the philosophy of basic goals of Environmental Education and are connected with quality education (Papadimitriou 1994: 49).

The institution of EECs is directly related to the environmental movement and is now considered internationally one of the main entities of education outside school. The aim is to act as places of pluralistic actions which will contribute to the education of all population groups with the development of a sense of shared responsibility and the development of actions to protect the environment and improve their quality of life through the rational use of the environment. As we noticed above, in “Agenda 21” and the 5th action program entitled "Sustainability is the Target", in the 6th environmental action plan of the European Union (“Environment 2010: Our future, our choice”) and the Strategy on “Education and Sustainability in Europe” a special emphasis is placed on the need to establish campuses which can contribute to the linkage of education with society, aiming at the formulation of environmentally responsible and active citizens.

Greece, according to the law 1892/90, had formally institutionalize Environmental Education into the educational system and had predicted the establishment of EECs, making reference to the purposes, objectives, activities, infrastructure and staffing of EECs. With this law foresaw the creation, from Ministry of Education itself, of an autonomous coordinating entity for the environment which would have both the responsibility of running EECs and the direct responsibility of the more efficient application of Environmental Education in all educational grades throughout the country (minedu.gr).

At present, according to the updates 11941/23-08-2010 and 11942/23-08-2010 of the Ministry of Education, Environmental Education Centers change form and function and are expected to be renamed to "Training Centers for the Environment and Sustainability, which will implement two types of activities: “actions for students” and “lifelong learning for adults”.

11.3.3.1. Objective

Programs that EECs organize and implement are aimed at the creation of a set of values and interests to pupils for active participation in the protection and improvement of the environment, heritage conservation, and consequently the improvement of the quality of life and sustainable development.

In addition, (with the founding decision Γ2/3219/11-5-95) EECs plan and implement environmental education programs for primary and secondary schools aimed at pupils ' awareness. Their objectives also include the production of educational information material for schools, the support of Environmental Education programs for schools in their region, the link with the Universities and other Educational Institutions and organizations at local, national and international level for scientific research and cooperation for producing educational programs, organizing and conducting educational meetings for teachers of Environmental Education, the development of international partnerships with relevant foreign entities, the promotion of research in the field of Environmental Education and finally the creation of Environmental Education Networks (Skanavi 2004: 204).

11.3.3.2. Staffing

In accordance with the relevant ministerial decision, in each centre are seconded a total of five teachers of primary and secondary schools for four years. They constitute the pedagogical team and one of them is operating as managing director of EEC. One teacher of the Pedagogical Group of EEC may be defined as a Deputy Manager. Candidates for the positions responsible for the EEC can be teachers of Primary or Secondary Education with a university degree, with an overall educational service eight years of which at least six years practiced as teachers in schools of the respective echelon. For the members of the pedagogical group is required six-year experience from which at least four years practiced at instructional service of the respective echelon (Ministry of Education Ministry Decision 2011 with Protocol No. 83691/Γ/7). It is clearly stated that priority is given, through points' accumulation, at placing teachers with doctoral and master's degrees. However, there are also more qualifications that must be taken into consideration.

11.3.3.3. Funding

At first, the financing of EEC originated from the reserve of the regular budget of the Ministry of Education. From 2007 to 2013 it was financed under the operational program "Education and Lifelong Learning" of ESPA, the act of "Lifelong Learning Actions for the Environment and Sustainability" (espa.gr) with co-financing of European Union and national resources.

The expenditure for the countries that operate EECs is handled by the relevant prefectures which can be subsidized with credits that are registered for this purpose in the budget of the Ministry of National Education and Religious Affairs. For the accommodation of EECs school buildings which are not used may be available, by decision of the prefect, acting on a proposal from the relevant municipal or community education committee (1892/90 (GOVERNMENT GAZETTE 101A') Article 111 par. 13).

11.3.3.4. Infrastucture

As far as the infrastructure is concerned, (M.D Φ 16/102/G308/3-4-1991) were identified as principal classrooms and the associated lab equipment, computers, library, multi-purpose, logistics, materials and storage for the provincial EECs, restaurant and guesthouse accommodation. In June 1997, the Minister of Education Gerasimos Arsenis signed in an open event at the forecourt of the EEC of Argyroupoli fifteen-year agreements' contract and membership in the CDP (Co-financed Development Programmes funding schemes of six new centers together with the mayors and the President of EIN (Faraggitakis 2010: 4).

The same decision identified the duties of instructors, the economic issues, the connection with the local community and other entities by the operation of the Advisory Committee as well as the issues of administrative and secretarial support.

11.3.3.5. Actions

In each centre are seconded teachers of primary and secondary education for three years. They constitute the pedagogical team. In this context, they can suggest, plan and implement the various actions that are decided in cooperation on the basis of the objectives and the institutional framework, the particularities of the region, the needs of students and teachers, and by utilizing the particular qualifications of its members.

The actions of each centre are not only addressed to students and teachers of the county in which it is located but also in most neighbouring prefectures (who are called districts or counties within range). This gives the possibility to participate in the actions of the EEC and in schools of surrounding counties while encouraged the EECs to expand a 30% of their actions throughout Greece (Tsalikis 2004, 641). Certain objective difficulties to expand the action of EECs throughout Greece are the programs that can an EEC implement within one school year, the number of schools that will have the opportunity to participate and the distance, which is in the case of insular Greece a crucial problem in the networking of EECs.

The various actions of EECs are summarized below.

11.3.3.6. Environmental Education Programs for Students

A basic action of EECs is the design and implementation of programs for students who visit them. Their duration may be from one up to six days and their theme differs and can be modified from region to region. As far as these programs are concerned, the main disagreement is the design and effectiveness of these one-day programs. The above mentioned is based on the argument that their very short duration makes it quite difficult to organize and create them, so that they can combine all dimensions and all the goals of an environmental issue. However, one-day programs are also the most popular in schools, since they do not have special requirements regarding the accommodation and hospitality of the students.

11.3.3.7. Training

Training is another dimension of the role of EECs. The form, structure, content and collaborations concerning the training programs are determined by regulatory circulars and the Ministerial decisions (Γ2/5921/2-11-98, Γ2/57905/4-6-02, 41643/Γ7/24-4-03) and from the technical specifications of the project sheets. The proposed duration is from 20 to 40 hours, without excluding shorter periods of time or workshops. Trainers can be teachers of institutes, academics, people from governmental and non-governmental organizations, collaborators with specific expertise, responsible persons for environmental education, teachers etc. The list is open so that in each case the most suitable person for each environmental issue can be found.

At this point, it is highlighted the fact that in order for the training to be fully-realized, it must be supported by the active involvement of the teachers involved therein, both in the design and in the pedagogical workshops that are conducted.

11.3.3.8. Educational Material

EECs have contributed significantly to the output of packages of educational material that is supportive of school programs. These packages of educational material of the centers can be distinguished into two types. Those relating to school programs implemented in each centre and are usually versions of each EEC and those that have nothing to do with these programs but are supporting material regarding a specific topic.

11.3.3.9. Thematic Networks

The creation of networks in the context of environmental education is quite important. Besides, that constitutes one of the objectives for the creation of EECs. The centers organize and support networks at local, regional, national or even international level. These networks enable a group of schools to share a common theme and work on developing partnerships and actions (Tsalikis, 2004: 649).

The EECs support thematic units of networks that have been created for students who are going to visit them. These thematic units deal with issues concerning a broader context such as forests, rivers, traditional settlements, etc. The Ministry of Education with the following Ministerial Decisions Y.A./Γ2/46672/9-5-02 &Y.A./Γ7/47587/16-5-2003 has issued detailed guidelines for the thematic networks and their partnerships with the responsible of University Education and for international collaborations with a criterion the anticipated benefits for schools. In the appendix, it is presented the document of the Ministry of Education concerning the function of the national thematic networks of the EECs for the school year 2013-2014.

The aim of the function of these networks is to provide an opportunity for students from different areas to work on a theme having a specific goal, to exchange experiences, to highlight common issues, to feel the inclusivity, maintain and enhance diversity, to collaborate in the development of actions at local, national or international level.

However, as stated "EECs have an advantage as moderators of thematic networks, because they are statutory entities of existence, have the infrastructure and people that can support schools from a pedagogical and educational aspect, to ensure communication and to develop partnerships with entities ' (Tsalikis, 2004: 649).

The actions of the EECs are limited within their county. It's quite difficult to expand their actions throughout Greece, since there are objective difficulties, such as the distance and the number of schools. However, the value of visits to distant centers, especially when they have developed their own actions and their own programs tailored to the characteristics of their region, is significant. Today, with the establishment of EECs across Greece there is great overlap in areas within their range. This is definitely a positive element since the programs and actions can be examined under the prism of complementation.

If there is a more permanent relationship in the cooperation between EECs and schools this might be achieved sometime as well. For the time being, the emphasis and priority to the participation of schools that haven't participated before in such programs is that all children have the same opportunities.

11.3.4. Collaborations

Collaboration at local, national and international level can grow in all sectors of action of an EEC within the framework of achieving the central goal. All the above mentioned actions i.e the design of programs, educational activities, the output of educational material, the thematic networks are areas where they can achieve collaborations with individuals and organizations. The utilization of the centre of local or international experience is necessary in order to have best results in its function.

Furthermore, under the prism of complementation of the actions of EECs, collaborations between these Centers can be achieved. A typical example is the cooperation, within the framework of international cooperation and training June 2003, of four EECs of Central Macedonia (Arnea, Eleftherio-Kordelio, Naoussa and Poroiwn) for the organization of a several-day training seminar for teachers from Balkan countries, in which each Centre contributed in its own way in a combined training program (Tsalikis 2004: 642).

However, the collaborations between the centers are made opportunistically in cases like the above mentioned. Such activities could have been expanded and systematized including other actions of these centers, such as programs and educational materials. We tend to believe that this problem is due to the fact that there are no fixed members in setting up the Group of EECs, but they change every three years. Maybe if this can be changed, the centers will gain a greater activity in educational and scientific reality.

11.3.5. Evaluation

The evaluation is a process that deals with the actions of EECs, as is the case of any other educational process. At the level of formal evaluation, concerning actions such as environmental programs, questionnaires are used and filled in by students and accompanying teachers at the end of their visit to the EEC. In addition, questionnaires are filled in by teachers who take part in training seminars.

Another level of evaluation is done through the same teachers of the pedagogical groups of centers, where they discuss and exchange experiences on the implementation of the programs or when it becomes an account of actions EEC. Another form is the assessment meetings with teachers or with those responsible for environmental education, where it is examined whether the actions that a centre develops meet the needs of the educational community.

11.3.6. Course of Creation a Network of EECs in Greece

The first EEC was founded and operated experimentally in the municipality of Kleitoria, Achaia (M.D./1242/1993). The staffing was difficult but the problems were overcome and gained the acceptance of teachers, students and society. Teachers were intrigued by its experiential and interthematic that the educational activity required while local residents saw the visitors under the prism of the region's sustainable development.

The EEC was staffed by two teachers and offered eight-day programs all year round. These programs were attended by school units of secondary grade who were interested to do so. This happened after a draw from the Ministry of Education with the presence of a representative of OLME (Greek Federation of Secondary Education State School Teachers). It was also a place for teachers of Educational Administration of Achaea where they could be further trained. (kpe-kleit. sch.gr).

In May of 1995 with the Ministerial Decision YAΓ2/3219/11-5 were founded six new EEC at Argyroupolis, at Eleftherio- Kordelio, at Kastoria, at Mouzaki, at Konitsa and at Soufli. It was also founded the department of Kleitoria's EEC at Akrata. The EEC of Argyroupolis is operating since 1995. All the others since 1996.

The successful operation of the first eight EECs created increased demand from other regions of the country as well. So after expertise processes in order to meet the criteria of the MD C2/5861/10-1997 five new EECs at Arnaia-Chalkidiki, Drapetsona, Spetses, Kalamata and Lithakia were established. By the year 2000 more EECs were established at the regions of Makrinitsa, Naoussa, Thermo of Aitoloakarnania, Stylida-Ypati, Porroiwn-Serres and Kimi.

Under the MD/72942/C2/11-7-2002 and with the co-financing of the 3rd KPS (Co-financed Development Programmes, in 2002 16 new EECs were established at Vamos-Chania, Arhanes-Herakleion, Korthi-Petaloudwn, Kambos-Chios, Evergetoulas-Lesvos, Ithaca, Amaroussion-Athens, Ypati-Fthiotida, Amfissa, Arachthos, Meliti, Eastern Olympus, Bertiskou-Edessa and Paranesti-Drama. Also in 2002 according to the law 2,896/2002 these centers were administratively subject to the Relevant Regional Directorates of Education. In November 2004 according to the MD 134908/C7 ten new EECs were founded. The new EECs were the following: Laurio, Nea Kios, Theodoros Ziakas at Grevena, Karpenissi, Krestena, Anogeia and Neapoli in Crete, Velventos-Kozani, Molawn-Lakonia and Agia-Larissa. In July 2006 followed the establishment of 15 more new EECs. At Vistonida-Maronia, Philippi, Giannitsa, Kilkis, Grevena, Siatista, Pramanta-Ioannina, Iraia-Arcadia, Kastri-Kinourias, Messolonghi, Thinalia-Corfu, Ierapetra, Smynos-Laconia and Troizina.

The map below presents the CCI by geographic region:

For the school year 2013 – 2014 will operate the following fifty EEC with related programs:

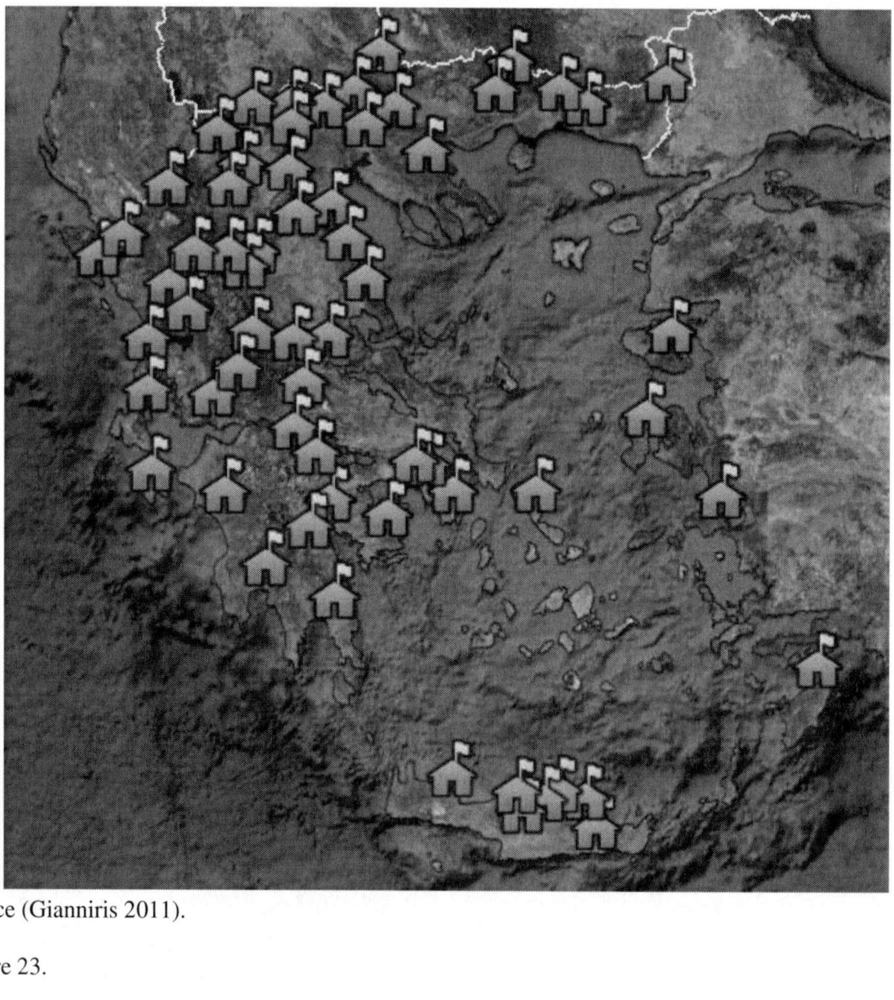

Source (Gianniris 2011).

Figure 23.

Table 1.

East Macedonia and Trace 1) Maronia- Rodopi 2) Paranestio 3) Soyfli 4) Filippi 5) Maronia	West Macedonia 1) Velvendo- Siatista 2) Ziaka- Grevena 3) Kastoria 4) Melitini- Florina	Central Macedonia 1) East Olympos 2) Arnaia 3) Edessa- Giannitsa 4) Eleftheriou- Kordelio & Vertisko 5) Kilkis 6) Naousa 7) Poroi
Thessaly 1) Kissavo- Mavrovounio & Elassona 2) Makrinitsa 3) Mouzaki 4) Pertouli- Trikala	Epirus 1) Araxthos 2) Konitsa- Prammanton 3) Filiata 4) Filippiada	West Greece 1) Akrata- Kleitoria 2) Thermos- Messologi 3) Krestena
Central Greece 1) Amfissa 2) Karpenisi 3) Stylida- Ypati	Attiki 1) Argyroupolis 2) Drapetsona- Trizina- Methana 3) Lavreotiki 4) Elefsina	Peloponese 1) Kalamata 2) Kastri- Arkadia 3) Molei- Lakonia 4) Nea Kios 5) Sikioni
North Aegean 1) Evergetoulas- Lesvos 2) Omiroupolis- Chios	South Aegean 1) Korthio- Andros	Ionian Islands 1) Kerkira 2) Lithekia- Zakynthos 3) Ithaka 4) Sfakiotes
Creta 1) Anogia 2) Arhanes- Rouva- Gouves 3) Neapolis- Ierapetra Vamos		

Source: minedu.gr.

However, although a total of sixty Environmental Education Centers were established, fifty are functional at present and the rest ten have suspended their operation. Part of our research is in a small percentage and the examination of the criteria why something like this is happening.

11.3.7. Problems in Operation of EECs

One of the main problems regarding the operation of EECs is their funding. As mentioned above the EECs operate now with 75% co-financing from the European Union. The program in which they are embedded is ESPA 2007-2013. Taking into consideration the economic crisis that plagues Europe, resources for the continuation of their operation should be ensured from another source. In addition to knowing that European funding programs have specific duration makes it difficult to set long-term objectives in their operation and action as well.

Another weakness of the proper operation of EECs is staffing. In EECs, teachers of all fields of expertise are transferred on condition that they have received any relevant training. Another disputable aspect is that requests for staffing of the EECs are accredited by the relevant Regional Administrations of Education rather than the Ministry of Education, since EECs belong to the former.

Environmental Education Centers are also not located in the immediate vicinity of the trainees, i.e., located away from most school units and offer education and learning through the natural surroundings. In addition, as mentioned earlier, the danger for EECs to constitute merely an occasion for a free trip is existent in many occasions.

Conclusion

Nowadays, 20 years after the founding of the first EEC in Greece, the institution of the EEC is becoming stronger and stronger since these centres are established in every corner of Greece. The environmental education has become a key element and this is the most important step in creating people up-to-date on social happenings with judgement and respect, who can contribute a great deal to the environment.

Making an assessment of the actions of the EEC, it can be said that they play a crucial role in informing, raising awareness and the mobilization of students, teachers and the wider society on critical ecological and environmental issues. Furthermore, the contribution to the provision of corresponding educational material and the set up of environmental projects, which in turn is an integral part of the educational action, are all essential as a matter of fact.

Concerning the three dimensions of environmental education (i.e.,, learning about the environment, within the environment and for the sake of the environment) the centres make their work worthily. And this is evident from the feedback we receive through requests made each year for school participation in the programs.

Our present action and the future action of students who participate in such programs for the sake of the environment is something that it cannot be said with certainty

It's all about personal choices. Either way, environment is a "sensitive" meaning and should be treated accordingly.

References

Chaleplis, S. (2008). «Environmental Education: A dimension of education that contributes to the building of a new worldview for the environment and humans." *Epistimoniko Vima. 40*, 159-174.

Environmental Education Center of Kleitoria, Available at: http://kpe-kleit.ach.sch.gr/ [Last accessed 04/01/2014]

Faraggitakis G. (2010).Environmental Education Centers in Greece: The objectives, the means to achieve them, and the development of the institution from 1993 to today, in

Proceedings of the 5th Conference on PEEKPE: Environmental Education : The crossroadsof Education for Sustainable Development. *Ioannina.*

Georgopoulos (2005). *Environmental Ethics.* Athens: Gutenberg

Gianniris (2011). Environmental education in Greece from 1995 to today, attitudes and positions of teachers in environmental education. The role of science teachers. Patras

Gittins J. (2005). 'Local Agenda 21 in theory and practice: The emerging story" in Environmental Education: The new culture that is emerging (677-696), Athens, Gutenberg.

minedu.gr Ministry of Education, Culture and Sport, Available at: www.minedu.gr [Last accessed 02/04/2013]

Papadimitriou. (1994). Environmental Education and school: A longitudinal view. Athens: Typothito

Rontos, Nagopoulos. (2013). "Endogenous development and the social economy as a means of reversing the traditional model of regional development", 1-5

Skanavi- Tsampoukou (2005). *Environment and Society: A link to incessant evolution.* Athens: Kaleidoscope

Tsalikis (2004). "Environmental Education Centers: Luxury or Necessity? A brief description and evaluation of the operation of the UI on Greece 'in A. Georgopoulos (ed.), *Environmental education: the new emerging culture* (635-654). Athens: Gutenberg

ZachariouA., Kadis K. (2008). "Centres of Environmental Education and Education for Sustainable Development: Report on Network of Environmental Education in Cyprus", in Proceedings of the 4th Conference PEEKPE on Towards Sustainable Development-Natural Resources, Society, Environmental Education. *Nafplio.*

In: Towards a Society with a More Fair Economy
Editors: J. A. Filipe, N. Nagopoulos, K. Rontos et al.
ISBN: 978-1-63482-900-7

ABOUT THE CONTRIBUTORS

Nikolaos Bloskas

Nikolaos Bloskas was born in 7/1/1990 in Chalkidiki, Greece. In 2007 he started his bachelor degree in sociology in the department of Sociology of the University of the Aegean. In 2011 he completed his undergraduate studies with honors. Afterwards, in the same year, he continued with his master studies in the same department in the program of: Social Research on Regional Development and Social Cohesion, the title of his thesis was: The governing framework for CSR and its implementation in Greece at a time of crisis. In 2013 he completed his master degree, also with honors. During the course of his studies he focused in matters of law, political sociology, development and European affairs having published various articles in different scientific journals and books. He also have participated as a member in organizational committees of various scientific seminars and events.

Manuel Pacheco Coelho

Manuel Pacheco Coelho is Professor of the School of Economics and Management at University of Lisbon (ISEG/UL) since 1984. He holds a Bachelor's, a Master's and a PhD degree in Economics from Technical University of Lisbon. He teaches disciplines of Economic Theory, particularly in the area of Microeconomics. He also coordinates and teaches courses in the area of specialization of Natural Resources Economics, Environment and Sustainable Development. He is the Coordinator of the Master in Development and Cooperation (ISEG/UL) as well as of the Post Degree in Economics of Energy, Environment and Sustainable Development (IDEFE/ISEG). He is also Professor of the Doctoral Program MIT/Portugal in "Sustainable Energy Systems". He is researcher at SOCIUS/ISEG and CIRIUS/ISEG research centers with special connection to Sociology and Regional and Urban Economics. He has guided several master thesis and doctorate dissertations. He has significant research work published in books, book chapters and articles in peer-review journals and proceedings of national and international conferences.

Vassiliki Dimitriou

Vassiliki Dimitriou is a graduate of the Department of Economic & Regional Development (Panteio University of Athens) and she has a Master of Science in Tourism Business Administration (Hellenic Open University). As executive in a company which specializes in caring out studies, she is qualified with a significant experience in reviews and evaluations, in management and studies development. She is experienced in project's management and supervision from national and community co-financed programs, regarding corporate social responsibility, gender equality, social economy, employment policies and social integration. Moreover, she is experienced in planning, management and evaluation of national and community programs. She has taught as instructor in a series of continuous vocational training for agents and organizations.

Manuel Alberto M. Ferreira

Manuel Alberto M. Ferreira has studied Electrotechnic Engineering in Lisbon Technical University. He holds a Master Degree in Applied Mathematics by Lisbon Technical University, PhD in Management-Quantitative Methods by ISCTE-Lisbon University Institute and Habilitation in Quantitative Methods by ISCTE-Lisbon University Institute. He used to be Chairman of the Board of Directors and Vice- President of ISCTE-Lisbon University Institute. He is Full Professor at ISCTE-Lisbon University Institute and the Director of the Department of Mathematics in ISTA-School of Technology and Architecture. His research interests are Mathematics; Statistics; Stochastic Processes-Queues and Applied Probabilities; Game Theory; Applications to Management, Finance and Social Problems; Bayesian Statistics-Application to Forensic Identification. He has published 367 papers, in Scientific Journals and Conference Proceedings and 35 book chapters. He has presented 163 communications in International Scientific Conferences. Personal page: https://ciencia.iscte-iul.pt/public/person/mamf

Ivo C. Figueredo

Ivo Cunha Figueredo holds an International MSc in Business Administration at ISTCE/Instituto Universitário de Lisboa in Portugal. He earned his Bachelor's degree in Financial Management by PUC MG - Pontifícia Universidade Católica de Minas Gerais. He has attended an English course at the Auckland University in New Zealand in addition to an English course at the University of Missouri – Kansas City (UMKC) in the U.S.A. He has also attended a postgraduate course in Accounting/Tax Management at CESUPA – Centro de Estudos Superiores do Pará, an MBA course in Accounting and Finance at FGV – Fundação Getúlio Vargas, a course of Accounting sciences by PUC MG - Pontifícia Universidade Católica de Minas Gerais as well as an Accounting Technician Course by IMACO - Instituto Municipal de Administração e Ciências Contábeis. Moreover, he has participated in IFRS 2010 by BDO Trevisan auditors and in the Latin American meeting of Accountants. He has also attended lectures concerning Total Quality Management and seminars on ISO 14000 by Mineração Rio Norte. He has significant experience on Account Systems and Computer Systems Account Implementation. He is Director in FACEPA-FÁBRICA DE PAPEL DA AMAZÔNIA S/A, where he works since 2000. He has several research papers published in prestigious international scientific journals.

José António Candeias Bonito Filipe

José António Candeias Bonito Filipe is Assistant Professor with Aggregation at ISCTE-IUL. He is also Member of BRU-IUL research group. He graduated in Economics by ISEG/UTL - Instituto Superior de Economia e Gestão, Universidade Técnica de Lisboa. He holds a Master in Management Sciences by ISCTE-IUL (Instituto Universitário de Lisboa). He obtained his PhD in Quantitative Methods (Operations Research) by ISCTE-IUL. He is also Subdirector of the Department of Mathematics in ISTA - School of Technology and Architecture at ISCTE-IUL. His research interests include Mathematics; Statistics; Stochastic

Processes - Queues and Applied Probabilities; Game Theory; Applications to Economics, Management, Finance and Social Problems; Environmental and Natural Resource Economics, Tourism, among others. He has published 250 papers in Scientific Journals and Conference Proceedings, 15 book chapters and 7 books. He has presented 80 communications in International Scientific Conferences. He has been leadership awarded by a United States Organization. Moreover, 18 scientific papers awarded, other awarded and distinguished academic achievements. He cooperates with many International Journals, Publishing Houses and Conferences, being Editorial Board Member, Reviewer, Final Evaluator, Judge, Track Chair, Chair of Sessions, Discussant of papers, Invited Speaker, etc. He is member of more than 20 International Organizations, Mentor and Patron of some of them and Country Head for Portugal of an International Academic Organization. He is examiner of PhD Theses in Portugal and abroad as well as participant in PhD Theses Intercalary Evaluation Panels, examiner of Master Theses and President of Board of some of them. He is the supervisor of PhD Theses and Master Theses of students from Portugal and abroad. He cooperates in International Projects and has some scientific partnerships with Scientists and Universities around the world. He is invited Professor in Universities abroad (Spain and Slovakia).

Selvarasu A. Mutharasu

Selvarasu A Mutharasu (born, 1970), has been a Professor of Marketing at the Asia's largest Residential University Annamalai University's Business School as 'Innovative Teacher' for over 20 years. His Wharton-Marketing online course and Research tools, Canada helped his contributions in the field of innovative teaching, advertising in the classroom, shopping in classroom, conducting innovative programmes, making new product 'AΩA' Zipped Collar&Cuff shirt, consultancy on branding, documenting idea of 'Amphi – Floating House', using USDA tool for subsector study, 'Herbal Diaper Market study', incubation of 'Napkin Machine', India paved way for disruptive innovations. His initiative of establishing MRSI.AU.Marketing Forum-2011, has paved way for Real Marketing Simulation physical Game-2012, 'StudentS' shoppee- Walmart India 2013 & 2014 'as Marketing Venture Innovation project, for academic, research excellence are milestones. His paper on Internal Marketing Mix was adjudged as 'First Prize' in AIMS10 International (U.S.A.) Conference-2013 held at IIMB, Bangalore, India. His paper on E-marketing vis-à-vis E-procurement has been certified with 'Excellence Award' 2014 for originality, novel, current and suitable for extension of research applications. His staff training programme on 'Strategic Leadership' 2014, registration of provisional patent of 'Oceanic Translucent tri-Aquarium [OTTAM] (6212/CHE/2014-India Patents), are remarkable social marketing contributions. His e-learning case on 'e2e-employee communication at Annamalai University:iAUs.iDea sharing.Walk the Talking' is in action and progress (http://iaus.blog.com) from October 2014. His membership with AIMS International-USA, Strategic Management Society-USA, New Economic Papers–RePEc as Author 'pmu263' and editor for Central and West Asia 2013, added value to the University. His initiation for Memorandum of Understanding [MoU] with Valaya Alongkorn Rajabhat University, Thailand and Walmart India for academic, research excellence are milestones. His qualitative research paper on 'Service Design Innovation on aquarium customer value' using QSR NVivo has helped him to claim new directions in research on services marketing in addition to his research fronts on Viral marketing Power social networks.

Nikos Nagopoulos

Nikos Nagopoulos completed studies in Sociology and Sociolinguistics in Heidelberg University. Currently, he is working as an Associate Professor in the Department of Sociology at the University of the Aegean, teaching the following: Sociology of Knowledge, New sociological Theory, Methodology and Theory of Social Sciences. He was Director of the post-graduate program "Research in local social development and cohesion", in the same Department. He also teaches the course "European policies for employment and social protection" in the post-graduate program "European societies - European integration" in the same Department. During the period 2014-15 he is working as researcher at the "Lazarsfelds Archive of Social Science" , teaching "New forms of Sociology of Knowledge " at the Vienna University (Austria) - Institut of Sociology.

He has been an academic consultant, evaluator and researcher of the ministries of Labour and social protection of Greece and Cyprus for the use of scientific knowledge in the national action plans for employment and social protection and the integration of the principles of equal treatment in national legislations. He has certified knowledge in vulnerable groups of social exclusion and culturally differentiated groups and he worked for many years as a scientific expert in programmes aimed at these groups. He is author of many books, scientific articles and has been responsible of scientific researches in the field of social science.

Niki Psoma

Niki Psoma was born in Mitilene. She completed her graduate studies at the Department of Primary Education of the University of the Aegean. She continued her post-graduate studies in Sociology at the University of the Aegean, for which she was offered a scholarship from the State Scholarship Foundation of Greece, and in Science of Education (Special Education) of the University Roma Tre. Since 2009 she has been working as a teacher in Greek Primary Education Schools with particular interest in preparing school activities in Environmental Education.

Kostas Rontos

Kostas Rontos is a Professor of Social Demography and Statistics at the Department of Sociology of the University of the Aegean. He is the President of the aforementioned Department and the Director of the MSc program "European Societies and European Integration". He is the Director of the Laboratory of Social Informatics, Statistics and Research Infrastructure, of the e-learning program "Empirical Research in Social Sciences" and of the Summer School "Quantitative and Qualitative Research Methods for Social Sciences". He used to be a Director at the National Statistical Service of Greece, where he had being working for 24 years (1981-2005).

He has participated in several research projects, carried out by several prestigious organizations, regarding statistical research, regional and demographic analysis and information systems. He has been the writer or co-writer of 199 publications, including books, as for example "Statistical Survey: Theory and Applications", "Analysis of Statistical Data and Socio-Demographic Implications", "Tools and Techniques for Decision Making", Psychology-Sociology of Work and Human Resources Management", "Introduction to Economics and Management" and "Managerial Economics" "Methodology of the Design and Construction of an Integrated Information System for the Description of the Foreigners Integration Policy in Greece", monographs such as ''Regional Employment, Projects for Young People and Local Initiatives: A statistical Approach of Employment in Greece'',

"Information Systems as a Supporting Tool of Regional Programming" and "Regional Programming and Spatial Analysis", contributions to books such as 'Social Groups with Xenophobic behaviour", "Theoretical and technical documentation of the integration policy of the foreigners in Greece into the framework of an Integrated Information System" articles, such as "Understanding Xenophobia in Greece: A Correspondence Analysis", "Crime and the (Mediterranean) City: Exploring the Geography of (In)security in Rome, Italy", "Generalised Social Trust in Greece and its Association with Demographic and Socio-economic Predictors", "Demographic trends, young people's attitudes towards marriage and socio-economic changes related to family formation in Greece and in the European Union: A comparative analysis based on official and survey research data, and survey studies in Greece and abroad".

Based on this frame, his research interests emphasize mainly to statistics, regional development and migration, social research, Demography and Information Systems.

Luca Salvati

Luca Salvati has two degrees (ecology: 2000; demography and social sciences: 2004), master's degree in economic statistics, specialization degree in Geography and Environment, PhD in Economic Geography. He is contract Professor of Cartography and GIS, multivariate statistics, and Strategic Environmental Assessment at Third University of Rome. He collaborates with University of Rome 'La Sapienza' in the field of urban and rural geography. He is currently permanent researcher at the Italian Council for Research in Agriculture (CRA); He has also collaborated, as a research fellow, with various research institutions in the framework of both national and European projects on the following themes: desertification, sustainable agriculture, land-use, climate change, urban sprawl and polycentric development at the regional scale, with reference to the Mediterranean basin. He is the author of more than 100 scientific articles in English, 12 books, essays and cartographical atlases.

Miltiadis Stampoulis

Dr. Miltiadis Stampoulis is a Labour Economist and graduate of the Economics School of the Aristotle University of Thessaloniki. He has MSc and PhD in Human Resources Economics from the University of Paris I – Sorbonne. He is Assistant Professor of the Department of Educational and Social Policy of the University of Macedonia, teaching labour economics and employment policies. His scientific interests and his substantial work on a wide range of scientific journals and publications include the relation between education and employment, the human resources management policies, the decentralized employment policies, the economic and social policy, the sectional / regional development, working relationships and adaptable forms of production and employment organization, etc.

Maria-Eleni Syrmali

Maria-Eleni Syrmali is a PhD Candidate at Panteion University of Social and Political Sciences. She received her MSc in Economic Theory from the Department of Economics of the Athens University of Economics and Business. She also completed her undergraduate studies in Economics at the same University. She has delivered lectures in Universities and Higher Technological Education Institutes. She has also presented her research findings in a number of international scientific conferences. Her scientific research has been published in academic journals, collective volumes and conference proceedings.

Flora Tsapala

Flora Tsapala is a Sociologist, MSc in Social Research and Ph.D. candidate in University of Aegean. She is social researcher of University of Aegean. She has been a researcher at a number of EU research projects. She has been participated in collective volume with article: "Analysis of the regional population and the demographic factors in Greece 1951-2011" and "The Quality of statistical data needed to support immigration integration policy in Greece". She has been co-author in papers in Greek Journals such as: "Social elites and new communication methods/ information technologies", "Socioeconomic and political aspects of overall development worldwide: Measurement and interconnections", "European and national policies for the integration of people with disabilities: A review of special education in Greece" and "Review of European and national policies for people with disabilities and criticism of the new Law on special education in Psychiatric Notebooks". She has organized National and International Conferences. She has participated in Greek and English International Conference with objectives such as Regional Demographic Analysis of Greece 1951-2011", Educational impacts of internet", "Educational techniques and methods", "Social and Psychological Causes for School Failure", "International society of sociology". Her research interests include qualitative and quantitative research methodology, the study of social and psychological phenomena and demographic analysis

Ioannis Vavouras

Ioannis Vavouras is Professor of Economic Policy at Panteion University, Department of Public Administration. He has studied at Panteion, from which he received his First Degree and his Ph.D. and at the University of Leicester, Department of Economics, from which he received his Master of Arts in Economics of Public Policy. His CV is included in Marquis Who's Who in the World and in Hübners Who is Who in Greece. He was elected as Head of the Department of Public Administration for three terms and as Rector of Panteion University for two terms. His main fields of research are economic policy, institutional economics, economic governance, macroeconomic analysis, public sector economics and economics of integration. He has more than 100 scientific publications (books, journal articles, volume chapters, etc.). Among his more recent English language publications are included: *Corruption in the Mediterranean and Balkan countries: Main determinants and regional differences*, with K. Rontos and P. Sioussiouras, Nova Science Publishers, Inc., New York, 2013, "Corruption, globalization and development: How are these three phenomena related", with D.A. Lalountas and G.A. Manolas, *Journal of Policy Modeling,* Vol. 33, 2011, "Political rights, development and corruption in the Balkan and Arab Mediterranean countries", with P. Sioussiouras, *Mediterranean Quarterly Journal*, Vol. 23, 2012, and "Modeling the factors that determine the phenomenon of corruption in the Mediterranean and Balkan region", with K. Rontos and P. Sioussiouras, in *Progress in Economics Research. Volume 26*, A. Tavidze (ed.), Nova Science Publishers Inc., 2012, Ch. 4, "The determinants of the shadow economy: The case of Greece", with G. Manolas, K. Rontos and G. Sfakianakis, *International Journal of Criminology and Sociological Theory,* Vol. 6, 2013, "Socioeconomic and political development: Their measurement and connections", with K. Rontos, *Global Journal of Human Social Science*, Vol. 13, 2013 and "Mediterranean countries and corruption: Political, economic and social factors", with K. Rontos, L. Salvati and P. Sioussiouras, *Mediterranean Quarterly Journal,* Vol. 24, 2013.

Desislava I. Yordanova

Desislava Ivanova Yordanova is an Associate Professor in Entrepreneurship and Management at the Department of Business Administration of Sofia University "St Kliment Ohridski". She obtained her Doctoral degree in Entrepreneurship, Strategy and Management from Autonomous University of Barcelona. She has published books, book chapters, and articles in various international journals including Journal of International Management, International Journal of Entrepreneurial Behaviour & Research, Journal of Developmental Entrepreneurship, International Journal of Latest Trends in Finance and Economic Sciences, International Journal of Management, Service Business, and Journal of Applied Economic Sciences. Her research interests include corporate social responsibility, entrepreneurship, small business management, and family business management.

INDEX

#

20th century, 104
21st century, 83, 110, 113, 216

A

abuse, 6, 36, 41
access, 11, 33, 41, 43, 63, 74, 75, 80, 118, 121, 126, 128, 168, 169, 170, 178, 179, 182, 188, 189, 193, 194
accommodation, 220, 221
accountability, 1, 2, 4, 5, 15, 30, 31, 33, 42, 98, 112, 172, 185
accounting, 85, 179, 180
activated carbon, 206
active citizens, 62, 66, 115, 218
actuality, 115
adaptation, 176, 190, 194
adjustment, 58, 140
administrative support, 166
administrators, 191
adults, 219
advancement, vii, 2, 9, 39, 40
adverse effects, 199
Afghanistan, 47, 48
Africa, 2, 34, 35, 36, 48, 50, 138
age, 90, 125, 217
agencies, 2, 3, 9, 41, 64, 74, 82, 97, 122, 123, 166, 167, 169, 170, 171, 172, 182, 187, 189, 199
aggregation, 10
aggression, 180
aging population, 65
agricultural sector, 167
agriculture, 63, 112, 120, 122, 123, 136, 155, 156, 233
AIDS, 200, 201
air quality, 187
Albania, 47
Algeria, 47
alters, 179
aluminium, 143
American culture, 138
American Psychological Association, 209
ammonia, 180
Angola, 47
ANOVA, 49
anti-commons, 127, 128, 130
APA, 209
appetite, 200
aquaculture, 120, 128
aquarium, 231
Argentina, 47
Aristotle, 233
Armenia, 47, 48
Asia, 36, 37, 48, 50, 131, 211, 212, 231
Asian countries, 50
assessment, 8, 133, 154, 155, 160, 169, 223, 226
assets, 113, 168, 179, 180
asthma, 206
atmosphere, 89, 180, 192
attachment, 85
attitudes, 99, 104, 106, 112, 115, 144, 188, 211, 217, 227, 233
audit(s), 86, 196, 197
Austria, 47, 49, 232
authority(s), 4, 5, 6, 9, 41, 76, 81, 98, 99, 120, 123, 177, 184
autonomy, 65
avoidance, 99
awareness, 3, 85, 87, 91, 93, 94, 96, 97, 104, 108, 110, 111, 112, 134, 135, 166, 187, 196, 201, 204, 207, 219, 226
Azerbaijan, 47, 210

B

back pain, 201
backwardness, 134, 137
Bahrain, 47, 49

ban, 206
Bangladesh, 48
banking, 63, 126, 169, 170
banks, 136, 167
Barbados, 47
barriers, 55, 136, 158
base, 7, 58, 64, 71, 82, 109, 120, 134, 172, 179, 183
basic needs, 194, 208
bauxite, 195
behaviors, 104, 133
Belarus, 47
Belgium, 47, 49, 193
benefits, 5, 64, 66, 73, 76, 83, 91, 93, 94, 95, 99, 119, 122, 123, 126, 145, 151, 166, 178, 180, 183, 190, 192, 199, 205, 208, 222
Bhutan, 47
bias, 10
biodiversity, 110, 121, 187, 188, 195
black hole, 127
blueprint, 32
Bolivia, 48
bonuses, 205
Bosnia, 47
Botswana, 30, 47
bottom-up, 62, 169
bounds, 192
brand image, 203
Brazil, vi, 47, 106, 131, 175, 183, 194, 200, 208
Britain, 108
budget line, 217
Bulgaria, vi, 47, 50, 130, 131, 175, 183, 189, 190, 191, 192, 193, 208, 209
bureaucracy, 8, 42, 70, 71, 72, 120, 128, 129, 130
bureaucratic procedures, 77
bureaucratization, 69, 77
Burkina Faso, 48
Burundi, 47
business education, 99
business environment, 83, 93
business ethics, 87, 190, 204
business management, 208, 235
business model, 57, 65, 196
business strategy, 95
businesses, 63, 64, 65, 71, 73, 74, 75, 76, 81, 82, 83, 84, 85, 86, 87, 88, 89, 90, 91, 92, 93, 94, 95, 96, 97, 98, 99, 101, 102, 118, 125, 126, 144, 145, 166, 176, 177, 178, 179, 198

C

CAD, 191
CAM, 191, 192
Cambodia, 47
Cameroon, 47, 49
campaigns, 91, 201, 202, 203, 207
cancer, 201
cane sugar, 180
capacity building, 2, 5
capital accumulation, 3, 70
capitalism, vii, 70, 71, 72, 118, 124, 125, 126, 181
carbon, 159, 186, 188
carbon dioxide, 159, 188
carbon emissions, 186
cardiovascular risk, 201
Caribbean, 36
case study(s), 160, 195, 204, 208, 211, 215
cash, 186, 188
catalyst, 190, 197
category a, 190
causal relationship, 7
Central African Republic, 47, 49
Central Asia, 160
central planning, 60
certification, 69, 71, 77, 86, 182, 193
Chad, 47
challenges, 33, 64, 87, 95, 107, 116, 122, 124, 131, 179, 190, 205
changing environment, 33
charities, 92, 167
checks and balances, 32
chemicals, 200, 206
child labor, 179
children, 90, 187, 193, 194, 222
Chile, 30, 47, 160
chimneys, 207
China, 47, 49, 80, 152
chlorine, 188
circulation, 194
city(s), 74, 80, 81, 95, 96, 97, 98, 100, 116, 134, 136, 137, 138, 139, 140, 141, 142, 181, 200, 230, 233
citizens, vii, 4, 6, 8, 31, 32, 33, 40, 41, 58, 60, 62, 66, 90, 97, 115, 120, 166, 205, 215, 217, 218
citizenship, 87, 137, 178, 207
civil liberties, 4, 8, 9, 11, 12, 15, 18, 21, 24, 27, 30, 31, 39, 40, 42, 44, 52
civil service, 5
civil society, 4, 6, 64, 66, 76, 86, 100, 166, 167, 183, 208
civil war, 10
civilization, 109, 144
clarity, 116, 173
classes, 192, 203
classification, 137, 141, 201
classroom, 105, 231
cleaning, 207
clients, 193, 194

climate, 74, 136, 154, 155, 156, 159, 180, 182, 185, 186, 187, 188, 233
climate change, 154, 180, 185, 186, 187, 188, 233
cluster analysis, 39, 44, 46, 48, 53
clustering, 44, 49, 50
clusters, 44, 48, 49, 50, 53
CO_2, 186, 187, 188
coal, 144, 195
codes, 179
codes of conduct, 179
coherence, 5
Cold War, 2
collaboration, 74, 96, 124, 125, 177, 189, 218
collective bargaining, 178
Colombia, 47, 49
color, 194
combustion, 145, 146
commerce, 65
commercial, 63, 64, 123, 136, 139, 168, 202
Common Market, 160
commons, 117, 118, 120, 121, 124, 126, 127, 128, 129, 130, 131, 210
communication, 82, 93, 136, 188, 189, 192, 201, 210, 212, 218, 222, 231, 234
communication technologies, 82
communism, 72
Communist Party, 79
communitarianism, 125
community relations, 73, 178
compaction, 139
comparative advantage, 119, 158
comparative analysis, 233
compensation, 63, 117, 124, 202
competition, 41, 59, 61, 83, 93, 99, 119, 126, 137, 138
competitive advantage, 101
competitive conditions, 121
competitive markets, 125
competitive regions, 139
competitiveness, 65, 72, 81, 83, 84, 85, 88, 94, 99, 139, 141, 158, 185, 191, 203
competitors, 177
complement, 109
complexity, 85, 134, 135, 158, 161
compliance, 177, 185
composition, 206
computation, 151
computer, 193
conceptualization, 63, 183
conditioning, 186
conference, 109, 233
conflict, 58, 136, 157, 216
Congo, 47
Congress, 79, 108, 130, 202
consciousness, 59, 142, 215, 217
consensus, 3, 34, 36, 129
conservation, 105, 110, 121, 179, 196, 197, 219
consolidation, 54, 81, 90, 94, 96, 155
construct validity, 10
construction, 180, 187
consumers, 71, 72, 78, 83, 84, 88, 89, 92, 125, 126, 145, 175, 182, 183, 189, 203, 209
consumption, 66, 86, 92, 110, 112, 121, 124, 139, 169, 171, 186, 187, 188, 196
consumption patterns, 86, 139
contamination, 139, 141
contract enforcement, 5, 31
controversies, 114
convergence, 50, 134, 137, 139, 142, 153, 154, 155, 156, 157, 158, 159, 160
conviction, 184
cooperation, 33, 64, 76, 90, 92, 94, 96, 97, 98, 106, 110, 117, 118, 119, 120, 121, 122, 123, 126, 127, 129, 131, 173, 190, 197, 219, 220, 222
coordination, 123, 124, 176
copper, 143, 195
corporate governance, 207
Corporate Social Responsibility (CSR), v, 69, 73, 74, 78, 79, 80, 81, 82, 83, 84, 86, 87, 89, 90, 92, 93, 95, 96, 97, 100, 101, 102, 131, 175, 176, 177, 182, 183, 184, 204, 209, 210, 211, 212, 213
correlation(s), 1, 10, 30, 31, 32, 44, 53, 71, 76
corruption, vii, 1, 2, 5, 7, 24, 30, 31, 32, 33, 35, 36, 39, 40, 41, 42, 43, 52, 54, 55, 177, 178, 179, 234
cost, 7, 10, 72, 85, 88, 89, 93, 125, 126, 145, 149, 151, 154, 171
cost of living, 10
Costa Rica, 47
cost-benefit analysis, 149, 151
cotton, 206, 207
Council of Europe, 107
Council of Ministers, 185
covering, 43, 74, 97, 178, 197, 201
CPI, 43, 45, 49
creativity, 192
crises, 71, 119, 122
critical thinking, 103, 112
criticism, 84, 117, 135, 138, 234
Croatia, 47
cross-cultural education, 113
Cuba, 47, 49
cultural conditions, 106
cultural differences, 136
cultural heritage, 193, 197
cultural identities, 199
cultural tradition, 199

cultural transformation, 201
cultural values, 60
culture, 3, 55, 71, 84, 85, 87, 88, 91, 104, 114, 134, 136, 142, 168, 179, 189, 190, 197, 199, 200, 208, 211, 227
cures, 55
currency, 179
curricula, 108, 109
curriculum, 103, 104, 105, 107, 108, 113, 191
customer service, 205
customers, 143, 146, 147, 148, 177, 183, 185, 186, 187, 188, 189, 190, 202, 204, 205
CV, 234
cycles, 189
Cyprus, 47, 227, 232
Czech Republic, 47, 49

D

danger, 226
data analysis, 180
data collection, 201
data set, 156
database, 55, 59, 194, 205
debts, 119
decay, 72
decision makers, 129
decision-making process, 6, 125, 176
deconstruction, 136
defence, 59
deficiencies, 199
deficit, 53, 166, 199
deforestation, 59, 139
degradation, 139, 154, 156, 157, 158, 159, 160
degradation process, 158
degraded area, 66, 196
Delta, 206
democracy, vii, 10, 11, 30, 32, 33, 40, 42, 43, 53, 54, 55, 76, 110, 137
democratisation, 85
democratization, 2, 42
demographic factors, 234
demographic transition, 134, 139
demographic trends, 61, 65
demography, 233
dengue, 201
Denmark, 47, 49, 82, 108
Department of Education, 233
dependent variable, 9, 11, 12
deprivation, 31
depth, 64, 70, 154, 158, 215
deregulation, 57, 62, 85
destruction, 114
developed countries, 119, 120, 122, 186
developing countries, 10, 33, 34, 77, 85, 100, 122, 140, 198
developing economies, 30
development model, 62, 63, 88, 99, 166, 185, 208
development policy, 109, 111
deviation, 138
diabetes, 201
dialogues, 165
diamonds, 144
dichotomy, 134
diffusion, 59, 76, 100, 107
dignity, 112
directives, 91, 129
directors, 97
disaster, 105, 110
disclosure, 75, 77, 90, 100, 101, 135, 178
discrimination, 166, 176, 179, 205
diseases, 201
disparities, 7, 58, 59, 66, 133, 136, 137, 154, 155, 156, 157, 160, 172, 176
dispersion, 156
distribution, vii, 14, 17, 20, 24, 26, 29, 40, 58, 59, 61, 66, 124, 146, 151, 156, 157, 158, 159, 160, 181, 188
distribution function, 146
distribution of income, 58, 159
divergence, 134, 156, 158, 159
diversification, 82, 172, 197, 198
diversity, 63, 90, 112, 140, 157, 205, 222
DOI, 78, 80, 151, 152
dominant strategy, 121
Dominican Republic, 47
donations, 92, 168, 190, 211
draft, 95, 102
drawing, 66, 96, 155
drought, 139, 160
duality, 140
dynamism, 125

E

East Asia, 101
Eastern Europe, 50, 193
ecological processes, 157
ecology, 160, 168, 233
economic activity, 6, 7, 34, 40, 61, 63, 64
economic change, 65, 106, 124, 137, 233
economic consequences, 180
economic cooperation, 130
economic crisis, 40, 61, 81, 82, 94, 100, 137, 216, 225
economic development, 1, 2, 8, 10, 11, 30, 31, 36, 39, 41, 42, 43, 49, 53, 109, 111, 129, 133, 139,

155, 156, 167, 176, 177, 178, 180, 183, 185, 195, 197, 207, 208
economic efficiency, 42, 82
economic growth, vii, 3, 6, 7, 34, 36, 37, 40, 42, 53, 54, 55, 61, 62, 63, 107, 109, 111, 119, 128, 154, 155, 156, 157, 160, 165, 167, 199, 202
economic growth rate, 128
economic indicator, 160
economic institutions, 3, 6
economic integration, 142
economic performance, 3, 34, 35, 64, 126, 157, 160
economic policy, 58, 62, 63, 66, 73, 94, 234
economic problem, 83, 117, 120, 129
economic reform(s), 119
economic relations, 6, 72
economic resources, 166
economic sociology, 78
economic systems, 137, 139
economic theory, 176
economic transformation, 64, 67, 125
economics, 3, 36, 121, 153, 154, 160, 181, 233, 234
economies of scale, 3
ecosystem, 154, 157
ECs, 218
Ecuador, 47
education, vii, 3, 11, 32, 40, 75, 103, 104, 105, 106, 107, 108, 112, 113, 114, 115, 158, 168, 186, 188, 190, 191, 192, 197, 199, 201, 205, 215, 217, 218, 219, 220, 221, 223, 226, 227, 233, 234
educational attainment, 8, 32
educational institutions, 218
educational materials, 223
educational opportunities, 113
educational policy, 217
educational process, 112, 223
educational programs, 219
educational system, 104, 108, 109, 217, 218
educators, 217
egg, 184
Egypt, 47, 49
El Salvador, 47
elaboration, 110
e-learning, 231, 232
electricity, 125, 146, 186, 187
emission, 145, 159, 186, 187
empirical studies, 43, 127, 133
employees, 61, 63, 71, 73, 83, 85, 88, 93, 98, 168, 171, 175, 177, 178, 183, 185, 186, 187, 189, 192, 193, 194, 195, 196, 197, 198, 201, 202, 204, 205, 209
employers, 192, 194
employment, 59, 60, 61, 62, 63, 64, 65, 66, 67, 74, 82, 84, 85, 90, 127, 129, 140, 166, 168, 169, 171, 172, 179, 182, 191, 194, 198, 199, 230, 232, 233
employment growth, 182
employment status, 166
empowerment, 74
encouragement, 82, 205
endogenous growth, 57, 58, 60, 61, 62, 67, 172
endowments, 155, 168
energy, 91, 124, 126, 143, 144, 145, 146, 152, 180, 186, 187, 188, 189, 196, 202, 205
energy consumption, 186
energy efficiency, 186, 187, 188
enforcement, 32, 75, 122
engineering, 191
entrepreneurs, 63, 66, 86, 93, 97, 99, 126, 177
entrepreneurship, 58, 60, 63, 65, 74, 78, 82, 86, 94, 95, 99, 117, 120, 165, 166, 167, 168, 169, 170, 172, 176, 181, 182, 204, 209, 235
environmental aspects, 195, 196
environmental awareness, 82, 100, 104, 109, 205, 207, 217
environmental conditions, 176
environmental control, 195, 196
environmental degradation, 105, 153, 154, 155, 157
environmental education, 103, 104, 105, 106, 108, 113, 114, 115, 158, 215, 217, 218, 219, 221, 223, 226, 227
environmental effects, 206
environmental impact, 83, 86, 157, 180, 186, 195, 196, 197, 207
environmental issues, 74, 83, 85, 103, 104, 137, 139, 153, 180, 196, 204, 217, 218, 226
environmental management, 179, 180, 195, 196
environmental movement, 104, 109, 110, 115, 218
environmental organizations, 207
environmental policy, 103, 108, 115, 195, 196
environmental protection, 76, 98, 107, 111, 114, 177, 195, 196, 197, 204
environmental quality, 104, 154, 155, 156, 157, 158, 196, 197
environmental standards, 75
environmental sustainability, 176, 184, 189, 195, 207, 208, 209
environmental variables, 154, 155, 156, 157, 158, 160
environmentalism, 111, 181
EPC, 202
equality, 66, 111, 204
Equatorial Guinea, 47
equilibrium, 62, 72, 121, 197
equipment, 144, 180, 189, 196, 200, 220
equitable distribution, 66

equity, 157, 161
Eritrea, 47
erosion, 54
estimation problems, 9
Estonia, 30, 47
ethical issues, 121
ethical standards, 175, 182
ethics, 65, 140, 185, 190
Europe, 50, 59, 63, 64, 65, 66, 67, 74, 78, 80, 84, 86, 87, 90, 105, 119, 128, 133, 134, 138, 141, 142, 160, 178, 187, 203, 217, 218, 225
European Commission, 3, 5, 74, 83, 84, 102, 177, 210
European Community, 115, 138
European integration, 232
European market, 74
European Parliament, 34, 84, 90, 217
European policy, 63, 85, 94
European Regional Development Fund, 59
European Union (EU), 34, 49, 59, 63, 64, 67, 70, 73, 75, 76, 77, 79, 83, 84, 94, 103, 104, 107, 115, 159, 167, 168, 170, 182, 185, 187, 212, 217, 218, 220, 225, 233, 234
everyday life, vii
evidence, 34, 36, 81, 127, 153, 154, 158, 160, 185
evolution, 8, 58, 86, 106, 109, 110, 114, 115, 127, 139, 153, 154, 181, 188, 197, 216, 227
exclusion, 63, 64, 127, 135, 136, 167, 169, 173, 232
execution, 171, 200
exercise, 2, 5, 59, 61, 66, 135, 141, 207
expertise, 83, 91, 94, 125, 170, 221, 223, 226
exploitation, 62, 72, 121, 122, 144, 145, 160, 176
explosives, 200
external environment, 71, 86, 97, 183, 218
externalities, 118, 179
extraction, 44, 61, 144, 195

F

Facebook, 125
factor analysis, 39, 41, 42, 44
factories, 127, 207
faith, 112, 134
families, 65, 119, 120, 123, 128, 177, 183, 187, 206
family budget, 189
family life, 183
farmers, 63, 123
fauna, 112, 180
federal law, 108
fever, 202
fibers, 206
financial, 58, 61, 62, 69, 72, 82, 83, 84, 85, 88, 90, 93, 94, 99, 100, 101, 111, 119, 124, 126, 128, 151, 165, 166, 167, 169, 170, 173, 179, 184, 185, 186, 188, 193, 196, 202, 207, 208, 216
financial capital, 72, 126
financial crisis, 62, 69, 82, 99, 119
financial data, 84
financial planning, 58, 216
financial resources, 83, 88, 94
financial sector, 119, 184
financial support, 169, 193, 207
financial system, 111, 185
Finland, 47, 49
fires, 188
fixed costs, 125
flaws, 32, 167
flexibility, 72, 140, 188
flooding, 105
flora, 112, 180
fluid, 33
food, 122, 181
force, 61, 72, 217
Ford, 146
foreign aid, 34
forest management, 187
formal education, 113, 115, 217, 218
formation, 8, 113, 155, 193, 233
formula, 9
foundations, 65, 84, 109, 166, 170, 182, 197, 200
fragments, 71
France, 47, 49, 73, 82, 100, 108
franchise, 204
free goods, 124
free market economy, 72, 73
freedom, 4, 11, 30, 32, 33, 42, 44, 54, 121, 139, 178
friction, 136
funding, 65, 126, 168, 169, 170, 172, 215, 220, 225
funds, 4, 64, 151, 152, 167, 168, 171, 188

G

Gabon, 47
GDP, 10
gender equality, 112, 230
genetic code, 184
geography, 3, 36, 135, 136, 153, 233
geometry, 135
geo-political, 138
Georgia, 47, 49, 106
Germany, 34, 47, 49, 73, 108
GHG, 185
GIS, 233
global competition, 119
Global Competitiveness Report, 35, 37
global economy, 85, 94, 126, 212
global village, 118

globalization, 2, 34, 35, 41, 54, 64, 71, 119, 139, 178, 202, 234
GNP, 10
goods and services, 98, 125, 188
governance, 1, 2, 3, 4, 5, 6, 7, 8, 9, 10, 12, 30, 31, 32, 33, 34, 35, 36, 40, 41, 43, 54, 55, 62, 99, 154, 172, 184, 185, 208, 234
government effectiveness, vii, 1, 27, 30, 32, 39, 41, 42, 43, 52
government intervention, 95
governments, 2, 4, 7, 32, 41, 72, 75, 82, 99, 107, 119, 122, 127, 128, 129, 144
grades, 219
graduate program, 232
grants, 169
Great Britain, 105, 217
greed, 109
greenhouse, 185
greenhouse gas(s), 185
groundwater, 139, 180
grouping, 44
growth, vii, 2, 3, 9, 33, 34, 35, 39, 42, 53, 55, 57, 58, 59, 60, 61, 62, 63, 65, 67, 84, 85, 88, 94, 99, 109, 110, 111, 112, 119, 120, 139, 154, 156, 159, 160, 172, 176, 177, 178, 181, 184, 185, 199, 205
growth rate, 154, 156
Guatemala, 47
guidance, 1, 7, 85, 218
guidelines, 1, 2, 75, 76, 108, 178, 179, 184, 185, 195, 196, 197, 222
Guinea, 47, 48
Guyana, 48

H

Haiti, 47
harmonization, 136, 183
harmony, 136
health, vii, 32, 40, 41, 63, 91, 112, 151, 167, 168, 197, 200, 201, 202, 203, 206
health care, 168
health risks, 201
hearing loss, 201
hegemony, 140
height, 200
hepatitis, 201
heterogeneity, 49, 136, 140
heteroscedasticity, 11
hiring, 171, 197, 198, 205
history, 35, 41, 103, 122
HIV, 200, 201
homes, 125, 126
homogeneity, 136
Honduras, 48
Hong Kong, 31, 47, 49
hospitality, 221
host, 59, 77, 88
House, 10, 11, 30, 34, 43, 44, 54, 231
housing, 66, 98, 184, 188, 198
human activity, 114
human behavior, 216
human capital, 166, 192
human development, 1, 3, 8, 9, 11, 18, 30, 31, 32, 33, 36, 39, 41, 42, 43, 52, 55, 177, 197, 208
human development index, 1, 8, 9, 11, 31, 32, 43
human experience, 112
human resource development, 183
human resources, 88, 91, 93, 95, 99, 172, 182, 185, 194, 207, 233
human right(s), 2, 74, 76, 112, 177, 178, 202, 205
human security, 112
human welfare, 144
Hungary, 47
hybrid, 73, 126, 146
hydrogen, 145, 146
hygiene, 201
hypocrisy, 88
hypothesis, 7, 44, 52, 53, 77, 89, 154, 157

I

ICC, 106
Iceland, 47, 50
ideal(s), 72, 73, 88, 115, 121, 140, 205
identification, vii, 40, 61, 165, 169
identity, 112, 136, 138, 140
ideology, 35, 71, 111
IEA, 55
image(s), 77, 83, 93, 96, 97, 98, 100, 102, 113, 118, 177, 182, 189, 203, 204, 212
imbalances, 59, 126, 158
IMF, 6, 35, 36, 55
immigration, 234
Impact Assessment, 197
improvements, 127, 200, 201, 205
impulsive, 92
in transition, 142
income, vii, 3, 8, 9, 10, 11, 12, 15, 18, 21, 24, 27, 30, 31, 37, 39, 40, 41, 42, 43, 49, 52, 58, 63, 128, 140, 141, 154, 155, 159, 168, 197, 198, 217
income inequality, 37
increased competition, 61
independence, 5, 65
independent variable, 9, 12, 16, 20, 22, 26, 29
India, vi, 48, 131, 175, 183, 202, 203, 208, 209, 211, 231
individual action, 124, 125
individual rights, 32, 44

individualism, 70, 125, 137, 139
individuals, 6, 64, 71, 76, 90, 97, 120, 122, 124, 176, 206, 222
Indonesia, 48
industrial revolution, 138, 139
industrialization, 140
industrialized countries, 30, 61, 159
industry(s), 60, 61, 71, 98, 144, 145, 155, 180, 192
inefficiency, 2
inequality, 59, 85, 111, 159, 160
infancy, 86
inflation, 34, 128
informal sector, 140
information economy, 124
information technology, 124
infrastructure, 4, 6, 32, 64, 125, 183, 198, 199, 207, 215, 218, 220, 222
ingredients, 32
initiation, 231
innovation, 3, 57, 63, 64, 65, 67, 84, 89, 94, 99, 120, 144, 172, 185, 188, 190, 192, 216
innovator, 192
insecurity, 89
inspections, 202
institutional change, 6, 35
institutional economics, 3, 54, 234
institutional framework, 2, 41, 42, 73, 167, 171, 173, 182, 220
institutional quality, 1, 4, 6, 7, 30, 37
institutional reforms, 6, 32
institutions, 1, 2, 3, 4, 5, 6, 7, 30, 31, 32, 33, 34, 35, 36, 41, 42, 53, 54, 57, 64, 65, 70, 71, 73, 76, 77, 87, 94, 109, 115, 119, 121, 135, 178, 181, 184, 193, 197, 217, 218, 233
integration, 36, 61, 63, 64, 65, 74, 75, 82, 85, 87, 89, 91, 95, 107, 113, 168, 182, 183, 189, 197, 203, 207, 232, 233, 234
integrity, 172, 200
intellect, 115
intellectual capital, 190
intellectual property, 127
intelligence, 137
intensive farming, 139
Inter-American Development Bank, 85, 101
interdependence, 82, 110
interest groups, 6
interference, 11, 198
intermediaries, 97
International Bank for Reconstruction and Development, 34
International Chamber of Commerce, 106
international competition, 138
international financial institutions, 184
international law, 76
international meetings, 104
International Monetary Fund, 35
international relations, 3
international standards, 203
international trade, 120
internationalization, 61, 185
internship, 190, 191
interpersonal relations, 81
interpersonal relationships, 81
interrelatedness, 104
intervention, 59, 66, 100, 184, 208
inversion, 216
investment(s), 2, 42, 65, 86, 128, 129, 151, 165, 170, 171, 177, 178, 180, 182, 183, 184, 186, 195, 196, 198, 199, 200, 203
investment capital, 65
investors, 83, 89, 125
iodine, 206
Iran, 47, 49
Iraq, 47, 49
Ireland, 47, 50
iron, 143, 195
Islam, 32, 35
islands, 172
isolation, 8, 61, 172, 216
Israel, 47, 139
issues, vii, 2, 3, 4, 6, 10, 33, 35, 54, 62, 66, 72, 77, 82, 85, 86, 87, 88, 89, 94, 97, 98, 99, 103, 104, 105, 107, 108, 113, 114, 134, 136, 139, 153, 154, 166, 173, 176, 184, 185, 188, 189, 190, 193, 201, 203, 205, 217, 218, 220, 222
Italy, 30, 47, 49, 133, 139, 141, 153, 159, 233

J

Jamaica, 47
Japan, 31, 47, 49, 79, 80, 211
job creation, 66, 128
joint ventures, 168
Jordan, 47
judiciary, 2
jurisdiction, 72

K

Kazakhstan, 47
Kenya, 48, 101
Keynes, 59
Keynesian, 58, 59
Keynesian model, 59
kindergarten, 217
knowledge-based economy, 74, 190
Korea, 31, 47
Kuwait, 47, 49

Kuznets Curve, 154
Kyoto Protocol, 187
Kyrgyzstan, 47

L

labor market(s), 61, 67
labor relations, 176, 182
labour market, 57, 61, 62, 64, 66, 159, 165, 167
landfills, 180
landscape(s), 134, 136, 137, 139, 157
languages, 3, 203
Laos, 47
Latin America, 36, 48, 54, 101, 230
Latvia, 47
laws, 59, 91, 169, 180, 195, 207
lead, 40, 55, 59, 72, 75, 94, 106, 110, 112, 139, 157, 172, 177, 191, 194, 208
leadership, 82, 91, 99, 231
leakage, 198
learners, 213
learning, 79, 105, 112, 113, 126, 193, 226
Lebanon, 47
legislation, 75, 76, 77, 94, 127, 195
leishmaniasis, 201
level of education, 217
liberalisation, 82, 85
liberalization, 72
Liberia, 48, 49
life expectancy, 8, 11
life quality, 154, 177
lifelong learning, 83, 115, 218, 219
lifetime, 197, 217
light, 74, 103, 134, 135, 139, 182
linear dependence, 14, 17, 21, 24, 27, 29
linear model, 156
linen, 206
liquidity, 88
Lisbon Strategy, 73, 84
literacy, 186, 188
Lithuania, 47, 80
livestock, 123, 136
living conditions, 63, 194, 216
loans, 167, 184, 193
local authorities, 60, 81, 95, 97, 100, 123, 166, 167, 173
local community, 98, 165, 167, 170, 182, 207, 218, 220
local development, 60, 61, 62, 63, 99, 182, 197
local government, 81, 82, 88, 92, 95, 96, 99, 100, 198
local labor markets, 57
local networking, 81
local production systems, 57, 61
logistics, 125, 195, 220
loneliness, 135
long-term services, 90
love, 125

M

Macedonia, 47, 81, 190, 191, 192, 222, 225, 233
machinery, 180
macroeconomic policy, 40
major issues, 181
majority, 9, 85, 93, 95, 137
malaria, 200, 201
Malaysia, 47, 100
man, 104, 111, 114, 136, 139, 194
management, 4, 5, 34, 62, 63, 64, 78, 85, 87, 89, 101, 112, 121, 124, 139, 152, 160, 161, 170, 176, 183, 185, 188, 189, 190, 192, 195, 197, 199, 200, 201, 205, 206, 208, 210, 229, 233, 235
manganese, 180, 195
manufacturing, 136, 167
mapping, 170
marginal costs, 125, 126, 129
marginalization, 64, 135, 166
market failure, 140
market share, 84, 125
marketing, 77, 78, 88, 89, 178, 202, 203, 207, 211, 231
marketplace, 126
marriage, 233
Marx, 70, 71, 79
mass, 76, 126, 146, 176, 189, 217
mass media, 76
materials, 105, 180, 191, 193, 204, 206, 220
mathematics, 113
matrix, 45
matter, 35, 36, 54, 74, 75, 105, 107, 157, 180, 187, 196, 206, 226
Mauritania, 47
Mauritius, 47, 202
measurement(s), 7, 9, 10, 34, 36, 55, 61, 77, 88, 136, 138, 179, 180, 181, 234
media, 4, 88, 98, 102, 126, 203, 217
median, 47, 48, 49
Mediterranean, v, 123, 133, 134, 135, 136, 137, 138, 139, 140, 141, 142, 160, 161, 233, 234
Mediterranean countries, 133, 134, 137, 141, 234
Mediterranean regions, 123
melting, 135
membership, 46, 47, 184, 220, 231
mental disorder, 168
metaphor, 137
methodology, 10, 35, 43, 50, 73, 77, 88, 112, 113, 115, 166, 197, 234

Mexico, 47
Microsoft, 191
middle class, 140
Middle East, 49, 78, 138, 202
migrant population, 139
migration, 59, 123, 233
military, 194
Ministry of Education, 108, 217, 218, 219, 220, 222, 223, 226, 227
mission, 87, 185, 187
Missouri, 230
misuse, 41
mixed economy, 64
model specification, 53
modelling, 159, 161
models, 3, 11, 30, 58, 73, 89, 111, 134, 137, 138, 145, 146, 154, 155, 178
moderators, 222
modern capitalism, 70
modern economies, 117
modernism, 138, 142
modernity, 136, 138
modernization, 139
modifications, 151
modules, 178, 190
Moldova, 48
Mongolia, 48
Montenegro, 47
Moon, 96, 101, 178, 210, 211
morality, 42
Morocco, 47, 139
morphology, 133
Moscow, 106
motivation, 8, 82, 99, 190
Mozambique, 48, 49
multidimensional, 3, 33, 41, 97, 103
multimedia, 193
multinational companies, 203
multinational corporations, 76
multinational enterprises, 71, 212
multiplier, 95
multiplier effect, 95
multivariate statistics, 233
musculoskeletal, 201
museums, 217
music, 126
Myanmar, 47

N

Namibia, 47
narratives, 135
national debt, 119
national income, 8, 10, 11, 43
national interests, 119
national policy, 58, 75, 216
National Research Council, 131
national strategy, 90, 91, 94, 95, 102
native species, 187
NATO, 193
natural environment, 91, 105, 107, 108, 113, 126, 183
natural gas, 144
natural resource exploitation, 121
natural resources, 62, 105, 110, 111, 112, 125, 127, 130, 144, 157, 176, 181, 184, 185, 195, 199, 210
negative consequences, 176
negative effects, 53, 144
negative relation, 156
negativity, 77
negotiation, 183, 186
neoliberalism, 72
Nepal, 48, 131
Netherlands, 47, 49, 64, 67, 82, 100, 160
network operators, 167
networking, 62, 81, 96, 97, 220
neural network, 125
New Deal, 72, 120
New Zealand, 47, 55, 79, 230
next generation, 120
NGOs, 64, 66, 76, 78, 88, 96, 97, 106, 109, 169, 183
Nicaragua, 48
nickel, 195
Nigeria, 48
nodes, 134, 151, 152
non-renewable resources, 144
normal distribution, 13, 17, 24, 26
North America, 50
Norway, 47, 108
nursing, 128
nursing home, 128

O

objective criteria, 179
obstacles, 95, 115, 120, 128, 145, 170, 205
OECD, 3, 5, 34, 35, 36, 41, 54, 63, 67, 75, 178, 212
oil, 49, 144, 145, 146, 180
one dimension, 1
OPA, 94
open markets, 119
openness, 5, 32, 176
operations, 74, 165, 177, 178, 184, 188, 195, 196, 197, 198, 199, 201, 215
opportunities, 66, 83, 93, 95, 140, 141, 144, 173, 183, 190, 196, 199, 205, 222
oppression, 10
optimism, 114

optimization, 59
organ(s), 202, 205
organism, 176
organizational culture, 207
organize, 120, 125, 128, 191, 219, 221
originality, 231
OSHA, 201
output per worker, 34
outreach, 173
outsourcing, 139
overlap, 95, 114, 222
overpopulation, 59
ownership, 101, 126, 127, 145
ox, 79

P

Pacific, 79
Pakistan, 47
Panama, 47
paradigm shift, 118
Paraguay, 47
parallel, 31, 109, 177
parasites, 201
participants, 106, 122, 176, 179, 192, 217
partition, 127
pasture, 123
peace, 112
per capita income, 3, 155
perfect competition, 59
performance indicator, 86, 180, 200
permit, 5, 120, 184
personal achievements, 205
personal autonomy, 11, 32, 44
personal choice, 226
personality, 85, 205
persuasion, 212
Peru, 47
petroleum, 202, 210
pharmaceutics, 127
Philippines, 48
phosphate, 143
photovoltaic panels, 152
physical environment, 180
platform, 63, 67, 125, 181
Plato, 3
playing, 75, 135
pluralism, 82
pneumoconiosis, 201
Poland, 47, 50, 108
polar, 59, 60, 61, 189
polarization, 60, 61, 138, 157
police, 5, 7
policy choice, 10
policy framework, 1, 31, 57, 157
policy initiative, 178
policy making, 64, 66, 73, 173
policy options, 159
policy recommendations, 2, 32
policymakers, vii, 3, 33
political aspects, 31, 40, 45, 234
political crisis, 40
political democracy, 53, 55
political development, 2, 30, 32, 36, 39, 40, 42, 46, 49, 50, 52, 53, 55, 234
political freedom, 1, 30, 31, 33, 42
political instability, 31, 53, 137
political institutions, 2, 4, 6, 32, 53
political parties, 10
political pluralism, 32, 43
political power, vii, 2, 5, 33, 72
political problems, 128
political rights, vii, 8, 9, 10, 15, 30, 31, 39, 40, 42, 43, 52
political stability, 1, 4, 7, 12, 14, 31, 55
political system, 4, 8, 31, 42, 49
politics, 185
pollution, 83, 114, 139, 144, 145, 156, 180
population, 32, 58, 59, 60, 106, 120, 123, 127, 128, 129, 139, 140, 144, 157, 180, 181, 194, 198, 208, 216, 218, 234
population group, 60, 218
population growth, 139, 157, 181
population structure, 127
portfolio, 188
Portugal, vi, 47, 50, 117, 121, 128, 130, 131, 143, 175, 183, 184, 185, 187, 188, 189, 208, 210, 211, 229, 230, 231
positive attitudes, 108, 115
positive correlation, 53
potential output, 144
poverty, 42, 63, 67, 85, 90, 112, 120, 123, 140, 170, 177, 181, 184
poverty alleviation, 181
poverty reduction, 112
power plants, 126, 180
predictor variables, 31
preparation, 107, 185
preservation, 121, 176, 181, 187
President, 74, 83, 184, 220, 230, 231, 232
prevention, 106, 183, 200, 201
primacy, 36
primary sector, 66
principles, 5, 30, 33, 63, 64, 65, 70, 73, 75, 76, 83, 87, 90, 91, 112, 113, 114, 115, 170, 172, 177, 178, 179, 181, 182, 184, 185, 197, 203, 204, 208, 215, 217, 218, 232

private enterprises, 63, 96, 117
private ownership, 127
private sector, 5, 6, 10, 41, 85, 95, 120, 166, 167, 181, 198
privatization, 4, 72
probability, 11, 147, 148, 149
procurement, 169, 171, 231
producers, 63
professional development, 183, 205
professional growth, 191
professionals, 87, 88, 191, 193
profit, 6, 41, 63, 64, 65, 70, 71, 72, 82, 87, 88, 94, 110, 111, 117, 125, 169, 170, 176, 178, 181, 182, 203, 204
profitability, 62, 176, 185, 208
project, 30, 81, 96, 97, 98, 128, 169, 173, 188, 192, 193, 194, 198, 199, 203, 207, 221, 229, 231
promoter, 207
property rights, 5, 31, 35, 118, 127
protection, 7, 31, 90, 91, 98, 107, 110, 111, 112, 178, 187, 188, 199, 200, 205, 218, 219, 232
prototype, 136
psychological phenomena, 234
psychology, 60, 209
public administration, 3, 94, 129
public authorities, 5, 99, 120, 177, 184
public awareness, 86, 106
public debt, 62
public goods, 6
public institutions, 2, 33
public interest, 64, 96, 208
public officials, 8
public opinion, 71, 74, 76, 78, 177, 196
public policy, 82, 86, 91, 120, 136
public resources, 5, 81, 96, 202
public sector, 4, 5, 6, 40, 41, 42, 54, 63, 66, 87, 88, 95, 140, 185, 234
public service, 5, 32, 54, 64, 198
pulp, 180
purchasing power, 8, 9, 10, 43
purchasing power parity, 10
purity, 206

Q

qualifications, 205, 219, 220
qualitative research, 231
quality control, 73
quality of governance, 1, 10, 30, 31, 34, 41
quality of life, 41, 103, 107, 111, 114, 128, 159, 180, 183, 184, 185, 197, 202, 208, 218, 219
quantitative research, 234
queuing networks, 151, 152
queuing theory, 151

R

race, 121
radio, 187, 203
ratification, 73
rationality, 70, 71, 136, 140, 176, 181
raw materials, 171, 206
reactions, 110
reading, 135
real estate, 193
real income, 9, 40, 41
reality, 7, 59, 73, 75, 76, 86, 98, 115, 118, 124, 127, 128, 166, 167, 186, 189, 209, 223
reallocation of resources, 111
recall, 134, 217
recession, 57, 61, 64, 69, 81, 85, 89, 216
recognition, 112, 140, 167, 169, 171, 178, 179, 184, 202, 205, 218
recommendations, 2, 32, 106
reconciliation, 114
recovery, 99, 180, 187, 196, 197, 199
recycling, 125, 139, 143, 144, 145, 148, 149, 151, 152, 180, 189, 206
redistribution, 7, 126, 141
reform(s), 2, 4, 6, 32, 33, 36, 54, 62, 67, 88, 90, 118, 119, 184
refugees, 205, 207
regeneration, 188
regional inequalities, 59, 60, 62
regional policy, 59, 60, 61, 66, 172
regional problem, 66
regions of the world, 199
regression, 8, 11, 12, 14, 18, 21, 24, 27, 30
regression equation, 30
regression model, 8, 11
regulations, 5, 75, 76, 119, 166, 172
regulatory affairs, 5
regulatory framework, 63, 166
regulatory quality, 1, 18, 31, 32
rehabilitation, 196, 197
relatives, 201
relevance, 154, 185
reliability, 43, 64
relief, 91
religion, 11
renewable energy, 126, 145, 186
rent, 128
repair, 151, 152
reproduction, 72, 112, 114
reputation, 72, 83, 98, 183, 186
requirements, 33, 186, 200, 201, 221
research institutions, 57, 233
researchers, vii, 3, 189, 208

Residential, 231
residuals, 13, 17, 20, 24, 26, 29
resistance, 136, 138
resolution, 155, 158
resource management, 121, 158, 177
resource utilization, 60
resources, 4, 5, 8, 41, 58, 59, 60, 82, 84, 88, 100, 118, 120, 121, 122, 123, 124, 127, 128, 129, 130, 143, 144, 145, 154, 160, 168, 173, 180, 181, 184, 191, 193, 194, 196, 200, 202, 210, 216, 220, 225
respiratory problems, 206
response, 94, 111, 140, 158, 180, 212
restaurants, 123
restoration, 114, 199
restrictions, 120, 151
restructuring, 83, 111
revenue, 88, 128, 180
rights, vii, 8, 9, 10, 11, 15, 30, 31, 39, 40, 42, 43, 44, 52, 75, 76, 87, 91, 118, 120, 127, 142, 178, 183, 234
risk(s), 31, 86, 88, 90, 135, 140, 159, 160, 170, 185, 186, 195, 197, 198, 200, 201
risk assessment, 160
risk management, 185, 186
Romania, 47, 50, 80
root(s), 3, 32, 125
Royal Society, 131
rubber, 206
rule of law, 1, 5, 6, 7, 11, 21, 31, 33, 44
rules, 2, 5, 6, 8, 33, 58, 72, 75, 115, 118, 120, 121, 122, 138, 185, 201, 204
rural areas, 140, 171
rural development, 155
Russia, 47, 49, 73
Rwanda, 47

S

safety, 90, 91, 196, 197, 200, 201, 203
Samoa, 48
saturation, 59
Saudi Arabia, 47, 49
savings, 184, 187, 188, 189, 199
scale system, 64
scaling, 60
scarcity, 139, 156, 157
scatter, 14, 17, 20, 24, 26, 29, 155
scatter plot, 155
scholarship, 192, 232
school, 59, 103, 104, 105, 107, 108, 109, 113, 115, 187, 218, 219, 220, 221, 222, 223, 224, 226, 227, 232
school activities, 232
schooling, 11
science, 3, 58, 59, 118, 189, 211, 212, 227, 232
scientific knowledge, 232
scientific papers, 231
scientific publications, 234
scope, 8, 30, 31, 33, 55, 93, 155, 166, 208
secondary education, 220
secondary school education, 108
secondary schools, 219
secularism, 137
security, 8, 64, 171, 185, 233
self-employed, 99
self-interest, 122, 125, 151
seminars, 192, 205, 223, 229, 230
sensitivity, 87
sensors, 125, 126
Serbia, 47
servers, 143, 145, 146, 147, 151, 152
service provider, 201
services, 4, 6, 40, 59, 61, 62, 63, 64, 65, 66, 67, 73, 88, 89, 91, 93, 97, 98, 124, 126, 134, 139, 146, 147, 148, 149, 150, 168, 169, 171, 180, 181, 182, 190, 194, 196, 198, 200, 201, 203, 207, 216, 231
settlements, 222
sexually transmitted diseases, 201
Seychelles, 47
shadow economy, 234
shape, 8, 172
shareholders, 63, 83, 84, 182, 202, 208
sheep, 123
shores, 136
showing, 49, 204
Sierra Leone, 48, 49
signalling, 200
significance level, 18, 24
signs, 179
Singapore, 31, 47, 49, 100
single currency, 137
skewness, 13, 17, 20, 24, 26, 29
Slovakia, 47, 49, 151, 152, 231
small businesses, 99
smoking, 201
social activities, 65
social behavior, 6, 78
social benefits, 73
social capital, 60, 126, 173
social care, 204
social change, 65, 112, 156
social cohesion, 57, 60, 63, 64, 65, 74, 83, 84, 85, 90, 98, 168, 176
social conflicts, 157
social consequences, 65
social contract, 77, 172
social control, 141

social development, 1, 5, 49, 57, 61, 62, 63, 64, 69, 70, 74, 77, 165, 166, 167, 168, 173, 181, 182, 183, 185, 207, 212, 232
social economy, 57, 61, 62, 63, 64, 65, 66, 165, 166, 167, 168, 170, 171, 173, 181, 216, 227, 230
social enterprises, 57, 62, 63, 64, 65, 96, 165, 167, 169, 170, 171, 172, 173
social environment, 32, 91, 94
social events, 61
social exclusion, 63, 67, 83, 90, 166, 170, 171, 173, 194, 208
social fabric, 57, 216
social group, 64, 91
social image, 98
social inequalities, 33
social infrastructure, 32, 199
social institutions, 65, 73
social integration, 74, 230
social interactions, 4, 41
social isolation, 61, 216
social justice, 65, 110, 177, 181
social life, 72, 168
social model, 63, 64, 118
social needs, vii, 66, 82, 88, 98, 100, 176, 183, 207
social network, 231
social norms, 177
social organization, 176
social participation, 65, 172, 173
social phenomena, 135
social policy, 57, 59, 64, 65, 66, 70, 72, 73, 83, 84, 182, 233
social problems, 57, 83, 88, 109, 119, 128, 172, 217
social programs, 199
social reality, 118, 195
social relations, 58, 72
social relationships, 58, 72
social resources, 4
social sciences, 3, 233
social security, vii, 40, 168
social services, 60, 63, 65, 66, 74, 96, 98
social solidarity, 58, 64
social structure, 8, 31, 71
social trust, 57, 60, 173
social values, 104, 112, 114
social welfare, 97, 168, 176, 182, 197, 207, 208
socialism, 125
sociology, 3, 70, 75, 80, 153, 229, 234
software, 124, 190, 191, 192, 193, 194
soil erosion, 105, 187
solar collectors, 186
solidarity, 58, 64, 65, 66, 73, 171, 184, 189, 208
Solomon I, 48
solution, 59, 66, 121, 129, 151, 181, 188, 189, 217
Somalia, 47
South Africa, 47
South America, 50
South Korea, 49
Southern Europe, 133
Soviet Union, 205
Spain, 47, 49, 50, 139, 231
special education, 234
specialisation, 63, 64, 67
specialists, 105, 191
specialization, 64, 67, 119, 176, 179, 229, 233
species, 121, 122, 187
specifications, 156, 221
speculation, 198
spending, 180, 203
spontaneity, 140
Spring, 84
Sri Lanka, 48, 202
stability, 1, 4, 5, 6, 7, 12, 14, 31, 55, 64, 159, 183, 184, 185, 201
Stability and Growth Pact, 65, 66
stabilization, 200
staffing, 215, 218, 223, 226
stakeholders, 74, 83, 90, 91, 96, 97, 155, 177, 178, 179, 187, 196, 201, 204, 208
standard deviation, 10, 155
standard of living, 11, 43, 120
standardization, 182
state(s), vii, 2, 4, 5, 6, 8, 11, 31, 32, 33, 36, 40, 41, 42, 58, 63, 66, 72, 73, 75, 77, 82, 86, 94, 113, 122, 127, 128, 138, 139, 140, 141, 143, 154, 156, 160, 167, 169, 179, 195, 202
state enterprises, 167
state intervention, 73
statistics, 9, 12, 13, 16, 17, 20, 22, 24, 26, 29, 43, 135, 155, 166, 170, 233
steel, 143
stereotypes, 138, 166
stigmatized, 72
stimulation, 60, 75
stimulus, 194
storage, 220
strategic planning, 89, 172, 176, 208
stress, 189
structural adjustment, 32
structural changes, 60, 172, 184
structural characteristics, 7
structural weaknesses, 2
structure, 1, 4, 30, 32, 41, 61, 71, 76, 83, 117, 120, 127, 136, 139, 176, 204, 217, 221
structuring, 185
style, 64, 87, 100
subjectivity, 10

submarines, 146
substitutes, 73, 111, 145
Sudan, 48, 159
sulphur, 144
supervision, 72, 75, 229
supervisor, 231
suppliers, 83, 85, 177, 182, 183, 196, 197, 198, 199
supply chain, 89, 90, 91, 94, 95, 99
surplus, 65
survey design, 10
survival, 31, 88, 89, 118, 122, 140, 194, 208
sustainability, 4, 5, 33, 62, 75, 77, 82, 95, 103, 104, 109, 110, 111, 112, 113, 114, 115, 116, 126, 176, 178, 181, 184, 185, 195, 203, 209, 210, 211
sustainable economic growth, 63, 74, 83
sustainable energy, 202
sustainable growth, 6, 36, 74, 155
Sweden, 47, 49
swelling, 62
Switzerland, 47, 213
synchronize, 203
Syria, 48

T

tactics, 59
Taiwan, 213
Tajikistan, 48
tanks, 10
Tanzania, 48
target, 2, 33, 90, 97, 117, 158, 188, 190
tax collection, 199
tax evasion, 99
taxes, 91, 111, 128, 197, 198
taxonomy, 30
Tbilisi, 106, 116
teachers, 106, 107, 108, 109, 112, 219, 220, 221, 222, 223, 226, 227
teaching experience, 94
teams, 189
techniques, 105, 145, 158, 234
technological change, 64, 145
technological developments, 144
technological progress, 106
technological revolution, 125
technology(s), 111, 114, 118, 125, 127, 176, 179, 187, 190, 191, 192, 193, 194, 195, 196, 202
technology transfer, 190
terminals, 195
territorial, 63, 81, 96, 134, 136, 137, 138, 142, 153, 154, 155, 156, 158
territory, 135, 136
terrorism, 5, 12, 14
tertiary education, 217
tertiary sector, 139
testing, 159
textbook, 191
Thailand, 48, 231
theoretical approaches, 59, 66
thoughts, 139
time periods, 156
time series, 158
Togo, 48
Tonga, 48
top-down, 62
tourism, 96, 97, 98, 121, 123, 128, 139, 155, 166
Toyota, 146
toys, 194
trade, 65, 71, 84, 85, 91, 136, 138, 157, 159, 171, 191, 195
trade agreement, 65, 84, 171
trade union, 91
trade-off, 157, 159
traditionalism, 137
traditions, 4, 41, 112
trainees, 191, 193, 226
training, 75, 87, 88, 91, 93, 97, 98, 106, 107, 112, 113, 158, 180, 183, 191, 192, 193, 194, 198, 201, 205, 207, 215, 221, 222, 223, 226, 231
training programs, 193, 198, 221
traits, 32, 136
trajectory, 138
transaction costs, 7, 124
transactions, 74, 90, 138, 179, 188, 197
transformation(s), vii, 40, 52, 79, 139, 194
transition, 33, 99, 111, 119, 122, 134, 139, 142
transition economies, 33
transition period, 111
transmission, 105, 113
transparency, 10, 32, 35, 55, 90, 91, 94, 96, 172, 178, 179, 180, 185, 189
transport, 144, 188, 206
transportation, 61, 115, 207, 216
treaties, 76
treatment, 166, 205, 206, 232
Trinidad, 47
Trinidad and Tobago, 47
tuberculosis, 200
Turkey, 47, 139, 160, 205
Turkmenistan, 48
turnover, 194, 203

U

Ukraine, 47
UL, 229
unemployment rate, 128
UNESCO, 105, 106, 110, 112, 115, 116

uninsured, 99
United, 3, 5, 10, 11, 30, 36, 41, 43, 47, 49, 63, 67, 85, 86, 102, 105, 106, 109, 110, 160, 177, 180, 184, 201, 231
United Kingdom (UK), 47, 49, 54, 73, 82, 85, 101, 131, 213
United Nations (UN), 3, 5, 11, 36, 41, 43, 63, 67, 75, 79, 85, 86, 102, 105, 106, 109, 110, 112, 115, 177, 178, 180, 181, 184, 185, 216
United Nations Development Program (UNDP), 5, 6, 11, 36, 41, 43, 55
United States, 10, 47, 49, 160, 201, 231
universe, 187
universities, 189, 190, 191, 192
updating, 104
urban, 60, 96, 133, 134, 135, 136, 138, 139, 140, 141, 142, 157, 169, 171, 172, 199, 215, 216, 233
urban areas, 139, 140
urban hierarchy, 136
urban policy, 96
urbanization, 105, 112, 133, 134, 135, 138, 139
Uruguay, 47
USA, 73, 105, 108, 116, 210, 231
USDA, 231
Uzbekistan, 48

V

Valencia, 141
valuation, 207
Vanuatu, 48
variables, 7, 9, 11, 13, 17, 20, 23, 26, 29, 30, 31, 39, 41, 42, 43, 44, 45, 49, 52, 53, 153, 154, 155, 156, 157, 158
variations, 7, 73
vector, 112
vegetation, 136, 155
vehicles, 125, 126, 144, 145, 146, 152, 200
vein, 1, 5
Venezuela, 47
versatility, 140
victims, 207
videos, 126
Vietnam, 48, 49
violence, 1, 5, 12, 14, 31
vision, 117, 124, 126, 129, 134, 135, 136, 184, 204
vocational training, 230
voluntarism, 70, 75, 76, 79, 178
volunteerism, 218
vote, 10, 168
voting, 191
vouchers, 171
vulnerability, 160
vulnerable groups, 66, 83, 98, 167, 168, 171, 205, 232

W

wages, 58, 198
war, 133
Washington, 34, 35, 36, 55, 80, 101, 131, 193, 209
waste, 139, 144, 180, 196
waste disposal, 196
wastewater, 139, 207
water, 139, 146, 155, 156, 180, 186, 187, 196
water quality, 180
weakness, 32, 62, 135, 136, 138, 139, 226
wealth, vii, 40, 55, 58, 118, 120, 122, 123, 127, 135, 185
web, 80, 125, 191, 193, 194
websites, 193
welfare, 8, 31, 64, 70, 72, 73, 74, 78, 121, 126, 128, 182, 203, 204
welfare state, 70, 72, 73, 74
well-being, 41, 128, 201
Western Europe, 50
whales, 121
wind power, 189
wool, 206
workers, 88, 97, 140, 177, 182, 187, 204, 205
workforce, 176
working conditions, 62, 205
working hours, 205
working population, 63
workplace, 61, 83, 88, 115, 176, 201, 205
World Bank, 2, 4, 5, 9, 10, 33, 34, 35, 36, 37, 41, 43, 54, 55, 80
World Development Report, 2, 36
worldview, 226
worldwide, 8, 9, 10, 30, 35, 36, 39, 40, 42, 43, 53, 54, 55, 61, 83, 113, 129, 185, 234
worms, 201

Y

Yale University, 54, 130
yellow fever, 201
Yemen, 48
young people, 90, 187, 189, 190, 201, 233

Z

zero growth, 109
Zimbabwe, 48